Nationalism in the New World

With admiration, for two great teachers:
George M. Fredrickson and Herbert S. Klein

Contents

Acknowledgments

We are grateful to several institutions for their generous support of this project. The Bogliasco Foundation generously provided a meeting place at Villa Pina in the Liguria Study Center for the Arts and Humanities in Bogliasco, Italy. There the Grupo Bogliasco, as we took to calling ourselves, met for a week to share ideas about nationalism, the Americas, and the Atlantic exchange and to lay plans for future events. The 51st International Congress of Americanists provided an opportunity for us to organize a stimulating symposium, "Nationalism in the New World," at their meeting in Santiago, Chile, in July 2003. Vanderbilt University provided a site and generous support for our conference in October of that year. A grant from the Collaborative Research Division of the National Endowment for the Humanities covered the lion's share of the expenses involved with this conference and the work involved in producing the book. We are especially grateful to Joel Schwartz and Elizabeth Arndt of the NEH for their helpful guidance and their confidence in our endeavor. The Fulbright Scholar Program administered by the Council for the International Exchange of Scholars awarded Don Doyle a Fulbright professorship at the Pontifícia Universidade Católica–Rio de Janeiro, which allowed the two editors to work together during several months in 2004. We are grateful to PUC-Rio, its Department of History, the Fulbright Commission of Brazil, and the United States Embassy in Brazil for supporting the Fulbright Chair in American History and for all they have done to facilitate our collaboration. Not least, we are very grateful to the authors of this book and all those involved in our expanded conversation on nationalism during these past few years.

This book is dedicated with great appreciation to our mentors, George M. Fredrickson and Herbert S. Klein, who, by chance, are both now at Stanford University. During our graduate student careers at Northwestern University and Columbia University they played an instrumental role in shaping our understanding of history as something that happens internationally.

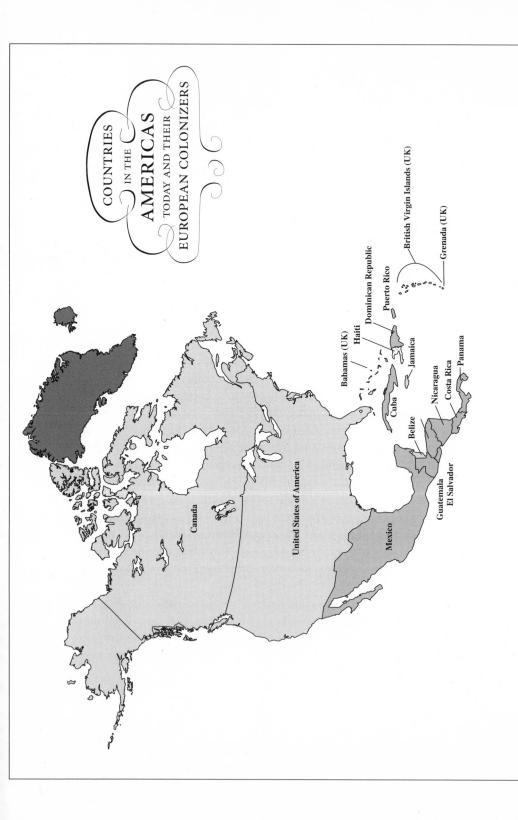

COUNTRIES IN THE AMERICAS TODAY AND THEIR EUROPEAN COLONIZERS

Canada

United States of America

Mexico

Guatemala
El Salvador

Belize

Nicaragua
Costa Rica
Panama

Cuba

Jamaica

Bahamas (UK)

Haiti

Dominican Republic

Puerto Rico

British Virgin Islands (UK)

Grenada (UK)

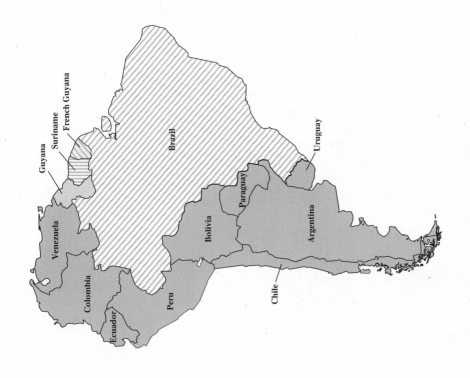

EUROPEAN
COLONIZER

United Kingdom

Spain

Portugal

France

Netherlands

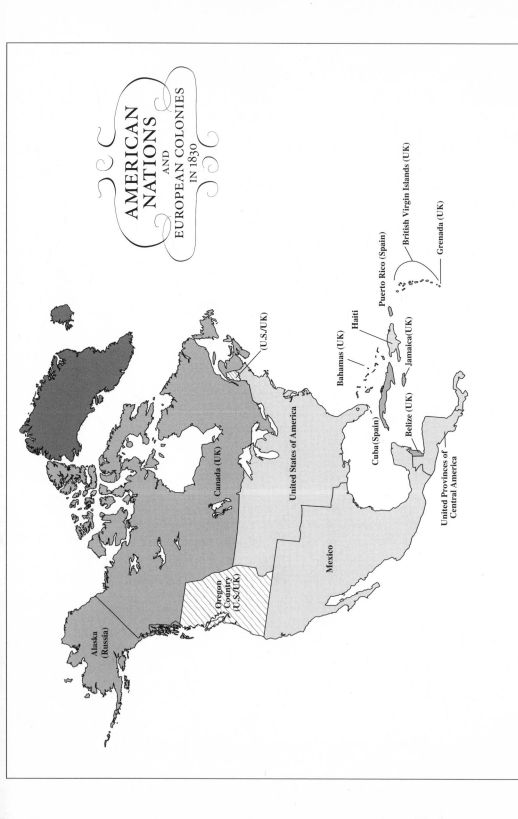

AMERICAN
NATIONS
AND
EUROPEAN COLONIES
IN 1830

Alaska
(Russia)

Oregon
Country
(U.S./UK)

Canada (UK)

(U.S./UK)

United States of America

Mexico

United Provinces of
Central America

Belize (UK)

Cuba(Spain)

Bahamas (UK)

Haiti

Jamaica(UK)

Puerto Rico (Spain)

British Virgin Islands (UK)

Grenada (UK)

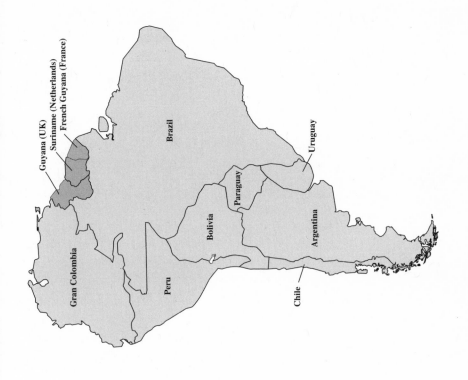

Guyana (UK)
Suriname (Netherlands)
French Guyana (France)

Brazil

Uruguay

Paraguay

Bolivia

Argentina

Gran Colombia

Peru

Chile

Colonies
Nations
Joint U.S./UK
Territory

Dates of Independence in the Americas

Nation	Date	European Colonizer
Argentina[1]	9 July 1816	Spain
Bahamas	10 July 1973	United Kingdom
Belize	21 September 1981	United Kingdom
Bolivia	6 August 1825	Spain
Brazil	7 September 1822	Portugal
British Virgin Islands		United Kingdom
Canada[2]	11 December 1931	United Kingdom
Chile	18 September 1810	Spain
Colombia[3]	20 July 1810	Spain
Costa Rica[4]	15 September 1821	Spain
Cuba[5]	20 May 1902	Spain
Dominican Republic[6]	27 February 1844	Spain
Ecuador[3]	24 May 1822	Spain
El Salvador[4]	15 September 1821	Spain
French Guyana		France
Grenada	7 February 1974	United Kingdom
Guatemala[4]	15 September 1821	Spain
Guyana[7]	26 May 1966	United Kingdom
Haiti	1 January 1804	France
Honduras[4]	15 September 1821	Spain
Jamaica	6 August 1962	United Kingdom
Mexico	16 September 1810	Spain
Nicaragua[4]	15 September 1821	Spain
Panama[8]	28 November 1821	Spain
Paraguay	14 May 1811	Spain
Peru	28 July 1821	Spain
Suriname	25 November 1975	Netherlands
United States of America	4 July 1776	United Kingdom
Uruguay	25 August 1825	Spain
Venezuela[3]	5 July 1811	Spain

1. Spanish viceroy displaced during the Revolution of May on 25 May 1810 but formal independence recognized in 1816.

2. Union of British North-American Colonies, a self-governing dominion retaining ties to the British Crown, founded 1 July 1867; formal independence recognized in 1931.

3. Part of Gran Colombia until 1830.

4. Part of Central American Federation until 1839.

5. Liberated from Spain 10 December 1898; under U.S. administration, 1898–1902.

6. Independence won from Haiti in 1844; during the colonial era, the island of Hispaniola passed between Spanish and French hands.

7. Originally Dutch.

8. Part of Colombia until 3 November 1903.

Nationalism in the New World

Introduction

Americanizing the
Conversation on Nationalism

DON H. DOYLE AND

MARCO ANTONIO PAMPLONA

*T*his book of essays grew from a meeting in Rio de Janeiro one beautiful afternoon in March 2001 between two historians who shared an interest in
the subjects of nationalism and comparative history. Our conversation that day
has continued at several international conferences and has enlarged to embrace
many other scholars, several of whose essays appear here. This book is our way
of bringing others into that expanding conversation.

Our concern with nationalism in the Americas has revolved around two
ideas: that the Americas have been neglected in the discussion on nationalism
and that there was something worth knowing about the American experience
that would benefit the general understanding of nationalism.

The lively discussion of nationalism that has taken place since the 1980s has
largely ignored the Western Hemisphere. Looking at the major anthologies published in English designed to introduce students to the study of nationalism,
one would wonder if any work had been done on the Western Hemisphere.
Three leading collections are John Hutchison and Anthony Smith, *Nationalism*
(1994); Geoffrey Eley and Ronald Grigor Suny, *Becoming National* (1996); and
Gopal Balakrishnan, *Mapping the Nation* (1996). Except for one essay on Latin
American literature in the Eley and Suny collection, not one of the dozens of
essays and excerpts in these three collections focuses on American nations. The
leading journal in the field, *Nations and Nationalism*, founded in 1995 by the
Association for the Study of Ethnicity and Nationalism (ASEN), focuses mainly
on Europe and has included only a handful of articles on American nations.[1]
The *Canadian Review of Studies in Nationalism* is the only journal in the Western Hemisphere devoted to nationalism studies, and while it includes more on

the Americas than other journals, especially on Canada and the Québec question, even in it the European tilt is evident.[2]

It is not that scholars are failing to produce worthy studies of nationalism in the Americas. As we discovered in the making of this book, there are a good number doing brilliant work on a variety of subjects dealing with nationalism, national identity, and related topics in the Western Hemisphere. Perhaps the subject does not have the same compelling urgency for Americanists that it does for those who study more troubled areas of the world such as Eastern Europe or the Middle East, but they recognize it as a topic of central significance to our times and demonstrate familiarity with the major currents of debate on nationalism. It would seem an opening reference to Benedict Anderson's *Imagined Communities* is an almost ritualistic requirement of any scholarly presentation on the subject. Americanists, in other words, are not ignoring the nationalism debate, but it is ignoring the Americas.

Underlying the neglect of the Americas is the assumption that American nations do not fit the traditional European paradigm for nationhood.[3] Walker Connor put this most explicitly when he wrote: "Whatever the American people are (and they may well be *sui generis*), they are not a nation in the pristine sense of the word." The "unfortunate habit" of referring to the United States as a nation and thus "equating American with German, Chinese, English," he tells us, "has seduced scholars into erroneous analogies."[4] Connor is referring to the United States, but the point he is making would apply as well to any multiethnic, immigrant country of the Americas. Most would find this usage of the term *nation* too confining, especially since the main thrust of contemporary scholarship has been to deconstruct the myths of an enduring ethnic core underlying the nation. Most American nations certainly do not qualify as nations by this standard in any case. Instead, they openly acknowledge the plurality of their immigrant populations, and while they may celebrate assimilation, they do not pretend to be based on coherent ethnic descent. If nationalism tends to reify ethnonationalist identities elsewhere in the world, in the Americas it typically strives to encompass plural ethnic identities.

The Americas also defy the current paradigm because nationalism in the Western Hemisphere has not produced the degree of violence and repression within and between nations that it has in Europe, the Middle East, Africa, or Asia. Underlying the iconoclastic deconstruction of nationalism by contemporary scholars is their judgment that it has been a pernicious force in these parts of the world. They blame nationalism for a host of atrocities: imperialism, wars, Fascism, and the Holocaust, to name a few. Most scholars of nationalism disparage, as Robert Wiebe put it, "the moral and intellectual emptiness of nationalist programs, the imbecility of their mass followings, and the suffocating effects of nationalism's success."[5]

To bring the Americas into the discussion on nationalism involves a new look at the historic role of the Americas in the Age of Nationalism and a reconsideration of the variety of roles nationalism has played around the globe. Due to the concern with nationalism's role in the atrocities of the modern world, we have forgotten its far more benign origins. In its youth nationalism was firmly aligned with a liberal humanitarian movement for liberty, equality, and self-rule, and the American nations that came into being in the wake of the revolutions that shook the Atlantic world beginning in 1776 provided models of what the modern world might become. Benedict Anderson described the American nations as the "*creole* pioneers": "Not only were they historically the first such states to emerge on the world stage, and therefore inevitably provided the first real models of what such states should 'look like,' but their numbers and contemporary births offer fruitful ground for comparative enquiry." "Out of the American welter," Anderson added, "came these imagined realities: nation states, republican institutions, common citizenships, popular sovereignty, national flags and anthems, etc., and the liquidation of their conceptual opposites: dynastic empires, monarchical institutions, absolutisms, subjecthoods, inherited nobilities, serfdoms, ghettoes, and so forth." In the new nations of the Americas "a 'model' of 'the' independent national state was available for pirating."[6]

In so many ways Anderson's *Imagined Communities* shaped the course of discussion on nationalism that followed its 1983 publication, but the "fruitful ground" Anderson charted for the Americas and their seminal role in the spread of nationalism has remained mostly unexplored territory. The exchange of ideas, leaders, and models of government that flowed both ways across the Atlantic throughout the nineteenth century was crucial to the contagious spread of nationalist movements in the Americas and Europe. Leaders in these movements were aware of being part of a broader experience in which the "national idea" was integral to the larger struggle against tyranny and in favor of self-rule. American independence leaders borrowed from European ideas, while the new nations of the Americas provided examples in which Europe might imagine its future.

Americans learned from one another as well, for they shared a common problem in forging new nations from former European colonies. Out of a world of empires and colonies the American states—most of them republics—emerged within a remarkably short span of time, between 1776 and 1825. As former colonial settler societies the new American nation-states had to stake their claim to independence on grievances and interests rather than on ethnonationalist ideas of primordial differences with the mother country or myths of some previous common history as a nation. Brazilian historian Sérgio Buarque de Holanda explains that it is not easy to spot the precise time when the inhabitants of Portuguese America, dispersed by distance, communication difficulties, mutual ignorance, ethnic diversity, and local interests, began to consider themselves united by bonds stronger than the many contrasts and differences that kept them apart. He wonders when this motley aggregate of groups and individuals began wanting to associate this sentiment with the desire for political emancipation. In Brazil, he wrote, "the two aspirations—independence and unity—were not born together and for a long period of time would not go hand in hand."[7]

Benedict Anderson used the independence of Latin America as an example of the new nationalism associated with the nineteenth century. Yet he may be incorrect in claiming that the anticolonial movements were national, if by that we are to understand that each country was aware of its own particular identity prior to independence. It is true that the administrative boundaries of the Spanish Empire and the daunting geographical challenges to communication and transport had begun to create intracontinental differences. But so did the diverse indigenous populations and the uneven spread of African slavery along with the variety of European immigrant backgrounds.

The presence of previous *ethnies* functioned as a general pattern, but differences were to develop everywhere. Mexico and the Andean nations, for instance, where large Indian and mestizo populations persisted, made more of their pre-European heritage than did other American nations. Also, due to the intensity of chattel slavery in their past, countries such as Brazil, the United States, and Cuba—not to mention Haiti—were to incorporate different African cultural traits deep within their traditions and national constructs. For all American nations, however, the languages, laws, religions, and customs came overwhelmingly from their former European rulers.

In Iberian America, with internal ethnic and racial divisions and in the absence of clearly identified external "others" that could be used to strengthen a sense of common identity, patriotism and nationalism took specific paths. By the time of independence nationalism had developed as a by-product of the Enlightenment and sought a liberty grounded (and granted theoretically) in universal rights. It sought recognition and defense of these rights but never based them on claims to a special identity. The model was the French Revolution, not Napoleonic chauvinism but an underlying civic nationalism. Simón Bolívar's brand of nationalism, for instance, lacked references to ethnic or cultural dimensions and made the ultimate criterion of nationality political in nature. Distinct from patriotism, which did not necessarily have anything to do with formal political organizations, nationalism was associated with a specific institutional goal—the nation-state. As such, it needed to be celebrated through some more well defined or elaborate canon—nationhood or nationality. Conversely, patriotism did not imply any particular institutional arrangement, and one's *patria*, or native land, could be a valley, a region, an institution, or a country. Moreover, patriotism did not necessarily imply obedience to either a collective will or its institutional representative, such as in the case of nationalism. Since links between conationals tended to be abstract (unlike the concreteness of skin color or socioeconomic resources), they were most often defined by their shared occupation of a territory.

The Latin American pattern of constructing nations and collective identity has also been shaped by the linguistic and cultural homogeneity of the continent following the conquest. Elite cultures did not experience deep divisions and struggles among themselves or any competition between languages (and the states representing them) that could inform the subsequent conflicts between political claims over territory.

Despite the differences between the various countries, until relatively recently there was no such thing as a national culture in Latin America. Self-hatred and European emulation were not uncommon in the aftermath of independence, and it was only much later in the nineteenth century and even well into the twentieth that literature (according to Anderson, a favorite vehicle of nationalist sentiments) and other artistic forms began to express a local as opposed to a continental belonging.

The populations of North America and Latin America were both different from those of the mother countries. All were multiethnic populations with varying proportions of Indians, Africans brought in as slaves, and diverse European and, later, Asian immigrants. The pluralism as well as the newness of American nations undermined any attempt to envision the nation along the lines of the European paradigm as a people bound and distinguished by common descent, a deep collective past, or homogeneous cultural traditions. Massive and sustained immigration continually accentuated the ethnic and cultural pluralism of many American nations. More than anything, immigration underscored the voluntary nature of nationality for the immigrants.

Ethnicity is of paramount importance for nation formation, as Anthony Smith has frequently noted.[8] The fact that modernists systematically overlooked the persistence of earlier myths, symbols, values, and memories in many parts of the world and their continuing significance for a large number of people cannot erase the influence of *ethnies*, which, once formed, have proved exceptionally durable. This does not mean that racial and other social attributes of specific human groups travel across history without undergoing any changes, especially with regard to their demographic composition and/or cultural contents. We wonder what happened to the many original Amerindian populations after the harsh ethnification or ethnicizing process was imposed on them by colonial rulers of European descent. Smith asserts that certain events more than others generate profound changes in the cultural contents of ethnic identities; among these events are war, conquest, exile, enslavement, religious conversion, and the massive influx of immigrants.[9] In short, we need to recall how intense these well-known episodes in the Americas were and how they have profoundly marked the history of the hemisphere. Since the conquest military mobilization, organized religion, and state making have eroded old and crystallized new ethnic identities, forming the so-called ethnic cores, cohesive and self-consciously distinctive *ethnies*. These ethnic cores developed diverse superior and subordinate relationships with the other *ethnies*, thus forming the basis of the sovereign nation-states of later periods.

To be sure, once American nation-states were formed, like those elsewhere they busied themselves with creating a unifying national identity. They wrote heroic histories and honored national heroes; they memorialized the nation's victories and lamented its defeats. They sought evidence of a distinctive national culture in their literature, music, and cuisine. Indeed, the need to construct a common national identity was every bit as pressing in the multiethnic immigrant societies of the Americas as in other countries, but immigrant nations had to work with different materials.

If ethnic nationalism was of necessity less important as an adhesive source of nationhood in the Americas, it was also less powerful as a source of division within and between nations. Compared to the rest of the globe, conflicts rooted in ethnonationalist disputes have been rare in the Western Hemisphere. American independence movements generally did not rest on claims of primordial differences with the mother country. For the most part, they stressed their grievances against imperial rule and their aspirations for self-government rather than fundamental ethnic or even cultural conflicts. Creole resentment of imperial rulers and the demands of forging a new national identity naturally inspired the language of difference. But if genuine differences existed between the colony and metropolis, they did not provide plausible claims to nationhood among colonial leaders whose language, religion, legal system, and core identity came largely from the mother country.

The question of territorial definition for the new nation-states developed differently in the New and Old Worlds. In Iberian America especially the previous political and administrative apparatus (which concentrated coercion and the organized bureaucracy of the old colonial state) was not dismantled; it was appropriated and reused by the new elite rulers. The boundaries of the new Iberian American nations were not given; they were produced. The size of the territorial domains under the jurisdiction of the new governments could vary, since they could express municipal, provincial, or regional polities. However, this previous image of a given territory (even if a dreamed-of one) informed the construction of the new boundaries of the sovereign nation-state formed after independence, which occurred simultaneously with the enforcement of the new political order. Not in vain were struggles for political independence profoundly militarized.

The new political boundaries, whether inherited from the colonial bureaucracy or reconfigured during and after independence, were not thought of as delineating deep ethnic and cultural differences between nations or peoples in the Americas. Border conflicts have been sporadic, sometimes violent, but ethnonationalism has only rarely been a source of international conflict among American nations. When compared to the rest of the world, the borders between American states have been remarkably stable and peaceful. There have been important exceptions; differences in language, religion, and race inflamed the conflict between Mexico and the United States in the 1840s, and at the end of a long war the border between them was drawn in blood.[10] There have been several other border disputes during the nineteenth century between American nations, several of them extremely violent. The Paraguayan War (1864–70) was the bloodiest conflict among South American nations. It set Paraguay against the Triple Alliance (Brazil, Argentina, and Uruguay) in a prolonged bloodbath that wound up shifting territory to Brazil and Argentina at the expense of Paraguay. The War of the Pacific (1879–83) was another violent border conflict that set Bolivia and Peru against Chile, but this conflict was over minerals and land, not primordial differences thought to divide peoples.

If ethnicity and religion played an important role in the formation of American nations, they have rarely sparked conflict *between* nations, and they have rarely inflamed separatist movements *within* nations of the Americas. Never mind that the independence of most American countries was initially won in what can only be called separatist revolts against their European rulers. The independence movements of the Americas, we argued previously, were anticolonial and were not fueled by ethnonationalism. Once independence was achieved separatist movements were rare—and rarely successful—in the Americas. In the turbulent region between Argentina and Brazil the provinces of the Banda Oriental del Uruguay fought Dom Pedro I's consolidating Brazilian government in 1828 and declared independence. Also, after the monarch returned to Portugal in 1831 during the Regencies (1831–40) rebellions erupted in different Brazilian provinces: Pará, Bahia, Maranhão, and Rio Grande. In the latter, a republican movement unleashed a fierce revolt known as the Farroupilha Revolution that resulted in a ten-year war (1835–45) before it was quelled by the emperor's forces. Simón Bolívar's dream of Gran Colombia had fallen apart by 1830 when disputes among its parts led to the separate nations of Venezuela, Colombia, Panama, and Ecuador, but none of these new states could be described as the product of separatist rebellions. In Central America some formerly autonomous cities and regions opposed the centralizing policy of the short-lived Mexican Empire (1822–23), banded together, and in 1823 declared the independence of the United Provinces of Central America. Other attempts to consolidate new nation-states in other parts of the Americas suffered equally serious losses. Indeed, different "national" projects competed in the late eighteenth and early nineteenth centuries in Iberian America. Some succeeded and others failed. To interpret separatist conflicts as regional patriotic struggles can be misleading in this context.

There were, however, important secession attempts in the Americas, the most violent separatist conflict in the Western Hemisphere being the U.S. Civil War. There were other border disputes and separatist movements of less consequence, but (with the exception of Texas) none were based on ethnonationalist ideology. In Texas Protestant Anglo-American settlers made ethnic and religious differences a vital part of their movement for independence from Mexico. For Confederates in the U.S. South white supremacist ideology was of paramount importance, but the Civil War was primarily a political conflict of interests that divided whites who otherwise shared a common ethnic and cultural heritage.

Those killed in wars over politics and interests are just as dead as those who die in wars fueled by ethnonationalist fanaticism, and of course all wars generate their own blood feuds. But conflicts over interests and even territory can be negotiated and resolved more readily than those thought to be over immutable primordial differences of blood, religion, or language, and this seems important to understanding the tradition of relative peace between nations in the Americas.

If ethnonationalism has not stirred constant international conflict in the Western Hemisphere, American nations have experienced tremendous ethnic tensions *within* their borders. Though, as we have argued, these have rarely evolved into genuine subnational separatist movements, the American pattern has more often involved some form of subjugation or exclusion of non-European ethnic minorities that remain as *ethnies* within the nation but are excluded from full and equal membership in it. Indians and Africans began as involuntary subjects of a nation and its colonial antecedent and then remained as excluded *ethnies* in nations whose membership was otherwise voluntary. The United States has not been alone in devising formal policies to segregate or remove these *ethnies* from the national community.

This exclusionary nationalism could also extend to voluntary immigrants, including Europeans, during debates on immigration restriction, which raised fundamental questions about the ethnic basis of the nation. In the United States, which received the lion's share of immigrants from Europe and Asia, the movement to restrict immigration began with outright prohibition of Chinese in 1882 and then turned against the so-called new immigrants from eastern and southern Europe. The arguments for restriction usually revolved around the capacity of certain ethnic groups to assimilate. All nations receiving large numbers of immigrants—Germans, Italians, and Japanese in Brazil, Italians in Argentina,

Chinese in Peru—have had similar debates over this issue, whether or not they imposed restrictions.[11]

When one considers the massive migration of different ethnic groups, languages, religions, and historic grievances that poured into American nations from outside, the potential for ethnic conflict seems greater, not less, than in Europe and other more historically settled parts of the world. Instead, the immigrant societies of the Americas seem built to absorb ethnic conflict or at least channel it into internal political and cultural contests instead of territorial separatist movements. Consider language, one of the main areas of culture where the state rules what is official and what will be taught in school. Hundreds of languages and dialects poured into the Americas from all over the world, and it is not difficult to imagine immigrants forming permanently separate language communities that might have taken on nationalist aspirations—language, in exile, acquires the power of territory and location.[12] Instead, the general pattern among immigrants from Argentina to Canada was to adopt the official language of their new home, even if they retained their own dialects and perhaps corrupted and renewed the host language. Controversies over bilingualism in parts of the United States and Canada are heated, and language has been a key feature of Québécois nationalism. But the general pattern has been that language has served to integrate rather than divide American nations. That the entire Western Hemisphere now communicates in the four official languages of the Americas—English, French, Spanish, and Portuguese—is testimony to the remarkable capacity of immigrants to assimilate a great diversity of citizens as well as the determination of American nation-states to impose some degree of cultural homogeneity upon their new citizens.

Nationalism tells people who they are and who belongs. It can be a force for violent conflict, repression, and exclusion, but it can be a powerful impetus for assimilation as well. It seems that nationalism is inherently neither one nor the other of these forces but is instead an ideological tool that in different political and historical contexts can be put to radically different uses. How American nations created and used nationalism and national identity is what this book of essays seeks to examine.

So again we ask, Why is nationalism in the Americas so important to understand on its own terms? What can we learn from the experience of different nation-states that grew out of a well-known common history as European colonies that broke with the ancien régime? What about the continuing relationship with their earlier European metropolises, which reinforced the spread of Western culture in these societies? How did the presence of varied *ethnies* among the many Native Americans who inhabited the continent before the arrival of colonists of European descent influence nation formation? The growth of African American populations during the last three centuries of colonial order certainly mattered. How and where? How did the late-nineteenth-century waves of immigrants to countries like the United States, Argentina, and Brazil affect the formation of national identity? Were the accommodation of various religions and the toleration among multiethnic groups achievements of civic nationalism? What different blends of ethnicity, racism, and civic nationalism were to be developed in the aftermath of independence in American societies at large?

We do not intend to offer ready-made answers to any of these questions, but we hope that the essays presented here will help advance some new thinking about what makes nationalism in the Americas a subject for international discussion and how the experience of the American hemisphere can illuminate the current understanding of nationalism around the world.

The essays in this book were first presented at two international conferences at which dozens of people presented their own work, discussed the work of others, and joined in conversation about the subject of nationalism in the New World. Our first conference took place as part of the 51st International Congress of Americanists held in Santiago, Chile, in July 2003. Another in October of the same year took place at Vanderbilt University in Nashville, Tennessee. Our call for papers went out over the H-Net discussion groups on the internet to as many scholars working in different specialties as possible; dozens responded with proposals. They came from Canada and Argentina, Cuba and Brazil, all parts of the United States, and Britain and Italy to join in what developed into a lively spirit of exchange and collaboration. The conversation we began in Rio in 2001 has continued in Santiago and Nashville and over the vast distance of cyberspace as we worked toward transforming conference papers into a coherent book. The conversations have taken place across boundaries of language, academic specialty, and nationality, and we have all learned more by crossing those frontiers.

The essays in this book are but a sampling of the larger body of papers presented at our conferences, and they in turn represent only a fraction of the scholarship emerging in this field. In our final selection of essays we sought diversity and balance among different national and topical studies. At the same time we looked for papers that addressed common themes of central importance to the understanding of American nationalism. The essays presented here often deal with specific subjects within particular nations, but we believe they have broad application to the more general subject of nationalism in the Americas and the modern world. We did not set out to cover the subject of American nationalism here but instead to bring together some exemplary work being done in the field and to stimulate the Americanization of the conversation on nationalism.

Craig Calhoun sets the stage with a broad theoretical and historical survey not only of the evolution of nations and nationalism in Western civilization but also of the efforts of scholars to interpret this phenomenon. Calhoun dissects the negative bias of contemporary scholars who see nationalism as a pernicious force and warns us not to view it as a passing phase likely to go away. Most of his essay focuses on the European background to the Age of Nationalism, which prepares us to see American nationalism as part of a broad transatlantic development.

T. H. Breen's essay deals with the early formulation of nationalist ideology in what became the first of the American independence movements when loyal citizens of the British Empire, joined in revolution by shared grievances and resentments, suddenly found themselves improvising a new political identity as Americans. The links Breen establishes with eighteenth-century European political thought—liberalism, civic humanism, and Protestantism—help immensely in the historicizing of the whole discussion on nationalism. It is this revolutionary nationalism, infused with such ideas of equality, liberty, and rights, that gave a nascent American nationalism ideological vitality.

Jack P. Greene shows just how frail and tentative this revolutionary nationalism was in the newly independent United States, which he characterizes as a "composite of old polities in the colonies." For many Americans victory made the alliance, which had been forged to make war against a common enemy, seem unnecessary. The weakness of national identity and power combined with what seemed to be fundamental conflicts between the new states suggested that the nation might cleave into four or more different nations. That it did not, at least until the 1860s, was due to the temporary absence of strong centrifugal forces for separation.

Susan-Mary Grant's essay analyzes the U.S. Civil War and addresses the political appeal of war and its role in the development of nation building. Other huge conflicts in the Americas such as the Paraguayan War, the War of the Pacific between Chile and Peru, and the Mexican Revolution were also important in stirring up national sentiments and collective identities, even though these events alone did not make nations. The particularity of the U.S. Civil War is magisterially explored by Grant, who shows us how easily patriotism can be turned into a faith and nationalism become its church. Grant discusses the recent historiography on the subject, with its alternative narratives on the effect of the Civil War on U.S. national identity. In addition, she provides a fine selection of excerpts from veterans' memoirs and letters the soldiers sent home during the conflict. These lend the whole discussion of the war that crucial humanizing dimension scholarship on nationalism often lacks and remind us the war was also about people who lived ordinary lives.

The violent struggles for independence in the United States and much of Latin America contrast markedly with their North American neighbor, Canada, as Phillip Buckner illustrates in his informative essay. Canada is one of the most interesting cases of American nationalism because of the deep and prolonged identity of Anglo-Canadians with Britain and, of course, because of French Québec and its challenge to national unity. Canada was the only major American nation *not* born in revolt against the mother country. As Buckner shows, Anglo-Canadians saw themselves as proud members of the British Empire, and their concern over the French minority reinforced their loyalty to Britain. With the rise of the Québécois separatist movement in the 1960s Anglo-Canadian nationalism began to give way to an official multiculturalism.

If in Canada the hesitant movement toward independence was conditioned by fears of the French minority, in other nations of the Americas the influx of immigrants prompted alternating responses of amalgamation and nativism. The essays by Jorge Myers and Jeane DeLaney focus on Argentina and at the same time deal with a subject of relevance to all the multiethnic immigrant nations of the Americas. Myers explores the strategies Argentina's nineteenth-century intellectuals pursued in the construction of a national identity, especially in the realms of language, history, and politics. Given its past—three centuries of colonial order—Argentina has found limited materials with which to concoct any glorious heritage. Immigration brought threatening diversity and cultural corruption to the inherited Spanish culture, but it also inspired a new imagining of a hybrid and superior Argentine culture. This did not prevent Argentines from suffering constant anxiety about preserving themselves from ethnocultural "corruption" associated with foreign immigrants. DeLaney comments on a select group of Argentine intellectuals who embraced romantic nationalist ideas from Germany in their effort to preserve the so-called *raza argentina* at a time when the country was effectively facing massive immigration from Italy and elsewhere. It is worth noting that these German romantically molded ideas of ethnicity, which strongly influenced a specific wing of late-nineteenth-century nationalists, were not exclusively Argentine but could be found in other Latin American countries at the same time.

Hayley Froysland's essay explores a parallel concern about a nation's racial integrity in Colombia, where elites perceived a threat not from foreign immigrants but from their own lower classes. The elites' harsh judgment of racial degeneracy among the poor was ameliorated by the confluence of religious charity and nationalism in a government reform program that aimed at nothing less than the "regeneration" of the whole "race." Women reformers, in league with the Catholic Church, assumed a leading role in this mission to regenerate the nation.

Eric Van Young suggests a parallel development in Mexico, where a weak national identity accompanied a move toward national independence followed by the slow evolution of nationalism during the nineteenth century. He finds

Benedict Anderson's theory of an imagined national community emerging through print media inadequate in explaining the Mexican movement for independence. At least for the masses of Indians and mestizos, their motives for fighting the Spanish rulers had more to do with resentment than with nationalist imaginings.

Wilma Peres Costa highlights the importance of the European travelers and interpreters who came with Dom João and the Portuguese court to Brazil in 1808. She analyzes the writings of French botanist Auguste de Saint-Hilaire and shows how that French "mirror" aided Brazil's elites in imagining their new nation. Just as Alexis de Tocqueville's evaluation of the United States helped provide a European mirror for North America, Saint-Hilaire gave Brazil a new understanding of itself, one that continued to shape national identity in subsequent decades.

Heather Thiessen-Reily discusses the invention of national tradition through the political career of a popular Bolivian leader. Her essay explores the complexity of caste and class in Latin America and how President Manuel Isidoro Belzú wisely and successfully appropriated and resignified symbols from the past, including those from nature and the Indian past. She also reveals the role of monuments and literature (oral culture included) in the shaping of this state-sponsored nationalism, in which a whole set of iconographic elements and rituals were put together to support a specific form of secular religion and liturgy to which people adhered in order to worship their national community.

Though nationalism, we argue above, was very much an international project, most scholars continue to study it within the confines of particular nations. The essays by Barbara Weinstein and Gary Gerstle, however, dare to take an international comparative approach. Each addresses fundamental issues of race and slavery in the making of American nations. Weinstein analyzes the impact of the destruction of slavery for the slaveholding elites of the American Republic and the Brazilian monarchy.

At the very least an awkward presence and at the very worst a serious threat to the survival of the modern nation, slavery was dealt with differently in each society. Whether it was the strong proslavery argument in the United States or the more lax rhetoric in Brazil, it is astonishing to find the ease with which both the Brazilian and the U.S. South's elites adapted the framework of modern nationhood to the reality of their slaveholding societies. Few studies have considered the decline of slavery in the Americas as a process intricately linked to nation formation and the question of national identity. Weinstein leads the way by bringing this discussion to center stage.

Gerstle also successfully ventures into the comparative approach and analyzes the ways in which racial identities and ideologies shaped the construction of nationhood in the United States, Mexico, and Cuba in the late nineteenth and early twentieth centuries. Being careful to treat these three countries in their historical contexts as neighbors unequally endowed with power and enmeshed in each other's affairs, Gerstle explores both the similarities in their official nationalist discourses and the particular conceptions of race and nation that emerged in each.

Our conversation that began in Rio in 2001 has now expanded to include dozens of scholars, each bringing a particular knowledge and perspective into the mix. One of the fruits of our exchange and collaboration is a new international organization aimed at further expanding the community of scholars and students who share an interest in nationalism. The Association for Research on Ethnicity and Nationalism in the Americas (ARENA; www.cas.sc.edu/arena) will have an institutional base at the Richard L. Walker Institute of International and Area Studies at the University of South Carolina, and it will continue to grow as an international association of scholars and serve to further stimulate the conversation on nationalism in the Americas that this book hopes to begin. Meanwhile, we invite readers to join the conversation on a subject of compelling importance to our world.

NOTES

1. See Blackwell Publishing, *Nations and Nationalism,* http://www.blackwell-synergy.com/loi/nana (18 September 2005).

2. *Canadian Review of Studies in Nationalism,* http://www.upei.ca/crsn (18 September 2005).

3. Peter J. Parish, "An Exception to Most of the Rules: What Made American Nationalism," *Prologue* 27 (1995): 219–29.

4. Walker Connor, "A Nation Is a Nation, Is a State, Is an Ethnic Group, Is a . . . ," *Ethnic and Racial Studies* 1 (1978): 379–88, reprinted in John Hutchinson and Anthony D. Smith, eds., *Nationalism* (Oxford, 1995), 36–46.

5. Robert H. Wiebe, "Imagined Communities, Nationalist Experiences," *Journal of the Historical Society* 1 (Spring 2000): 33.

6. Benedict Anderson, *Imagined Communities,* rev. ed. (London, 1991), 46, 81.

7. Sérgio Buarque de Holanda, "A herança colonial—sua desagregação," in *História Geral da Civilização Brasileira,* bk. 2, *O Brasil Monárquico,* vol. 1, *O Processo de Emancipação* (São Paulo, 1962), 9.

8. Anthony D. Smith, *The Ethnic Origins of Nations* (London, 1986), is one of several important publications by Smith on ethnicity and nationalism.

9. Anthony D. Smith, "Opening Statement: Nations and Their Pasts," *Nations and Nationalism* 2, no. 3 (1996): 358–65.

10. Don H. Doyle, "Manifest Destiny, Race, and the Limits of American Empire," *Studies in Ethnicity and Nationalism,* special issue, *Nation and Empire* (2005): 24–42.

11. Roger Daniels, *Guarding the Golden Door: American Immigration Policy and Immigrants since 1882* (New York, 2004); Jeffrey Lesser, *Negotiating National Identity: Immigrants, Minorities and the Struggle for Ethnicity in Brazil* (Durham, N.C., 1999).

12. Susana Rotker, *The American Chronicles of José Martí: Journalism and Modernity in Spanish America* (Hanover, 2000), 85. See her comments on Cubans living in the United States.

Nationalism Matters

CRAIG CALHOUN

*N*ationalism is easily underestimated. To start with, in its most pervasive forms it is often not noticed. Analysts focused on eruptions of violence, waves of racial or ethnic discrimination, and mass social movements fail to see the everyday nationalism that organizes people's sense of belonging in the world and to particular states and the methodological nationalism that leads historians to organize history as stories within or of nations and social scientists to approach comparative research with data sets in which the units are almost always nations. It is important not to start inquiries into nationalism by selecting only its most extreme or problematic forms for attention. Equally, it is important not to imagine it as exceptional, about to vanish, a holdover from an earlier era lacking in contemporary basis; it is hardly good scholarship to wish nationalism away.

On the contrary, nationalism is a discursive formation that gives shape to the modern world.[1] It is a way of talking, writing, and thinking about the basic units of culture, politics, and belonging that helps to constitute nations as real and powerful dimensions of social life. Nations do not exist "objectively" before they exist discursively. Equally, however, nations conjured out of talk and sentiment are also "real" material structures of solidarity and recognition. To say that nationalism is part of a social imaginary is not to say that nations are mere figments of the imagination to be dispensed with in more hardheaded analyses. As a discursive formation, nationalism (like, say, individualism) generates ever more discussion because it raises as many problems, aporias, and questions as it resolves.

There have been long and generally fruitless debates about the antiquity and origins of nationalism. Attempts to resolve them turn in large part on definitions, each of which is tendentious. Is nationalism essentially political and linked to the emergence of the modern state? Elie Kedourie writes that

> nationalism is a doctrine invented in Europe at the beginning of the nineteenth century. It pretends to supply a criterion for the determination of the unit of population proper to enjoy a government exclusively its own, for the legitimate exercise of power

in the state, and for the right organization of a society of states. Briefly, the doctrine holds that humanity is naturally divided into nations, that nations are known by certain characteristics which can be ascertained, and that the only legitimate type of government is national self-government.[2]

But one might as well argue that nationalism is essentially cultural and as old as fellow feeling among members of linguistic and ethnic communities. Or, more moderately, one might suggest that modern nationalism is a transformation wrought on such ancient ethnic identities by the new circumstances of modernity, including not only states but popular literacy, and with it newspapers and novels, mass educational systems, museums, and histories. Though their arguments are in other important ways opposed, two of the most prominent contemporary analysts of nationalism, Anthony Smith and Benedict Anderson, seem to agree on this, with the former stressing continuity with the past and the "reality" of ethnic traditions and the latter stressing imaginary construction, the novelty of mass media, and the role of the state.[3]

In this context it is perhaps instructive to note that we draw the word "nation" from ancient Roman usage, in which nations were preeminently subject peoples and barbarians. Romans understood these nations to be organized in terms of common descent and ways of life rather than properly political institutions. The Romans themselves, thus, were not in an important sense a nation, at least not from the mature Republic on. Nor was nationality as such the basis for political community, though it was a basis for exclusion. One might then locate the origins of nationalism—or at least of Europe's characteristic nations—in the dissolution of the Roman Empire and the development of a variety of different politico-cultural groupings in medieval Europe.[4] This has the advantage of reminding us that there is nothing "natural" about either the link between community and cultural commonality and the development of nationalism or the nation-state, either as actual (in varying extent) or as idealized in doctrine. As a way of organizing political life and cultural or ethnic claims (themselves commonly political), nationalism grows neither in primordial mists nor in the abstract. It grows in relationship to other political, cultural, and ethnic projects.

Nationalism is pervasive in the modern world because it is widely *used*, not merely found, but it is used in different projects—claiming or contesting the legitimacy of governments, demanding reorganization of educational curricula, promoting the elimination of ethnic minorities in the pursuit of cultural or racial purity. Its meaning lies in the interconnections among these various uses, not in any one of them. There is no common denominator that precisely defines the set of "true" nationalisms or "true" nations by virtue of being shared by all and by no other political or cultural projects or formations. Yet nationalism is real and powerful. Nationalism matters because it is a vital part of collective projects that give shape to the modern world, transform the very units of social solidarity, identity, and legal recognition within it, and organize deadly conflicts.

Nationalism flourishes in the wake of empires but also in active relationship to empires, including Austro-Hungarian, Spanish, Portuguese, British, French, German, and non-European empires. It flourishes also in competition among ostensible nations. It organizes both domestic and international struggles and indeed the very distinction of domestic from international. It matters more because it matters in so many different contexts. This gives added resonance and life to the rhetoric of nationalism even while it renders definitions problematic.

Theoretical and historiographical arguments about nationalism are heavily reliant on European examples as well as European political projects and debates and European misunderstandings. This collection of new studies of nationalism in the Americas is welcome because it contributes to a better recognition of the ways in which nationalism matters and the mutability of the ways in which the category of nation is deployed. In particular, it may help overcome not only a Eurocentric selection of examples but also biases and blind spots built into theory by thinking in terms of certain prototypical European arguments and categories. These are deeply integrated into the theory and historiography as they have developed throughout European modernity. This is not to say that there are not comparable confusions in studies of the Americas or in the use of "nation" as a category in American political projects or academic research, and indeed many of these come in large part from importing European analytic perspectives too uncritically. Merely fitting the New World examples into an Old World framework won't help and indeed may add confusion by reproducing the opposition of old to new and with it the implication that nationalism emerges as a process of maturation, the collective *Bildung* of peoples as they gain the capacity for sovereignty and with it the overcoming of older political forms like empire (or, relatedly, that further "maturation" overcomes nationalism itself in the production of cosmopolitan politics and identities).

European nationalism has from early on been deeply invested in three misrecognitions that different constructions of European history and politics helped to embed in more general theories of nationalism. The first of these is that nations are relative equals. The second is that nation and empire are sharply opposed and incompatible political formations. The third is that nations are always already available only to be called forth in new mobilizations for action or discourses of legitimacy. Some analysts of Europe have recognized how each of these assertions misleads. Nonetheless, they have been important themes in the discursive formation by which nationalism is reproduced in and among European countries and, indeed, elsewhere.

The New World has lessons to teach on each of the themes about which European self-understanding has been misleading. Let me evoke these briefly with reference mainly to Europe, leaving the development of or contestation over the New World cases to the other chapters in this book. I shall then turn to a review of general themes and debates structuring theories of nationalism. It is important, I think, for studies of nationalism in the New World to engage these debates well, grasping the overall range of arguments and positions and putting these ideas to use in a new empirical context. But it is important too for scholars to be skeptical of the ways in which many issues and debates are posed in the dominant literature on nationalism. Among other things, for a scholarly literature it has been unusually caught up with praising or—recently much more often—debunking the objects of its study.

Three Misrecognitions

European nationalism developed simultaneously as an account of internal integration and legitimacy of rule and external differentiation and sovereignty. It had ancient roots but took its dominant forms in a modern era shaped by inconclusive wars and economic competition. It is important to see the shaping influence of a Europe in which many different states had long existed without any attaining domination over the whole. That Germany's Third Reich came closer than any previous project of Continental integration since the dissolution of the Roman Empire only reveals the primary historical fact of a plurality of powerful states. But more on empire in a moment. Here we should note the relatively unusual character of Europe and its major influence on thinking about nationalism.

In few other regions of the world, if any, were several comparably powerful states forced to coexist with each other in relative equality without the peacekeeping and integrating influence of an overarching or at least central empire. Where empire was absent, either state making was modest or state projects collided in wars, conquests, and expansion. The latter was indeed Europe's pattern, and who is to say that it is not still—that the peace produced after World War II in part by projects of European union will not ultimately result in a supra-European state, whether imperial or national or in some sense more novel?

European nationalism reflected, however, the relative stalemate in which a variety of different states could achieve relative independence and pursue distinctive policies. This was not simply an inheritance from feudalism, which did indeed produce diverse polities but not the boundaries or domestic integration of modern states. On the contrary, it was only in the early modern period that this mode of political and social organization took shape. Through most of the nineteenth century patterns of procreation and family life varied more within states than among them.[5] As late as the middle of the nineteenth century the majority of French citizens spoke regional languages, not the standard French that first the royal court and then the revolutionary Republic was concerned to perfect.[6] In other words, before the nineteenth century states organized less of social life and coincided less with cultural integration. Just as important, the Peace of Westphalia that ended the Thirty Years War in 1648 established a principle of independent sovereignty and mutual recognition that became basic to the flourishing of nationalism. A variety of relatively small countries gained recognition in the Peace or, later, on the terms it outlined; most prominent initially were the Netherlands and the Swiss Confederation. The latter of these reminds us that the principle established at Westphalia was not yet that of the nation-state but of the autonomous or sovereign state for which nationalism could grow in importance as a discourse of domestic legitimacy and external recognition. The principle, moreover, was hardly the empirical actuality. And of course borders could be made more and more salient—not just by making them harder to cross but by building infrastructure and institutions that offered people benefits but stopped sharply at their edges.

The idea of nationalism, and indeed theories of nationalism, have been enormously shaped by the extent to which the big European states reached a balance of power and through alliances and wars managed almost despite themselves to sustain it. The importance of Spain faded after the Thirty Years War, and the long process of constructing countries out of the Holy Roman Empire and eventually the other Hapsburg dominions began.[7] France was especially strong at first, and it is arguably at the moment of the French Revolution of 1789 that all the most frequently evoked elements of nationalism were first fully and clearly in play on the European Continent.[8] But France was never strong enough to dominate, Napoléon notwithstanding. Germany was long locked into a struggle to catch up in political integration and military might but with increasing clarity became the Continental counterweight to France. If Germany was initially the negative example in ideas of nationalism because it lacked France's central state, its very projects of integration and their philosophical articulations (notably, e.g., by Johann Gottlieb Fichte during the early nineteenth century) became extremely influential. The contrasts between France and Germany loomed extremely large in the development of nationalism in theory and practice and to this day structure basic conceptual divides such as the overblown contrast between civic and ethnic nationalism. England, still in the early stages of integration or transformation into Britain, became a third exemplar of a powerful nation-state.

Of course, there were a number of smaller European states, and the number grew as various former Hapsburg dominions gained or struggled for independence. For at least three hundred years, though, the crucial fact was the absence of an integrating Continental power. The issue for smaller states, then, was not so much to gain shelter under one or another empire as to gain recognition as a sovereign state. While there was always a lot of realpolitik to this, it was always bound up with the capacity to project identity as a nation. It is worth noting that this has remained a powerful factor in the politics of international recognition. When Slovenia and Croatia announced their independence from the former Yugoslavia, the United States (and Germany, leading the European powers) immediately recognized their sovereignty. When Bosnia-Herzegovina did the same, recognition was withheld, apparently on the grounds that it did not represent a "real nation," despite a longer history of territorial integrity and civic life, including five hundred years of peace.

Doctrines of nationalism long included the notion of the equivalence of each nation, at least each "real" or "historical" nation (and debates over what to do about "nationalities" that fell short of that constitute another story). This doctrine was influenced by and paired with that of individualism. The nation was conceptualized in part as a person, including a legal person on the model of kings as sovereigns. And as domestic law came increasingly to recognize human persons as equals, so international law recognized national persons as equals. But of course they weren't. East Timor and the People's Republic of China, Luxembourg and the United States are all recognized members of the United Nations and sovereign equals before international law. Yet it takes a rather grand leap of imagination to consider them equal in other senses. This act of imagination was made possible significantly by a specific phase of European history. It was extended by the processes of decolonization that ended European overseas empires through the production of putative nation-states conceived on the model of such equivalence.[9]

The second misrecognition to which I pointed was the sharp contrast of nation to empire. We have already seen one source of this in the Peace of Westphalia. Though there was no clear-cut military triumph in the Thirty Years War, to a considerable extent the war marked the defeat of empire—represented by Spain and the Holy Roman Empire—by powers that would increasingly style themselves and organize themselves as nations, notably France and Sweden. During the ensuing period European social theorists wrote extensively about foreign empires and the instructive lessons they offered to European countries. Montesquieu's *Persian Letters* (1721) is only one of the most famous such treatises to mark out the alleged contrast between the tyranny of empire and the liberties of European political arrangements. Of course, many of these works, including Montesquieu's, were written at least as much to point out bits of tyranny at home as to criticize those abroad. But the fact that empire became so basic a foil was influential. It was in this discourse, for example, that the Ottoman

Empire became (in European eyes) paradigmatically non-European and non-Western, with implications to the present day. To an important extent the same is true of Russia, and certainly China, Japan, and others were not merely exoticized but analyzed specifically as empires (and it is a somewhat tendentious question whether this was the right category to use in all cases).

The most important misrecognition in all of this was that it helped underwrite two hundred years of European discourse in which discussions of national identity and citizenship were constructed in contrast to other "bad" empires without being much troubled by the fact that the emerging national states were themselves imperial powers. Even France in its most republican phases was also an empire. Think only of the repression of Haiti's revolution or note that though republican France set up nominally republican institutions in Egypt it was still a conqueror. One of the challenges for current analysis of European history is coming to terms with the extent to which the forging of European national states was never purely a domestic affair or even simply a combination of domestic affairs with European international relations. It was importantly tied up with the development of colonial empires. If this is true for France, Britain, and Germany (as it certainly is), it applies with equal force in the different cases of Spain and Portugal. The case of Britain is complicated also by the extent to which the British Empire began with English rule over the Celtic countries of Scotland, Ireland, and Wales. These were formally treated as imperial dominions before they were integrated into any project of British nationalism.

The extent to which nationalism should be recognized as almost always interwoven with empire may seem self-evident in some ways in some parts of the New World. If so, this is a good thing, for this recognition could help produce a necessary corrective. But it is not always self-evident in all ways, as the very image of the United States as a republic suggests. It is hard for U.S. citizens to grasp either westward expansion or overseas conquests like the Philippines as part of an imperial history. And in the context of contemporary U.S. projections of global power pundits commonly describe as something new the notion that the United States might act like an empire.

The third misrecognition is perhaps most easily stated, though it is hard to deal with theoretically. This is the notion that nations are always already available to political projects as their prepolitical grounds. Put another way, the idea of "nation" is basic to the idea of "the people" as the source of political legitimacy. Far from being clearly opposed to democracy, national identity is in many ways one of its conditions. The idea of nation does work for democratic political theory (and practice) that it is hard for most democrats to acknowledge openly. For example, it answers the question of why particular people in a particular place benefit from the putatively universal rights identified by democratic theorists. Let me take just a moment to explicate the significance of this for liberal theory, partly because it matters not just theoretically but because of the extent to which liberal theory suffuses modern state practices and the construction of international relations.

Relying at least tacitly on the idea of "nation" to give an account of why particular people belong together as the "people" of a particular state has historically done the double work of explaining the primary loyalty of each to all within the state and the legitimacy of ignoring or discriminating against those outside the state. Liberal discussions of citizenship and political obligation relied on the background presumption of common nationality to minimize troubling questions about ethnic or other intermediate solidarities (or relegate these to treatment as special cases). Moreover, liberal theory allowed the differentiation of domestic from international affairs on the basis of the same background assumptions. So long as the fiction of a perfect match between nations and states was plausible, liberalism faced relatively few problems of political identity or the constitution and significance of groups, though it meant liberal theory was sociologically impoverished.

Most reasoning about justice, political obligation, and other problems thus assumed the context of "a society," while reasoning about international relations addressed relations among such societies. It is instructive to see how John Rawls, the most important liberal theorist of the current era, addressed these issues. Rawls's classic theory of justice presumed an individual state as the necessary context of analysis.[10] A well-ordered society, Rawls insisted, was precisely not a community or an association: "We have assumed that a democratic society, like any political society, is to be viewed as a complete and closed social system. It is complete in that it is self-sufficient and has a place for all the main purposes of human life. It is also closed, in that entry into it is only by birth and exit from it is only by death."[11] Rawls knew, of course, that this was in some ways a fiction, but he initially thought it plausible, since his major focus was on what made "a" society just. Accordingly, he postponed examination of relations among states and transnational phenomena to a later step in analysis. Social changes of the 1990s—commonly summed up under the notion of intensified globalization—forced him to undertake that examination. Rawls's own approach was to retain the notion of "peoples" or discrete societies and then to propose a "law of peoples" regulating relations among them.[12]

Jürgen Habermas also responded to the same social changes that were making it hard to presume nation-states as the automatic contexts for democracy, rights, or political order. His reflections were informed not only by German and global affairs but by the project of European integration. Debates over whether Europe needed a constitution became the focus of many of his analyses.[13] Introducing his concept of "constitutional patriotism," he stressed the idea of political loyalty to a constitutional arrangement as such, an idea important both as a commitment to procedures that would limit loyalties to substantive social groups (nations or ethnicities) and as a referent for public discourse in which the public itself assumes some of the legitimating function otherwise assigned to nations.[14] Habermas insists that within all modern societies, and thus even more in international amalgamations such as the European Union, there will necessarily be multiple different substantive conceptions of the good life, and these will often be associated with different social groups (though he does not stress the latter point). Constitutional patriotism does not underwrite any of these in their specificity but is instead a general commitment to justification of collective decisions in terms of fairness. It thus allows for debate over how to balance direct reference to universal rights and procedural norms with more specific political culture. But, insisting on a more "comprehensive" rights-based theory of justice, Habermas is unwilling to accept the extent of variation among quasi-autonomous political cultures that Rawls's theory allowed.[15] Habermas's approach is more "cosmopolitan" in clearly favoring a global institutionalization of the sort of system of rights that has so far been institutionalized mainly (and often still incompletely and problematically) within individual states. Accordingly, Habermas approaches relations beyond nation-states in the same way as he approaches domestic affairs within states: as a matter of achieving a comprehensive, universalistic set of procedures and then motivating political loyalties to them that transcend all substantive identities or groupings without prejudice for or against any.

Rawls and Habermas are only two among a wave of liberal theoreticians to propose solutions to the problems of identity, belonging, and sovereignty in the context of the growing globalization of the post-1989 era. Many of these theoreticians have assumed the label "cosmopolitan." To a considerable extent this cosmopolitanism has involved trying to apply what had been basically "domestic" liberal theory to tackle more global questions. To their credit, the various theorists of a new cosmopolitan liberalism recognized that it was no longer tenable to rely so uncritically on the idea of nation. Many realized that their presumption of the internal integration and external singularity of "societies" did not match reality well. This was, of course, not just a result of social change. Nations had never been as sharply bounded as nationalism suggested. And nationalism itself was always produced in international affairs. In the Americas nationalism was a product of inter-American relations and relations with Europe; it was never entirely domestic.

One of the problems with the proposed cosmopolitan solutions is that they do not give adequate weight to the work done by notions of nationalism (and other projects of collective identity) in enabling people who are not well empowered to participate in global affairs as individuals to participate through collectivities. I have argued this point elsewhere, criticizing in particular the extent to which cosmopolitan thought exemplifies the "class consciousness of frequent travelers."[16] But here what I would stress most is the extent to which such cosmopolitan thinking, and liberal theory in general, approaches nations as inheritances rather than creations. If nationalism is approached as a new product, it is generally debunked as an "invented tradition" or denigrated as a manipulation by opportunistic political entrepreneurs. But this underestimates the extent to which national identities have always and everywhere been created through a variety of historical projects. Nationalism has been implicated in the structure of the discipline of history organized as so many national histories, thus generally implying the prior existence of the object studied. But of course the writing of national history has also been part of the creation of nations. Nationalism as a project has been seen under the problematic heading of "late nationalism," especially the ethnonationalisms of Europe's East. And the idea of founding nations rather than discovering them has been left to other parts of the world and poorly integrated in the theoretical self-understanding of European theory.

Nationalism and Social Theory

Social theory has approached nationalism first as a political ideology structuring relations of power and conflict. It has focused on nationalism's relationship to ethnic violence and war, on the production of beliefs that one's own country is the best, and on the invocation of national unity to override internal differences. It has seen nationalism first through bellicose international relations and second through projects by which elites attempt to mobilize mass support. This has been an influential view both among scholars of nationalism and among general social theorists who have tended to see nationalism largely as a problem to be overcome.[17]

A second strain of social theory associated with modernization theory and anticipated by both Max Weber and Émile Durkheim has seen nation building as a crucial component of developing an effective modern society, one capable of political stability and economic development. Nationalism, as the ideology associated with such nation building, is thus an important part of one phase in the process of becoming modern and is also a normal reflection of industrialization and state formation.[18] But however normal to this phase, it is also deeply implicated in power relations and conflicts and is prone to problematic manipulation by state elites.[19] Accounts of non-European nation building have generally assumed a "natural" European model (though there are important exceptions, like Anderson's *Imagined Communities*).

These first two lines of theory both emphasize politics and the state and treat nationalism mainly as a feature of the modern era. A third strain of social theory recognizes the role of nationalism in politics and conflict but stresses also its more positive contributions to the production of culture, the preservation of historical memory, and the formation of group solidarity. Many of the most influential theorists in this group also place much greater stress on the sources of nationalism in ancient ethnicities that provide the basis for identities prior to any specific political mobilization.[20] A related point is that nationalism ought not only to be approached through its most extreme manifestations but also grasped in its more banal forms—in a variety of ceremonial events, for example, and the organization of athletic competitions.[21] These contribute not only to specific group loyalties but also to the reproduction of the general view that the world is organized in terms of nations and national identities.

Here the study of nationalism as a topic of social theory intersects with the more reflexive question of how nationalism has shaped a crucial unit of analysis in social theory, that of society. While "sociality" may be universal to human life, the idea of discrete, bounded, and integrally unitary "societies" is more historically specific. It appears in strong form as one of the characteristic, even definitive, features of the modern era. This form reflects political features as, for example, both state control over borders and intensification of state administration internally help to produce the idea of bounded and unified societies and as arguments for political legitimacy increasingly claim ascent from the people rather than descent from God or inherited office.[22] It also reflects cultural features, though many of these are not ancient inheritances but modern inventions or reforms, such as linguistic standardization, common educational systems, museums as vehicles of representation, and the introduction of national media. Anderson, in one of the most influential studies of nationalism, has described it as productive of "imagined communities."[23] By this he means that nations are produced centrally by cultural practices that encourage members to situate their own identities and self-understandings within a nation. Reading the same news, for example, not only provides people with common information and common images of "us" and "them" but helps to reproduce a collective narrative in which the manifold different events and activities reported fit together like narrative threads in a novel, interweaving them all with the life of the reader. Practices and institutions of state administration are central to this production of nations as categories of understanding and imagining, but they are not exhaustive of it, and those who wield state power do not entirely control this production.

To simplify the field, then, we can see four main themes in theories of nationalism, which may be combined in different ways by different authors: (1) nationalism as a source or form of conflict, (2) nationalism as a source or form of political integration, (3) nationalism as a reform and appropriation of ethnic inheritance, and (4) nationalism as a new cultural creation. These themes are deployed in debates over "civic" versus "ethnic" nationalism and over the "modernity" or "primordiality" of nations. But before we turn to debates within the field we should consider further the underlying problem of nationalism as a source and a shaper of the notion of society itself.

Nationalism and the Production of Societies

Human beings have always lived in groups. The nature of these groups has, however, varied considerably. They range from families and small bands through clans and other larger kin organizations to villages, kingdoms, and empires; they include religions and cultures, occupational groups and castes, nations, and, more recently, even global society to the extent it knits all humanity into a single group. In most of these cases the self-understanding of members has been crucial to the existence of the group: a kingdom, a religion, or a caste is both an "objective" collection of people and pattern of social organization and a "subjective" way in which people understand how they belong together and should interact. This clearly is true of the idea of nation. Without the subjective component of self-understanding, nations could not exist. Moreover, once the idea of nation exists, it can be used to organize not just self-understanding but categorizations of others.

The most basic meaning of nationalism is the use of this way of categorizing human populations both as a way of looking at the world as a whole and as a way of establishing group identity from within.[24] In addition, nationalism usually refers not just to using the category of nation to conceptualize social groups but also to holding that national identities and groups are of basic importance (and often that loyalty to one's own nation should be a commanding value). Nationalism is thus simultaneously a way of constructing groups and a normative claim. The two sides come together in ideas about who properly belongs together in a society and in arguments that members have moral obligations to the nation as a whole, perhaps even to kill on its behalf or die for it in a war.

Nationalism, then, is the use of the category "nation" to organize perceptions of basic human identities, grouping people together with fellow nationals and distinguishing them from members of other nations. It is influential as a way of helping to produce solidarity within national categories, as a way of determining how specific groups should be treated (e.g., in terms of voting rights or visas and passports), and as a way of seeing the world as a whole. We see this representation in the different colored territories on globes and maps and in the organization of the United Nations. At the same time, clearly the boundaries of nations are both less fixed and more permeable than nationalists commonly recognize.

Central to nationalist discourse is the idea that there should be a match between a nation and a sovereign state; indeed, the nation (usually understood as prepolitical and always already there in historical terms) constitutes the ground of the legitimacy of the state. This is Kedourie's point in the passage I quoted near the beginning of this chapter. Ernest Gellner likewise avers that nationalism is "a political principle, which holds that the political and the national unit should be congruent."[25] Yet nationalism is not merely a "political principle," and its reproduction is a matter of banal practices (Olympic competitions, pace Michael Billig) and imaginative construction (museums, censuses, and habits of reading, pace Anderson) as well as political ideology.[26] Moreover, whether or not ethnicity explains nationalism (or the origins of nations, pace Smith), common language and culture facilitate national integration and identification.[27] And whether nationalism was born first as a doctrine or as less articulated practices or indeed born in Europe rather than, say, Spain's American colonies is also subject to dispute.

A variety of claims are made about what constitutes "proper" nations. For example, they are held ideally to have common and distinct territories, common and distinct national cultures (including especially languages), and sovereign states of their own. It is very difficult to define nations in terms of these claims, however, since there are exceptions to almost all of them. To take language as an example, there are both nations whose members speak multiple languages (Switzerland) and languages spoken by members of different nations (Spanish, Portuguese, English). Likewise, nationalist ideologies may hold that all members share distinctive common descent, constituting in effect a large kin group, but this is not definitive of nations in general. Nations are organized at a scale and with an internal diversity of membership that transcend kinship. No definition of nation (or of its correlative terms such as nationalism and nationality) has ever gained general acceptance.[28]

This is why I have argued that nationalism is better understood as a "discursive formation."[29] It is a way of speaking that shapes our consciousness, but it is also problematic enough that it keeps generating more issues and questions. As a discursive formation nationalism is implicated in the widespread if problematic treatment of societies as bounded, integral wholes with distinctive identities, cultures, and institutions. Charles Tilly has referred to the "pernicious postulate" that societies are bounded and discrete; Rogers Brubaker has similarly criticized "groupism"; Brubaker and Frederick Cooper have called for a relational approach in contrast to ideas about clear collective identities; and Michael Mann has similarly argued for seeing social life in terms of multiple and overlapping networks rather than discrete societies.[30] Their critiques have hardly ended the problematic usage, partly because it is so deeply embedded in the way we speak and think. This is not an unmotivated error by social scientists; it is a participation, perhaps unwitting, in the nationalist rhetoric that pervades public life and contemporary culture.

Moreover, something of the same problem has long been apparent in studies of nationalism. Author after author has slipped from showing the artificially constructed and sometimes false character of national self-understandings and histories into suggesting that nations are somehow not real. Traditions may be no less real for being invented, however, or even for incorporating falsehoods. The critique of these claimed histories—and especially claims that they justify contemporary violence—is important. But it is a sociological misunderstanding to think that the reality of nations depends on the accuracy of their collective self-representations.[31]

Ethnic and Civic Nationalism

The category of nation has ancient roots. As we saw, both the term and two of its distinctive modern meanings were in play in the Roman Empire.[32] For the Romans the term referred to descent groups, usually understood to have a common language and culture as well. But the Romans commonly used such ethnic categorizations to designate those who were not Roman citizens. National origins, in this sense, were what differentiated those conquered by or at war with the Romans from those fully incorporated into the Roman state, not what the Romans claimed as the source of their own unity. But in the very distinction we see two sides that have become part of the discourse of nations ever since: first, an attribution of common ethnicity (culture and/or biological descent) and an idea of common membership of a state (citizenship and, more generally, respect for laws and standards of behavior, which can be adopted, not only inherited).

These two sides to the idea of nation shape an enduring debate over the extent to which a legitimate people should or must be ethnically defined or can or should be civically constituted and what the implications of each might be. Ethnic nationalist claims based on race, kinship, language, or common culture have been widespread throughout the modern era. They sometimes extend beyond the construction of identity to the reproduction of enmity, demands that members place the nation ahead of other loyalties, and attempts to purge territories of those defined as foreign. As a result, ethnic nationalism is often associated with ethnic violence and projects of ethnic cleansing or genocide. However, ethnic solidarity is also seen by many as basic to national identity as such and thus to the notion of the nation-state. While this notion is as much contested as defended, it remains influential.

In such usage ethnic nationalism is commonly opposed to civic nationalism.[33] The latter is understood as the loyalty of individual citizens to a state based purely on political identity. Habermas has theorized this as constitutional patriotism, stressing the extent to which political loyalty is to a set of institutional arrangements rather than to a prepolitical culture or other extrapolitical solidarity.[34] Ethnic nationalism in such usage refers precisely to rooting political identity and obligation in the existence of a prepolitical collective unit—the nation—that achieves political subjectivity by virtue of the state. The legitimacy of the state in turn is judged by reference to the interests of the nation.

The contrast of ethnic to civic nationalism is heavily influenced by that of Germany to France.[35] The contrast has been enduring and has resulted in different understandings of citizenship. France has been much more willing, for example, to use legal mechanisms to grant immigrants French citizenship, while Germany—equally open to immigration in numerical terms—has generally refused its immigrants German citizenship unless they are already ethnic Germans.[36] Other countries vary on the same dimension (and in Europe the European Union is developing a mainly civic, assimilationist legal framework), but it is important to recognize that the difference is one of proportion and ideological emphasis.[37] As Smith has remarked, "All nations bear the impress of both territorial and ethnic principles and components, and represent an uneasy confluence of a more recent 'civic' and a more ancient 'genealogical' model of social cultural organization."[38] Not all scholars accept the distinction or hold it to be sharp; those who do use it often attribute ethnic nationalism to countries that are "late modernizers."[39]

Central to the idea of civic nationalism is the possibility for citizens to adopt national identity by choice. This is most commonly discussed in terms of the assimilation of individual immigrants into nation-states; civic nations can in principle be open to anyone who agrees to follow their laws. Citizenship in the state is seen as primary rather than prior membership in a descent group or cultural tradition. The distinction is fuzzy, though, as a rhetoric of civic nationalism and citizenship can mask underlying commitments to particularistic cultural or racial definitions of what counts as a "proper" or good citizen. Thus (in a recently prominent example) even law-abiding Muslims may not seem sufficiently French to many; conversely, the French state may pass laws ostensibly enforcing neutrality on religion but in fact expressing particular ethnocultural mores. It is particularly difficult to frame rationales for limits on immigration in civic nationalist terms without falling back on ethnic nationalism.

At the same time, the civic nationalist tradition contains another thread. This is the notion that the nation itself is made, is a product of collective action. This is symbolized by revolutions and the founding of new states (which may include more or less successful efforts to call forth national solidarities). The idea of choice here is not simply that of individual membership but of collective determination of the form and content of the nation itself—the effort to take control of culture as a historical project rather than merely receiving it as inheritance. When the revolutionary French National Assembly reformed the calendar and systems of measurement, it was engaged not merely in administration of the state but in an effort to make a certain sort of nation, one with a more modern, rational culture. And, of course, the tension between attempting to make a new culture and preserve an old one has been played out in the educational system ever since.

While much nationalist ideology has claimed definitive ethnic roots, social scientists are divided on the question, and most prominent twentieth-century analysts of nationalism have sought to challenge the explanation of nationalism by ethnicity. Hans Kohn and Hugh Seton-Watson stress the crucial role of modern politics, especially the idea of sovereignty.[40] Eric Hobsbawm treats nationalism as a kind of second-order political movement based on a false consciousness that ethnicity helps to produce but cannot explain because the deeper roots lie in political economy, not culture.[41] The dominant approach in contemporary scholarship views nationalism largely as an ideological reflection of state formation.[42] Gellner emphasizes industrialization and also stresses the number of cases of failed or absent nationalisms: ethnic groups that mounted either little or no attempt to become nations in the modern sense.[43] This suggests that even if ethnicity plays a role it cannot be a sufficient explanation (though one imagines that the nineteenth-century German romantics would simply reply that there are strong, historic nations and weak ones destined to fade from the historic stage). Carlton Hayes argues for seeing nationalism as a sort of religion. Michael Hechter analyzes it in terms of strategic individual action aimed at maximizing mostly economic and political benefits. Kedourie approaches nationalism as an ideology and attempts to debunk nationalism by showing the untenability of the German romantic cultural-ethnic claims. Indeed, in their different ways all these thinkers have sought to debunk the common claims nationalists themselves make to long-established ethnic identities.[44]

Against this backdrop Smith acknowledges that nations cannot be seen as primordial or natural but nonetheless argues that they are rooted in relatively ancient histories. Smith argues that the origins of modern nationalism lie in the successful bureaucratization of aristocratic *ethnies* that were able to transform themselves into genuine nations only in the West. In the West territorial centralization and consolidation went hand in hand with a growing cultural standardization. Nations, Smith thus suggests, are long-term processes, continually reenacted and reconstructed; they require ethnic cores, homelands, heroes, and golden ages if they are to survive. "Modern nations and nationalism have only extended and deepened the meanings and scope of older ethnic concepts and structures. Nationalism has certainly universalized these structures and ideals, but modern 'civic' nations have not in practice really transcended ethnicity or ethnic sentiments."[45]

The ethnic similarities and bonds that contribute to the formation of nations may indeed be important and long-standing, but in themselves they do not fully constitute either particular nations or the modern idea of nation. While some critics of ethnic explanations of nationalism emphasize the influence of state formation or other "master variables," a number assert that nations are created by nationalism—by this particular form of discourse, political rhetoric, or ideology—and are not merely passively present and awaiting the contingent address of nationalists.[46]

An emphasis on preexisting ethnicity—even where this is rightly identified— is unable to shed much light on why so many modern movements, policies, ideologies, and conflicts are constituted within the discourse of nationalism. Indeed, as Gellner has suggested, the very self-recognition of ethnicities or cultures as defining identities is distinctively modern.[47] Walker Connor uses a similar point (ironically reversing the Roman roots of the term *nation*) to distinguish ethnic groups as "potential nations" from real nations: "While an ethnic group may, therefore, be other-defined, the nation must be self-defined."[48]

Explanations of nationalism thus need to address the contemporary conditions that make it effective in people's lives and that affect both their attempts to orient themselves in the world and their actions. Such conditions are, of course, subject to change, and nationalist constructions are apt to change with them. Thus East Indian nationalists from the nineteenth century through Nehru were able to make a meaningful (though hardly seamless or uncontested) unity of the welter of subcontinental identities as part of their struggle against the British.[49] The departure of the British from India changed the meaning of Congress nationalism, however, as this became the program of an Indian state, not of those outside official politics who resisted an alien regime. Among other effects of this, a rhetorical space was opened up for "communal" and other sectional claims that were less readily brought forward in the colonial period.[50] Similarly, the proliferation of nationalisms in eastern Europe attendant on the collapse of Communist rule involved a "reframing" of older national identities and nationalist projects; the nationalisms of the 1990s were neither altogether new nor simply resumptions of those that predated Communism.[51] The opposition between primordiality and "mere invention" leaves open a very wide range of historicities within which national and other traditions can exert real force. As Ernst Renan famously stressed, nationalist histories are matters of forgetting as well as remembering, including forgetting the "deeds of violence which took place at the origin of all political formations."[52] At the same time, not least because academics commonly devote a good deal of energy to debunking popular nationalism, it is important to recall not only the deeds of violence but the cultural productivity that goes into nationalism—the symphonies and tangos, films and poetry.

Nationalism is partly a matter of narrative construction, the production (and reproduction and revision) of narratives locating the nation's place in history.[53]

As Anderson puts it, nations move through historical time as persons move through biographical time; each may figure in stories like characters in a novel.[54] This is one reason why the continuity of ethnic identities alone does not adequately explain nationalism: the narrative constructions in which it is cast change and potentially transform the meaning of whatever ethnic commonalties may exist. Ironically, the writing of linear historical narratives of national development and claims to primordial national identity often proceed hand in hand. Indeed, the writing of national historical narratives is so embedded in the discourse of nationalism that it almost always depends rhetorically on the presumption of some kind of preexisting national identity in order to give the story a beginning. A claim to primordial national identity is, in fact, a version of nationalist historical narrative.

Modernity versus Primordiality

A long-running debate in the literature on nationalism pits arguments that it is an extension of ancient ethnicity against those who argue that it is essentially modern.[55] Majority scholarly opinion tends toward the latter view, though explanations differ. "Modernists" variously see nationalism rooted in industrialization (Gellner), state formation (Tilly and Mann), the rise of new communications media and genres of collective imagination (Karl Deutsch and Anderson), and the development of new rhetorics for collective identity and capacities for collective action.[56] While many favor specific factors as primary explanations, most recognize that several causes are interrelated.

Many nationalists but few scholars see nationalism as ubiquitous in history and simply the "normal" way of organizing large-scale collective identity. Most social scientists point instead to the variety of political and cultural forms common before the modern era (e.g., empires and great religions) and the transformations wrought by the rise of a new kind of intensive state administration, cultural integration, popular political participation, and international relations. Many of these social scientists argue that nations and nationalism in their modern sense are both new. In particular, they would argue that ethnicity as a way of organizing collective identity underwent at the least a substantial reorganization when it began to be deployed as part of ethnonationalist rhetoric in the modern era. Others, however, including notably Anthony Smith and John Armstrong, argue that there is more continuity in the ethnic core of nations, though they too would agree that modernity transformed—if it did not outright create— nationalism.[57]

The attraction of a claimed ethnic foundation to nations lies largely in the implication that nationhood is in some sense primordial and natural. Nationalists typically claim that their nations are simply given and immutable rather than constructions of recent historical action or tendentious contemporary claims. Much early scholarly writing on nations and nationalism shared in this view and sought to discover which were the "true" ethnic foundations of nationhood.[58] It is no doubt ideologically effective to claim that a nation has existed since time immemorial or that its traditions have been passed down intact from heroic founders. In no case, however, does historical or social science research support such a claim. All nations are historically created.

Noting this, one line of research emphasizes the manipulation of popular sentiments by the more or less cynical production of national culture by intellectuals and state-building elites. Hobsbawm and Terence Ranger, for example, have collected numerous examples of the ways in which apparently definitive cultural markers of national identity can in fact be traced to specific acts of creation embedded in political (or sometimes marketing) projects rather than reflecting preexisting ethnicity.[59] The Scots tartan kilt is a famous example, dating not from the mists of primordial Highland history but from eighteenth-century resistance to Anglicization and early-nineteenth-century romantic celebrations of a no longer troubling ethnic Scottishness.[60] Likewise, nineteenth-century Serbian and Croatian intellectuals strove to divide their common Serbo-Croatian language into two distinct vernaculars with separate literary traditions. But as this last example makes clear, it is not obvious that because the "traditions" of nationalism are "invented" they are somehow less real or valid. Anderson finds the same fault with Gellner: "Gellner is so anxious to show that nationalism masquerades under false pretenses that he assimilates 'invention' to 'fabrication' and 'falsity,' rather than to 'imagining' and 'creation.' "[61]

Hobsbawm and Ranger imply that long-standing "primordial" tradition would somehow count as legitimate, while by contrast various nationalist traditions are of recent and perhaps manipulative creation. Many ideologues do claim origins at the dawn of history, but few scholars have doubted that cultural traditions are constantly renewed. What so-called primordialists have argued is that certain identities and traditions—especially those of ethnicity—are experienced as primordial.[62] Sociologically, what matters is less the antiquity of the contents of tradition than the efficacy of the process by which certain beliefs and understandings are constituted as unquestioned, immediate knowledge. This has more to do with current bases for the reproduction of culture than with history as such. Tradition needs to be distinguished from the "traditionalism" of those who claim to be its authoritative representatives and who—especially in contexts of literacy and record keeping—often enforce an orthodoxy foreign to oral tradition.[63]

Ethnicity and cultural traditions are bases for nationalism because they effectively constitute historical memory, because they inculcate it as "prejudice," not because the historical origins they claim are accurate (prejudice means not just prior to judgment but constituting the condition of judgment).[64] Moreover, all traditions are "invented" (or at least, in a more diffuse sense, created); none are truly primordial. This was acknowledged, though rather weakly, even by some of the functionalists who emphasized the notion of primordiality and the "givenness" of cultural identities and traditions.[65] All such traditions also are potentially contested and subject to continual reshaping, whether explicit or hidden. Some claims about nationality may fail to persuade because they are too manifestly manipulated by creators or because the myth that is being proffered does not speak to the circumstances and practical commitments of the people in question.

Notions of nations as acting subjects are distinctively modern, part of a new way of constructing collective identity. This said, there is no scholarly agreement about when nationalism began. Greenfeld dates it from the English Civil War, Anderson from Latin American independence movements, Peter Alter from the French Revolution, and John Breuilly and Kedourie both from German romanticism and reaction to the French Revolution.[66] I have previously suggested that rather than trying to identify a single point of origin scholars should see nationalism as drawing together several different threads of historical change.[67] As a discursive formation it took on increasingly clear form through the early modern period and was fully in play by the Napoleonic era.

The idea of nation became a fundamental building block of social life during the early modern period, especially the eighteenth and nineteenth centuries. While it is fruitless to search for a precise origin point for modern nationalism, it is possible to identify some of the social changes and conditions that helped to make it important.

First, nationalism reflected a distinctive scale of social organization larger than cities (which had previously been primary units of belonging and common culture for elites), villages, or kin groups. This was made possible partly by improved communication, which enabled larger populations to interact with greater density—a matter simultaneously of roads, the spread of literacy, and wars that brought large populations together in common military organizations and movements.[68] It was also facilitated by increased integration of trade among different regions within contiguous territories and by the mobilization of new kinds of military and state power.[69]

Second, nationalism constituted a new ideology about primary identities. In this it competed not only with localism and family but with religion.[70] In fact, nationalism was often furthered by religious movements and wars (notably, in the wake of the Reformation), and national self-understandings were frequently religiously inflected (as in the Catholicism of Poland or the Protestantism of England). But nationalism involved a kind of secular faith and a primary loyalty to the nation that was and is distinct from any religion that may intertwine with it.

Third, nationalism grew hand in hand with modern states and was basic to a new way of claiming political legitimacy. States furthered social integration among their subjects by building roads, mobilizing militaries, sponsoring education, and standardizing languages.[71] But they also were shaped by a cultural change that introduced a new, stronger idea of "the people" who were both governed and served by a state. Indeed, the idea of the state as providing necessary services for the "commonwealth" was basic, and with it came the notion that the legitimacy of the state depended on its serving its people effectively and/or being recognized by them. Political legitimacy was to "ascend" from the people rather than descend from God or proper dynastic ancestry. This placed a new stress on the question of who the people might be. The notions that they were those who happened to have been born into the domain of a monarch or conquered in war were clearly inadequate. The idea of nation came to the forefront. It represented the "people" of a country as an internally unified group with common interests and the capacity to act.

The last point is crucial. The idea of nation not only laid claim to history or a common identity but purported to describe (or construct) a collective actor. As Charles Taylor has put it, statements like "We the people," as articulated in the U.S. Constitution, are performative: they put in play a strong claim to cohesion and the capacity to act in concert.[72] Similarly, the *levée en masse* of the French Revolution symbolized the capacity of the people not merely to act but to shape history.[73]

The constitution of nations—not only in dramatic revolutionary acts of founding but in the formation of common culture and political identities—is one of the pivotal features of the modern era. It is part of the organization of political participation and loyalty, of culture and identity, of the way history is taught and the way wars are fought. It not only shapes practical political identity and ideology, it also shapes the very idea of society in which much social theory is rooted. If nations are obsolete, this will matter a lot. But however troubled and troubling the national organization of politics is, there is not much evidence that nations are fading from the global scene.

NOTES

1. This argument is developed at more length, though differently, in Craig Calhoun, *Nationalism* (Minneapolis, 1997). The idea of a discursive formation comes from Foucault's account of the development of modern individualism and more generally of the ways in which knowledge and social relations were focused, produced, and reconstructed by clusters of concepts and usages that could only partially stabilize the pro-

duction of knowledge because they included enough contradictions and tensions to keep generating ever more discourse. See Michel Foucault, *The Archaeology of Knowledge* (New York, 1969) and *Power/Knowledge: Selected Interviews and Other Writings, 1972–1977* (New York, 1977).

2. Elie Kedourie, *Nationalism*, 4th ed. (Oxford, 1993), 1.

3. Anthony Smith, *The Ethnic Origins of Nations* (Oxford, 1986), and Benedict Anderson, *Imagined Communities*, rev. ed. (London, 1991).

4. Patrick J. Geary, *The Myth of Nations: The Medieval Origins of Europe* (Princeton, N.J., 2002).

5. Susan Cott Watkins, *Provinces into Nations: Demographic Diversity in Europe, 1880–1960* (Princeton, N.J., 1992).

6. Eugen Weber, *Peasants into Frenchmen* (Stanford, Calif., 1976).

7. This is precisely the era of the formation of what Immanuel Wallerstein described as the modern world-system, with its global economic structure mediated by a characteristic political form of competing states (*The Modern World-System* [La Jolla, Calif., 1984]).

8. For example, bounded territories, indivisibility, sovereignty, legitimacy rooted in the people, a high level of popular participation in political affairs, direct individual membership (rather than mediation through intermediate associations or feudal hierarchies), common culture, ideologies of shared descent, an image of the nation in historical time, and sacralization of the "homeland." No one of these, to reiterate, is definitive, but together they are the main themes in the discourse of nations and the basis of a family resemblance among nationalist claims. See Calhoun, *Nationalism*.

9. The equivalence is not just a legal formality. It is also reflected in the "isomorphism" of institutional structures within nation-states—the ways in which they imitate each other in the organization of government, for example, with comparably structured ministries and social service organizations. This may be even more important than the building of museums and the celebration of national folklore to gaining international recognition. See Walter Powell and Paul Dimaggio, eds., *The New Institutionalism in Organizational Analysis* (Chicago, 1991), especially the chapters by Meyer and Rowan and Jepperson and Meyer.

10. John Rawls, *A Theory of Justice* (Cambridge, Mass., 1971).

11. John Rawls, *Political Liberalism* (New York, 1993), 41.

12. John Rawls, *The Law of Peoples* (Cambridge, Mass., 1999).

13. Many of Habermas's most theoretically developed analyses are collected in *The Inclusion of the Other* (Cambridge, Mass., 1998). But this was a theme Habermas also pursued in a variety of less theoretical political interventions. Some of these are collected in *The Postnational Constellation* (Cambridge, Mass., 2001). The theme remains current for him and for Europe, however, as shown by his leadership of a transnational effort to produce a European-wide debate about the nature of the European public itself in the context of opposition to the U.S. invasion of Iraq. A collection of these interventions is translated in Daniel Levy, Max Pensky, and John Torpey, eds., *Old Europe, New Europe, Core Europe* (London, 2005).

14. In "Belonging in the Cosmopolitan Imaginary," *Ethnicities* 3, no. 4 (2003): 531–53,

I argued that it is important to develop the notion of "public" as itself a form of social solidarity, not just a realm of discourse based on solidarities and identities established "before" it, and also that unifying Europe suffers a lack of such a public as well as its more famous "democratic deficit." See also the discussion of constitutional patriotism in Craig Calhoun, "Constitutional Patriotism and the Public Sphere: Interests, Identity, and Solidarity in the Integration of Europe," in Pablo De Greiff and Ciaran Cronin, eds., *Global Ethics and Transnational Politics* (Cambridge, Mass., 2002), 275–312.

15. See the discussion in Thomas McCarthy, "Reconciling National Diversity and Cosmopolitan Unity," in De Greiff and Cronin, *Global Ethics*, 260–74.

16. Craig Calhoun, "The Class Consciousness of Frequent Travelers: Toward a Critique of Actually Existing Cosmopolitanism," *South Atlantic Quarterly* 101, no. 4 (2002): 869–97.

17. For example, see Michael Hechter, *Containing Nationalism* (New York, 2000); and Habermas, *The Postnational Constellation*.

18. Ernest Gellner, *Nations and Nationalism* (Oxford, 1983); Charles Tilly, ed., *The Formation of National States in Western Europe* (Princeton, N.J., 1975); and Liah Greenfeld, *Nationalism: Five Paths to Modernity* (Cambridge, Mass., 1992).

19. Michael Mann, *Sources of Social Power*, vols. 1 and 2 (Cambridge, 1986, 1993).

20. Smith, *The Ethnic Origins*; see also Anthony Smith, *National Identity* (London, 1991) and *Nationalism and Modernism* (London, 1998); John Armstrong, *Nations before Nationalism* (Chapel Hill, N.C., 1982); John Hutcheson, *The Dynamics of Cultural Nationalism*, rev. ed. (London, 1994).

21. Michael Billig, *Banal Nationalism* (London, 1995); Lynette Spillman, *Nation and Commemoration* (Cambridge, 1997).

22. Anthony Giddens, *The Nation-State and Violence* (Berkeley, 1984).

23. Anderson, *Imagined Communities*.

24. Calhoun, *Nationalism*.

25. Gellner, *Nations and Nationalism*, 5.

26. Billig, *Banal Nationalism*; Anderson, *Imagined Communities*.

27. Smith, *The Ethnic Origins*.

28. Peter Alter, *Nationalism* (London, 1989); Calhoun, *Nationalism*; Walker Connor, *Ethnonationalism* (Princeton, N.J., 1994); John Hall, "Nationalisms, Classified and Explained," in Sukuman Periwal, ed., *Notions of Nationalism* (Budapest, 1995); Alexander J. Motyl, "The Modernity of Nationalism: Nations, States and Nation-States in the Contemporary World," *Journal of International Affairs* 45 (1992): 307–23; and Smith, *Theories of Nationalism*.

29. Calhoun, *Nationalism*, following Foucault, *The Archaeology of Knowledge* and *Power/Knowledge*.

30. Charles Tilly, *Big Questions, Large Processes, Huge Comparisons* (New York, 1984); Rogers Brubaker, "Ethnicity without Groups," *Archives Européenes de Sociologie* 40, no. 2 (2002): 163–89; Rogers Brubaker and Frederick Cooper, "Beyond 'Identity,'" *Theory and Society* 29 (2000): 1–47; Mann, *Sources of Social Power*, vol. 1.

31. Calhoun, *Nationalism*.

32. Geary, *The Myth of Nations.*

33. This contrast was influentially developed by Hans Kohn in *The Idea of Nationalism* (1929; New York, 1967); see also my introduction to the new edition (New Brunswick, N.J., 2005).

34. Habermas, *The Inclusion of the Other.*

35. Kohn, *The Idea of Nationalism*; and Alter, *Nationalism.*

36. Rogers Brubaker, *Citizenship and Nationhood in France and Germany* (Cambridge, 1992).

37. Calhoun, *Nationalism;* and Saskia Sassen, *Guests and Aliens* (Chicago, 1999).

38. Smith, *The Ethnic Origins,* 149.

39. Reinhard Bendix, *Nation-Building and Citizenship* (Berkeley, Calif., 1964); Tom Nairn, *The Break-up of Britain: Crisis and Neo-Nationalism* (London, 1977); John Schwarzmantel, *Socialism and the Idea of the Nation* (Hemel Hempstead, 1991).

40. Hans Kohn, *The Age of Nationalism* (New York, 1944); Hugh Seton-Watson, *Nations and States* (Boulder, Colo., 1977).

41. Eric Hobsbawm, *Nations and Nationalism since 1780: Programme, Myth, Reality* (Cambridge, 1990).

42. Tilly, *The Formation;* Charles Tilly, *Coercion, Capital and European States, AD 990–1990* (Cambridge, 1990); Hall, "Nationalisms"; Mann, *Sources of Social Power,* vol. 2.

43. Ernest Gellner, *Nations and Nationalism* (Oxford, 1983).

44. Carlton J. H. Hayes, *The Historical Evolution of Modern Nationalism* (New York, 1931); Michael Hechter, *Containing Nationalism* (New York, 2000); Elie Kedourie, *Nationalism* (1960; Oxford, 1993).

45. Smith, *The Ethnic Origins,* 216.

46. Kedourie, *Nationalism*; Gellner, *Nations and Nationalism*; Anderson, *Imagined Communities*; Partha Chatterjee, *Nationalist Thought and the Colonial World: A Derivative Discourse?* (Atlantic Highlands, N.J., 1986).

47. Gellner, *Nations and Nationalism,* 8–18, 61.

48. Connor, *Ethnonationalism,* 103.

49. This happened contrary to the predictions of numerous pundits, including George Orwell, *Talking to India* (London, 1943), and is only partly contradicted by the partition that created Pakistan.

50. Partha Chatterjee, *The Nation and Its Fragments: Studies in Colonial and Post-Colonial Histories* (Princeton, N.J., 1994).

51. Rogers Brubaker, *Nationalism Reframed: Nationhood and the National Question in the New Europe* (Cambridge, 1996).

52. Ernst Renan, "What Is a Nation?" in Homi Bhabha, ed., *Nation and Narration* (London, 1990), 11.

53. Bhabha, *Nation and Narration.*

54. Anderson, *Imagined Communities.*

55. Those who argue for the extension of ancient ethnicity include Smith, *The Ethnic Origins*; Armstrong, *Nations before Nationalism;* and John Hutcheson, *The Dynamics of Cultural Nationalism,* rev. ed. (London, 1994). Those advocating the modern nature of

nationalism include Gellner, *Nations and Nationalism*; Hobsbawm, *Nations and Nationalism*; and Greenfeld, *Nationalism*.

56. Gellner, *Nations and Nationalism*; Tilly, *Coercion*; and Mann, *Sources of Social Power*, vol. 2; Karl W. Deutsch, *Nationalism and Social Communication: An Inquiry into the Foundations of Nationality*, 2nd ed. (Cambridge, 1966); Anderson, *Imagined Communities*; Calhoun, *Nationalism*.

57. Smith, *The Ethnic Origins*; Smith, *National Identity*; Smith, *Nationalism and Modernism*; and Armstrong, *Nations before Nationalism*.

58. Joan S. Skurnowicz, *Romantic Nationalism and Liberalism: Joachim Lelewel and the Polish National Idea* (New York, 1981); Joseph F. Zacek, "Nationalism in Czechoslovakia," in Peter F. Sugar and Ivo J. Lederer, eds., *Nationalism in Eastern Europe* (Seattle, Wash., 1969).

59. Eric Hobsbawm and Terence Ranger, eds., *The Invention of Tradition* (Cambridge, 1983).

60. Hugh Trevor-Roper, "The Invention of Tradition: The Highland Tradition of Scotland," in Hobsbawm and Ranger, *The Invention of Tradition*, 15–42.

61. Benedict Anderson, "Introduction," in Gopal Balakrishnan, ed., *Mapping the Nation* (London, 1996), 6.

62. Clifford Geertz, *Old Societies and New States* (New York, 1963).

63. The distinction is made by Max Weber in *Economy and Society*, trans. W. Schluchter and G. Roth (1922; Berkeley, 1968), 4. See also the discussion in Pierre Bourdieu, *Algérie 60: Structures économiques et structures temporelles* (Paris, 1977), and in Craig Calhoun, *The Roots of Radicalism* (Chicago, forthcoming).

64. Hans-Georg Gadamer, *Truth and Method* (New York, 1981).

65. See Shmuel Eisenstadt, *Modernization, Protest and Change* (Englewood Cliffs, N.J., 1966) and *Building States and Nations* (Beverly Hills, Calif., 1973); Geertz, *Old Societies*; Ernest Gellner, *Thought and Change* (London, 1964).

66. Greenfeld, *Nationalism*; Anderson, *Imagined Communities*; Alter, *Nationalism*; John Breuilly, *Nationalism and the State* (1982; Chicago, 1993); and Kedourie, *Nationalism*.

67. Calhoun, *Nationalism*.

68. Deutsch, *Nationalism*.

69. Tilly, *Coercion*.

70. Hayes, *The Historical Evolution*; Anderson, *Imagined Communities*.

71. Breuilly, *Nationalism*.

72. Charles Taylor, "Modern Social Imaginaries," *Public Culture* 14, no. 1 (2002): 91–123.

73. William Sewell Jr., "Political Events as Structural Transformations: Inventing Revolution at the Bastille," *Theory and Society* 25 (1996): 841–81.

Interpreting
New World Nationalism

T. H. BREEN

*T*his essay addresses an interpretive problem that has long obstructed our ability to compare nationalism across the boundaries of time and space. In a nutshell, the issue is the relationship between nationalism and the political languages it speaks—in other words, its ideological voice.

As a character from *Alice in Wonderland* might have said, it seems curious that the problem of defining a persuasive connection between nationalism and political ideas would present itself at all. Presumably, no one would deny that the two are linked in some significant way. Nevertheless, however clear the relationship may appear, it remains nebulous. Within the vast literature of history and social science these categories of analysis are like twin stars in some distant galaxy.[1] They seem to follow separate interpretive orbits without ever quite escaping the other's gravitational pull. Perhaps uncertainty about the nature of the interaction has convinced scholars working in different disciplines—political science and history, for example—that they can explore one topic without paying too much attention to the other. Whatever their reasoning, they frequently generalize about the ideological face of nationalism without fully exploring the particular social and historical contexts in which intense feelings of national identity acquired a political vocabulary.

One can appreciate the rationale driving this interpretive strategy. Judging from the histories of very different systems of government throughout the world, nationalism has almost always shown itself able to accommodate a wide range of political ideologies. Over the last several centuries, in fact, nationalism has transformed the face of political culture in monarchies and republics, in oligarchies and democracies, and in oppressed colonies and imperial states. And yet, however profound the impact of nationalism on ideology may have been in these different situations, we still find scholars paying greater attention to the external symbols of nationalism—to the design of flags and the organization of parades—than to the political language it speaks.[2]

As a way to address this problem and to think in broader comparative terms we might start our analysis with several innocuous observations. It seems clear enough that nationalism—however we define the term—serves to intensify a people's commitment to a dominant political ideology, making men and women more fervently monarchist or republican, fascist or communist than they were before the heating up of political identity. Viewed from this perspective, we might say that nationalism has functioned as a kind of catalyst, amplifying political ideas and assumptions already present within a political culture. It is true, of course, that in certain circumstances nationalism has the capacity to deflect the dominant ideology, in other words, to bring out or exaggerate aspects of the political culture that no one might have predicted in advance. But even so, nationalism has readily accommodated different political ideologies, so that, if nothing else, we should recognize that while the fundamental organizing categories of nationalism do not change dramatically over time—categories of personal loyalty and sacrifice for the common good—the political content of patriotism is remarkably protean. Throughout history people calling themselves patriots have pledged undying allegiance to kings, presidents, dictators, clans, and spiritual leaders. It follows, therefore, that by focusing attention on the specific historical context of nationalism we may better comprehend how it interacted with political ideas in different settings.

The experiences of late-eighteenth-century North Americans—first as British colonists and then as citizens of an independent country—provide an excellent window onto the changing ideological face of nationalism. We immediately see in this literature an unfortunate division of interpretive labor. Historians who have reconstructed the political ideas of this period have shown only passing interest in nationalism. They have generally devoted themselves to tracing a single strand of political ideas that they believe defined mainstream American political culture roughly from the middle of the eighteenth century to the ratification of the Constitution of the United States.

The candidates for the dominant political discourse have changed from time to time. It was once confidently asserted that John Locke and his disciples guided the colonists to nationhood. Within this framework liberal notions about rights informed political resistance to the British Empire and, later, energized the young republic. Locke has recently given way to Machiavelli, liberalism has surrendered to republicanism, so that a literature that once resonated with talk of human and natural rights now insists that Americans spoke a republican language that stressed the need for virtuous citizens to stand vigilant against the corruption of power. When the historiographic battle between liberalism and republicanism threatened to degenerate into scholasticism, some participants suggested that Americans had, in fact, blended liberalism and republicanism and, by adding a seasoning of evangelical religion, created a synthetic political discourse.[3]

The merits of these rival positions are not matters of immediate concern for us. Rather, what catches our attention is that within this ongoing scholarly conversation political ideas seem to have acquired the character of master narrative, so that liberalism or republicanism—or whatever political ideology we have selected—receives credit for structuring everyday political life roughly from the middle of the eighteenth century to the election of Thomas Jefferson. The shifting contexts in which these ideas may have stirred nationalistic passion or sparked patriotic sacrifice are in this literature of less concern than are abstracted genealogies of ideas.

By the same token, historians of American nationalism have not shown much interest in political ideology. They have largely divorced themselves from the debate over the primacy of republican or liberal ideas during the late eighteenth century. Instead, they usually start their narratives with the actual establishment of a new nation—the United States of America—and thus do not intersect in interesting ways with the investigation of late colonial and revolutionary political thought.

The decision to begin accounts of American nationalism with the Declaration of Independence or with the Constitution, of course, has a compelling logic. Without a real nation to define it would seem to make little sense for anyone to bother working out the contours of nationhood. Moreover, the embryonic nationalism of the 1780s and 1790s seems part of a familiar teleological history that anticipates a political culture of the early nineteenth century, the Civil War, and the role of the United States in current world affairs. To be sure, although those who explore the early manifestations of American nationalism recognize that it initially defined itself against Great Britain, aristocratic privilege, and hereditary monarchies, these investigations have focused principally on what might be called the performance of nationalism—such as urban celebrations, Fourth of July orations, language reform, and patriotic symbols— without paying much attention to the content of its political ideology.[4]

It is, of course, possible to reunite what historians of ideology and nationalism have put asunder. In fact, I shall argue that nationalism has indeed affected the articulation of political thought, often in ways that provide fresh insight into how ordinary people translated ideological abstractions into emotional commitments and mutual trust. To make a persuasive case for this proposition it is necessary at the start to stipulate two conditions. First, the assertion of political identity to a high level of nationalistic intensity does not require the existence of a sovereign state. Nationalism can be a vision, a hope, a utopian blueprint for a future nation. In that sense it can energize the language of political resistance. Long before colonial Americans actually achieved independent political status they found that nationalism stoked popular imagination and brought forth what has felicitously been called a nation of the mind.[5] Moreover, like colonial peoples in Africa and South America the British Americans championed the rhetoric of imperial nationalism long before they imagined independence. Within an interpretive framework defined largely by colonial dependency imperial nationalism provided a positive and reassuring sense that the colonial or Creole settlers were full members of the larger cosmopolitan community, however distant they may have been from the European seat of power. The point is that eighteenth-century nationalism took on different ideological faces (imperial, revolutionary, and republican), each a reflection of how men and women responded creatively to shifting political circumstances.

The second stipulation at the heart of my argument is that no single political ideology dominated mainstream public discussion in America during the entire second half of the eighteenth century. At any given moment during this long period political thought reflected evolving social conditions and available cultural resources. In other words, although several political discourses coexisted in a kind of open marketplace of ideas, those assumptions and beliefs that seemed best suited to address the current challenge resonated with the greatest credibility. Thus it is possible for me to agree with historian J. G. A. Pocock that postrevolutionary America experienced a "Machiavellian Moment" while at the same time insisting that the 1760s and 1770s—in other words, the run-up to independence—should properly be described as a "Lockean Moment." Moreover, from the more flexible perspective we should appreciate that relatively contented mainland British colonists at midcentury spoke an entirely different political language from that which flared up at the time of the Revolution, one that was neither republican nor liberal in content. As a cultural anthropologist might observe, Americans chose to over- or underarticulate political beliefs as the context of nationalism shifted.[6]

What we discover, therefore, is that between the 1740s and the 1790s American nationalism gave voice to three distinct ideologies. These were not stages in a progressive development, and it would be misleading to suggest that the imperial nationalism of the mid-eighteenth century directly anticipated the establishment of an independent republic. More significant for this line of reasoning is the fact that each variety of nationalism expressed its own aspirations through a different political language. The nationalism of a provincial culture, for example, called forth a vocabulary that would have made no sense at all during the Revolution or the establishment of a new republic. It is from this perspective that we might say that while nationalism did not invent political ideology, it did determine within changing contexts which bundle of ideas was most appropriate for the mobilization of the populace and the forging of an effective political identity.

In each case the meaning of patriotism depended upon a shifting conversation between nationalism and political ideology. At midcentury colonial Americans participated in a heightened sense of *imperial nationalism*. As subjects of the Crown they merged their own political aspirations with those of a powerful metropolitan state (in this case, with Great Britain), and like other colonial peoples at certain moments in their histories they celebrated the power, prosperity, and security that the core state seemed to guarantee. The ideological component of imperial nationalism was mainstream Whiggish thought, an amalgam of broadly shared ideas about a balanced constitution, Protestant succession, and the glories of commerce.

Revolutionary nationalism was a different phenomenon altogether. Angry colonists rejected the myths and traditions of an earlier provincial identity, and as they mobilized to resist what they now regarded as British oppression they reached out to distant strangers—other Americans scattered throughout thirteen separate colonies—in the name of an imagined community, in other words, of a country of the mind. Without the energizing force of nationalism during these years Americans could never have successfully confronted the military might of Great Britain. The language of revolutionary nationalism was profoundly Lockean. It turned on the universalizing possibilities of human and natural rights; it rejected historical arguments in favor of an inclusive ideology that championed equality and liberty.

And after Americans had made good on their claim for independence they focused their attentions on *republican nationalism*. State building called forth the language of citizenship, and whereas revolutionary nationalism had assumed that patriots were people prepared to sacrifice self-interest in the name of the rights of the community, republican nationalism raised barriers to the kind of inclusive political participation associated with revolutionary mobilization. It amplified a political discourse that stressed the importance for the new state of independent, agrarian, male property holders. These were proper republican citizens who possessed sufficient political virtue to preserve the republic from moral corruption. The ideal patriot was a modern-day Cincinnatus, the brave yeoman who put down the plow to serve a community made up of other yeomen. Republican nationalism served, therefore, to remove from the public conversation about national identity those whose race, gender, or poverty excluded them from ever becoming genuine citizens of the republic.

This interpretive scheme provides a rough guide to the shifting connection between nationalism and political ideology. The framework acknowledges the perils of pushing generalization at the expense of specific detail. No doubt, many Americans throughout this period resisted the force of nationalism in any form; others may not have had the slightest notion what distinguished republicanism from liberalism. On one central point, however, my argument makes no concessions. It assumes that ordinary men and women were always capable of articulating multiple identities. Searches for a single master identity—a cultural project usually governed by essentialist logic—only muddles our understanding of the issues at stake. For eighteenth-century Americans the experience of living in a specific place—a tightly bounded little community where shared genealogies and historically sanctioned customs gave meaning to human existence—crosscut other, larger possibilities for personal identity.[7] Daily life defined itself around neighborhood affairs, colonial events, and imperial exchanges. These various levels of experience were not in competition; they were not mutually exclusive. One could sing the praises of Great Britain, for example, and still think of oneself as a Virginian or a New Englander, and we can assert with confidence that the claims of nationalism—whatever its character at that moment—were always woven into a complex web of other loyalties.

The first nationalism to affect large numbers of Americans radiated out from a European imperial core. Sometime during the mid-eighteenth century ordinary British people became intensely aware of themselves as being British. By their own lights they had accomplished more than had any of their Continental rivals. The British bragged about their personal liberties and material well-being, and when they gathered in pubs to sing the words to "Rule, Britannia" they had no doubts about the sources of their remarkable success. For one thing, they were neither French nor Spanish. For another, they were Protestant. As historian Linda Colley has explained, a swaggering, self-satisfied generation fabricated a "British national identity." They literally invented "Britishness."[8]

A number of different elements fed this powerful surge of nationalism. The economy was doing well; the British navy had scored a series of splendid victories. A robust new middle class sustained a consumer marketplace that provided satisfactions that had seemed for most people only a generation earlier completely out of reach. Moreover, a rapidly expanding popular press kept ordinary men and women informed about a larger British world where persons like themselves fought the French and defended the Protestant faith. The sudden outburst of British chauvinism seemed to have had no counterpart in contemporary Continental regimes. Of course, the French thought of themselves as superior to the British in every particular, but their nationalistic rhetoric never had the aggressive, uncompromising quality of the British. In his study of eighteenth-century French nationalism David A. Bell explains that the French who visited England expressed "amazed horror at the Francophobia and excessive patriotism of the English." Other foreign travelers to Britain were repelled by "the astonishing strength of xenophobia."[9]

Although we might take French complaints with grains of salt, we cannot ignore the striking intensification of the British patriotism. Like the sudden heating up of a solar core, the energy of this heightened identity transformed how satellite communities calculated the benefits and burdens of association with a mighty empire. In each region the calculus of political identity played out in different ways, a reflection of local traditions and perceived vulnerability. Historians of Scotland and Ireland have explored the effects of this aggressive British nationalism more thoroughly than have their counterparts who focus on mainland North America.[10] But even from this comparative disadvantage we can state with certainty that although Americans accommodated themselves to the altered relationship with the mother country in different ways, none of them could disclaim the surge of British nationalism. This new force redefined the gravitational field of empire.

Some historians have described this process as a kind of reabsorption in which the Puritans and adventurers who had once perceived themselves as beyond the pale of English authority were drawn back like colonial moths to the illumination of the mother country. The recolonization of the American imagination is sometimes called Anglicization. This term, however, does not seem adequate to the interpretive task. While it alerts us to a renewed American interest in English culture (in other words, in the development of a polite cosmopolitan society that offered material pleasures and innovative forms of public entertainment), it does not quite capture the hard edge of British nationalism. After all, imperial nationalism at midcentury involved more than selecting the proper tea service or acquiring the latest epistolary novel. It also stirred hatred for the French and contempt for those outside the circle of Protestantism.

The ideological component of imperial nationalism drew heavily on mainstream English political thought. Like the great majority of English men and women, Americans accepted the Glorious Revolution of 1688–89 as one of the grand turning points in the history of liberty. Parliament had constrained the Crown's prerogatives and secured the Balanced Constitution, a governing structure that quickly acquired near-mythic status in contemporary political theory. An English ruling class grown weary of Stuart flirtations with Catholicism made sure that future monarchs would be Protestant. And, according to the reasoning of the day, these reforms allowed the British to turn their attentions to making money, celebrating individual freedoms, and creating an invincible navy. These elements served as the foundation of a broadly accepted political ideology associated with England's dominant Whig party or, perhaps more precisely, with England's ruling class.[11]

In terms of patriotic identity, therefore, Americans subscribed to mainstream English beliefs. This is a significant point to establish, since some historians have argued that the colonists picked up various strands of a strident dissenting English political discourse. It is alleged that instead of echoing a strikingly self-congratulatory Whig perspective, Americans favored polemicists such as John Trenchard and Thomas Gordon. Their works warned of dark conspiracies and abuses of power. Their influence in America, however, has been greatly exaggerated, for while Trenchard and Gordon's *Cato's Letters; or, Essays on Liberty,*

Civil and Religious, and Other Important Subjects (1720–23) circulated widely throughout the colonies, provincial newspapers seemed far more interested in the activities of the royal family and the success of the British military in remote corners of the empire. And Americans certainly accepted the notion that commerce and liberty went hand in hand. As historian David Armitage has observed, "The classic conception of the British Atlantic Empire as Protestant, commercial, maritime, and free flourished . . . from the mid-1730s to the mid-1760s, when the Atlantic Empire began to unravel in the aftermath of the Seven Years' War."[12]

Imperial nationalism was no less a genuine expression of nationalism for being a metropolitan construction. In fact, depicting it as a faux or inauthentic political identity serves only to undervalue its influence for ordinary colonial Americans. For them full membership in the British Empire was not a theoretical proposition. It brought them material comforts in the form of consumer goods and welcome military support during the wars against the French in Canada. Historian John Murrin was certainly correct when he argued, "To the extent that the settlers were self-conscious nationalists, they saw themselves as part of an expanding *British* nation and empire. Loyalty to colony meant loyalty to Britain."[13]

The editor of the *New-Hampshire Gazette* fully accepted this logic. In the first issue of his newspaper in 1764 he gave voice to self-confident provincial patriotism. A colonial journal like his provided a means by which "the spirited *Englishman*, the mountainous *Welshman*, the brave *Scotchman*, and *Irishman*, and the loyal *American*, may be firmly united and mutually RESOLVED to guard the glorious Throne of BRITANNIA. . . . Thus Harmony may be happily restored, Civil War disappointed, and each agree to embrace, as *British Brothers*, in defending the Common Cause."[14] Others agreed. The Reverend Jeremy Belknap, an accomplished historian, reminded a generation of Americans who had experienced revolution against the empire of an earlier moment when colonists gloried in their imagined Britishness. According to Belknap, the brilliant leadership of William Pitt during the Seven Years War "had attached us more firmly than ever, to the kingdom of Britain. We were proud of our connection with a nation whose flag was triumphant in every quarter of the globe. . . . We were fond of repeating every plaudit, which the ardent affection of the British nation bestowed on the young monarch [George III], rising to 'glory in the name of Britain.'"[15] This statement reflected neither nostalgia nor irony. Belknap faithfully captured an earlier moment when Americans truly wanted to be accepted as "*British Brothers*." Unless we understand the powerful attraction of Britishness at midcentury and the sacrifice that Americans were willing to make for the British Empire, we will not fully comprehend the extraordinary fury unleashed when Americans discovered that their beloved brothers actually regarded them as lesser beings.

Anger born of a profound sense of rejection and betrayal did not in itself spark revolutionary nationalism. But the humiliating discovery that Americans were not regarded as true "*British Brothers*" created a social environment in which new forms of patriotism took root, in time replacing the imperial nationalism that had only recently bound them to a sprawling commercial empire. The chronicle of growing disaffection is, of course, well known. Fresh from the victory over France in the Seven Years War, Americans assumed that they were full partners with Great Britain in a grand colonial project. They were mistaken. Faced with mounting debt, Parliament decided that the time had come to exercise firmer authority over its distant possessions, and, to the shock of the Americans, the British began taxing the colonists in ways that radically revised the implicit understandings of the former imperial relationship. The shift came suddenly. As David Ramsay recounts in his wonderful history of the American Revolution, "The change of the public mind of America respecting connection with Great-Britain, is without parallel. In a short space of two years, nearly three millions of people passed over from the love and duty of loyal subjects, to the hatred and resentment of enemies."[16] Another contemporary historian, Mercy Otis Warren, shared Ramsay's dismay at the swift erosion of imperial loyalty. After all, the Americans had tried so hard, and "while a friendly union existed, they had, on all occasions, exerted their utmost ability to comply with every constitutional requisition from the parent state."[17]

Such analysis, however insightful, does not quite plumb the depths of revolutionary nationalism. Its intensity of feeling reflected more than annoyance over taxation and representation. After all, to mobilize a colonial population it had to foster a shared sense of political identity. It had to provide the backbone of resistance. Revolutionary nationalism held out a vision of independence even as it transformed one strand of eighteenth-century discourse into a powerful ideology that justified patriotic sacrifice for a new political order. The process of reimagining popular political identity was slow, much slower than Ramsay allowed. It began sometime during the later stages of the Seven Years War, when Americans for the first time came fully to appreciate the burden of being colonists.

We might counter that this was hardly a discovery of great significance. A colonist was a colonist, of course. Not surprisingly, *colonist* is a descriptive term that revolutionary historians generally take for granted. The problem is that they do not really regard Americans as ever having been colonists, certainly not in the same way that nineteenth-century Colombians or Mexicans, for example, were once colonists. Unlike them, Americans downplay their colonial past, real or imagined, electing rather to treat it as a period during which colonists—hearty yeomen all—were somehow preparing for real nationhood. Within this familiar account American colonialism has lost its sting. It evokes a popular form of architecture, a quaint Georgian world that we have lost, or perhaps merely an invitation to enjoy a patriotic vacation.

For the purposes of this investigation, however, such benign images of pre-revolutionary American society serve largely to obscure a critical shift in popular political consciousness that occurred only at the very end of the so-called colonial era.[18] To give colonialism a grittier quality—in other words, to capture the precise context in which revolutionary nationalism radically recast popular political ideology—we might stipulate that the 1780s were, in fact, a genuine *postcolonial* period in the history of the United States. This thought experiment raises provocative questions about the relationship between popular ideas about political power and traditional assumptions about a long, largely undifferentiated era known commonly as the *colonial period* of American history. For example, had a genuinely postcolonial mentality expressed itself in the United States after 1783, we might now feel obliged to determine more accurately than we do at present the precise content of America's colonial experience. We might want to know more about the defining characteristics of the colonial society against which the revolutionaries reacted. From the perspective of a postcolonial culture it would surely make little sense to define the colonial period as everything that happened between the founding of Virginia in 1606 and the Declaration of Independence in 1776. Rather, in terms of the history of political consciousness our colonial period would shrink to a few years following the 1757 defeat of the French in Canada and the Declaration of Independence in 1776. We would recognize that it was during these years that ordinary Americans became more fully aware of themselves as being colonists, not as they had once assumed equal partners in empire but, rather, as politically and economically dependent on a powerful European state. Of course, we might properly observe in passing that the rulers of eighteenth-century Great Britain did not bring to white American colonists the same oppressive violence that their nineteenth- and twentieth-century successors would visit on the indigenous peoples of Africa and Asia. But comparative repression is outside the purpose of this essay. We must remember that however mild the hand of British imperial power may now seem, we still have to explain the ideas and passions that sparked what was, in fact, a successful colonial rebellion.

The key ingredient in persuading Americans that imperial nationalism was a sham, therefore, was an element that anyone working in the field of comparative colonialism would immediately recognize as the *discovery of dependence.*[19] When ordinary people began asking about the empire in terms of cost-benefit, they were on the road to constructing an alternative political identity. Ramsay understood these mental processes. Reflecting on colonization as an historical phenomenon in the early modern world, he observed, "By these means Europeans have made the riches both of the east and west, subservient to their avarice and ambition. Though they occupy the smallest portion of the four quarters of the globe, they have contrived to subject the other three to their influence or command."[20] Others came to the same conclusion. Events persuaded them that Americans were, in fact, simply colonists, perhaps *nothing more* than colonists—subjects of the Crown who did not quite measure up to the men and women who happened to reside in England. Put another way, the study of revolutionary nationalism forces a recognition that the colonists could not have imagined independence until they had first experienced the psychological burden of political dependence.

Once we appreciate this moment as a time of perceived betrayal and doubt, of relegation into second-class status in the empire, we begin to understand why respected Americans sometimes depicted their relationship with Great Britain in crude racist language. This is not the kind of rhetoric that usually finds its way into discussions of political thought. If we are concerned, however, with how the breakdown of one set of national identities encouraged the development of a new political culture, then these complaints acquire interpretive significance. "We won't be their Negroes," snarled a young, rising John Adams, writing in the *Boston Gazette* on 14 October 1765 as "Humphrey Ploughjogger." Like others of his generation, Adams maintained that Providence had never intended white Americans "for Negroes . . . and therefore never intended us for slaves. . . . I say we are as handsome as old English folks, and so should be as free." James Otis Jr., the fiery Boston lawyer, inquired, "Are the inhabitants of British America all a parcel of transported thieves, robbers, and rebels, or descended from such? Are the colonists blasted lepers, whose company would infect the whole House of Commons?"[21] Like the anonymous author of a piece that appeared on 8 August 1765 in the *Maryland Gazette*, an essay originally published in a Boston journal, colonists throughout America found themselves asking an embarrassing question of immense and cultural consequence: "Are not the People of *America*, BRITISH Subjects? Are they not *Englishmen*?"

There is something slightly embarrassing about Americans of the intellectual stature of Adams and Otis worrying about whether they were as handsome or as white as contemporary Englishmen. But such leaders soon turned humiliation to more constructive ends as resentment transformed itself into a shared sense of pride. They began to reach out to each other across the boundaries of class and space, learning to trust people whom Benedict Anderson has called "distant strangers." Through a number of highly innovative mechanisms such as consumer boycotts they mobilized men and women who in normal times would have had nothing to do with each other. In their little communities they began to imagine larger solidarities.[22] At first these invented collectivities had no name, certainly none upon which Americans from New Hampshire to Georgia could immediately agree. But in a fumbling creative way they experimented, looking for an abstract vocabulary commensurate with the promise of revolutionary nationalism. During the period of popular mobilization Americans everywhere effectively made contact with each other through the channel of print, most aggressively and imaginatively through newspapers. On the vital role of print in the construction of national political identity Anderson was absolutely correct.[23]

Soon, even in small, relatively isolated communities people began to situate themselves within a continental conversation that assumed that the members of local committees and associations belonged to an American public that spoke for the interests not of a single village or county, not even of a particular colony, but of something greater, a solidarity provoked originally by the rhetoric of betrayal and resistance and soon taken for granted by the very people it was intended to persuade. In this extraordinary political environment the "respectable inhabitants" of Middletown, Connecticut, together with "the major Part of the Merchants & Traders of the Colony," could declare with remarkable insouciance, "This meeting [takes] into Consideration the unmerited Distress which the People of America and the Inhabitants of this Colony in particular suffer and are further exposed to from the operation of several Acts of Parliament Imposing Duties." No one doubted, apparently, that "the People of America" actually existed or that they might suffer as one. Perhaps even more revealing, the Middletown group inserted in "the public News Papers of the Colony" an announcement of its intention to cooperate with "our Sister Colonies, in preserving just natural rights, Liberty, and the Welfare of America."[24]

Similar meetings throughout the colonies responded to the imperial challenge in precisely the same manner as did the inhabitants of this Connecticut community. They published their decisions; they protested their uncompromising resolve. And, increasingly, they thought of themselves as Americans. A proliferation of collective nouns and phrases reflected a pressing need among people who previously had not had much to do with each other to describe what they were becoming. This development in the political language of the day did not signal that the colonists had replaced older, local identities with a new sense of self. They still thought of themselves as New Englanders or Virginians, as rice planters or urban mechanics, as Lutherans or Congregationalists. Rather, an inventive terminology suggested that the extraordinary difficulties of coordinating massive resistance to Great Britain over such a large territory had raised a tough question of diction for those many popular newspaper writers who now presumed to speak within a public sphere about a much broader although as yet ill-defined collectivity that seemed to be taking shape.

The tentative choice of words employed to meet this challenge reflected the problem of representing a people who were not really a people who lived in a country that was certainly not yet a country. These were men and women who had no burning desire for independence from Great Britain and who would have been shocked before 1773 to learn that they were on the high road to forming a nation of the mind. Some authors used the word "country." Others seemed more comfortable referring to the "British Colonies in America," but however the union with the "Sister-Colonies" originated, the goal of the whole was the promotion of "American Happiness." After all, "Every Lover of Liberty on the Continent" strove to advance "the general Cause of American Liberty" or the "Common Cause of American Liberty." If "our brethren in North-America" did anything less, they would be incapable of defending "the present and future INTEREST, LIBERTY AND WELL-BEING OF AMERICA."[25] A leading Boston newspaper reported that other colonists had urged that "we become one DETERMINED PEOPLE."[26] A New York City author went over the top, advocating in 1769 an *"American Magna Charta and a Bill of Rights."* As this person explained in screaming uppercase letters:

> Every SON AND DAUGHTER OF LIBERTY IN AMERICA, must inevitably, FIRMLY RESOLVE NOT TO BE SLAVES FOR CONTINUANCE, but immediately subscribe to, and immediately PRACTICE the wearing of the *cheapest Cloathing*, THE VERY CHEAPEST CLOATHING that can possibly be invented. AMERICAN REPRESENTATIVES should immediately begin and set the EXAMPLE; it must strongly be promoted, become *fashionable*, and universally be esteemed POPULAR, till the Time shall arrive that EVERY GRIEVANCE IN AMERICA is justly removed.[27]

Equating revolutionary nationalism with patriotic dress was a clever though not altogether unpredictable move in a society no longer content with colonial dependence.

Revolutionary nationalism spoke the universal language of rights. It is possible, of course, that it might have attached itself to another political discourse such as republicanism, but it did not do so, at least not for a broader public whose participation in organized resistance to the empire was absolutely essential. The ideological content of revolutionary patriotism was profoundly Lockean.[28] During the period when Americans increasingly identified themselves as American, revolutionary nationalism injected passion and energy into talk of rights, liberty, and equality. A political vocabulary that had been circulating throughout the Anglo-American world for more than a century took on fresh vitality. The lesson here is obvious. Those who attempt to separate the history of political thought from the history of nationalism generally fail to appreciate how these two elements interacted in ways that allowed old ideas suddenly to acquire exciting utopian possibilities.

What we discover, therefore, is that in this particular colonial setting nationalism promoted a persuasive political ideology that transformed abstractions about the contractual foundations of society into the stuff of commitment, trust, and sacrifice. As colonists pitting themselves against a European imperial state, they could not very well draw upon British history to make a persuasive case for their own cause. Instead, they championed rights that stood outside the flow of time, rights that people possessed before the institution of government, and rights that all people shared simply as human beings. This kind of revolutionary rights talk has struck some modern historians as undisciplined, even perhaps intellectually incoherent. And they are correct. The colonists were quite content to proclaim their God-given, universal, egalitarian rights without being too specific about which rights they had in mind. William Patten understood the problem. In a speech celebrating the repeal of the Stamp Act in 1766 he noted, "As freedom and liberty are so comprehensive terms, it may be necessary to specify in what sense they are used in this discourse. When I say that every man is by nature free, I intend, that he has a natural right to life, to safety, to judge, determine and act for himself, to such things as are common, to enjoy what by the blessing of providence on his own industry, he has acquired."[29]

What angry colonists revealed, therefore, was that revolutionary nationalism gave rights talk unprecedented emotive power. It was a catalyst for liberal values. Over time this bundle of ideas would prove intellectually unstable, since there were always some people in the society who wanted to claim natural or human rights that others insisted were utterly out of bounds. But these problems did not greatly perplex the men and women caught up in the revolutionary ferment. As the anonymous authors of a 1770 broadside published in New York City announced, they intended "to meet, and associate with People of all reputable Ranks, Conditions, and Denominations. . . . And that for the sole Purpose of supporting the Rights of America, which we conceive to be similar to those of his Majesty's Subjects of Great Britain:—And we have justly, as indefeasible a Right to them, as we have to the Air we breathe: Justice being every where immutable, whatever the Circumstances and Situations of Life may be."[30]

Victory over the British in 1783 dramatically recast the face of nationalism. For the people who had waged colonial war against an empire insistence on human and natural rights had stiffened resistance. During the years when calls for reform turned into thoughts of genuine independence, American patriots still described themselves as subjects. And in the mobilizing rhetoric of the moment they insisted that all subjects should properly enjoy equal rights. It made no matter that subjecthood was a category of monarchy. The colonists had been excited by the possibility of creating a society in which all British brothers might become American brothers, and it is not surprising that African Americans—many of them still slaves—responded to the clarion call of rights. Months before

Thomas Paine invited a people empowered by revolutionary nationalism to remake the world. Gen. Thomas Gage, then head of the British forces in Boston, received a petition drafted by "a Grate Number of Blackes in the Province . . . held in a state of Slavery within a free and Christian Country." They reminded imperial authorities—as well as white Americans—that we "aprehind we have in common with all other men a naturel right to our freedoms without being deprived of them by our fellow men[,] as we are a freeborn Pepel and have never forfeited this Blessing by aney compact or agreement whatever. . . . We therefore Bage your Excellency and Honours will . . . cause an act of the legislative to be pessed that we may obtain our Natural right[,] our freedoms[,] and our children to be set at lebety."[31]

The slaves who penned this document had been touched by the extraordinary possibilities contained in rights talk. For other colonists who heard such appeals it seemed as if a Lockean Moment had opened a Pandora's Box. Rights had an electrifying effect on men and women who never before had thought of themselves as possessing a political voice. As John Adams recognized as early as 1776, rights within the context of revolutionary nationalism could be disruptive. He feared, for example, that the slightest relaxation of franchise rights would open a door to more radical demands for political participation. "New claims will arise," Adams complained. "Women will demand a vote; lads from twelve to twenty-one will think their claims not closely attended to; and every man who has not a farthing will demand an equal vote with any other, in all the acts of the state."[32]

The new sovereign republic—the United States of America—discouraged people from thinking in radical terms of universal rights and equality. The key word in defining republican nationalism was *citizen*, not *subject*, and since not everyone could become a citizen in the independent government of the United States, it swiftly became clear that the challenge was determining who would qualify as a citizen. Republican nationalism thus encouraged an exclusionary turn of mind.[33] As Ramsay explains, "Subject is derived from the latin [*sic*] words, *sub* and *jacio*, and means one who is under the power of another; but a citizen is an unit of a mass of free people, who, collectively, possess sovereignty. Subjects look up to a master, but citizens are so far equal, that none have hereditary rights superior to others. Each citizen of a free state contains, within himself, but nature and constitution, as much of the common sovereignty as another."[34] The stress in this commentary was on free or, perhaps in terms of classic republican ideology, on being fully independent. From Ramsay's perspective, African Americans could not be citizens. Native Americans, women, and many poor white men were also barred from full participation. This narrowing of the political horizon was most certainly not a reflection of a conscious conspiracy among propertied males to discriminate against other Americans. Prejudices against blacks and women had a long history. The point is that republican nationalism had an agenda different from that of revolutionary nationalism. And in this changed context rights were domesticated, written down, ordered, enumerated, and constrained by procedures. All of this was perfectly predictable. For a postrevolutionary society the major goals were drafting a constitution, strengthening the bonds of republican identity, and achieving fiscal stability.

In this republican context, one that awarded a privileged role to independent agrarian property holders, even people like Thomas Jefferson began to express second thoughts about the kind of open-ended rights talk that had inspired the black slaves of Boston. To be sure, he still claimed to believe that all men were created equal and were endowed by their creator with certain unalienable rights, but like many contemporaries after 1780 he carefully explained that since blacks were not fully human they could not possibly share the same natural rights as did the white yeomen farmers who figured so prominently in his strangely tortured *Notes on the State of Virginia.* Republican patriots were white men who cultivated the land, who had sufficient real property to preserve an independent political judgment, and who had enough virtue to resist the soft, effeminate manners of a European aristocracy.

Historians of the young republic have usually adopted an upbeat approach to the analysis of republican nationalism. They have reconstructed a political culture in which feisty white males insisted that they were as good as any other white man. In their celebration of personal independence these citizens refused to pay the slightest deference to those who claimed special privilege on the basis of superior education or birth. But the story of postrevolutionary nationalism had a less appealing side that has seldom received close scholarly attention. To be sure, there have been exceptions. More than thirty years ago historian Winthrop Jordan made an arresting suggestion. "The search for national self-identity after the Revolution," he claimed, "and particularly the crisis of 1787–88, was intimately linked with white American attitudes toward Negroes. . . . [I]t would be preposterous to suppose that efforts at cultural independence and national unity had no connection with American thoughts and feelings about a category of the populace which was so distinctly different and separate."[35] A parallel argument has recently been made about how gender influenced republican nationalism. Rosemarie Zagarri, Jeanne Boydston, and Linda Kerber, for example, have observed that new political identities were crafted within "a deeply gendered community" in which "the best that women could do was to fashion an indirect political status through their roles as mothers of future citizens."[36]

From empire to revolution to nationhood we have explored a shifting conversation between nationalism and political thought. We have advanced a framework for reflection upon this relationship. Like a fire whose embers are never quite extinguished, nationalism threatens at any moment to ignite a blaze capable of transforming the lives of even the most ordinary people. It has the capacity to stir extraordinary ideological passions, to justify violence in the name of the community. It offers an inspiring sense of belonging. It encourages the invention of reinforcing rituals and symbols.

But nationalism does not create political thought. It works with the cultural resources that it finds at hand, giving new intensity to old ideas, and then, as the context of politics changes, so too does the character of nationalism. The connection holds true now as it did during the age of the American Revolution, when patriotism wore three different faces.

NOTES

1. I explored this theme in an article focused exclusively on the period before the American Revolution, "Ideology and Nationalism on the Eve of the American Revolution: Revisions *Once More* in Need of Revising," *Journal of American History* 84 (1997): 13–39.

2. Works that have shaped my thinking on these problems are Eric J. Hobsbawm, *Nations and Nationalism since 1780: Programme, Myth, Reality* (Cambridge, 1990); Ernest Gellner, *Nations and Nationalism* (Oxford, 1983); Benedict Anderson, *Imagined Communities: Reflections on the Origin and Spread of Nationalism* (London, 1991); and Colin Kidd, *British Identities before Nationalism: Ethnicity and Nationhood in the Atlantic World, 1600–1800* (Cambridge, 1999). In *For Love of Country: An Essay on Patriotism and Nationalism* (Oxford, 1995) Maurizio Viroli offers useful insights into the shifting intellectual frameworks in which various European nationalisms have found meaning. Less valuable for these purposes is Liah Greenfeld, *Nationalism: Five Roads to Modernity* (Cambridge, Mass., 1992).

3. Some of the major titles in this debate are Bernard Bailyn, *Ideological Origins of the American Revolution* (Cambridge, 1967); Gordon S. Wood, *The Creation of the American Republic, 1776–1787* (Chapel Hill, N.C., 1969); J. G. A. Pocock, *The Machiavellian Moment: Florentine Political Thought and the Atlantic Republican Tradition* (Princeton, N.J., 1975); Joyce Applyby, *Liberalism and Republicanism in the Historical Imagination* (Cambridge, 1992); and James T. Kloppenberg, "The Virtues of Liberalism: Christianity, Republicanism, and Ethics in Early American Political Discourse," *Journal of American History* 74 (1987): 9–33.

4. The most valuable of these studies is David Waldstreicher, *In the Midst of Perpetual Fetes: The Making of American Nationalism, 1776–1820* (Chapel Hill, N.C., 1996).

5. See Anthony Pagden, *Peoples and Empires: A Short History of European Migration, Exploration, and Conquest, from Greece to the Present* (New York, 2001), 166.

6. See Fredrik Barth, *Ethnic Groups and Boundaries: The Social Organization of Difference* (Prospect Heights, Ill., 1998).

7. Jack P. Greene, "Changing Identity in the British Caribbean as a Case Study," in Nicholas Canny and Anthony Pagden, eds., *Colonial Identity in the Atlantic World, 1500–*

1800 (Princeton, N.J., 1987), 215. See also Rogers Brubaker and Frederick Cooper, "Beyond 'Identity,' " *Theory and History* 29 (2000): 1–47.

8. Linda Colley, *Britons: Forging the Nation 1777–1837* (New Haven, Conn., 1992), 1–3. See also Kathleen Wilson, *The Island Race: Englishness, Empire and Gender in the Eighteenth Century* (London, 2003).

9. David A. Bell, *The Cult of the Nation in France: Inventing Nationalism, 1680–1800* (Cambridge, Mass., 2001), 44, 46.

10. See, for example, Eliga H. Gould, "Revolution and Counter-Revolution," in David Armitage and Michael J. Braddick, eds., *The British Atlantic World, 1500–1800* (London, 2002), 203–4. See also S. J. Connolly, "Varieties of Britishness: Ireland, Scotland and Wales in the Hanoverian State," in Alexander Grant and Keith J. Stringer, eds., *Uniting the Kingdom? The Making of British History* (London, 1995); J. T. Leerssen, "Anglo-Irish Patriotism and Its European Context: Notes Toward a Reassessment," *Eighteenth-Century Ireland* 3 (1988): 7–24; J. L. McCracken, "Protestant Ascendancy and the Rise of Colonial Nationalism, 1714–60," in T. W. Moody and W. E. Vaughan, eds., *Eighteenth-Century Ireland, 1691–1800*, vol. 4 of *A New History of Ireland* (Oxford, 1986); and Colin Kidd, *Subverting Scotland's Past: Scottish Whig Historians and the Creation of an Anglo-British Identity, 1689–c. 1830* (Cambridge, 1993).

11. H. T. Dickinson, *Liberty and Property: Political Ideology in Eighteenth-Century Britain* (London, 1977).

12. David A. Armitage, *The Ideological Origins of the British Empire* (Cambridge, 2000), 193–94.

13. John Murrin, "A Roof without Walls: The Dilemma of American National Identity," in Richard Beeman, Stephen Botein, and Edward C. Carter III, eds., *Beyond Confederation: Origins of the Constitution and American National Identity* (Chapel Hill, N.C., 1987), 334–38.

14. *New-Hampshire Gazette*, 13 July 1764.

15. Jeremy Belknap, *The History of New-Hampshire*, 3 vols. (Dover, N.H., 1812), 2:246.

16. David Ramsay, *The History of the American Revolution*, ed. Lester H. Cohen, 2 vols. (Indianapolis, 1990), 1:317.

17. Mercy Otis Warren, *History of the Rise, Progress and Termination of the American Revolution*, ed. Lester H. Cohen, 2 vols. (Indianapolis, 1989), 1:15–16.

18. This theme is developed in much more detail in T. H. Breen, *Marketplace of Revolution: How Consumer Politics Shaped American Independence* (New York, 2004), chaps. 6 and 7.

19. For example, see Uday Singh Mehta, *Liberalism and Empire: A Study in Nineteenth-Century British Liberal Thought* (Chicago, 1999). See also Jack P. Greene, "Transatlantic Colonization and the Redefinition of Empire in the Early Modern Era: The British-American Experience," in Christine Daniels and Michael V. Kennedy, eds., *Negotiated Empires: Centers and Peripheries in the Americas, 1500–1820* (New York, 2002), 267–82.

20. Ramsay, *History*, 1:311.

21. James Otis Jr., *A Vindication of the British Colonies* (1765), in Bernard Bailyn, ed., *Pamphlets of the American Revolution* (Cambridge, 1965), 568.

22. The creation of revolutionary trust and popular mobilization is the theme of Breen, *Marketplace of Revolution.*

23. Anderson, *Imagined Communities.*

24. Silas Deane Papers, 1753–1842: Correspondence 1761–76, box 1, folder 2, Connecticut Historical Society, Hartford.

25. "To the Gentlemen Select Men of Leicester, Massachusetts, 25 December 1769," Revolution Collection, box 1, folder 3: 1754–73, American Antiquarian Society, Worcester, Mass.; [Anonymous], *At a Town-Meeting Called by Order of the Town-Council* (Newport, R.I., 1767); *Pennsylvania Gazette*, 31 May 1770; "John Neufville, Chairman, General Committee of the Sons of Liberty in North Carolina (25 April 1770)," in William J. Saunders, ed., *Colonial Records of North Carolina*, 9 vols. (Raleigh, N.C., 1890), viii, 197–98; *South-Carolina Gazette*, 9 August 1770; "The New-Castle [Delaware] County COMPACT," *South-Carolina Gazette*, 12 October 1769; "At a Meeting of the Principal Merchants and Traders of the Colony of Connecticut," broadside, Connecticut Historical Society.

26. *Boston Gazette*, 23 November 1767.

27. *New-York Gazette and Weekly Mercury*, 29 May 1769.

28. The case for Locke is made in T. H. Breen, *The Lockean Moment: The Language of Rights on the Eve of the American Revolution* (Oxford, 2001). See also Daniel T. Rodgers, *Contested Truths: Keywords in American Politics since Independence* (Cambridge, 1987), 46–65, and "Republicanism: The Career of a Concept," *Journal of American History* (1992): 11–38.

29. William Patten, *A Discourse Delivered at Halifax in the County of Plymouth, July 24, 1766* (Boston, 1766), 7. For a fuller discussion of the specific context of the language of rights during this period see Philip A. Hamburger, "Natural Rights, Natural Law, and American Constitutions," *Yale Law Review* 102, no. 4 (1993): 907–60. See also Michael J. Lacey and Knud Haakonssen, eds., *A Culture of Rights: The Bill of Rights in Philosophy, Politics, and the Law—1791 and 1991* (Cambridge, 1991).

30. Broadside, New York 1770, "Forasmuch as it is manifest," John Carter Brown Library, Providence, R.I.

31. Cited in Sidney Kaplan, *The Black Presence in the Era of the American Revolution, 1700–1800* (Washington, D.C., 1973), 13 (original spelling).

32. John Adams to James Sullivan, 26 May 1776, in Charles F. Adams, ed., *Works of John Adams*, 10 vols. (Boston, 1850–56), 9:375–76. For a discussion of the rights of women in this society see *Massachusetts Gazette and Boston Post-Boy*, 30 May 1774.

33. This argument is made in great detail in T. H. Breen, "Subjecthood and Citizenship: The Context of James Otis's Radical Critique of John Locke," *New England Quarterly* (1998).

34. David Ramsay, *A Dissertation on the Manner of Acquiring the Character and Privileges of a Citizen of the United States* (Charleston, 1789), 3.

35. Winthrop D. Jordan, *White over Black: American Attitudes Toward the Negro, 1550–1812* (Chapel Hill, N.C., 1968), 335. See also James Oakes, " 'Whom Have I Oppressed?' The Pursuit of Happiness and the Happy Slave," in James Horn, Jan Ellen Lewis, and Peter Onuf, eds., *The Revolution of 1800: Democracy, Race and the New Republic* (Charlottesville, 2002), 220–39.

36. See Linda K. Kerber, " 'I have Don . . . much to Carrey on the Warr': Women and the Shaping of Republican Ideology after the American Revolution," in Harriet B. Applewhite and Darline G. Levy, eds., *Women and Politics in the Age of the Democratic Revolution* (Ann Arbor, 1993), 228; see also Jeanne Boydston, "Making Gender in the Early Republic: Judith Sargent Murray and the Revolution of 1800," in *The Revolution of 1800* (Charlottesville, 2002), 240–66; Rosemarie Zagarri, "The Rights of Man and Woman," *William and Mary Quarterly*, 3rd ser., 55 (1998): 203–30; and Rosemarie Zagarri, "Gender in the First American Party System," in Doran Ben-Atar and Barbara B. Oberg, eds., *Federalists Reconsidered* (Charlottesville, 1998), 118–34.

State and National Identities in the Era of the American Revolution

JACK P. GREENE

*H*ow a nation forged out of a composite of old polities develops a national identity and sense of loyalty among its citizens is an intricate and fascinating problem that deserves more attention than it has so far received in the new literature on the history of early modern and modern state formation. This problem is perhaps even more intriguing when, as in the case of the United States, the new national state is an unintended consequence of an unplanned political movement. Obviously, there could have been no specifically *American* nationalism based on loyalty to an American national polity before there was such a polity or at the very least the imminent prospect of such a state. And the new United States, initiated in the throes of political resistance against White-hall and military resistance against a trained army, jointly intent on bending colonists to the metropolitan will, did not come into existence until 1776 and was not even in prospect before the fall of 1774.

To unravel the problems of national identity emerging in the United States during the revolutionary era—what kind of identity and how it emerged—it is first necessary to understand the nature of the corporate identities and loyalties extant in the several polities that came together to form the nation. Insofar as the inhabitants of these polities had a larger national identity, that identity was not, contrary to the implicit assumption of a couple of generations of American studies students, pervaded by a longing for the nascence of an American national self, engendered by an American national state. Rather, it revolved around the colonists' pride in their attachment to the highly successful national state of Great Britain.

This attachment was a function of the very nature of early modern English colonization. As Richard Helgerson and Liah Greenfeld have recently emphasized, a distinctive and well-articulated sense of national identity was a product of the late Elizabethan and early Jacobean eras, the very time when English people were beginning to form the first English colonies in America. Protestantism and, increasingly during the late seventeenth and eighteenth centuries, the slowly expanding commercial and maritime superiority of the English nation were significant components of this identity. Far more significant, however, was the English system of law and liberty. Epitomized by the consensual institutions of juries and parliaments and by the tradition of the subordination of the monarch to law, this system, contemporary English and many foreign observers agreed, constituted the principal distinction between English people and all others on the face of the globe.[1]

The overwhelmingly English people who created and organized all of the English or, after 1707, British colonies in America took with them to their new homes explicit and deeply held claims to the culture they left behind and to the national identity implicit in that culture. Everywhere they went to colonize they manifested their powerful determination to express and preserve their Englishness by reordering existing physical and cultural landscapes along English lines, imposing upon them English patterns of land occupation, economic and social organization, cultural practices, and political, legal, and religious systems, and making the English language the language of authority. This was true even of those settlements formed by those who, like Massachusetts Puritans, hoped to improve upon English institutions. Far from being moderated by the contemporary immigration of significant numbers of people from other parts of Britain, Ireland, and Germany, this Anglicizing impulse seems actually to have been reinforced during the decades after 1740 by growing communication and commercial links between the colonies and Britain and by the colonies' important participation in the imperial wars against Catholic and allegedly despotic France and Spain between 1739 and 1763. Probably at no time during the colonial era had colonial British patriotism and nationalism been more intense than they were at the conclusion of the Seven Years War.

For English colonists and their descendants, however, a variety of conditions operated during the long colonial years both to render colonial claims to Englishness problematic and to enhance the urgency of such claims among immigrants and their descendants. These included the colonists' great physical distance from England; the social and cultural contrasts, especially during the colonies' earliest decades, between the simple and crude societies they were constructing and the complex and infinitely more polite society from which they came; their situation on the outermost edges of English civilization in the midst of populations who to them appeared pagan, barbarous, and savage; the presence, if not the preponderance, in their societies of aliens in the form of indigenous Americans and, later, Africans; their frequent reliance upon new institutions, such as plantations and chattel, race-based slavery; their persistent conflicts with the parent state over whether they, as colonists, were entitled to

English laws and privileges; and, perhaps most important of all, a general tendency among people in the home islands to regard them as "others" who fell considerably short of metropolitan standards.[2]

Nothing brought home more forcefully to colonists the problematic character of their claims to a British identity than the various measures at issue between the colonies and Britain between 1764 and 1776. At bottom, the colonists objected to being taxed and governed in their internal affairs without their consent precisely because such measures were contrary to the rights and legal protections traditionally enjoyed by free or "independent" Britons and thus called into question their identity as British people. The vociferousness of their objections proclaimed the profound importance they continued to attach to maintaining that identity. Indeed, what came to be known as the American Revolution was to a significant degree a direct outgrowth of colonial resistance to those measures and should be understood as a movement by colonial Britons to secure metropolitan acknowledgment of their British identity. Before the winter of 1775–76, when sentiment for independence became widespread, union among the colonies was principally a means to this end.[3]

Important as it was, the colonists' shared identity as freeborn and Protestant Britons was always mediated through a set of colonial identities. Over the years each colony, as a separate and semiautonomous social and political entity, evolved a specific corporate identity peculiar to itself. Rooted in a particular physical space, manifested in a specific form of socioeconomic organization, extended, modified, and refined by decades of collective experience, and internalized by several generations of Creoles and immigrants, these colonial identities and the loyalties and commitments associated with them had, by the era of the American Revolution, become powerfully entrenched.

If the colonists shared a common British identity, that identity thus everywhere existed in symbiosis with another identity that was locationally and socially based, historically grounded, explained and justified, culturally transmitted from one generation to the next, and prescriptive. *Briton* was thus a category with many subcategories. To be a Virginian was to be different from a Pennsylvanian or a Rhode Islander. If colonists undertook political resistance to defend their claims to a British identity, they also brought to that resistance well-developed and deeply held provincial identities with which they were comfortable, of which they were proud, and about which they could be extraordinarily defensive.

If attacks upon their entitlement to a British national identity drove the colonists to resist, the strength of their provincial identities helps to explain why they were not more hesitant in 1776 to give up their British identity. Long ago, in most cases, they had found ways to fold their British identity—with its emphasis upon Protestantism, liberty, rule of law, consensual governance, civility, and commerce—into their provincial identities. For that reason, when the colonists abandoned their formal connection with Britain, they did not so much forfeit their national British identity as reaffirm their attachment to and exemplification of its principal components. Secure in their several provincial identities, colonial resistance leaders could relinquish the association with Britain and transform colonies into republican polities without fear of losing their long-standing and psychologically important sense of themselves as freeborn Protestant peoples and legitimate heirs to British traditions of consensual governance and rule of law. By asserting their distinctive provincial identities and pointedly carrying them over into the new states they created out of the old colonial polities, revolutionary leaders everywhere effectively staked out a claim for those states as the genuine repositories of all that was admirable about the British national identity and thereby reiterated their continuing *cultural* identification with the larger British world to which they had so long been attached.

Moreover, throughout the revolutionary era—and in the founding states probably for several decades thereafter—these provincial identities represented the principal form of collective consciousness. Before the mid-1770s the conventional wisdom, as expressed, for instance, by Benjamin Franklin in a 1760 pamphlet published in London, was that the colonies were too dissimilar even to act in concert for their own defense, much less to amalgamate into a single polity. The colonies were "not only under different governors, but have different forms of government, different laws, different interests, and some of them different religious persuasions and different manners," Franklin wrote, adding that the "jealousy of each other" was "so great that however necessary an union of the colonies has long been, for their common defence and security against their enemies, yet they have never been able to effect such an union among themselves, nor even to agree in requesting the mother country to establish it for them."[4]

When delegates from the continental colonies came together in the First and Second Continental Congress in 1774 and 1775, this insight hovered in the background. Those who were most cautious about resistance to Britain, including especially the Pennsylvania lawyer and future loyalist Joseph Galloway, stressed the profound differences among the colonies and the probable effects of those differences upon their ability to maintain a common resistance. "Their different Forms of Government—Productions of Soil—and Views of Commerce, their different Religions—Tempers and private Interests—their Prejudices against, and Jealousies of each other—all have, and," he predicted, "ever" would operate "to create such a Diversity of Interests[,] Inclinations, and Decisions" that they would never be able to "unite together even for their own Protection." In Galloway's view this disunity had two potentially harmful effects. First, it made the colonies "weak in themselves." Many of them, he noted in calling attention to the pervasive institution of chattel slavery in North America, already held "an

Enemy within their own Bowels ready to destroy" them. Second, it made them potential arenas for civil wars. When "Controversies founded in Interest, Religion or Ambition" erupted among them, Galloway warned, the colonies would become "an Easy Prey to every foreign Invader."[5]

Nevertheless, the strong and surprisingly pervasive feelings of identification with the "common cause" in 1774–76 provided a foundation for the early articulation of aspirations for the creation of a broader American identity. Thus did the Virginia lawyer and orator Patrick Henry announce at the First Continental Congress that the "Distinctions between Virginians, Pennsylvanians, New Yorkers, and New Englanders, are no more. I am not a Virginian, but an American."[6] Thus did the Pennsylvania physician Benjamin Rush in the days immediately after the Declaration of Independence urge his fellow delegates to give "up colony distinctions." "We are now One people—a new nation," he declared, arguing both that Americans were "not more divided" in their "Interests, language & trade" than were the people of Great Britain and that "the variety of interests" and productions among them was actually such an extraordinary "Advantage to us" as to suggest that "heaven [had] intended us for one people."[7] "One general Congress has brought the Colonies to be acquainted with each other," Connecticut delegate Silas Deane waxed optimistically in early 1775, "and I am in hopes another may effect a lasting Confederation which will need nothing perhaps, but time, to mature into a complete & perfect American Constitution."[8]

But such "national" enthusiasm always was tempered by recognition of the incredible diversity among the colonies. As the Rhode Islander Samuel Ward wrote to a correspondent back home, congressional delegates were certainly "very happy . . . that the common Good of our Country" seemed "to be the General Aim" of all the delegates.[9] Virginian Richard Henry Lee declared that "all the old Provinces, not one excepted," were "directed by the same firmness of union, and determination to resist [Britain] by all ways and to every extremity."[10] As they became better acquainted with one another, studied their collaborators' "Character and Tempers" and "Principles and Views," and learned ever more about the distinctive patterns of "Trade, Policy, and Whole Interest of a Dozen [separate] Provinces,"[11] however, they also rapidly came to the realization that "the different Forms of Government in the several Colonies, different Educations, Books, & Company naturally occasion[ed] the viewing political Objects in a light not always the same."[12]

These differences provided the foundation for unfavorable comparisons and growing jealousies. As delegates sized up representatives from other colonies and found them wanting, they also developed an enhanced appreciation for what it was about their own provincial society that made it superior to those in other regions, thus powerfully reinforcing the provincial identities that they had brought with them to Philadelphia. This process did little to alter existing stereotypes and suspicions. As the object of the Coercive Acts of 1774, Massachusetts was at the center of the firestorm of resistance, and New England delegates "found a strong Jealousy of Us, from New England, and the Massachusetts in Particular." Delegates from other regions, the Massachusetts lawyer John Adams wrote to his wife, Abigail, were suspicious that the New Englanders had "Designs of Independency," that they wanted to create and dominate "an American Republic," that they were religious bigots who acted on "Presbyterian Principles—and twenty other Things." The appointment of George Washington, a Virginian, as commander in chief of the army in the spring of 1775, Adams hoped, would allay such jealousies and "have a great Effect, in cementing and securing the Union of these Colonies."[13]

Washington's appointment may indeed have cemented relations between Virginia and Massachusetts, the two colonies that over the past decade had vied with one another to take the lead in resisting British efforts to tax the colonies and tighten up colonial administration, but it by no means eliminated the deep fissures and jealousies among the colonies. When the British government showed every sign that it was determined to secure colonial obedience by force and when throughout the first half of 1776 colonial leaders increasingly began to think in terms of political independence, they remained uneasy lest some recalcitrant colony break the unity of the resistance movement. Virginia, the two Carolinas, and the New England colonies all moved relatively quickly to support the movement for independence, but some of the middle colonies, including especially Maryland, Pennsylvania, and New York, acted with far more deliberation. This anxious situation aroused all the latent suspicions and distrust the colonies had of each other. Thus did James Duane in May 1776 caution his fellow New York delegate John Jay against moving too quickly for independence. We should wait to see "the Conduct of the [other] middle colonies before we come to a Decision," he wrote. "[I]t cannot injure us to wait a few weeks: the Advantage will be great, for this trying Question will clearly discover the true principles & the Extent of the Union of the Colonies."[14]

Such cautious behavior did not endear New Yorkers to their fellow resistance leaders. Before Maryland opted for independence John Adams described it as "so eccentric a Colony—sometimes hot sometimes so cold—now so high, then so low—that . . . I have often wished it could exchange Places with Halifax[, Nova Scotia]."[15] But Adams reserved his most negative judgments for New York, the last colony to opt for independence. "Is it Deceit, or Simple Dul[l]ness in the People of" New York "which occasions their eccentric and retrograde Politicks," Adams fumed to the New Hampshire politician John Sullivan in late June 1776.[16] "What is the Reason that New York must continue to embarrass the Continent? Must it be so forever? What is the Cause of it?" Adams asked

Connecticut leader Samuel Holden Parsons at the same time. "Have they no Politicians, capable of instructing and forming the Sentiments of their People? Or are their People incapable of seeing and feeling like other Men. One would think that their Proximity to New England, would assimilate their opinions and Principles," he observed. "One would think too that the [presence of units of the British] Army [in New York] would have some Influence upon them. But it seems to have none. N. York is likely to have the Honour of being the very last of all in imbibing the genuine Principles and the true system of American Policy. Perhaps," he despaired, "she will never entertain them [at] all."[17]

In a letter to his friend Cotton Tufts, Adams penetrated to what he thought was the fundamental explanation for New York's hesitant progress toward endorsing independence: its very character and collective identity. New York, he wrote,

> still acts in Character, like a People without Courage or sense, or Spirit, or in short any one Virtue or Ability. There is neither Spunk nor Gumption, in that Province as a Body. Individuals are very clever. But it is the weakest Province in point of Intellect, Valour, public Spirit, or any thing else that is great and good upon the Continent. It is incapable of doing Us much good, or much Hurt, but from its local situation. The low Cunning of Individuals, and their Prostitution plagues Us, the Virtues of a few Individuals is of some Service to Us. But as a Province it will be a dead Weight upon any side, ours or that of our Enemies.[18]

The more delegates to Congress came to realize that political disagreements among the various colonies to some important extent rested upon deep-seated social and characterological differences, the more attractive became the sort of explanation offered by Adams, founded as it was on the assumption that every colony had a distinctive corporate identity and character. If, culturally and politically, the colonists were all in a general sense Britons, the category *Briton*, they discovered, came in many varieties. John Adams, one of the most astute observers of his fellow delegates, wrote:

> The Character of Gentlemen in the four New England Colonies differ[s] as much from those in the others, as that of the Common People differs, that is as much as *several distinct Nations* almost. Gentlemen, Men of Sense, or any kind of Education in the other Colonies are much fewer in Proportion than in N. England. Gentlemen in the other Colonies have large Plantations of slaves, and the common People among them are very ignorant and very poor. These Gentlemen are accustomed, habituated to higher Notions of themselves and the distinction between them and the common People, than We are.

"An instantaneous alteration of that Character of a Colony, and that Temper and those Sentiments which its Inhabitants imbibed with their Mother[']s Milk, and which have grown with their Growth and strengthened with their Strength," Adams opined, could "not be made without a Miracle." Although he held out hope that "an Alteration of the Southern Constitution, which must certainly take Place if the War continues," would "gradually bring all the Continent nearer and nearer to each other in all Respects," he expressed his dread of the short-term "Consequences of this Dissimilitude of Character." "Without the Utmost Caution on both sides, and the most considerate Forbearance with one another and prudent Condescension on both sides," he worried, "they will certainly be fatal."[19] "In such a Period as this, Sir, when Thirteen Colonies unacquainted in a great Measure, with each other, are rushing together into one Mass," Adams wrote another correspondent, "it would be a Miracle, if such heterogeneous Ingredients did not at first produce violent Fermentations."[20]

The pronounced heterogeneity to which Adams referred proved to be a formidable challenge to those who hoped to create a durable political union. Although it did not prevent any colony from voting for independence and transforming itself into a republican polity, it profoundly affected the character of the general government they began to try to construct in the summer of 1776. In the weeks immediately after the Declaration of Independence, when Congress first took up the intricate problem of creating a durable political union among the former colonies it quickly discovered how fundamental these differences actually were. The delegates disagreed strongly over whether slaves should be counted as property or as people in apportioning government expenses, whether the carrying trade should be taxed, whether states with western land claims should give them up to the general government, whether voting in Congress should be by states or by population or wealth, and, most important of all, how authority should be distributed between the national government and the states.

Some delegates joined with John Witherspoon, president of the College of New Jersey, in urging a strong and permanent union. Arguing that a "common danger is the great and only effectual means of settling difficulties, and composing differences" and pointing out the efficacy of the current conflict with Britain "in producing such a degree of union through these colonies, as nobody would have prophesied and hardly any would have expected," Witherspoon urged that there would never be a more propitious time for the colonies to put aside their jealousies, transcend their local interests and attachments, and effect a vigorous and lasting union. "If the colonies are independent states, separate and disunited, after this war," he warned, "we may be sure of coming off the worse."[21]

But many delegates took a shorter-term view. Thus did the Virginian Benjamin Harrison advocate a confederation "in which the objects of the war should be defined, the terms of closing it delineated, and the colonies of the union bound to each other to contribute their respective force to obtain these objects, and when these objects were attained, that any one colony should have a right to say they will go no farther."[22] Harrison's advocacy of providing a clear exit strategy for those states that found confederation uncongenial scarcely betokened even a deep commitment to the idea of a *permanent* union, much less any deep sense of American nationalism.

The debate over confederation laid bare a fundamental difference between those states in which slavery was of paramount economic importance and those in which it was not. Thus did James Wilson of Pennsylvania vigorously insist that slaves ought to be taxed the same as free people. Some states, he noted, had "as many black as white [people]," and to exempt slaves from taxation would mean that those states "would not pay more than half of what they ought." Besides, he objected, such an exemption would "be the greatest Encouragement to continue Slave keeping, and to increase them," and slaves, he observed, "prevent[ed] freemen from cultivating a Country" and were "attended with many Inconveniences." "If it is to be debated, whether Slaves are their Property," the South Carolina planter Thomas Lynch angrily retorted, "there is an End of the Confederation. Our Slaves being our Property," he asked, "why should they be taxed more than Land, Sheep, Cattle, Horses, &c.?" Benjamin Franklin, Wilson's fellow Pennsylvania delegate, had a ready answer. Slaves, he said, "rather weaken[ed] than strengthen[ed] the State, and there is therefore some difference between them and Sheep. Sheep will never make any Insurrections."[23]

In these early days of the American national union, however, the extent of slavery was not the crucial divide. Delegates from the states from New York south had deep reservations about the designs of New England, or what they referred to as the "Eastern states." Thus did the Maryland delegate Samuel Chase worry that the "great Advantage in Trade" enjoyed by the "Eastern Colonies" would give them a Superiority."[24] Thus in a letter to New York delegate John Jay did Edward Rutledge of South Carolina express his dread of the New Englanders' "over-ruling Influence in Council" and "their low Cunning, and those levelling Principles which Men without Character and without Fortune in general Possess, which are so captivating to the lower Class of Mankind, and which will occasion such a fluctuation of Property as to introduce the greatest disorder." "If the Plan now proposed should be adopted," Rutledge declared in the summer of 1776, "nothing less than the Ruin to some Colonies will be the Consequence of it. The idea of destroying all Provincial Distinctions and making every thing of the most minute kind bend to what they call the good of the whole," he observed, "is in other Terms to say that these Colonies must be subject to the Government of the Eastern Provinces." Rutledge spoke for many delegates when he expressed his resolve "to vest the Congress with no more Power than what is absolutely necessary, and to use a familiar Expression to keep the Staff in our own [i.e., the states'] Hands, for I am confident if [it be] surrendered into the Hands of others a most pernicious use will be made of it." "Unless it is greatly curtailed," he predicted, the confederation could "never pass, as it is to be submitted to Men, in the respective Provinces who will not be led or rather driven into Measures which may lay the Foundation of their Ruin [as provinces]."[25]

Of course, the determination to keep the preponderance of power in the hands of the states was not entirely a function of state jealousies and fears of domination and ruin. It had solid intellectual underpinnings, arising from the logic of the American constitutional argument for exemption from metropolitan interference in the internal affairs of the colonies. No principle had been more important to the colonial case than the doctrine that government had to be founded on consent. As John Dickinson explained to the inhabitants of Quebec in late 1774, "the first grand Right" of British governance was the right "of the People" to have "a Share in the Government of themselves." By this right, he wrote, "is secured to them their own Government by their Representatives chosen by themselves and in consequence thereof of being ruled by *Laws* which they have themselves approved, not by *Edicts of Men* over whom they have no Controul." At this early stage of nation building, relatively few questioned that the state governments—in Dickinson's words, the people's "own Government"— and not some distant general government were the best vehicles for the protection of life, liberty, and property and most directly expressive of the people's interests and identities.[26]

The depth of this attachment to state governments combined with the expanding awareness of the dissimilarities among the states and the mutual suspicions and jealousies arising out of those dissimilarities to cause many delegates to despair of ever achieving a viable union. "I am inclined to think that we shall never modell" a confederation "so as to be agreed to by all the Colonies," observed the North Carolina delegate Joseph Hewes in late July 1776.[27] "The Ideas of North & South (or as now properly called East & West)," reported Connecticut delegate William Williams in August 1776, were "as wide as yer Poles." With "such clashing & jarring Interests, such diversity of manners &c. &c.," he declared, "I little expect any permanent Union."[28] The Pennsylvania lawyer John Dickinson, author of the initial draft of the Articles of Confederation, was one of the earliest of many analysts who questioned whether a formal union could ever be sustained and "whether in 20 or 30 Years this Commonwealth of Colonies may not be too unwieldy—& Hudson's River be a proper Boundary for a separate Commonwealth to the Northward." "I have a strong impression on my Mind," he said, that such a division "will take Place."[29]

At the same time that Congress was making so little progress in what John Adams called the "most intricate, the most important, the most dangerous, and delicate Business" of designing a workable national government, the individual colonies were rapidly and successfully transforming themselves into republi-

can polities.[30] By the fall of 1776, as Benjamin Rush reported to a French correspondent, "new governments" had been "instituted in all the states, founded on
the authority of the people."[31] By early 1777 only three states—New York, New
Hampshire, and Massachusetts—had failed to adopt formal constitutions, and
New York and New Hampshire would soon do so. Moreover, these constitutions
were expressive of local loyalties and pride, for the most part being warmly endorsed by the local populace. For example, after the South Carolina Provincial
Congress had promulgated a new constitution in the spring of 1776 and selected
new officers, the people reportedly responded "with Transports of Joy." When
the new officers walked through Charleston attended by a company of horse,
John Adams learned from two men who had recently come from South Carolina
to Philadelphia, "the People gazed at them, with a kind of Rapture. They both
told me," said Adams, "that the Reflection that these were Gentlemen of their
own Choice, whom they could trust, and whom they could displace if any of
them should behave amiss, affected them so that they could not help crying."[32]

Although the several state constitutions were similar to the extent of founding the polity on popular consent, assigning the predominance of power to the
legislature, and providing for annual elections of legislators, they differed from
one another in many particulars. These "particulars" were an expression of the
identities that each of the colonies had developed over the long colonial era.
Indeed, the extent to which these constitutions replicated, with a formal republican twist, the governing arrangements with which the colonists had been
familiar in the colonial era is remarkable. In general, those constitutions tended,
as the North Carolina delegate William Hooper remarked in the fall of 1776, to
be "as nearly as similar as possible to the old one[s], abolishing little else but the
regal & proprietary powers and deriving all power from the people."[33] In providing for a single-house legislature, which many delegates to Congress regarded
as "a visionary system,"[34] even the Pennsylvania Constitution, which contained
the most innovations and elicited the most opposition, replicated Pennsylvania's colonial constitution, which also operated without a second branch of the
legislature. To be sure, some states undertook some changes. Thus John Adams
praised the North Carolina and Virginia constitutions, prematurely in the case
of Virginia, for making "an Effort for the Destruction of Bigotry" by abolishing
"their Establishments of Episcopacy so far as to give compleat Liberty of Con-
science to Dissenters, an Acquisition in favour of the Rights of Mankind," he
thought, "which is worth all the Blood and Treasure which has been and will
be Spent in this war."[35] Throughout the colonies, however, constitution makers
tended to stay with the familiar. They did not reconstruct political boundaries,
change the nature of local governance, alter the structure of the judicial system, or undertake any wholesale overhaul of the ancient legal systems that had
evolved during the long colonial period to suit the specific conditions of life

and the "genius" or identity of the inhabitants of each state. Rather, they seem to have acted in the spirit of an observation of Connecticut delegate William Williams, who averred that it would be "impossible for us to get a better [constitution] on the whole than our Fathers chose for Us & we have long practised upon with great Peace & Happiness, and that any alterations or Innovations wo'd be attended with dangerous Consequence."[36]

The rapidity with which the state governments seized power and established their authority effectively dictated that provincial distinctions, with all "the local prejudices, and particular interests," and specific identities they involved, would gain in intensity and contribute to the perpetuation of those extreme "jealousies of each other" that had come to the fore in the early days of the Revolution.[37] This development both expressed and sharpened the older provincial identities by which people in all the original states continued to define themselves. In effect, the composite American federal state in its initial form thus created an arena for the reiteration and sharpening of provincial state identities. So fundamental were these identities and the distinctions on which they were based that many people came to think of them as definitional. Indeed, they came to believe, as the Rhode Island merchant Stephen Hopkins remarked in the early debates over the confederation, that "the Safety of the whole" depended "upon the Distinction of the Colonies."[38] The Revolution, as Silas Deane of Connecticut said early in the struggle, was fundamentally about securing "the particular, & local Privileges, Rights, & immunities of British American Subjects" as those rights had been enjoyed and legally embedded in the several colonies.[39] This deep attachment to local rights, manners, and identities enormously affected the nature of the national government and dictated that attachments people had to it would be secondary to the primary attachments they had to their own states.

While the congressional debates over the terms of confederation dragged on, congressional delegates showed considerable scrupulosity about infringing on the rights of the states. Thomas Burke from North Carolina was particularly articulate on this subject, denying that "provisions made by Continental Councils" should ever "be enforced by Continental authority." To do so, he asserted, would be to give "Congress a Power to prostrate all the Laws and Constitutions of the states" by creating "a Power within each [state] that must act entirely Independent of them, and might act directly contrary to them." "By virtue of this Power," he warned, Congress could "render Ineffectual all the Barriers Provided in the States for the Security of the Rights of the Citizens[,] for," he explained, if they gave "a Power to act Coercively it must be against the Subject of some State, and the subject of every state was entitled to the Protection of that particular state, and subject to the Laws of that alone, because to them alone did he give his Consent."[40] In a similar vein James Smith, a Pennsylvania delegate, objected to efforts to give Congress authority to institute wage and price controls because "such a recommendation would interfere with the domestic police of each State," which was a subject "of too delicate a nature to be touched by the congress."[41]

Given such attitudes, it is scarcely surprising that the articles upon which Congress eventually agreed left the balance of authority with the states. Ever on the alert for any provision that might leave "it in the power of the future Congress . . . to explain away every right before belonging to the States, or to make their power as unlimited as they pleased," Thomas Burke encountered surprisingly little opposition to his "amendment, which held up the principle, that all sovereign Power was in the States separately, and that particular acts of it, which should be expressly enumerated, would be exercised in conjunction, and not otherwise; but that in all things else each State would Exercise all the rights and powers of sovereignty, uncontrolled." Only Virginia voted against him, with New Hampshire abstaining. In its final form Burke's amendment, which became Article 2 of the Articles of Confederation, provided that "each State retains its sovereignty, freedom, and independence, and every power, jurisdiction, and right, which is not by this confederation expressly delegated to the United States, in Congress assembled."[42]

Burke interpreted his triumph as a necessary step for the perpetuation of a weak national government, and he was delighted that it came so easily. "I was much pleased to find the opinion of accumulating powers to Congress so little supported, and I promise myself, in the whole business I shall find my ideas relative thereto nearly similar to those of most of the States," Burke wrote to fellow North Carolinian Richard Caswell. "In a word, Sir, I am of opinion the Congress should have power enough to call out and apply the common strength for the common defence: but not for the partial purposes of ambition."[43] Nor did he think even that the jurisdiction of the national government should extend over commerce. "The United States ought to be as One Sovereign (power) with respect to foreign Powers, on all things that relate to War or where the states have one Common Interest," he argued in Congress in December 1777. "But in all Commercial or other peaceful Intercourse they ought to be as separate Sovereigns."[44] Following his victory, Burke referred to Congress as "the united Council of free, Independent, Sovereign States of America," thus pointedly emphasizing its limited character.[45]

The overwhelming desire to maintain the "separate independence" and identities of the states thus dictated that the national government should both have limited powers and command little affection within the United States at large.[46] Throughout the war and after, state and local governments continued to be the primary venues for the fulfillment of people's political goals and the principal sites at which citizens interacted with their governments. Even as the war itself drew attention to the common cause and stimulated the formation of a rudimentary national patriotism, these conditions operated to reinforce people's ancient identification with their states.

With the ratification of the Articles of Confederation in 1781 the United States attained a formal structure of national governance, but many congressional leaders doubted that it would last. When James M. Varnum became a delegate from Rhode Island in 1781, he found Congress hamstrung by the delegates' concern to protect the rights and interests of their respective states. This concern, he reported, "frustrate[d] every Attempt to introduce a more efficacious System." As a result, he complained, Congress spent its time "in trifling executive Business, while Objects of the greatest Magnitude" were "postponed, or rejected as subversive in their Nature, of democratical Liberty," which the delegates equated with the continuing supremacy of the states. "A Prudent Caution against the Abuse of Power," he noted, "is very requisite for supporting the principles of republican Governments, but when that Caution is carried too far, the Event may, and probably will prove alarming." The "Time is not far distant," he conjectured, "when the present American Congress will be dissolved, or laid aside as Useless, unless a Change of Measures shall render their Authority more respectable."[47] A few months later the Virginia delegate James Madison recommended to the legislature of his state that it should "presume that the present Union will but little survive the present war."[48]

Nor did the prospects for the continuance of the union change during the final years of the war or with the peace. Some states were notoriously slow to pay their shares of congressional requisitions for carrying on the war. Delegates committed to the perpetuation of union, like James Madison, argued in vain that such requisitions "were a law to the States, as much as the acts of the latter for complying with them were a law to their individual members: that the foederal constitution was as sacred & obligatory as the internal constitutions of the several States; and that nothing could justify the States in disobeying acts warranted by it."[49] But the states had the upper hand, and each one did as it pleased. "There was," lamented James Wilson, "more of a centrifugal than centripetal force in the States."[50]

This uncertain situation led to a demand to endow the national government with at least a limited taxing power, but such demands invariably encountered strong opposition. Thus did Arthur Lee, a delegate from Virginia, predict in the winter of 1783 that the states "would never agree to those plans which tend to aggrandize" national authority because they "were jealous of the power of Congress." Acknowledging "himself to be one of those who thought this jealousy not an unreasonable one," Lee asserted that "no one who had ever opened a page or read a line on the subject of liberty, could be insensible to the danger of surrendering the purse into the same hand which held the sword."[51] Lee evidently spoke for many delegates when he announced on a subsequent occasion that "he had rather see Congress a rope of sand than a rod of iron."[52]

In this situation many delegates thought that the union could not persist in its existing form. "It is now the general Idea in Congress," Massachusetts congressman Stephen Higginson reported in the summer of 1783, that "the present Confederation will not answer any longer" and that "a dissolution must take its place, . . . & I expect it will by common sense like the old money be declared unfit & laid aside."[53] Some people predicted civil war among the states.[54] Others assumed that the thirteen states would break up into several smaller confederacies united merely for defensive purposes. Thus early in 1783 Nathaniel Gorum of Massachusetts argued that "the Union could never be maintained on any other ground than that of justice" and pointed out that "some States had suffered greatly from the deficiencies of others," declaring that "if Justice was not to be obtained through the foederal system & this system was to fail as would necessarily follow, it was time this should be known [so] that some of the states might be forming other confederacies adequate to the purposes of their safety."[55]

Charles Thomson, longtime secretary to Congress, spelled out the forces and logic behind such a dissolution in the summer of 1783 and speculated about the form the separate confederacies would take and why. "The common danger which has hitherto held these states together being now removed, I see local prejudices, passions and views already beginning to operate with all their force," Thomson wrote in underlining the continuing primacy of state identities in organizing the political consciousness of Americans. "And I confess I have my fears, that the predictions of our enemies will be found true, that on the removal of common danger our Confederacy & Union will be a rope of sand. There must & will undoubtedly be, for the sake of security, some confederation of states," he continued, "[b]ut how many of the states will be comprehended in a Confederacy or how many confederacys there will be is yet uncertain."[56]

In speculating about the number and nature of these confederacies Thomson stressed the importance of similarities in interests, manners, demographic composition, and identities. He foresaw the formation of four separate confederacies. The "four eastern states" in New England, he predicted, "will form one confederacy" because their "manners, customs and government" were "very similar" and they were "an unmixed people, being all sprung from a common stock without any great accession of strangers or foreigners." New York, he thought, would "be compelled to join the confederacy either voluntarily or by force not from any of the causes aforementioned; [b]ut because the eastern states will not think themselves secure if Hudson's river & the northern lakes, which are the keys of the country, are kept by a people independent of and separated from them. For this purpose the state of Vermont, which has hitherto given NY some trouble, will be supported & encouraged & kept as a rod over the head of NY & if necessary used to chastise & compel it into the eastern Confederacy." Because they were "all states whose boundaries are fixed and confined and who have one common strong desire to possess a share of the great Western territory, which they now claim as their right and as an acquisition which the present confederacy has obtained by the expense of their blood and treasure," the middle states of New Jersey, Pennsylvania, Delaware, and Maryland, Thomson conjectured, would form a second union.[57]

Thomson thought that Virginia, the largest and most populous of the states, would comprise a nation unto itself. "The haughtiness of Virginia, its great extent and its boundless claims," he wrote, would "induce it to set up for itself," and "if ever royal government is set up in N. America," Virginia would be the place where it would "first erect its throne." Virginia's "first quarrel," he speculated, would "be with the middle confederacy about the western Country. Unless perhaps the people beyond the Allegheny Mountains should be induced first to set up for themselves and to claim an exclusive right to that country. In that case Virginia may attempt to subjugate them & the middle confederacy will support them against her. She may then attempt to form an alliance with the Eastern confederacy or the three Southern states." Finally, Thomson suggested, the three southern states of North Carolina, South Carolina, and Georgia would probably "league together but without any close confederacy. For," he explained, "such is the fiery pride of South Carolina, such the dissipation of her morals & her insolence occasioned by the multitude of slaves that she will not cordially join in any Union till she is taught wisdom by sore suffering." Thus divided into rival confederacies, "America," Thomson worried, "may be the theatre of war & her councils become famous for brigues [strife] & intreagues of policy."[58]

Thomson and other observers who predicted the early demise of the first American national union after the peace were wrong. The confederation did not collapse. Instead, it limped along much as it had done during the war. Theoretically, as Nathan Dane, a delegate from Massachusetts, noted in 1786, the confederation provided for "a Just division of power between a federal head and the Legislatures of the States," with Congress holding "the weapons of war & the palms of peace" and the states having jurisdiction over all other aspects of public and domestic relations. But this relationship was far from equal. As he went on to explain, "the respective States" retained the upper hand. They held "the purse strings of the Union, the power of creating Congress annually[,] . . . recalling its members at pleasure and regulating the rewards of their Services." As a result, delegates usually expressed the opinions and the identities of the states they represented. "We seldom see a member of Congress depart from the opinions of his State," Dane wrote. "Even tho he may be fully convinced that that opinion is founded on mistaken facts and would be given up by the State had it possess'd itself of the true State of things and of the information he has," Dane said, "he will ever harbour doubts whether it is in his power to induce his constituents to alter their opinion & think with him." Yet Dane had "little doubt that it will be always safest to leave the ballance of power inclining in favor of the respective Legislatures[,] it being then not quite so far removed from the people."[59] In the American scheme of governance as it operated between 1775 and 1787 Congress, as Nathaniel Gorham observed just over a year before the Federal Convention of 1787, was "but the shadow of a Government."[60]

The national governments that presided over the war and confederation periods were too feeble, too much in thrall to the states, and too remote from most people's lives to generate a national sense of collective identity strong enough to challenge the identities of the separate states. Formed in the shadows of and coexisting with those older and infinitely more immediate identities, American national identity remained embryonic and superficial. The manifold literary and cultural expressions of American patriotism during and after the Revolution are misleading.[61] In the new composite American national polity state identities would long continue to be central.

To understand in its fullest dimensions the nature of collective identity in the early republic, then, historians need to come to terms with its colonial roots and provincial variants. The powerful state identities inherited from the colonial era and the deep-seated provincial loyalties, habits, and prejudices they expressed represented a formidable challenge for those who hoped to create a durable national union. The war-oriented and contingent union thrown together in 1775–76 did little to foster a full-blown and deeply internalized rival national identity, and the constitution of 1787 provided a framework in which state identities could easily coexist with an emerging American national sense of self and even retain much of their vitality. How during the early nineteenth century those state identities interacted with demands for a larger national identity and whether, when, and how they might have merged with or been transcended by such an identity are interesting and difficult problems that scholars have scarcely begun to address. The American Civil War might be taken as an indication of how fragile American national sentiment yet was after ninety years of nationhood. Perhaps the search for answers to these questions should concentrate upon a much later era.

NOTES

1. See Richard Helgerson, *Forms of Nationhood: The Elizabethan Writing of England* (Chicago, 1992); and Liah Greenfeld, *Nationalism: Five Roads to Modernity* (Cambridge, Mass., 1992), 27–87.

2. These themes are elaborated more fully in Jack P. Greene, "Empire and Identity

from the Glorious Revolution to the American Revolution," in P. J. Marshall, ed., *The Eighteenth Century,* vol. 2 of *The Oxford History of the British Empire* (Oxford, 1998), 208–30.

3. This interpretation is developed at greater length in Jack P. Greene, *The British Revolution in America* (Austin, Tex., 1996).

4. Benjamin Franklin, *The Interest of Great Britain Considered* (London, 1760), in Leonard W. Labaree et al., eds., *The Papers of Benjamin Franklin,* 27 vols. to date (New Haven, Conn., 1959–), 9:90.

5. Joseph Galloway to Samuel Verplanck, 30 December 1774, in Paul H. Smith, ed., *Letters of Delegates to Congress 1774–1789,* 26 vols. (Washington, D.C., 1976–2000), 2:288.

6. Patrick Henry, speech, in John Adams's notes of debates, 6 September 1774, in ibid., 1:28.

7. Benjamin Rush's notes for a speech, 1 August 1776, in ibid., 4:598–601.

8. Silas Deane to Patrick Henry, 25 January 1775, in ibid., 1:291.

9. Samuel Ward to Henry Marchant, 7 October 1774, in ibid., 1:162.

10. Richard Henry Lee to William Lee, 10 May 1775, in ibid., 1:337.

11. John Adams to Abigail Adams, 7 October 1774, in ibid., 1:154–55.

12. Samuel Ward to Henry Marchant, 7 October 1774, in ibid., 1:162.

13. John Adams to Abigail Adams, 17 June 1775, in ibid., 1:497.

14. James Duane to John Jay, 18 May 1776, in ibid., 4:35.

15. John Adams to James Warren, 20 May 1776, in ibid., 4:41.

16. John Adams to John Sullivan, 23 June 1776, in ibid., 4:296.

17. John Adams to Samuel Holden Parsons, 22 June 1776, in ibid., 4:292–93.

18. John Adams to Cotton Tufts, 23 June 1776, in ibid., 4:298.

19. John Adams to Joseph Hawley, 25 November 1775, in ibid., 2:385–86, emphasis added.

20. Johns Adams to Samuel Osgood, 14 November 1775, in ibid., 2:342.

21. John Witherspoon, speech, 30 July 1776, in ibid., 4:584–86.

22. Benjamin Harrison to ———, 24 November 1775, in ibid., 2:382.

23. Speeches of James Wilson, Thomas Lynch, and Benjamin Franklin, in John Adams's notes of debates, 30 July 1776, in ibid., 4:568–69.

24. Speech of Samuel Chase, in John Adams's notes of debates, 30 July 1776, in ibid., 4:568–69.

25. Edward Rutledge to John Jay, 29 June 1776, in ibid., 4:338.

26. John Dickinson's draft letter to Quebec, 24–26 October 1774, in ibid., 1:238.

27. Joseph Hewes to Samuel Johnston, 28 July 1776, in ibid., 4:555–56.

28. William Williams to Ezekial Williams, 23 August 1776, in ibid., 25:587.

29. John Dickinson, notes for a speech in Congress, 1 July 1776, in ibid., 4:356. David C. Hendrickson, *Peace Pact: The Lost World of the American Founding* (Lawrence, Kans., 2003), 104–57, provides an excellent analysis of the jealousies and divisions that informed the construction of the Articles of Confederation.

30. John Adams to James Warren, 15 May 1776, in Smith, ed., *Letters of Delegates,* 3:678.

31. Benjamin Rush to Jacques Barbeu-Dubourg, 16 September 1776, in ibid., 5:183.

32. John Adams to Abigail Adams, 17 May 1776, in ibid., 4:18.

33. William Hooper to Joseph Hewes, 27 October 1776, in ibid., 5:410.

34. William Hooper to North Carolina Provincial Constitution, 26 October 1776, in ibid., 5:402.

35. John Adams to James Warren, 3 February 1776, in ibid., 6:201–2.

36. William Williams to Jabez Huntington, 12 August 1776, in ibid., 4:666.

37. John Witherspoon, speech, 30 July 1776, in ibid., 4:584–86.

38. Stephen Hopkins, speech, in John Adams's notes of debates, 1 August 1776, in ibid., 4:592–93.

39. Silas Deane to Thomas Mumford, 16 October 1774, in ibid., 1:201.

40. Thomas Burke's notes of debates, 25 February 1777, in ibid., 6:357–58.

41. Benjamin Rush's notes of debates, 14 February 1777, in ibid., 6:274–75.

42. Thomas Burke to Richard Caswell, 29 April 1777, in ibid., 6:673–74.

43. Ibid.

44. Thomas Burke's notes on the Articles of Confederation, 18 December 1777, in ibid., 8:435.

45. Thomas Burke to the North Carolina Assembly, 28 April 1778, in ibid., 9:534.

46. Thomas Burke to Richard Caswell, 23 May 1777, in ibid., 7:109.

47. James M. Varnum to William Greene, 2 April 1781, in ibid., 17:115–17.

48. James Madison to Thomas Jefferson, 18 November 1781, in ibid., 18:206.

49. James Madison, speech, in James Madison's notes of debates, 21 February 1783, in ibid., 19:720.

50. James Wilson, speech, in James Madison's notes of debates, 28 January 1783, in ibid., 19:625.

51. Arthur Lee, speech, in James Madison's notes of debates, 28 January 1783, in ibid., 19:630.

52. Arthur Lee, speech, in James Madison's notes of debates, 21 February 1783, in ibid., 19:722.

53. Stephen Higginson to John Lowell, 8 July 1783, in ibid., 25:751–53.

54. Philip Schuyler to Jeremiah Wadsworth, 16 July 1780, in ibid., 15:455.

55. Nathaniel Gorum, speech, in James Madison's notes of debates, 21 February 1783, in ibid., 19:722.

56. Charles Thomson to Hannah Thomson, 25 July 1783, in ibid., 20:453–54.

57. Ibid.

58. Ibid.

59. Nathan Dane to John Choate, 31 January 1786, in ibid., 32:121.

60. Nathaniel Gorham to Caleb Davis, 1 March 1786, in ibid., 23:167.

61. Len Travers, *Celebrating the Fourth: Independence Day and the Rites of Nationalism in the Early Republic* (Amherst, Mass., 1997); and David Waldstreicher, *In the Midst of Perpetual Fetes: The Making of American Nationalism, 1776–1820* (Chapel Hill, N.C., 1997) are the best recent studies of the development of American nationalism in the half century after 1776.

Americans Forging
a New Nation, 1860–1916

SUSAN-MARY GRANT

*J*ust over a month after the fall of Fort Sumter—the event that marked the beginning of the American Civil War—the *Boston Post* reflected on the recent turn of events. It was, announced the paper, "the age of nationalities. Fired by our example, the oppressed of the world would have aspired to the dignity of nationalities. Shall the first to set the example, and the grandest in the procession of nations, suffer its nationality to depart, at the bidding not of a foreign foe, but of rebel traitors of the soil?" Not everyone concurred with the paper's assessment of America's national existence. According to New York lawyer and famous diarist George Templeton Strong, "the bird of our country is a debilitated chicken, disguised in eagle feathers. We have never been a nation; we are only an aggregate of communities, ready to fall apart at the first serious shock and without a center of vigorous national life to keep us together." Strong hardly needed the excuse of Southern secession to bemoan his country's lack of cohesion. He had consistently harbored doubts about the viability of American nationality long before his worst fears were realized. Scornful of the American tendency to "venerate every trivial fact about our first settlers and colonial governors and revolutionary heroes," Strong nevertheless understood what this craving for history revealed. "We are so young a people," he argued, "that we feel the want of nationality, and delight in whatever asserts our national 'American' existence." When secession made civil war between North and South inevitable, Strong shamefully concluded that Americans were "a weak, divided, disgraced people, unable to maintain our national existence[,] . . . impotent even to assert our national life." The war's outcome found him in a better frame of mind. "The people has," he wrote " . . . just been bringing forth a new American republic— an amazingly big baby—after a terribly protracted and severe labor, without chloroform." Birth metaphors were clearly the order of the day. Addressing a group of young Republicans some two years after the end of the conflict, the radical politician Charles Sumner took as his subject the question "Are We a

Nation?" Sumner had no hesitation in answering it in the affirmative. "Even if among us in the earlier day there was no occasion for the word Nation, there is now. A Nation," he confidently asserted, "is born."[1]

Scholars have tended to concur with Strong's and Sumner's conclusions. America's Civil War, according to its foremost modern historian, "marked a transition of the United States to a singular noun. The 'Union' also became the nation." Whether the process of creating a nation also created an American nationality, however, remains less certain. Indeed, the belief that the Civil War represents the cornerstone of American national identity has been, over the years, rather stronger than the actual evidence supporting it. The lack of any sustained analysis of American nationalism has hindered our efforts to place the Civil War in its proper context. The link between the Civil War and American nationalism is further obscured by the emphasis that scholars—be they sociologists primarily interested in nationalism or historians whose focus is the war and its aftermath—place on the subject. If sociologists have tended to regard America as a nation apart, Civil War scholars are equally guilty of positioning the conflict as central to and yet simultaneously removed from the historical continuum of the nineteenth century. Regarded in some ways as America's own version of the birth of the modern, the Civil War's role in inculcating a robust and inclusive American nationalism needs more careful analysis than it has so far received. If the war forced Americans to reconsider the foundations of their nationhood, it is by no means obvious that it altered, in any significant way, the terms of the antebellum debate, although it did introduce a new and important element into the equation in the war experience itself. Indeed, what remained consistent in the American nationalist discourse is as important to our understanding of how Americans perceived their national identity as those elements introduced by the war itself. The period between the secession winter of 1860–61 and America's entry into World War I reveals a constant struggle on the part of Americans to define and defend a national identity stronger than the sum of its component and increasingly immigrant parts, an identity tempered by conflict, certainly, but essentially rooted in antebellum concerns over the democratic experiment that the nation represented.[2]

An enduring interest in their national identity preoccupied Americans before, during, and after the Civil War. As early as 1782 J. Hector St. John de Crèvecoeur had posed his now-famous question, "What, then, is the American, this new man?" His question proved to be of perennial interest. As the noted author Henry James put it, "Nothing could be well more characteristic of our nationality than the sight of a group of persons more or less earnestly discussing it." James was describing Americans abroad some ten years after the Civil War, but his comments could equally apply to Americans at home and at virtually any time. Nearly forty years later, with America on the verge of a very different conflict, the historian and author Agnes Repplier turned her attention to the subject. When she wrote, the Civil War semicentennial had just ended. Repplier acknowledged that American national life had received a boost from "the great emotions" of that conflict but nevertheless concluded that only the United States, "of all the countries in the world, . . . [has] any need to create artificially the patriotism which is the birthright of other nations." By leaving America on the sidelines of nationalism studies, modern scholars have reinforced the idea of American uniqueness as far as its national identity is concerned, predicating their argument either on some variant of the Turner thesis or, more usually, on America's cosmopolitan, immigrant population. Yet American uniqueness in this regard, although frequently asserted, does not stand up to comparison with the experience of other nations. In the course of his famous debates with Stephen A. Douglas, Abraham Lincoln had addressed the thorny question of national identity in a nation of immigrants. Reflecting on the importance of the Fourth of July to Americans whose ancestors had won American independence, he noted that many Americans could not trace their blood lineage back to the revolutionary generation. Nevertheless, Lincoln asserted, the moral sentiment of the Declaration "is the father of all moral principle in them, and . . . they have a right to claim it as though they were blood of the blood, and flesh of the flesh of the men who wrote that Declaration." As Don Doyle has argued, the "celebration of the nation as a new idea and a repudiation of the past was . . . central to the founding of the United States. . . . But it was also fundamental to the liberal nationalism of Europe that came out of the Enlightenment. European nationalists such as Giuseppe Mazzini," Doyle reminds us, "embraced the modern nation as an ideal that could unite and inspire people who may not belong to a community bound by blood." When Lincoln described the Declaration of Independence as the "electric cord" that held the Union together he was invoking just this idea of the nation.[3]

Writing about a very different nation, albeit one with strong ties to America, Linda Colley takes issue with "those who are accustomed to thinking of nations only as historic phenomena characterised by cultural and ethnic homogeneity." By restricting the definition of a nation in this way, she observed, "we shall find precious few of them available in the world either to study or to live in." Most nations, Colley argues, "have always been culturally and ethnically diverse, problematic, protean and artificial constructs that take shape very quickly and come apart just as fast." On those grounds, she avers, "we can plausibly regard Great Britain as an invented nation superimposed . . . onto much older alignments and loyalties." The parallels with the American case—as indeed with many others—are obvious. The American people, comprising, by the nineteenth century, a heterogeneous population of relatively recent immigrants both voluntary and involuntary in origin together with Native Americans, established under a federal system that encouraged state and local as well as national loyalties, of necessity approached the idea of the nation in a multitude of ways. America, like Great Britain, was an invented nation, and, like Great Britain, at the heart of its invention was war. "Time and time again," Colley argues,

> war with France brought Britons, whether they hailed from Wales or Scotland or England, into confrontation with an obviously hostile Other and encouraged them to define themselves collectively against it. They defined themselves as Protestants struggling for survival against the world's foremost Catholic power. They defined themselves against the French as they imagined them to be, superstitious, militarist, decadent and unfree. And, increasingly as the wars went on, they defined themselves in contrast to the colonial peoples they conquered, peoples who were manifestly alien in terms of culture, religion and colour.[4]

Perhaps the only difference between the British experience, as Colley describes it, and the American is that Americans, by the nineteenth century, no longer needed to look across a stretch of water to find the "Other." With that single exception, Colley's list reads the same for America as for Britain. In the rise of nativism throughout the antebellum era we can trace Protestant America's opposition to the perceived Catholic threat; the Native Americans, Mexicans, and African Americans within the nation certainly fulfilled all the requirements of a "manifestly alien" Other; and, by the 1850s, an influential element in the North certainly regarded the South as "militarist, decadent and unfree," while elements in the South saw in the North the main threat not only to their peculiar institution of slave labor but to an entire way of life predicated on that labor system.

Northern victory in the Civil War, of course, resolved the sectional issue in practical if not emotional terms. It also provided the opportunity and the stimulus for American national symbols and celebrations to reassert themselves, and scholars have begun to explore the ways in which patriotism manifested itself in both North and South at this time. The emphasis on Confederate nationalism is now, gradually, being supplemented by studies that focus on the Civil War North and on how various individuals and organizations worked to create a new national fabric that functioned on several levels and was capable of transcending and subsuming antebellum local, state, and regional loyalties. Via events such as the Sanitary Fairs, the Union League, and the Loyal Publication Society, Northern elites worked both to present the war in terms meaningful to the wider population—which translated, all too often, into an avoidance of any troubling discussions over slavery or race—and to create a "new version of American national identity" that "made room for the South and the rebellious portion of the North after the war." Many of these efforts—although by no means all—were aimed at the civilian population, the intention being to shore up morale for a conflict that was proving far costlier in terms of lives and matériel than had been anticipated. Soldiers' letters, in contrast, provide some indication of how the national cause was perceived by the men in the field, not all of whom evinced much belief in duty, honor, or country.[5]

For many Civil War soldiers financial considerations reinforced or perhaps even took precedence over any overtly patriotic sentiment. The Union bounties offered were relatively high, and for struggling farmers and unskilled workers such apparently easy money would be hard to resist. Still others saw in the war—at least in the early stages—the opportunity for excitement, for travel, for experiences far beyond the steady domesticity that they were used to. For still others peer-group pressure came into play. It would be hard to resist the inducements to join the army if almost everyone else in the town or village had decided to do so. The majority of men who marched off to war in 1861, in short, probably did not have either states' rights or the Union uppermost in their minds, even if they had some vague sense that these matters were important. In the process of fighting, of course, many of these soldiers would have reflected on what they were fighting for. Such reflections led some of them straight back home again. Volunteering, indeed, dried up relatively quickly in some areas, rather undermining the argument that Union soldiers felt strongly about the national cause. The most extreme example of initial enthusiasm dissipating in the face of battle concerned the First Minnesota Volunteers, whose troops suffered horrific casualties at First Bull Run, sustaining greater losses than any other Federal regiment that day. The result of this was that some of the survivors attempted to have their enlistments nullified, a case that eventually came to court in *United States v. Colonel Gorman*. The soldiers lost their case, but the initial period of the war certainly saw unbridled enthusiasm existing alongside a distinct reluctance to serve the cause of the nation. One Northerner wrote to his son about a meeting held in his town in August 1862 to drum up support for the war: "Volunteering has about ceased I don't hear of any volunteers for the Old Regiments," the father wrote. There were "a number of addresses made, and as much as seventy five dollars offered over and above the ninety dollars Bounty, to any who would volunteer, but they did not receive a man, it is thought now we will have to stand a Draft of near 40,000 men to fill up the Old Regiments in the State."[6]

What many of the Civil War soldiers' letters reveal is that blind, unquestioning loyalty was not part of their psychological baggage. Ulysses S. Grant noted, long after the war, that American armies were unlike their European equivalents: the latter were mere automatons, he concluded, compared to the free-thinking troops of America. Civil War soldiers were certainly not backward in coming forward with their opinions on the progress of the war and, in particular, on the conduct of their officers. But alongside their many criticisms of the way in which the war was being conducted lay views on why the war was being pursued at all. Many troops felt that the war, so far from being fought for a great cause, was little more than the work of fanatics on each side. Some could not see that there was much difference between North and South but only that "Bribery and Corruption [and] self-aggrandizement" dominated both sections. Some were unwilling to accept at face value the decisions of the Lincoln administration, even if they, on the whole, supported it. As James Maitland wrote to his son in 1863, "There are two ideas advanced which I cannot concur in. That is in regard to arbitrary arrests by the Military, and trying them before a Military Tribunal instead of the civil according to the provisions of the Constitution. And the other idea was that the present war could never be stopped until slavery was entirely eradicated, or that no settlement of the question would be entertained until Slavery was abrogated." The issue of slavery, of course, was a sensitive one, and Lincoln's Emancipation Proclamation of 1863 did not endear him to all. One Rhode Island private expressed his disgust at "officers triing to make young men believe that they are fighting for the Union it is false as hell," he wrote. The "Northern fanaticks do not care a dam for the union or country," he argued, but were motivated purely by abolitionist sentiments, sentiments that he most certainly did not share.[7]

Many soldiers, of course, did respond positively to the call to arms and expressed an appreciation that their national identity was bound up in the conflict. Robert Gould Shaw, for one, acknowledged that the war itself made him "look at the stars and stripes with new emotions," while William Haines Lytle declared, "God help the old flag! In no nobler or holier cause can a man's life be offered up." For him the Civil War was "the great war for Union and Liberty." In these cases out of conflict came consensus of a kind, a reappraisal of the value of a Union that some, certainly, had come to take for granted. For still others the war itself produced a degree of faith in the cause that had, perhaps, been absent at the outset. It must be remembered that if volunteering was not in itself sufficient to sustain military ranks, nevertheless some 2.5 million civilians fought in the Union army (about one in twelve of the white adult male population) and 1.6 million fought for the Confederacy (about one in three). Volunteer troops, even after conscription had been introduced, continued to make up the bulk of the armies. Whatever their reasons for joining up in the first place, something more than money or the hope of glory kept men in the war. The military experience itself in such cases inculcated a sense of national identity that had been, perhaps, lacking. The Union army, indeed, can be regarded as "one of the most potent agencies of American nationalism." Armed service introduced men who survived the experience to "places and people hitherto remote, but now fixed in their minds as part of the same American nation to which they belonged," while those who did not return "contributed to the nation that stock of heroes and memories which a sense of nationality demands."[8]

That military involvement should both create and strengthen a sense of nationalism is not unique to the Civil War, and the way in which it achieved this end has parallels with an earlier conflict. In assessing the impact of the Revolutionary War on British society, Stephen Conway observes that British society was "militarized" by the experience, both by the direct involvement of so many men in the war and by the public fascination with and vicarious involvement in events. The parallels with the American case are especially instructive in regard to what Conway terms "component patriotisms." Localism, he shows, so far from operating against this developing sense of Britishness, actually strengthened it. "The mobilization of manpower," he argues, "reflected and gave due recognition to the persistence of provincial feeling," and the deliberate acknowledgment of local loyalties served to encourage rather than discourage men from joining the nation's cause. Irish volunteers, for example, saw themselves as fighting to uphold "republican values" in their own communities at the same time as they fought under the British flag, while the Scots were induced to join the navy by the suggestion that to do otherwise would be to "allow themselves to be outdone by the English." National identity is, of course, both multifaceted and context sensitive; as Colley reminds us, identities "are not like hats. Human beings can put several on at a time." However, in the context of the Civil War and the development of national identity at this time, historians have frequently regarded state loyalties as a barrier to rather than a specific enabler of an overarching sense of American nationalism. In the concept of "component patriotisms," however, we can see that the means whereby the Union raised its regiments—although indicative of a lack of centralized resources—might actually have operated to its advantage. The ideal of a centrally organized volunteer army "fought a losing battle in practice in 1861 against state pride, state loyalties and local initiative." Yet losing this particular battle might just have helped the Union win the war.[9]

Away from the battlefield a variety of noncombatants struggled to understand and explain the function of the conflict for America's national future, prompted by a combination of the Copperhead challenge at home and the keen interest if not comprehension of foreign powers in America's struggle. At the same time antebellum concerns over immigration and its impact had not been forgotten; for some, indeed, the war had only exacerbated the problem. At the war's midpoint in 1863 Congregational minister John Abbott was simultaneously optimistic about the war's eventual outcome and daunted by the challenges to American nationality that lay ahead. "Our hands are full," he observed with a degree of understatement. "We have four millions of slaves, unlettered, debased by ages of oppression. . . . We have four millions of poor whites at the South, not one whit above the slaves. . . . And we have a flood of emigration pouring in upon us from the poor and the oppressed of Europe. . . . To receive all these into our National family—to instruct, to purify, to harmonize, will task to the uttermost all the energies of every patriot, philanthropist, and Christian in the land." Abbott's perception of southern whites as separate from the "national family" revealed ingrained antebellum sectional prejudices as much as contemporary concerns and was indicative of the shape of things to come as far as the debate over American national identity was concerned.[10]

The buildup of national sentiment in the North and its Confederate equivalent in the South came to rather an abrupt halt in 1865, something that the historiography tends to gloss over in its rush to get to the memorial industry that the Civil War in time became. Although Memorial Day was inaugurated almost immediately after the guns ceased and taken up by the Grand Army of the Republic in 1868, the impulse to honor the memory of those who had fallen went hand in hand with the quite understandable impulse to forget the horrors of war. This is hardly surprising. Albion Tourgee, the civil rights advocate who served as a judge in the South during the period of Reconstruction, observed that after any conflict, but especially a civil war, "there always comes a period when public interest in the causes and incidents of the strife may be said to lag. . . . The conqueror palls of triumph and the conquered shun whatever reminds them of defeat." The presence of Federal troops in the South, of course, made it difficult if not impossible for former Confederates to avoid reminders of defeat for quite some time to come. Beyond the South, however, many Americans effectively took up where they had left off when it came to the subject of their national identity and did not in any overt way link it to the conflict they had just experienced.[11]

The historiographical focus on Civil War memorializing tends, for obvious reasons, to concentrate on the many memorials, veterans reunions, and publications produced in response to the war. What is frequently overlooked is the fact that for some the war's impact on the debate over American nationalism was, at best, muted. Sometimes the war hardly registered at all. Only two years after Appomattox Henry James mused to fellow author Thomas Sergeant Perry about American national identity without bringing the war into the equation at all. Instead, James harked back to antebellum concerns over American identity, its component parts, and its probable future. "We have exquisite qualities as a race," he observed, "and it seems to me that we are ahead of the European races in the fact that more than either of them we can deal freely with forms of civilization not our own, can pick and choose and assimilate and in short . . . claim our property wherever we find it. To have no national stamp has hitherto been a defect and a drawback," he concluded, but no longer. His views found support only a few years later, when Thomas Wentworth Higginson, the former abolitionist and colonel of the first black regiment in the Civil War, turned his attention to the subject of "Americanism in Literature." Contrasting the American national character with that of the English, Higginson suggested that the "Englishman's strong point is a vigorous insularity which he carries with him. . . . The American's more perilous gift," he continued in an almost direct echo of James, "is a certain power of assimilation, through which he acquires something from every man he meets." At least Higginson acknowledged that a major civil war had taken place, but even then all he had to say on the subject was that Americans were "accustomed to say that the war and its results have made us a nation, subordinated local distinctions, cleared us of our chief shame, and given us the pride of a common career." What the war had clearly not done, in Higginson's view, was establish an American national identity. "It seems unspeakably important that all persons among us . . . should be pervaded with Americanism," he asserted, but clearly, as far as he was concerned, that lay in the future.[12]

Both James and Higginson, in common with Abbott, conceived of American national identity as something distinct from American nationalism. They were concerned with the inherent qualities of Americans as a people, and of the three only Higginson ventured to consider how these qualities, acquired from so varied a number of sources, might cohere to form not just an American character but an American nation. The Civil War's role in inculcating the kind of "Americanism" that Higginson believed was essential was, at best, tangential. Poet, travel writer, and composer of the "National Ode" for the Fourth of July in 1876, Bayard Taylor was similarly exercised by the question of how the national traits of European immigrants combined to produce an identifiably American "national character," but he was dismissive of the role played by the Civil War in creating a unified whole out of the disparate immigrant elements of the nation. "Ten years ago the two divisions of our country leaned upon their swords, breathless and bleeding from their long conflict," he recalled. One "half had been fighting and starving for what they believed their rights, long after hope was dead; the other had been truly battling for ideas, for the idea of country, of humanity, of justice, of liberty." Now, however, he noted with dismay, "the day of commemoration does not even bring a garland to their graves." The centennial celebrations of 1876, Taylor argued, constituted an "infallible test . . . an absolute gauge of the strength of our concrete enthusiasm. In eighteen months," he reminded his readers, "the first century of our national existence will be complete. Our after ages can see no anniversary so solemn as this. Our struggle into life is near enough for us to remember it with emotion; living memories link us to it still: it is distant enough to have become traditional, venerable." Taylor believed the centennial offered Americans the refuge of the Revolution, a conflict far enough in the past to have acquired the mystique necessary for national consolidation. Others concurred. One North Carolinian argued that if "there is any spot which should be consecrated by such an occasion, that spot is here in Philadelphia, where American liberty was born; and upon such an occasion the people of all parts of this country can drown out the memories of our unfortunate struggle with the more glorious memories of the struggle in which our forefathers engaged." With the memories if not the memorializing of a more recent conflict still fresh, however, the prospects for a genuinely national celebration were not promising.[13]

America's centennial celebrations can provide little more than a snapshot, albeit a revealing one, of the stage reached in the debate over American nationalism by 1876. This most overtly patriotic expression of national existence brought more than celebrations and pageants to America; it also brought its fair share of problems, including economic depression, Custer's defeat by the Sioux, continuing corruption in Washington in which Grant, the victorious war hero, was implicated, and no obvious healing of the breach between North and South. With Federal troops still stationed in South Carolina, Florida, and Louisiana there was little likelihood of sectional reconciliation that year, but this was only one factor among many that undermined the attempts by the centennial's organizers to "express an established national tradition in the United States." Indeed, they had "a comparatively tenuous basis for their claims about 'the nation's' century. While they were celebrating a century of formal sovereignty, this only served to emphasize that there was no simple association between political sovereignty and national identity. . . . By the time of the centennial," Lyn Spillman argues, "Americans were celebrating a century of formal sovereignty, but an uneven and contested cultural unity." The celebrations, when they got under way, did little to even things out and were notable for what they avoided as much as for what they celebrated. Immigrants and African Americans were hardly mentioned, and Native Americans were represented by a Smithsonian exhibit that acknowledged their existence as a colorful aboriginal presence in the United States but kept them firmly out of the imagined national community, portraying them, indeed, as "an interior other to national identity" at that time.[14]

America's centennial year is frequently presented as a turning point in the development and institutionalization of American national identity, an identity that looked less to the future than to what Michael Kammen has described as "a more serene and distant past, a golden age of fantasy." Spillman, too, has identified a growing "anxiety about nationality" in Gilded Age America, expressed in overt patriotic spectacles and "Americanization" campaigns that sought "to reinforce an image of national unity in large historical pageants." Almost a decade after the centennial a notable example of national pageantry occurred in response to the death in 1885 of Ulysses S. Grant. The way in which his funeral was handled in part influenced and in equal part reflected the direction that Civil War memory was taking. Carrying out the wishes of her husband, Julia

Grant had requested that "if any conspicuous Union generals were selected [as pallbearers] some equally noted Confederate officers should be chosen. . . . The spectacle of distinguished adversaries in a civil war walking side by side in honorable remembrance of the victorious general," *Harper's Weekly* enthused, "is a symbol of reunion whose significance can not be surpassed." The magazine contrasted Grant's funeral procession with an earlier attempt by Andrew Johnson to encourage sectional reconciliation: Grant's procession was not, the magazine stressed, "a sentimental effusion like Andrew Johnson's arm-in-arm convention in Philadelphia. That was a political trick, and implied a feeling which did not exist. But Grant, instinctively magnanimous in the field, and without a trace of vindictiveness, clearly comprehended the scope of the struggle and the nature of the result." And the nation's memory of Grant was kept alive for some time after his death. In 1892 the cornerstone was laid for the memorial that became Grant's Tomb in New York, itself dedicated five years later on Grant's Day, 27 April 1897, the seventy-fifth anniversary of the general's birth.[15]

Grant's funeral took place in a climate conducive to the kind of Civil War memorializing epitomized by veterans groups such as the Grand Army of the Republic, a phenomenon that took some people by surprise. The Union general William T. Sherman, indeed, professed himself amazed by the resurgence of interest in the Civil War that he noticed on a visit to Columbus, Ohio, in 1888. The reaction to his visit, he wrote, "convinces me that the young people, male and female, of the interior of our country feel an increased interest in the events of the Civil War. I did believe, and have so expressed myself in former years, that the interest, enthusiasm and élan would die out with one or two generations; but not so." "It is only within a very recent time," Albion Tourgee had noted in the previous year, that the "younger portion have awakened to a positive and active interest in the events in which their fathers participated or witnessed, animated by that pride which always exalts the exploits of an ancestor, while the survivors of those who fought have passed the period of satiety and are fast approaching the reminiscent stage which occupies itself in reviewing the rear."[16]

A wealth of recent scholarship has highlighted the way in which the Civil War entered American memory—and by extrapolation America's national story— on military terms. Through the efforts of veterans organizations and publications such as *Century Magazine*'s "Battles and Leaders" series, Civil War soldiers made their own particular peace, forged out of the memories of the battlefield horrors they had witnessed and the comrades they had lost. Joshua Lawrence Chamberlain—famous for holding Little Round Top on the second day of Gettysburg—epitomized the soldiers' perspective in this regard. According to Chamberlain, the war provided both North and South with a "rushing tide of memories which divided us, yet made us one forever." Yet the veterans' interpretation presented a particularist white view of the conflict, a version of the

Civil War in which states' rights, not the preservation of slavery, had created the Confederacy, and defense of the Union, not emancipation, had motivated the Federal side. Between the two, the role played by and the promises made to African Americans were lost. Out of conflict, scholars conclude, came compromise. But it was a very specific compromise, one based on male, white, combatant views of the war, one that ill prepared America to meet the needs of its black population and, in the long run, those of the multiethnic, multilingual nation that America would become.[17]

There is a problem with this interpretation in that it is an argument of ever-decreasing circles, forever returning us to the same point: Southern intransigence, Northern complicity resulting in, ultimately, the betrayal of America's black population. By concentrating on the veterans' viewpoint—understandable, since it is so readily, indeed exhaustively, available—we skew the picture. Soldiers' reminiscences and the specific ideological stance adopted by the Grand Army of the Republic do not tell the whole story as far as American national identity is concerned. Alongside the many battlefield reminiscences promulgated by *Century Magazine* in the 1880s and 1890s, a variety of other publications considered American national development from an essentially antebellum perspective that either took little account of the Civil War's impact on national construction or regarded it as detrimental to the construction of any valid and functioning national identity.

The debate over American national identity in the latter part of the nineteenth century cannot be fully understood solely within the context of Civil War memorializing. The issues of immigration, assimilation, and integration—now openly termed "Americanization"—remained a constant in American nationalist discourse from the antebellum era onward. The Civil War may have distracted attention from these themes for a time, but almost as soon as the guns ceased American writers and thinkers took up where they had left off in their analysis of the nationalism question. One writer in 1898 might as easily have been writing some fifty years earlier in his emphasis on the need for patriotism to "beget a race of citizens amalgamated into a community of sentiment" and his criticism of those "phrases that are very frequent in the mouths of men, classifying Americans by a qualifying adjective of a national sort, [which] are destructive of the best hopes of America. Partly because of youngness, partly because of the composite character of our population," he observed, "we are still in the process of forming, as a nation."[18]

Parallel to the veterans' memorializing of the war and their emphasis on its function as the war that had made the nation ran a more traditional discourse that took Europe as the obvious foil for America and wholly ignored the presence of nonwhites in the nation; on that latter point, the two streams of thought met. In some cases the war was recognized as the high point of American national awareness, for Northerners at least. Concerned about what he saw as "Certain Dangerous Tendencies in American Life," one writer observed that "since the civil war we have had new elements and conditions in our national life. . . . We had not, before the war, been prepared in any way for the tasks or difficulties which we have since encountered." He was especially dismayed at the decline of religious sentiment and the impact this was having on national identity. Looking back to the war, he suggested that a "society with a plan or method of work resembling that of the New England Loyal Publication Society, which did so much to reinforce the national sentiment during our civil war, could now render quite as efficient service." What was needed, he felt, was "a paper for the people, which shall have for its aim the development of a national spirit and temper." Another suggested that "perhaps the most unhappy legacy which our Civil War has left us, is the general neglect of the obligations and duties of citizenship." Still others thought that the war might teach America the much-needed lesson that "there is no peculiar exemption for the American people from the calamities that have befallen other peoples." Americans, the writer went on with a distinct air of disapproval, "have passed from the vain incredulity on the subject of war, the irritable assertion of its impossibility in the face of the currents that rendered it inevitable, to take a pride in the extraordinary extent and destructiveness of the warfare in which we were five years engaged." This view was echoed in part by Charles Dudley Warner, most famous as the coauthor, with Mark Twain, of *The Gilded Age*, who reflected on America's "absence of traditions . . . and flexible social condition." He took issue, however, with the "notion . . . that we are somehow a peculiar people, and that our condition, our government, our isolation, exempt us not only from the universal laws of political economy, but from the rules that other nations, by long experience, have found necessary to a healthful life." The orator, he noted, "always carries his audience with him when he says of anything, 'It is not suited to the genius of our people;' as if we had invented a new kind of intellect, and patented a new order of life." [19]

If some writers thought that America had failed to absorb the lessons of the Civil War and had not turned these to any obvious national effect, still others saw the war's outcome as offering a fresh start. Edward Bellamy, for one, believed the war "should be ranked the greatest in history, not merely on account of the extent of the territory—and of the vastness of the armies involved, but far more because it issued, as such a war never did before, in the speedy reconciliation of the foes. The reunion of the North and South after the struggle is the best proof of the progress of humanity that history records, the best evidence that the Nationalist motto, We war with systems not with men, is not in advance of the moral sense of the nation we appeal to." Walt Whitman, for another, believed that the Civil War had much to offer America, particularly as far as literature was concerned. What was needed, according to Whitman, was "Patriotism" and "Nationality." A national literature, he argued, "is, of course, in one sense, a great mirror or reflector. There must be something before something to reflect. I should say now, since the Secession War, there has been, and to-day unquestionably exists, that something." Southerners were, on the whole, more interested in and expressive of that "something" than Northerners proved to be. Yet Northern writers, too, harked back to the Civil War in an emotive and moving way.

Union general Daniel Sickles was a case in point. His Civil War activities—he fought in most of the major campaigns, lost a leg at Gettysburg but also received the Medal of Honor for his role in that most famous battle, and was active in securing Gettysburg's future status as a national park—have been somewhat overshadowed by the most dramatic incident of his life: his shooting in 1859 of his wife's lover. Yet Sickles, described by one biographer as an "American Scoundrel," was sensitive to the discrepancy of perspective between those who remembered the Civil War and those who did not. He eloquently if somewhat romantically viewed his troops from the perspective of 1890 as "men who had only a home to live for and a country to die for" but acknowledged that reactions to the Civil War were, by that time, mixed. Describing the reaction to a reception held in honor of a group of Union commanders in Gettysburg in October of that year, he noted: "To some, belonging to our generation, not only their names, but their faces were familiar, and it was not without emotion that this sight carried them back to the days of their youth. . . . But to most of them the sight was a perfectly novel one. To the new generation the battle of Gettysburg is an historical event, like the battle of Marathon."[20]

Sickles's belief that the Civil War had, by 1890, faded into historical legend contrasts sharply with Sherman's identification of renewed interest in the war only two years previously. This apparent contradiction highlights the fact that, despite the efforts of the Grand Army of the Republic, by the end of the nineteenth century no recognizable consensus on the meaning of the war had yet emerged. The Civil War generation, observed the U.S. commissioner of pensions, Green B. Raum, "will pass away as a tale that is told, but their work will endure forever." The passing of the Civil War generation provided, in theory, an opportunity for a reassessment of that conflict, for the conflicting views of it to merge into a coherent and "usable past." Yet the question remains as to how usable that past was to Americans in search of a national identity. There remains an unresolved tension in the historiography between the late-nineteenth-century trend toward what Kammen has identified as a "conservative, organic view of society" with its concomitant emphasis on the "importance of ancestors, memories, and legends" and the importance that so many contemporary writers placed on America's future and, more significantly, on the reception that this powerful brand of ancestor worship received from America's immigrant population.[21]

It may be constructive in this context to compare America's Civil War with World War I. Both conflicts are frequently seen as watersheds between a rose-tinted past and a chaotic future. The conservative vision of the Grand Army of the Republic, it has been argued, positioned the American nation in a place "not bound by the ordinary constraints of history[,] . . . a peaceable kingdom from which disorder and diversity were shut out." The "Great War," similarly, is still regarded as the dividing line between a rose-hued Edwardian England and the confusion and chaos of the later twentieth century, a perspective informed by the many reminiscences, diaries, and poetry that emerged from "Flanders fields." While there is clearly a great difference between Margaret Mitchell's *Gone with the Wind* and Robert Graves's *Goodbye to All That*, the role of both wars in national memories has proved to be of enduring interest. The "two basic components" in our understanding of World War I are, according to Jay Winter, the modernist and the traditional. The modernist view was the work of the elites and involved "the creation of a new language of truth-telling about the war in poetry, prose, and the visual arts." The traditional entailed "what many modernists rejected: patriotic constraints, 'high diction,' incorporating euphemisms about battle, 'glory,' and the 'hallowed dead,' in sum, the sentimentality and lies of wartime propaganda."[22]

The veterans' version of the Civil War clearly fits into the second of Winter's categories. Theirs was the very traditional view of conflict and of the "hallowed dead." What America lacked in the aftermath of the war was the modernist strain. The elites did not produce any alternative grand vision of the war's meaning. Instead, politicians backtracked on or avoided issues too tricky to deal with, while many of the leading lights at the center of the Union's patriotic wartime activities, men such as Frederick Law Olmsted of the Sanitary Commission, moved on to greener pastures, leaving many of the questions they themselves had raised about American national identity unresolved. As Thaddeus Stevens's and Frederick Douglass's generation died away, so too did the radical vision of what the Civil War had been about and what it had been on the verge of achieving. What remained were the fast-fading memories of the veterans themselves and the more permanent physical memorials to the conflict, both of which approached commemoration from the perspective of the battlefield. Again, this is not surprising, nor is it especially suspect. Other soldiers in other wars recalled their wartime experiences in similar ways and, it must be said, at similar length, and war memorials are a feature of all societies. Yet this "traditional" interpretation of the war diluted its role as a constructive force in American national identity by placing the conflict at the heart of and yet simultaneously insulated from the broader society around it. Both the veterans' construction of the conflict as a white man's war and the more theoretical arguments concerning American nationalism in the period between the outbreak of the war and America's entry into World War I revolved around an avoidance of the imperatives of national construction.

The quite natural impulse on the part of many writers to turn away from the trauma of the war and to couch their analysis in terms familiar to the antebellum debate over American nationalism hampered the process of coming to terms with the Civil War, of acknowledging its racial imperatives, and, ultimately, of reconstructing the national society in line with the ideals that, by the war's conclusions, many Northerners believed they were fighting for. In seeking to understand why the Civil War entered America's national story in the way that it did, more than the veterans' perspective has to be taken into account. In late-nineteenth-century America there was no modernist voice to help the nation lay the ghosts of its most destructive conflict, either interpret it in national terms or, more significantly, place it in an international context. By positioning America as sui generis among nations, many commentators failed to consider what might be learned from other countries' national struggles. Above all, they continued to describe American nationalism in civic terms when it was, and had been for many years prior to the Civil War, a mixed civic-ethnic construct: civic in form but very clearly ethnic in function.

In this context the examples of other New World nations, as explored elsewhere in this volume, are clearly apposite. Gary Gerstle shows how "Mexican and Cuban nationalists each developed an ideology that repudiated . . . race as a marker of their nationhood," although this achievement came at some cost and was successful in spite of rather than in any sense due to the influence of the United States. Gerstle's analysis offers a different perspective from that of James McPherson, for example, who has proposed that the American example of emancipation was exported and that other New World societies, including Mexico, Cuba, and Brazil, were encouraged to adopt a more inclusive form of nationalism by the victory of the Union in the Civil War. By the late nineteenth century there were certainly enough examples of alternative methods of national construction to give American commentators pause, to offer potential solutions to the racial divisions that blighted American society, and to suggest methods by which America's own brand of civic nationalism might live up to its stated ideals. The blame for the fact that the lessons offered by America's proximate neighbors were neither learned nor, it seems, ever heeded is too frequently laid at the door of the Reconstruction process, more specifically, the South. Certainly, the South, as Barbara Weinstein has argued elsewhere in this volume, can be regarded as unique among the New World "nations" in constructing a nationalism predicated on a proslavery ideology "as an exception to the otherwise historically inverse relationship between nation building and proslavery sentiment." Yet the reluctance to break the ethnic ties that bound America's civic ideals in the post–Civil War era neither originated with the South nor related to the African American postemancipation experience alone, as Gerstle has shown.[23]

Instead, American thinking on nationalism in the late nineteenth and early twentieth centuries continued along familiar tracks that had been laid in the antebellum era. By restricting the terms of the debate in this way, the search for "Americanism" in the post–Civil War period became itself a divisive process. Indeed, by the eve of America's entry into World War I American nationalism, at least according to the professionals, was in a parlous state. So far from conceiving of their nation as, in Benedict Anderson's words, "an imagined political community[,] . . . a deep, horizontal comradeship," at the turn of the twentieth century few Americans, according to contemporary sociologists, were able to "furnish credible evidence of sharing very largely in the knowledge, beliefs, and purposes of all Americans." This assessment was overly pessimistic, but at the same time it revealed that Americans were still alive to the importance of the subject, to its evolving nature, and to the challenges it presented. The history of nationalism reveals all too clearly that the dangers only arise once that debate stops.[24]

NOTES

1. *Boston Post*, 16 May 1861; George Templeton Strong, diary entries for 11 and 12 March 1861, 8 November 1854, and 1 June 1865, in Allan Nevins and Milton Hasley Thomas, eds., *The Diary of George Templeton Strong* (New York, 1952), vol. 2, *The Turbulent Fifties, 1850–1859*, 196–97; vol. 3, *The Civil War, 1860–1865*, 109; vol. 4, *Post-War Years, 1865–1875*, 2; Charles Sumner, "Are We a Nation? Address of Hon. Charles Sumner before the New York Young Men's Republican Union, at the Cooper Institute, Tuesday Evening, Nov. 19, 1867," New York, 1867, 4–5.

2. James M. McPherson, *Battle Cry of Freedom: The Civil War Era* (New York, 1988), 859.

3. J. Hector St. John de Crèvecoeur, *Letters from an American Farmer* (1782; London, 1986), 69–70; Henry James, "Americans Abroad," *Nation*, 3 October 1878, 208–9; Agnes Repplier, "Americanism," *Atlantic Monthly* (March 1916): 289–97; Abraham Lincoln, "Speech at Chicago, 10 July, 1858," in Roy F. Basler, ed., *The Collected Works of Abraham Lincoln* (New Brunswick, N.J., 1953), 2:499; Don H. Doyle, *Nations Divided: America, Italy, and the Southern Question* (Athens, Ga., 2002), 15.

4. Linda Colley, *Britons: Forging the Nation, 1707–1837* (1992; London, 1994), 5.

5. Melinda Lawson, *Patriot Fires: Forging a New American Nationalism in the Civil War North* (Lawrence, Kans., 2002), 13.

6. James W. Geary, *We Need Men: The Union Draft in the Civil War* (Dekalb, Ill., 1991),

6–7; James M. Maitland to son, 31 August 1862, in Maitland Papers, Gilder-Lehrman Collection, Pierpont Morgan Library, New York.

7. Ulysses S. Grant, *Personal Memoirs* (1885, 1886; New York, 1999), 639; James Maitland to brother, 6 April 1863, and James Maitland to son, 21 May 1863, both in Maitland Papers; George O. Bartlett to Mr. Ira Andrews, 7 January 1863, Bartlett Papers, Gilder-Lehrman Collection, Pierpont Morgan Library, New York.

8. Robert Gould Shaw to his parents, 23 April 1861, in Russell Duncan, ed., *Blue-Eyed Child of Fortune: The Civil War Letters of Robert Gould Shaw* (Athens, Ga., 1992), 77; Rith C. Carter, ed., *For Honor, Glory and Union: The Mexican and Civil War Letters of Brig. Gen. William Haines Lytle* (Lexington, Ky., 1999), 219; Peter J. Parish, *The American Civil War* (New York, 1975), 637.

9. Stephen Conway, *The British Isles and the War of American Independence* (New York, 2000), 170, 182; Colley, *Britons*, 6; Parish, *American Civil War*, 134; see also Bruce D. Porter, *War and the Rise of the State: The Military Foundations of Modern Politics* (New York, 1994), 264.

10. John S. C. Abbott, *The History of the Civil War in America* (New York, 1863), 615–16.

11. On Memorial Day see Michael Kammen, *Mystic Chords of Memory: The Transformation of Tradition in American Culture* (1991; New York, 1993), 102–3; Albion W. Tourgee, "The Renaissance of Nationalism," *North American Review* (January 1887): 1–11, 1.

12. Henry James to Thomas Sergeant Perry, 20 September 1867, in Leon Edel, ed., *Henry James: Letters*, vol. 1, *1843–1875* (London, 1974), 77; Thomas Wentworth Higginson, "Americanism in Literature," *Atlantic Monthly* (January 1870): 56–63, 56–57.

13. Bayard Taylor, "What Is an American?" *Atlantic Monthly* (May 1875): 561–67, 562, 565–66. Taylor actually wrote the piece in 1874; quotation in Lynette Spillman, *Nation and Commemoration* (Cambridge, 1997), 72.

14. Spillman, *Nation and Commemoration*, 25, 37, 43–45, 71–72.

15. Kammen, *Mystic Chords of Memory*, 138; Spillman, *Nation and Commemoration*, 37; *Harper's Weekly*, 15 August 1885, 531.

16. William T. Sherman, "Camp-Fires of the G.A.R.," *North American Review* (November 1888): 497–503, 497; Tourgee, "The Renaissance of Nationalism," 2, 4.

17. Joshua Lawrence Chamberlain, *The Passing of the Armies: The Last Campaign of the Armies* (1915; Gettysburg, Pa., 1994), 271; most recently, Stuart McConnell, *Glorious Contentment: The Grand Army of the Republic, 1865–1900* (Chapel Hill, N.C., 1992); Nina Silber, *The Romance of Reunion: Northerners and the South, 1865–1900* (Chapel Hill, N.C., 1993); Cecilia Elizabeth O'Leary, *To Die For: The Paradox of American Patriotism* (Princeton, N.J., 1999); and David Blight, *Race and Reunion: The Civil War in American Memory* (Cambridge, Mass., 2001) have all explored the impact of soldiers' interpretations of the war.

18. William Croswell Dome, "Patriotism: Its Defects, Its Dangers and Its Duties," *North American Review* (March 1898): 310–23, 316–17.

19. John Pope, "Some Legacies of the Civil War," *North American Review* (June 1887): 583–95, 593; Murat Halstead, "Our National Conceits," *North American Review* (Novem-

ber 1889): 550–60, 551; J. B. Harrison, "Certain Dangerous Tendencies in American Life," *Atlantic Monthly* (October 1878): 385–402, 386, 400; Charles Dudley Warner, "Aspects of American Life," *Atlantic Monthly* (January 1879): 1–9, 7–8.

20. Edward Bellamy, "Progress of Nationalism in the United States," *North American Review* (June 1892): 742–53, 743; Walt Whitman, "Have We a National Literature?" *North American Review* (March 1891): 332–38, 336–38; Daniel E. Sickles, "Further Recollections of Gettysburg," *North American Review* (March 1891): 258; Thomas Keneally, *American Scoundrel: Love, War and Politics in Civil War America* (New York, 2002).

21. Green B. Raum, "Pensions and Patriotism," *North American Review* (August 1891): 205–15, 206, 215; Kammen, *Mystic Chords of Memory*, 89, 93.

22. McConnell, *Glorious Contentment*, 220–22; Jay Winter, *Sites of Memory, Sites of Mourning: The Great War in European Cultural Memory* (Cambridge, 1995), 2.

23. Gary Gerstle, "Race and Nation in the United States, Mexico, and Cuba, 1880–1940," in this volume; James M. McPherson, "'The Whole Family of Man': Lincoln and the Last Best Hope Abroad," in James M. McPherson, *Drawn with the Sword: Reflections on the American Civil War* (New York, 1996), 227; Barbara Weinstein, "Slavery, Citizenship, and National Identity in Brazil and the U.S. South," in this volume.

24. Benedict Anderson, *Imagined Communities: Reflections on the Origins and Spread of Nationalism* (1991; New York, 1992), 6–7; "What Is Americanism?" *American Journal of Sociology* (January 1915): 433–86, 483.

Nationalism in Canada

PHILLIP BUCKNER

*L*ike other new nations in the Americas, Canada is essentially a product of the migration that flowed into the Americas between the seventeenth and twentieth centuries. During the first wave of migration from 1500 to 1800 almost all of the migrants came from Europe or were transported from Africa by Europeans to serve as slaves. The European migrants came in sufficiently large numbers that they were able to overwhelm the indigenous peoples, and the migrants and their descendants created a series of new societies that in many cases bore limited resemblance to the European societies from which the migrants were originally drawn. The colonies most recognizably European in their social composition and culture were those established in what became the United States and Canada, partly because the Native populations were smaller than elsewhere in the Americas, partly because the environment was particularly suitable for the development of European agriculture and the spread of dense European settlement, partly because they were able to achieve levels of affluence that equaled (and eventually surpassed) European levels, and partly because the ties between Britain and its colonies appear to have been stronger than those between the other European empires and their colonies in the Americas. As J. H. Elliott points out in *The British Atlantic World, 1500–1800*, the English Atlantic "may well stand out from the other European Atlantics in terms of the degree and process of exchange and communication between metropolis and colony."[1]

The process of how European colonies were transformed into a series of distinctive nation-states is an issue that rarely troubles those who write about the theory and practice of nationalism. For the primordialists Canada and the United States are by their definition not nations; they are merely states that can command a degree of patriotism from their citizens. But even those who find the primordialist definition of the nation too limiting accept that the new nations were fundamentally different from those established in Europe. In his 1991 study of the evolution of national identity Anthony Smith argues that most European nations are structured around a cohesive and self-consciously distinctive *ethnie*. In Europe these *ethnies* have roots in the distant past in a myth of shared ancestry, but in the Americas there were no immediate antecedent *ethnies*, and so nations were formed through "an attempt to coalesce the culture of successive waves of (mainly European) immigrants."[2] In *Nationalism and Modernism*, published in 1998, Smith develops this theme, arguing that "in the United States, Canada and Australia, colonists-immigrants have pioneered a providentialist frontier nationalism; and once large waves of culturally different immigrants were admitted, this has encouraged a 'plural' conception of the nation, which accepts, and even celebrates, ethnic and cultural diversity within an overarching political, legal and linguistic national identity."[3] The idea of "providentialist frontier nationalism" seems to work better in the case of the United States than in the case of Canada (or Australia, for that matter). But even in the case of the United States Smith's model underestimates the cultural importance of the original migrants who settled in the thirteen colonies and of their descendants in shaping the distinctive character of American nationalism. Smith's model also implies a smoother and easier transition to a "plural" conception of the nation than was the case in either Canada or the United States.

In the thirteen colonies the dominant white elites were largely drawn from the British Isles and even before the Revolution shared some sense of belonging to a common "British" culture. After 1783 the myth of a common pioneer experience in the colonial period and of a "manifest destiny" to spread American civilization across the continent, as well as the shared experience of the Revolution, formed the initial basis for the creation of an American national identity. In theory America was built around the concept of a civic nationalism that treated all of its citizens as equal and allowed for cultural diversity. In practice civic nationalism "contended with another potent ideological inheritance, a racial nationalism that conceives of America in ethnoracial terms, as a people held together by common blood and skin colour and by an inherited fitness for self-government."[4] And, of course, the people who were deemed to possess a "common blood" were those who could trace their descent back to the period of colonization in the seventeenth and eighteenth centuries or who came from the same ethnic background in northern Europe as the original settlers. In fact, in most of the new nations created in Central and South America the decision to break the tie with the mother country was taken by what can be described as an ethnic core. As in the United States the descendants of these original immigrants played a dominant role in shaping the identity of the new nations, and in each of these nations there was an ongoing conflict between those who defined the nation in civic nationalist terms and those who thought in ethnocultural terms.

The Canadian story in many respects is not dissimilar, but it has some unusual features that arise from its unique pattern of European settlement. The first unusual factor is the persistence of one of the most cohesive and self-conscious *ethnies* in the Americas. New France was a product of the first wave of

European migration to the Americas, but it did not follow what French Canadian historians like to think of as the "normal" pattern of evolution. Partly this was because New France did not attract a sufficient number of European settlers to be able to follow the example of the other European colonies and establish an independent state during the late eighteenth and early nineteenth centuries. At most 35,000 Europeans migrated to New France, and close to 70 percent were transients who did not stay long.[5] Initially, the French Crown placed responsibility for the colony in the hands of a succession of chartered trading companies that were given a monopoly over the fur trade in return for promoting colonization, but only the last of the chartered companies made a serious effort to encourage settlement as New France grew from a population of 107 in 1627 to over 3,000 in 1663. The colony was placed under royal control in 1663, and a substantial number of French soldiers, indentured servants, and women were sent to the colony. But after 1672 the French monarchy was distracted by costly wars in Europe, and the population of New France grew largely through natural increase, peaking at around 75,000 when it was conquered by the British in 1759–60 and ceded to the British Crown by the Treaty of Paris in 1763.

During the time that it was a colony of France, New France was not particularly distinctive in the kind of migrants it attracted. As in the other European colonies in the Americas, the vast majority of the migrants did not arrive free to sell their labor to the highest bidder; instead, they were under some form of constraint and were drawn overwhelmingly from the large pool of itinerant landless laborers that existed throughout Europe. A very high proportion of the migrants to New France were single males, mainly soldiers and indentured laborers. A proportion of the original migrants may have been Flemings, Germans, Swiss, Italians, and Iberians, but the vast majority of the migrants were drawn from a few core areas in France, and the population of New France was probably less diverse in its origins than most of the other European colonies established during the first wave of European migration. The Native population was small and easily segregated, and after the first few years of settlement there was virtually no intermarriage between the Native peoples and the French colonists. The role of French women (and virtually all of the women immigrants were from France) was particularly important in the transmission of French culture, as was the Roman Catholic Church, which was staffed by Frenchmen and was the only church allowed in the colony.

In the process of crossing the Atlantic there was what R. C. Harris has called a "simplification" of French institutions, but visitors from France did not feel as if they were visiting an entirely strange and alien land.[6] The towns were smaller versions of those found in the French provinces. Huge areas of the colony remained in a state of wilderness, but the countryside around the towns had been cleared of forest and supported the same crops as in France, for the migrants had brought with them their cabbages, turnips, and lettuce.[7] The peasants tilled the fields in similar ways wearing similar clothes. The traditional ruling classes—royal officials, seigneurs, merchants, and clergy—were still the ruling classes, even if there was more upward social mobility in New France than in Old France. Even before the conquest there was a growing split in the colony between mere sojourners and the mass of permanent residents who had begun to think of themselves as *canadien* as well as French. When New France was ceded to the British in 1763 and renamed Québec, the inhabitants had to choose between remaining French or *canadien*. Most of the military officers, the administrators, and the representatives of French commercial houses, as well as smaller numbers of artisans and seigneurs, returned to France. Those who remained became British subjects and adjusted their loyalties accordingly.

The *canadien* population grew rapidly after 1763, but there was virtually no further migration from France, and few foreign migrants ventured into the heartland of French Canada. Natural increase alone is sufficient to account for the rapid demographic growth of the rural areas of Québec in the late eighteenth and nineteenth centuries.[8] Although there were a few exogamous marriages with Native peoples in the West and with Scottish or Irish Catholics who settled in Québec, the vast majority of the *Canadiens* married members of their own ethnic community, and they would continue to do so well into the twentieth century. After 1763 a trickle of British migrants—mainly from the thirteen colonies—moved to Québec, and a few thousand Loyalists came after 1783, but migration directly from Europe only gained momentum after 1815. Initially, almost all of the newer migrants came from the British Isles, and by the 1850s the British minority formed close to a quarter of the population of Québec and for a time formed a majority in the urban centers of Montréal and Québec City. But in the latter part of the nineteenth century Québec attracted relatively few migrants from Britain. Many French Canadians immigrated to the United States during this period, but English Canadians left in even larger numbers. Gradually, the English-speaking population, even in the urban centers, was overwhelmed by the internal migration of French Canadians from the rural areas. Migration to Québec from Europe resumed on a substantial scale from 1900 to 1914, during the 1920s, and again after 1945. But the European migrants flowed almost entirely into Montréal, creating a multicultural minority numbering about 20 percent of the province and about half of the population of Montréal.[9]

Nearly 80 percent of those who live in Québec today (and well over 90 percent of those living in the rural areas of Québec) are thus directly descended from those who settled in New France prior to 1763. Québec is the only place in the Americas with such a homogeneous and geographically concentrated population descended directly from the first wave of European migrants. To call this population either an immigrant or fragment *ethnie* is rather misleading. Most of the French-speaking population can trace their roots back seventeen or eighteen generations to the small number of migrants who settled in New France in the mid-seventeenth century, and they would reject the notion that they are "immigrants." Moreover, for two centuries they have had very limited contact with France. From the mid-nineteenth century to the present French Canadian intellectuals, historians, writers, and artists have sought to identify themselves as a distinct people. In the process they have evolved founding myths and historical memories of their own that define their national identity.

Of course, the *Canadiens* have never inhabited an independent state. In 1791 the old Province of Québec was divided into two colonies: the area west of the Ottawa River that had an English-speaking majority became Upper Canada, and the area east of the Ottawa with a French-speaking majority became Lower Canada. In 1837–38 there was a substantial rebellion against British rule in Lower Canada, but the rebellion failed, and in 1841 the Canadas were reunited into the United Province of Canada, in which a clear majority of the combined population was British. The failure of the rebellion of 1837–38 convinced the *canadien* leadership that they would have to accommodate themselves to living in what was essentially a British world.[10] Within this world they were by no means a helpless minority, since they had the same political and legal rights as other British subjects. During the 1840s the British surrendered control over local affairs in the British North American colonies to the locally elected legislatures. Indeed, although the *Canadiens* formed only a minority in the United Province of Canada, they were a sufficiently powerful minority to be able to protect their interests within the colony and ensure the survival of their distinctive national culture. To distinguish themselves from the English-speaking majority in the United Province of Canada, who also began to describe themselves as Canadians, *les Canadiens* began to describe themselves as *les Canadiens français*. The French Canadian political elite, which benefited from the commercial prosperity generated by the 1841 Union and which was strongly influenced by the very conservative Roman Catholic Church, increasingly saw the advantages of the imperial connection, particularly if the alternative was annexation to the United States.

The confederation of the British North American colonies into the Dominion of Canada in 1867 added a new layer of complexity. Initially, neither the French-speaking Acadians in the Maritimes (who had been under British rule since Acadia had been surrendered to the British by the Treaty of Utrecht in 1713) nor the French-speaking Métis (the children of French fur traders and Native women) in western Canada were seen as part of the core French Canadian nation. Indeed, the major advantage of confederation from the perspective of the French Canadian majority was that it would create a federal union and divide the United Province of Canada into the Provinces of Ontario and Québec.

French Canadians would be the majority in Québec and thus would gain control over their own provincial state (albeit a state severely limited in its constitutional powers). Not all French Canadians were satisfied with the limited powers granted Québec under the 1867 constitutional arrangements, but the dissatisfaction was limited, since the government of Québec did have the powers that seemed crucial for the survival of French Canadian culture, notably, control over education and civil law. At the federal level the French Canadian minority was strong enough to ensure that French Canadian politicians played a key role in national politics and in the definition of national policies that brought economic benefits to the Province of Québec. The major source of contention was the treatment of French-speaking minorities outside of Québec and the imperial enthusiasm that swept English Canada during the late nineteenth century. French Canadians did not share the continuing enthusiasm of most English-speaking Canadians for the imperial connection, particularly when it involved participation in "the odious Boer War" and conscription during World War I. [11] Increasingly, they looked forward to the day when Canada would become an independent nation.

French Canadian politicians in the late nineteenth century liked to emphasize that whereas English Canadians had two loyalties, one to Canada and the other to Britain, they had only one—to Canada. This glossed over the fact that most French Canadians saw themselves as members of a distinctive and self-conscious national community that participated in the Canadian national community as a collectivity. They viewed Canada as a nation with two founding ethnic cores—a French Canadian core based in Québec and an English Canadian core based in the rest of Canada. We should not confuse this with some form of civic nationalism. While French Canadians in Québec came to incorporate the French-speaking minorities outside of Québec into their definition of the French Canadian cultural nation and sought to defend the rights of French-speaking minorities outside of Québec, they did not welcome the large-scale migration of Europeans from south and central Europe or of Asians into Canada. Indeed, they were probably less tolerant of ethnic and cultural diversity than most English Canadians. [12] Their vision of Canada was as racist and ethnocentric as that of the English Canadian majority and was essentially based upon the notion of "arm's-length racial cohabitation." [13]

Until the period after World War II the vast majority of French Canadians were content with their status as a cultural majority within the province of Québec and as a cultural minority within the larger Canadian nation. But in the 1950s and 1960s the French Canadian birthrate plummeted, and the rapid influx of large numbers of new immigrants turned the French Canadians into a smaller minority within Canada and even weakened their dominant position within Québec. The "Quiet Revolution" of the 1960s transformed and modernized

Québec society, removing the conservative influence of the Catholic Church and unleashing a new and more aggressive form of French Canadian nationalism. By the 1970s a majority of the French-speaking population of Québec had begun to describe themselves not as *canadien français* but as Québécois. A growing number came to believe that the existing constitutional relationship between Canada and Québec was undesirable, and a majority of the French-speaking population of Québec has come to reject provincial status and to call for separatism (or at least some form of sovereignty association). Many Québécois continue to have overlapping and to some extent conflicting loyalties both to Québec and to Canada, and it is still not clear whether the Québécois nation will remain part of a multicultural Canada in which they are defined as just another cultural minority. Québécois nationalism has, however, shed its overt racism, and if Québec separates from Canada, an independent Québec state will be based upon a form of civic nationalism that will give equal rights to all its citizens, regardless of their ethnic origins. But the dominant ethnic core in this "plural" nation will be the descendants of those who settled in New France during the mid-seventeenth century, and they will define the nature and identity of the new nation.

If the first distinctive feature in the evolution of Canada was the persistence of an unusually cohesive and self-conscious French Canadian *ethnie* within a larger English-speaking community, the second has been the long and intimate connection of Canada with the United Kingdom. Almost alone among the nations on the mainland of the Americas, Canada achieved its independence through evolution, not revolution. This too was a product of a distinct pattern of migration. Whereas most states in the Americas were a product of the first wave of European migration between 1500 and 1800, Canada was not. It remained a British colony throughout the nineteenth and early twentieth centuries, effectively becoming an independent state with the passing of the Statute of Westminster in 1931. Moreover, the dominant ethnic core in English-speaking Canada was a product not of the first wave of European migration but of the second wave of European migration between 1815 and 1914. Around fifty-five million people emigrated from Europe to the Americas, mainly to North America, between 1830 and 1930—nearly twenty times as many as in the previous three centuries.[14] Not only was the scale of the migration much larger, but the pattern of migration was very different. Although a majority of the migrants were still young single males, there was a much higher proportion of women and families. Once the practice of importing contract labor to North America had died out and the slave trade was abolished, migration to North America was in the vast majority of cases a voluntary act taken by those who had come to believe that their lives would be improved by it. This was true even of the minority of migrants who required financial assistance for the voyage across the Atlantic.[15] Migrants were rarely drawn from the most destitute classes in Europe. They usually paid their own passage, and in North America they were able to sell their labor to the highest bidder and move repeatedly in search of better economic opportunities.

Most European migrants moved as part of a chain migration. They were motivated to live and work among relatives, neighbors, and friends in an alien yet at the same time familiar environment. For this reason migration historians have raised questions about the validity of describing the migrants as "uprooted"—the title of Oscar Handlin's famous 1951 study of transatlantic migration; increasingly, they prefer the word "transplanted"—the title of John Bodnar's 1985 study.[16] Indeed, recent scholarship emphasizes that nineteenth-century migrants were far better able than earlier migrants to retain contacts with their ancestral homes in Europe and that acculturation involved a series of mainly voluntary steps "toward the intentional if gradual sinking of new roots, while almost imperceptibly the old roots began to wither away."[17] This withering-away process could be very slow, stretching over generations and in some cases never completed. Many migrants and their descendants (though certainly not all) can be described as transnationals, particularly if they belonged to migrant groups that faced discrimination, settled in ethnic clusters, and did not intermarry or merge with the dominant ethnic core.[18]

In one sense Canada was just another "New World" country that received a small share of the massive European migration to the Americas after 1815. Yet there were important differences between Canada and the other nations receiving migrants. Most of the latter, including the United States, had already declared their independence, and they had received their core European population during the earlier period of European migration. Only the sparsely populated French colonies of Acadia (Nova Scotia after 1713) and New France (Québec after 1763) had failed to follow this pattern. Even after they became British colonies they managed to attract only a small minority of the migrants flowing across the Atlantic. The largest flow of migrants came from the United States. About 5,000 to 7,000 New Englanders moved into Nova Scotia in the 1750s and 1760s, about 60,000 American Loyalists settled in what was left of the British Empire in North America after 1783, and perhaps another 50,000 to 60,000 Americans crossed, mainly into Upper Canada, between the 1790s and 1815. By 1815 the total population of British North America was only around 500,000, of whom over 300,000 (mainly concentrated in Québec) were of French ancestry. Most of the rest were migrants from the thirteen colonies or the United States and their descendants. A substantial minority of the non-French population could trace their roots to Scotland and even to Germany. In 1815 the British North American colonies, in Jack Bumsted's words, were "a collection of relatively and culturally distinctive provinces with weak colonial administrations incapable of melding their various emergent cultures into a coherent whole."[19]

It was the arrival of massive numbers of migrants from the British Isles that transformed the British North American colonies. Between 1815 and 1860 at least half a million British migrants settled in British North America. While the Francophone population increased about threefold to around one million, almost entirely through natural increase, the non-Francophone population increased tenfold to around two million, primarily through migration from the British Isles. Almost everywhere except in Québec the British-born and their descendants formed a majority of the population by the 1860s. The arrival of such large numbers of immigrants transformed the British North American colonies. In 1815, except in the older seigneurial areas in Québec and around the coastline of the Bay of Fundy in the Maritimes, the countryside consisted of a wilderness broken only by the occasional cluster of farms. By the 1860s every acre of arable land had been granted to settlers, and much of it was under cultivation. For most migrants the frontier experience was short. The forest was rapidly receding, and the countryside was dotted with small towns and villages linked by roads, telegraph lines, steamships, post offices, and, increasingly, railways. The migrants had not just reshaped the material landscape; they had also transformed the cultural landscape of British North America by the 1860s. They had destroyed the fragmentation that had been such a pronounced feature of the colonies in 1815 and had begun to forge a new sense of identity among the English-speaking population of British North America. Put crudely, they had made British North America *British*.[20]

Indeed, the act of migration was not the same for British migrants who settled in Canada as it was for the other migrants to the Americas. The British were not transferring to a foreign land but to a portion of the world that remained British. Until 1947 there was no such thing as a Canadian citizen, only a British subject resident in Canada. Even after 1947 Canadian citizens remained British subjects, and British subjects resident in Canada had all the rights of Canadian citizens whether they applied for Canadian citizenship or not. Until 1962 Canadian-born British subjects had an automatic right of entry to Britain, where they had the same legal status as British-born British subjects. British migrants could transfer easily across the Atlantic and back again if they wished, and their descendants could equally easily make the transfer the opposite way, which is why it is impossible to say with certainty who was a Canadian and who was not in the nineteenth and early twentieth centuries. Many British-born migrants came to view themselves as Canadians while retaining a sense of their British identity. A not insignificant number of their Canadian-born offspring ended up migrating to Britain in the late nineteenth century and came to view themselves as primarily British while retaining a sense of their Canadian identity. Just as

French-speaking Canadians thought of themselves as both Canadian and *canadien français*, English-speaking Canadians thought of themselves as both British and Canadian.

Within the British Empire migrants from the British Isles faced no legal or structural barriers preventing rapid integration into the local British community. Nor did the British migrants have to abandon their national identities in order to assimilate with the cultural majority, since they immediately formed part of that majority (although the Catholic Irish were to some extent a separate case). Within British North America by the 1860s the British migrants and their descendants were disproportionately represented in the colonial elites. British-born ministers provided the leadership in most of the Protestant churches, and British-born lecturers staffed virtually all of the institutions of higher education. British textbooks were increasingly used in the schools, and the children of the native-born as well as of more recent immigrants were sent to Britain to receive a specialized training not available at home. The bar and the bench and the commercial elites were drawn increasingly from the British migrants and their offspring. Moreover, the Atlantic had shrunk, and colonial newspapers carried up-to-date reports on British events that were seldom more than a few weeks old and by the 1860s usually only a few days old. British North Americans increasingly felt themselves to be part of the wider British world, encompassing not just Britain and British North America but the whole British Empire. They followed events in the Crimea and celebrated British victories with enthusiasm (especially since one of the imperial regiments fighting in the Crimea had been raised in Upper Canada). They viewed with horror and anger the atrocities committed during the Indian rebellion of 1859 (or at least those committed by the rebels).

In their efforts to replicate British culture in British North America the colonials often incurred the scorn of British visitors. But to British North Americans there was nothing ludicrous in their desire to show their loyalty and attachment to the empire. Henry J. Morgan proudly noted in *The Place British Americans Have Won in History* that the recipient of the first Victoria Cross, Lt. Col. A. R. Dunn, who had taken part in the Charge of the Light Brigade, was a native of Toronto and that in India and the Crimea "the tombs of a number of our countrymen, who sacrificed their lives for England's glory, speak more eloquently than I can do."[21] British Americans had little sympathy with those "Little Englanders" who called upon Britain to "emancipate" its colonies. Indeed, they denounced the term "emancipation," pointing out that Canadians were "not slaves, not even colonists in the old and popular sense of that term, but freemen and an *integral* part of a nation whose liberty, science, wealth and power are pre-eminent among the nations of the world."[22] Although Americans might view Canadians as "poor-relation British," that is not how they viewed themselves.[23] After the introduction of responsible government in the 1840s Canadians had effective control over their own internal affairs and were able to abandon those aspects of British culture that they did not want such as primogeniture and a state-supported church. They sought to build what has accurately been described as a "Better Britain."[24] They viewed their society as more liberal and more tolerant than that of the United States, a myth that still persists in Canada. Indeed, Canadians demonstrated during the War of 1812, the border conflicts of the 1830s and 1840s, and the U.S. Civil War that they did not want to be Americans but wished to remain British.

By 1871 the aboriginal population of Canada had shrunk to between 110,000 and 137,000, concentrated heavily in western Canada, and would continue to decline as the buffalo disappeared and settlers invaded western Canada, shrinking to not much above 1 or 2 percent of the population in the 1920s and 1930s. Indeed, by 1871 Canada was essentially composed of two clearly defined national groups: 60.6 percent of the nonaboriginal population of over 3.5 million was of British origin and 31.1 percent of French. Only just over 8 percent of Canadians were of neither British nor French origin. The only substantial group numerically were the 202,991 Canadians of German origin, who formed 5.8 percent of the Canadian population.[25] Except for the substantial German communities in Lunenberg County in Nova Scotia and in Waterloo County in Upper Canada, where well over 60 percent of Canada's German population was located, there were no substantial concentrations of non-British migrants. Scattered across British North America, the non-British migrants could not form self-contained communities, and intermarriage rates with British migrants and native-born Canadians of British descent were high.

The British majority was not monolithic, and the British community in Canada was more Scottish and far more Irish than in the mother country. But while the British migrants brought their national, regional, and local cultures with them, migration was inevitably a homogenizing experience. During the transatlantic crossing people from one part of the British Isles were usually mixed with people from other parts, and upon their arrival the British migrants rarely settled in self-contained ethnic communities and rarely worked, traded, or worshiped solely with people of the same ethnic background. The first generation usually came out as families or married people of the same ethnic origin, but over time there would be considerable intermarriage between the different British groups and the descendants of earlier migrants from the United States. This was particularly true among Protestants, since religion was a greater barrier to intermarriage than ethnicity. Over time more and more of the British population could trace their origins to several parts of the British Isles. Even among the first-generation immigrants ethnic identity was frequently fluid. Among later generations memories of the ancestral home blurred and faded, and many of the immigrants and their descendants began to define themselves as both British and Canadian.

Irish Catholics were undoubtedly the least easily integrated into the British American community. Except for French Catholics, Irish Catholics had the highest rates of endogamous marriages in British North America and showed a substantial degree of residential clustering in the emerging urban centers in British North America. But while there were Irish Catholics who hated the British Empire and everything it stood for and who joined Fenian societies, they were not the majority. There were bitter religious disputes between Protestants and Catholics, most notably over the issue of public funding for separate schools, but once this issue was resolved many Irish Catholics were prepared to identify themselves with the British majority. Thomas D'Arcy McGee, an Irish nationalist who in Canada became a defender of the imperial connection, argued that the Irish were better treated in Canada under British rule than they were in the United States.[26] McGee did not represent all the Catholic Irish in Canada. Indeed, he became the first founder of the Canadian Confederation to be assassinated, apparently for betraying the Irish nationalist cause. But by the 1860s there were few barriers to prevent the effective political integration of Irish Catholics into the majority British culture. In 1864–71 it was this shared British culture that enabled the British North American colonies to unite to form the Dominion of Canada. The British community in British North America was not seeking independence from Britain but a larger British colony better able to resist the annexationist pressures from an American republic dominated by the northern states. It also sought to oversee the expansion of British authority over the vast and as yet largely unsettled (at least by Europeans) territories west of the Great Lakes still nominally under the control of the Hudson's Bay Company.

The flow of British migration to Canada slowed after 1867. The older provinces in the East had little good land left and were only slowly urbanized in the late nineteenth century, while the Canadian West was only slowly developed. Both native-born Canadians and recent British immigrants tended to head south to the United States. Lloyd Reynolds has estimated that Canada retained only about 176,000 of the 673,000 British migrants who entered Canada between 1871 and 1901.[27] Quite likely, this 176,000 included a disproportionate number of the British women recruited as domestic servants by organizations like the British Women's Emigration Association and of the British children brought out by organizations such as Dr. Barnardo's Homes, since these groups were less likely to have the resources to enable them to join the exodus to the United States.

During this period of limited immigration to Canada from Europe and substantial emigration from Canada to the United States the proportion of native-born Canadians rose to 87 percent of the population in 1901. Of the 13 percent born outside Canada 405,883 out of 699,500 had been born in Britain or other British possessions (primarily Newfoundland) and the next largest number—127,899—in the United States. In 1901 barely 3 percent of the Canadian population had been born elsewhere, mainly in Germany, although there were a growing number of Poles, Jews, Italians, Ukrainians, and Chinese. Even in the sparsely populated West, where most of the non-British migrants settled, over three-quarters of the population were either native-born Canadians or British immigrants. By 1901 the population of those defined by the census as of neither British nor French ethnic origins had grown to barely 10 percent, and people of German origin still formed substantially over half of the non-British, non-French population. There were still few large or cohesive ethnic communities across Canada, and a substantial number (though certainly not all) of the children or grandchildren of the earlier migrants had been absorbed into the British-Canadian majority.

English-speaking Canadians were proud of their membership in a global empire and of their loyalty to the British Crown.[28] Yet a sense of being part of a wider British world did not preclude an equally strong sense of being Canadian, of being part of a distinctive national community within the empire. The union of the British North American colonies into a single state hastened the evolution of a new national identity, particularly as the new state spread across the continent and began to develop the Canadian West. In 1879 the Government of Canada introduced a new system of protective tariffs that Conservatives described as the National Policy that was designed to encourage industrialization and urbanization, even at the expense of trade with Britain. It also built a national railway that linked Canada from coast to coast and created a paramilitary federal police force, the North West Mounted Police. When Sir John A. Macdonald, the first prime minister of Canada and the architect of these policies, died in 1891, his supporters immediately began to turn him into a national hero.[29] English Canadian authors began to write histories that emphasized the importance of Canada to the empire, resurrecting myths about the Loyalists and about the role played by the Canadian militia in preserving Canada for the empire during the War of 1812, against the Fenian threat in the 1860s, and against the Métis who had supported the 1885 North West Rebellion. The South African War added a new myth of the superiority of the Canadian volunteers to the regular troops of the British Army. J. M. S. Careless once described late-nineteenth- and early-twentieth-century Canadian historians as "the Britannic, or Blood is Thicker than Water" school because their theme was "the emergence of a new Britannic community within the empire."[30] English-speaking Canadians had no doubt that they were creating a nation, one that would eventually achieve full autonomy, but they were determined that it should be a "British" nation that would remain part of a larger British world. Not surprisingly, the two most important public celebrations in early-twentieth-century Canada took place on 24 May, Queen Victoria's birthday, a celebration of empire, and on 1 July, a celebration of Canada's birthday.

The commitment of English-speaking Canadians to the British throne and British institutions was shown during World War I, when hundreds of thousands of English-speaking Canadians served and many thousands gave their lives for a Britain many of them had never seen but that they still regarded as their mother country. World War I is usually seen as a watershed in the evolution of English Canadian nationalism. Undoubtedly, English-speaking Canadians did emerge from the war with a stronger sense of Canadian identity and a desire to achieve complete self-government and international recognition of their national status. This new status was recognized after the war, and with the passing of the Statute of Westminster Canada became effectively an independent nation. But English Canadians did not abandon their desire to create a British nation. Indeed, it is arguable that participation in war strengthened the emotional ties between Canada and Britain and ensured the survival of the British connection even after the formal bonds were weakened during the 1920s, when Canada was given the right to control its own foreign policy and ceased even in theory to be a colony.[31]

The desire by English Canadians to remain British and to continue as part of the British Commonwealth of Nations also survived the huge wave of migrants that poured into Canada between 1900 and 1929. This migration is usually seen as transforming Canada into a truly multicultural society, and in one sense it did, for substantial numbers of migrants entered Canada from all parts of Europe, and a significant minority came from Asia. But it is important to remember that emigrants from the British Isles still formed a clear majority of the migrants. Between 1901 and 1921 well over 1.3 million British subjects entered Canada, and at least 870,000 of them became permanent residents. Even in 1911, at the end of the heaviest period of migration, the number of British-born in Canada (around 11.6 percent) exceeded the total number of migrants born in all other overseas countries combined (around 10.4 percent). In the 1920s, when migration resumed again on a smaller scale, the number of European migrants did slightly outnumber the British, but many of the European migrants were transients, and even in this decade Canada attracted and retained 276,000 British migrants. During the 1930s the gates were closed to virtually all but the British. Outside of Québec, the British and native-born Canadians of British origin continued everywhere to form a clear majority of the population; in Ontario and the Maritimes they formed a very substantial majority. The pressures encouraging (and coercing) non-British immigrants to assimilate remained strong. Even in the group settlements established by European migrants in western Canada one recent study has concluded that there was "significant cultural transformation" and "an inescapable reality to the melting pot" on both sides of the U.S.-Canada border.[32]

Of course, migrants faced different levels of discrimination and pressures to assimilate. In theory the British nationalism that had been transported to Canada was a civic nationalism. The United Kingdom itself was composed of four distinct national groups, and the British Empire encompassed an even wider range of nationalities and cultures. All British subjects were theoretically equal as long as they were prepared to pledge loyalty to the Crown and to the empire. In reality Britons everywhere accepted race as an objective category and drew a distinction between the British and other, inferior races. Whether this inferiority was genetic and therefore permanent and irreversible or whether it was cultural and environmental was unclear, for notions about race were frequently contradictory. But in Canada the British ethnic core was determined to perpetuate itself and its values (this does not mean that they agreed entirely on what those values were), and the distinction between a civic and an ethnic nationalism was blurred and ambiguous. Native Canadians were thus denied citizenship unless they were willing to renounce Native culture and embrace British "civilization." Blacks and Asians were discouraged or even prevented from immigrating to Canada and were discriminated against if they did immigrate. Central and southern Europeans had to overcome widespread prejudice. Each of these groups had to negotiate a place for themselves, with varying degrees of success, on the margins of English Canadian society, constructing their own sense of Canadian identity, one frequently at odds with that held by the English Canadian majority (or the French Canadian majority in the Province of Québec).[33]

In time most of the European migrants and their descendants were incorporated into the English Canadian majority, and they joined with the majority in support of going to war in 1939, again in defense of the British world and what it stood for. They also supported conscription in 1944 (over violent objections from French Canada). Even when the war came to an end it was far from self-evident that within two decades the commitment of the English-speaking majority in Canada to remaining a British community would be undermined, partly by the collapse of the British Empire, partly by changing patterns of migration, partly by Canada's growing economic and cultural integration with the United States, and partly by the rise of a more assertive Québécois nationalism.[34] In the 1960s English-speaking Canadians therefore sought to redefine Canada as a bilingual and bicultural nation based on the recognition that there were two founding peoples. When that failed to satisfy the Québec nationalists and the growing number of English-speaking Canadians whose origins were neither English nor French, English-speaking Canadians sought to reinvent Canada as a postcolonial, "plural" nation with a new set of historical symbols. This meant jettisoning much of Canada's British legacy. The Red Ensign, for many years Canada's unofficial national flag, was abandoned for an entirely new and distinctive Canadian flag. "God Save the Queen" was replaced by "O Canada" as the official national anthem. English Canadian historians began to rewrite the history of Canada to bring out its multicultural character.

Unfortunately, good politics does not always make for good history. Until at least the 1950s Canada was not a multicultural nation in any meaningful sense of that term. It was a predominantly British nation with a substantial French Canadian minority who were prepared to accept the constraints of living within a predominantly British nation in return for a substantial degree of provincial autonomy in Québec and a powerful voice in federal politics. Canada did include a smaller minority of people of European origin who were encouraged or coerced into becoming part of the English Canadian majority and an even smaller number of people of non-European origin who were denied full equality and, in the case of Asians, discouraged from assimilating. In reality—a reality that many Canadians still wish to deny—Canada was not more tolerant of diversity than the United States.

Much has changed since the 1960s. But the legacy of two centuries of being part of a British world has shaped the English Canadian national identity in ways not easily undone. The descendants of earlier British immigrants may no longer constitute a large majority of the population, as they once did, but outside of Québec they still constitute the ethnic core and play a predominant role in shaping the distinctive character of modern English Canadian nationalism, which English Canadians define as simply Canadian nationalism. And while English Canadians in general are not as racist as their ancestors, they are not as tolerant as they would like to believe. Ironically, they are particularly intolerant of the notion that Québec should be given any special powers within the Canadian federation or that French Canadians should be treated as anything other than just another ethnic minority in a plural nation. It is this problem—a legacy of the way in which Canada was formed by two different waves of European settlement and the creation of two different ethnic cores—that threatens the survival of Canada even in its reinvented "plural" form.

NOTES

1. J. H. Elliott, "Afterword: Atlantic History: A Circumnavigation," in David Armitage and Michael J. Braddock, eds., *The British Atlantic World, 1500–1800* (New York, 2002), 247.

2. Anthony D. Smith, *National Identity* (London, 1991), 38–40.

3. Anthony D. Smith, *Nationalism and Modernism* (London, 1998), 194.

4. Gary Gerstle, *American Crucible: Race and Nation in the Twentieth Century* (Princeton, N.J., 2001), 4.

5. Peter N. Moogk, "Reluctant Exiles: Emigrants from France in Canada before 1760," *William and Mary Quarterly*, 3rd series, 46 (1989): 462–505.

6. R. C. Harris, "The Simplification of Europe Overseas," *Annals of the Association of American Geographers* 67 (1977): 469–83.

7. See Ramsay Cook, "Cabbages not Kings: Towards an Ecological Interpretation of Early Canadian History," *Journal of Canadian Studies* 24, no. 4 (Winter 1990–91): 5–15.

8. Colin M. Coates, *The Metamorphoses of Landscape and Community in Early Quebec* (Montréal, 2000), 57.

9. See Bruno Ramirez, "The Crossroads Province: Quebec's Place in International Migrations, 1870–1915," in Rudolph J. Vecoli and Suzanne M. Sinke, eds., *A Century of European Migrations 1830–1930* (Urbana, 1991), 25–26.

10. See P. A. Buckner and Carl Bridge, "Reinventing the British World," *Round Table* 92 (2003): 77–88; and Carl Bridge and Kent Fedorowich, "Mapping the British World," in *The British World: Diaspora, Culture and Identity* (London, 2003), 1–15.

11. *Canadian Annual Review for 1909* (Toronto, 1910), 106.

12. Michael D. Behiels, *Quebec and the Question of Immigration: From Ethnocentrism to Ethnic Pluralism, 1900–1985* (Ottawa, 1986).

13. Alan Gordon, *Making Public Pasts: The Contested Terrain of Montreal's Public Memories, 1891–1930* (Montréal, 2001), 79.

14. See Walter Nugent, *Crossings: The Great Transatlantic Migrations 1870–1914* (Bloomington, Ind., 1992), 29–30, and "Demographic Aspects of European Migration Worldwide," in Dirk Hoerder and Leslie Page Moch, eds., *European Migrants: Global and Local Perspectives* (Boston, 1991), 25–26.

15. See Robin F. Haines, *Emigration and the Labouring Poor: Australian Recruitment in Britain and Ireland, 1831–60* (New York, 1997).

16. Oscar Handlin, *The Uprooted* (Boston, 1951); John Bodnar, *The Transplanted: A History of Immigrants in Urban America* (Bloomington, Ind., 1985). See also "John Bodnar's *The Transplanted*: A Round Table," *Social Science History* 12, no. 3 (1988): 217–68.

17. Dirk Hoerder, "International Labour Markets and Community Building by Migrant Workers in the Atlantic Economies," in Vecoli and Sinke, *A Century of European Migrations*, 79–80, 100.

18. For useful surveys of the whole issue of migration to and acculturation in the United States see Gary Gerstle, "Liberty, Coercion, and the Making of Americans," *Journal of American History* 84 (September 1997): 525–58, with lengthy comments by David Hollinger and Donna R. Gabaccia and Gerstle's response (559–80); and Gary Gerstle and John Mollenkopf, "The Political Incorporation of Immigrants, Then and Now," and Ewa Morawska, "Immigrants, Transnationalism, and Ethnicization: A Comparison of This Great Wave and the Last," in Gary Gerstle and John Mollenkopf, eds., *E Pluribus Unum: Contemporary and Historical Perspectives on Immigrant Political Incorporation* (New York, 2001), 1–30, 175–212.

19. Jack M. Bumsted, "The Cultural Landscape of Early Canada," in Bernard Bailyn

and Philip D. Morgan, eds., *Strangers within the Realm: Cultural Margins of the First British Empire* (Chapel Hill, N.C., 1991), 379, 392.

20. For a longer version of this argument see P. A. Buckner, "Making British North America British, 1815–1860," in C. C. Eldridge, *Kith and Kin: Canada, Britain and the United States from the Revolution to the Cold War* (Cardiff, 1997), 11–44.

21. Henry J. Morgan, *The Place British Americans Have Won in History: A Lecture* (Ottawa, 1866), 10.

22. [Egerton Ryerson], *Remarks on the Historical Mis-statements and Fallacies of Mr. Goldwin Smith* (Toronto, 1966), 3, 12, 15.

23. Robert Wiebe, *Who We Are: A History of Popular Nationalism* (Princeton, N.J., 2002). Wiebe's use of this phrase shows how this view of nineteenth-century Canada persists in the United States even to the present.

24. This is a key theme in James Belich, *Making Peoples: A History of New Zealanders from Polynesian Settlement to the End of the Nineteenth Century* (Auckland, 1996).

25. Unless otherwise stated, population figures given here and elsewhere in this chapter are taken from Census Canada official publications.

26. See Thomas D'Arcy McGee, *The Irish Position in Britain and in Republican North America: A Letter to the Editors of the Irish Press Irrespective of Party,* 2nd ed. (Montréal, 1866).

27. Lloyd G. Reynolds, *The British Immigrant: His Social and Economic Adjustment in Canada* (Toronto, 1935), 27.

28. See P. A. Buckner, "Canada," in David Omissi and Andrew Thompson, eds., *The Impact of the South African War* (Houndsmill, 2002), 233–50.

29. Gordon, *Making Public Pasts*, xi–xii.

30. J. M. S. Careless, *Careless at Work: Selected Canadian Historical Studies* (Toronto, 1990), 107.

31. I have developed this argument in "The Long Goodbye: English Canadians and the British Connection," in P. A. Buckner and R. Douglas Francis, eds., *Rediscovering the British World* (Calgary, 2005).

32. John W. Bennett and Dan S. Sherburne, "Ethnicity, Settlement and Adaptation in the Peopling of the American-Canadian West," in Jean Burnet et al., *Migration and the Transformation of Cultures* (Toronto, 1992), 214, 185.

33. See, for example, Patricia K. Wood, *Nationalism from the Margins: Italians in Alberta and British Columbia* (Montréal, 2002).

34. See the essays in P. A. Buckner, ed., *Canada and the End of Empire* (Vancouver, 2004). On the importance of changing migration patterns see Stephen Constantine, "British Emigration to the Empire-Commonwealth since 1880: From Overseas Settlement to Diaspora," in Bridge and Fedorowich, *The British World*, 16–35.

Language, History, and Politics in Argentine Identity, 1840–1880

JORGE MYERS

*W*hat is America?" Domingo Faustino Sarmiento asked near the end of his life.

> This is perhaps the first time we shall ask ourselves who we were when we were
> called Americans and who when we called ourselves Argentines. Are we Europeans?
> So many copper-colored faces refute us! Are we Indians? Smiles of scorn from our
> blonde ladies give us perhaps the only answer. Mixed? No one wants to be, and there
> are thousands who don't even want to be called Americans or Argentines. Are we
> a nation? A nation without an amalgam of accumulated building materials, without
> adaptation or cement? Argentines? Whither and whence: it would be good to become
> aware of this. [1]

This question, voiced by Sarmiento at a time when the political and social
changes taking place in Argentina before his very eyes had led him to adopt a
melancholy, even despondent, tone in his writings, rages through all the works
of the Generation of 1837 and before as well. Argentines had been wrestling since
independence with the complex question of their own identity, only to discover
that as they sought to define it in opposition to the legacy of the colonial past
and of the colonizing country, Spain, it only seemed to become more and more
clouded by paradox and contradiction.

The National Problematic

A number of factors caused the Argentine difficulty in forming a national identity. The first and initially by far the most significant was the failure of the
state-building process in the half century after 1810. Unlike the United States
(and, indeed, unlike most of the other Latin American republics, with the exception of Central America), the construction of the state destined to replace
the imperial polity in the River Plate region proved exceptionally difficult. The

traditional networks for the allocation and exercise of political power crumbled under the stress of the struggle for independence, civil war, and the emergence of a violently factional politics. The result was a simultaneous tendency toward a progressive fragmentation of the successor polity to the viceroyalty accompanied by an equally progressive weakening of the legitimacy of the formally sovereign central authority of that polity. Although the United Provinces of South America continued to be at least nominally subordinate to a central government between 1810 and 1820, civil wars (such as those that broke out in the Banda Oriental, now Uruguay, and the littoral region of the River Plate) and the outright rejection of that subordinate status (as occurred in the case of the ruling elites of Paraguay, large portions of Upper Peru, and, sporadically, the Banda Oriental) steadily eroded the governing capacity of the authorities in Buenos Aires. Moreover, in the course of the constitutional debates and civil wars taking place during that first decade of independence, a permanent political dynamic had emerged that pitted the claims of the provinces of the interior against those of the city (and later of the province of Buenos Aires) and that would later lead all the provinces to see their goals and interests as essentially opposed to those of the central government. As a result of this situation, the central state authority collapsed in 1820, and from then until 1853 the Argentine territory would lack any de jure "national" government (with the brief exception of the not entirely constitutional presidency of 1826–27). Only in 1852–53 would the number of sovereign polities occupying Argentine territory be reduced to two, the Argentine Confederation and the Free State of Buenos Aires, and only in 1861–62 would the country now known as Argentina be united under a single constitutional government. Even then, one very thorny constitutional issue would remain unsolved: that of the site of the national capital. Federalization of the city of Buenos Aires was not to be decreed until 1880 as a result of the defeat of the last uprising of the province of Buenos Aires against the federal government. Hence one of the dominant elements in the Argentine national problematic was the emergence of strong political identities centered on the provinces, which competed with and obstructed the consolidation of a single overriding national identity.[2]

A symptom of this situation was the contested nature of the new nation's name. If in the case of roses their olfactory perception is not unduly affected by the name one applies to them, for nations the situation seems entirely reversed. In terms of national identity the name adopted by a people is more than simply a geographical marker; it is a condensation of the historical and projectual intention of its members (or at least of its elites), and, if successful over time, it is also a powerful instrument for triggering the sentiments associated with nationalism and patriotic fervor. As in the case of maps and other symbols through which the abstract content of the national idea is rendered concrete, but even more so given its epigrammatic succinctness, the name of a nation is a central element in and perhaps even a necessary starting point for defining its identity. For this reason the fact that the name of the new nation that gradually took shape on the right bank of the River Plate was itself a cause of conflict indicates the indefinite and controversial nature of Argentine national identity throughout the nineteenth century. As in most of Spanish America, the collective identity of the people seeking emancipation from the colonial rule of Spain had tended to be defined in very general and not necessarily specifically regional terms: the Revolution had been carried out by Creole or American patriots whose identity had been defined in opposition to that of the hated "Goths," the Spaniards.[3] When individuals sought to identify themselves in more precise regional terms, the reference was usually to a city and a province, not to any of the larger regions of the empire that eventually became nation-states. In Argentina even norms governing citizenship expressed this reference to an essentially *American* identity: the 1824 constitution of the province of Corrientes granted the right to vote and hold office to all individuals born in the Americas, and even as late as the 1870s (although by then such instances had become the object of growing criticism) Peruvian, Chilean, and Paraguayan nationals sat in provincial legislatures in Argentina on the basis of their American origin. When individuals sought a more precise regional definition of their identity, they did so through reference to their city, their province, or their *pago* (hometown). As a result, the term *argentino* initially had restricted geographical reference: it applied, with some degree of ambiguity, to the inhabitants either of Buenos Aires or of the banks of the River Plate and its littoral. But to contemporaries in the first half of the nineteenth century it was clear that *salteños, cordobeses,* or *cuyanos* were not the same as *argentinos.* Only very gradually, and through an extremely tortuous process, was *argentino* replaced by *porteño* and/or *bonaerense* as a denomination for the inhabitants of Buenos Aires, while the latter term was transformed into the name of all the inhabitants of the Republic of Argentina.[4] It was only after the 1860s and 1870s—ultimately as a result of the efforts of the state educational system—that it came to be accepted by all as the name of the nation to which they belonged.

If Argentina's national identity, understood in political terms, was so indeterminate as to become a subject of intense discussion and military conflict, it was no less indeterminate when framed in cultural terms. Three elements were central in this regard. First, the traditional cultural division between the city and the countryside, common throughout Spanish America, assumed, at least in the perspective of local elites, a more dramatic contrast as a result of the nature of Spanish colonization in the River Plate region. The poor inhabitants of the cities, the destitute and the outcast, had gradually settled the countryside, which had remained sparsely settled and economically stagnant until the middle of the eighteenth century, giving rise to a specific rural culture, that of the gauchos or wandering *paisanos*. Seminomadic and fiercely independent, the gauchos employed styles of dress, habitation, and speech that contrasted strikingly with those of city dwellers. This cultural difference, of which elite Argentines were all too aware throughout the nineteenth century (until economic modernization and the agency of the state imposed a more homogeneous cultural pattern by eliminating the gauchos as a specific cultural group, a process that culminated in their absorption into the proletarian workforce of the *estancias* [ranches]), formed one of the central focuses of discussion concerning Argentine national identity throughout the nineteenth century. Moreover, the particular speech patterns of the gauchos, reelaborated by elite writers as part of the *gauchesco* genre of poetry, underpinned an especially intense discussion during the last decades of the nineteenth century and first of the twentieth century concerning the possibility that a specifically Argentine language might develop—clearly differentiated from its Spanish trunk—and (although it is important to note that this argument did not always accompany the former) that said genre might constitute the point of departure for a national literature to emerge in Argentina.[5]

Second, the immense distances separating one city from the next and the added experience of political autonomy between 1820 and 1853 had generated very strong regional cultures in the provinces of the interior. Local patriotism, awareness of certain cultural differences (such as the attitude to Catholicism, more liberal in Buenos Aires and the littoral, more traditional in Córdoba and the northern provinces), and the hatreds fanned by the long period of civil war between the *federales* and the *unitarios* contributed to the formation of strong provincial identities. Even after national unification in the 1850s these factions continued to resist absorption into the single "national" identity proposed by the elites that controlled the federal state.[6]

Third, as a result of its condition as a backwater throughout most of its colonial history, the territory that later became Argentina was very sparsely populated. At the moment of independence it had the smallest population of any of the new Latin American states, approximately 400,000 inhabitants. Hence, from the 1820s onward a dominant theme in Argentine discourse came to be the issue of the "desert." The great empty solitudes that overwhelmed the small, precarious cities of the region were blamed by the elites for the former viceroyalty's economic backwardness and for the antisocial habits and propensity toward violence that they ascribed to the inhabitants of the countryside. The solution— proposed in the 1810s, refloated by Bernardino Rivadavia's government in the 1820s, and converted into a leitmotif of Argentine statesmanship by the intellectuals of the Generation of 1837 and their post-1852 political allies—was mass immigration from Europe. This, it was believed, would both galvanize the local economy by reducing the cost of labor and increasing the overall capacity of the nation to undertake economic enterprises of a varied sort and transform the native Creole culture through a process of accelerated "Europeanization."[7] The growing influx of immigrants from the 1840s onward, which after the 1870s became—to use José Luis Romero's graphic metaphor—a flood, added yet another element of cultural indeterminacy to Argentine identity: alongside the native *gauchesco* dialect, new vernaculars composed of syntheses of Neapolitan and Spanish, Basque and Spanish, or Genoese and Spanish seemed, at century's end, poised to become the new national language of Argentina.[8]

In the successive battles to define Argentine national identity waged by intellectuals and politicians, cultural and political elements often overlapped. A persistent theme in Argentine life from independence onward had been the emergence of a powerful republican discourse. Whether this was expressed in protoliberal terms, as in the Rivadavian regime's (1821–27) emphasis on the *representative* character of the Republic of Argentina, or in classical republican terms, as in the Rosista regime's (1829–52) emphasis on civic virtue, subordination to the established order, and political unanimity, the tendency was toward the establishment of a national identity that should be defined primarily in terms of political principles and objectives rather than in those of the cultural attributes of the country's inhabitants. From the perspective of the elites in the Rivadavian period, the elements that constituted a specifically Argentine identity were essentially political and ideological: first, the republican representative form of government through which—in the province of Buenos Aires, at least—the entire adult male population had been incorporated into the citizenry; second, the modernizing impulse made possible through independence from Spain and directed at the creation of financial, commercial, educational, and political institutions until then absent from the Spanish world; and third, the "new" character of the polity created after 1810. The Revolution was seen as a laboratory in which political and social patterns newer and better than those of Spain or even of other European countries were to be created.

The Rivadavian elite expressed national identity, therefore, in terms of political sovereignty rather than in those of cultural attributes. During the Rosista regime, at the same time as an emphasis on classical republican rhetorical topics was introduced into the political language of the period, with a concomitant emphasis on republican virtue and political unanimity, the "Americanist" strand in the regime's discourse presaged the future "cultural turn" adopted by the first romantic generation. The insistence on uniform styles of dress and ornament contributed—albeit in a highly authoritarian manner—to the creation of a consciousness of a shared republican identity: red bows were to be worn by all women at all times; a red jacket was to be worn in public by all men at all times; the official Rosista emblem, the *cintillo punzó*, with its slogan of "Death to the Savage, Disgusting Unitarians, Long Live the Holy Confederation!" was to be the obligatory badge for all men; and the fronts of all the houses in Buenos Aires were to be painted red.

The Rosista order was not only proclaimed to be the embodiment of republican enthusiasm, it was also represented as the expression of an intense American sentiment. An American identity was starkly contrasted with that of the Europeans. A rough equality, civic virtue, freedom from the weight of obscurantist tradition, love of independence—such were the positive attributes that the publicists of the regime ascribed to the *American* citizens of the Argentine Confederation. And on the basis of that identity, a stern and watchful patriotism was enjoined on the confederation's citizens: not only European aggression—as in the two blockades of Buenos Aires in the 1830s and 1840s—but also European ideas, values, and styles of dress were to be resisted.[9] As a result of the powerful imprint of republican discourse and ideologies left by the Rivadavian and Rosista regimes, discourse on the nature of the national identity would tend to oscillate in the second half of the nineteenth century (even as the institutions of the nation-state were being constructed) between an emphasis on cultural and political definitions. Even when it was the cultural attributes that were stressed, these were almost always encompassed within or subordinated to the language of republicanism.

The Nation Desired and the Generation of 1837

The first consistent discourse on the subject of Argentine nationhood, understood both in cultural and political terms, only coalesced as part of the agenda of the initial generation of romantic writers in the River Plate, the Generation of 1837.[10] This was the first intellectual movement in Argentina to assume as its primordial task a project of cultural transformation centered on the need to construct a national identity. "To study what is national," a task singled out and emphasized by Juan Bautista Alberdi in his lecture in the Salón Literario of 1837, became the leitmotif of this generation of intellectuals. Deeply imbued in the historicist doctrines that had circulated so intensely in the French intellectual universe after the July Revolution, Esteban Echeverría, Alberdi, and other members of the initial core of this movement proclaimed in their early writings of the 1830s the need for a *national* literature, a *national* philosophy, a *national* history, and, more generally, a *national* culture and intellect.[11] The task they assigned themselves as initiators of that "nationalization" of Argentine culture was logically dependent on their reading of the previous events of Argentine history. They argued, first, that the Argentine Revolution had achieved political independence but that the task of emancipating Argentine culture from its Spanish cage remained as yet unaccomplished. This was a sentiment that echoed through the writings of this generation: José Mármol, author of Argentina's first fully fledged novel and a poet of Byronic inspiration, claimed, "We must struggle against the Spaniard who lives in all of us."[12] In the words of Alberdi, "Our fathers gave us material independence: it is our task to conquer a form of civilization of our own, the conquest of our American genius."[13] Moreover, as Echeverría (and his unnamed coauthor, Alberdi) stated in 1838 in the *Dogma socialista*, the complete fulfillment of the promise held out to Argentines by independence would only become possible when the intense factional struggle dividing the country's two parties, the *unitarios* and the *federales*, was overcome. To achieve this end the authors of the dogma argued that a synthesis of both would be necessary, a synthesis that would improve on the originals through its combination of the best elements contained in the centralist and federalist positions within a single, superior political movement. This, of course, would be the political organization representing the intellectual and generational movement of which they were a part: the Asociación de la Joven Generación Argentina, loosely patterned on Giuseppe Mazzini's Giovane Italia and Giovane Europa movements.[14]

Hence, the mission of the New Generation was dual. First, it was to explore and appropriate those preexisting elements in River Plate culture that seemed most apposite to the task of elaborating a unique Argentine national identity, a task that would be carried out through the agency of the most recent and prestigious theoretical and methodological perspectives developed in European (non-Spanish) philosophical and social thought. Argentine cultural emancipation from Spain would thereby be achieved, or so they believed. The second part of their mission consisted in the development of an ideology and a politics of conciliation: in constitutional debate they would pursue synthesis rather than factional confrontation, and in their post–Rosas era politics they proposed to emphasize the need for consensus over the ties of party loyalty, although in this case they would find that this was easier said than done.

The nation was interpreted in two distinct ways by the authors enrolled in this movement. One was descriptive and the other—the dominant strand in their thinking—was prospective and, hence, normative. In the first mode the American identity of the Argentine people was stressed. All those characteristics that as a result of the American landscape and social environment had come to form part of a peculiarly "Argentine" way of life were to be sought after and studied as so many marks of national identity. Sarmiento, despite his negative appraisal of the political and social impact of the gauchos on Argentina's postrevolutionary development, was among the first to take seriously this line of enquiry, asking himself in the pages of *Facundo* and other works what it was that made Argentines who they are.[15] The answer, the ultimate theoretical roots of which lay in Montesquieu's theory of the determinism of climate and in Tocqueville's model interpretation of U.S. mores and institutions, was to be found in the geography of the River Plate provinces and in the specific human types to which that geography had given rise: the "civilized" city dwellers, on the one hand, and the "barbarous" rural inhabitants, the gauchos with their idiosyncratic culture, on the other.

Seeking to explain why the May Revolution had gone astray, producing the despotism of Rosas instead of the rule of liberty its participants had envisaged, Sarmiento argued that the opposition between the cities and the countryside had been decisive. The Revolution had gone through two phases: the revolt of the Europeanized cities against Spain and the revolt of the "barbarous" countryside against the cities. The rural world had conquered the cities and imposed its own cultural patterns on them. Hence, any understanding of Argentine national identity required a careful exploration of the cultural universe of the countryside and its inhabitants. Two factors were stressed in *Facundo*: the ubiquity of violence—a product of the cattle frontier—and the weakness of social ties—a result of the "desert." Hence, geography and history had combined to produce a national culture unsuited for modern liberal institutions, which would have to be radically transformed for the ideals of the May Revolution to become a reality.

Sarmiento endorsed two solutions: first, the creation of a system of free public education, modeled in part on that of Massachusetts, which he had studied as part of his research mission financed by the Chilean government (1845–47). Schools were "factories of citizens" and hence had to be made available to the entire population of Argentina. Sarmiento, during his post-1852 political career as head of the school board of the province of Buenos Aires (1855–58), as governor of his home province of San Juan (1862–63), as president of the republic (1868–74), and finally as president of the National Council of Education, the governing body of the entire newly created federal public school system, in the 1880s would collaborate directly in the transformation of that ideal into a reality. Second (and in this respect he was merely endorsing a measure already proposed by Alberdi and by the followers of Bernardino Rivadavia before him, in the 1820s), he agreed that mass emigration from Europe (needed to people the pampas and to gradually replace cattle ranching with agriculture) should be promoted by the Argentine state. Such policies were not explicitly directed against the gauchos and their lifestyle, and, in fact, Sarmiento's own attitude toward them in his writings was ambivalent (as were those of most elite intellectuals of the period). Nevertheless, until the early twentieth century, when authors such as Leopoldo Lugones sought to rescue the gaucho as a national cultural archetype, most members of the educated elite saw gaucho culture and society as part of the problem rather than the solution to the issue of national identity.[16]

The other mode of interpretation became the more important of the two from the perspective of defining the new nation in the nineteenth century precisely because of this wholesale rejection of possible origins and models. As was the case in other parts of the fallen Iberian empires, the cultural heritage of Spain was spurned by the intellectuals of the Generation of 1837 as constituting precisely that against which the revolutionary wars had been waged. Just as in contemporary Mexico, where hatred of the *gachupín* (peninsular Spaniard) was still very much alive years after independence, at least among the nonconservative segments of Mexican public opinion, in Argentina the Spanish legacy had been subjected to virulent criticism from the revolutionary decade onward. A central feature of the ideology and rhetoric of the Revolution had been the theme of caesura and new beginnings, a theme that underscored the identification of Spain with all that was "arbitrary" and corrupt in the system of the ancien régime. The fact that until 1834, moreover, the absolutist regime of Fernando VII continued to exercise power in Spain (despite the brief Liberal Triennium) simply served to reinforce that rejection, which would only begin to be revised in the last decades of the nineteenth century.

The Argentine romantics emphasized culture, however, rather than politics and institutions in their own critique of the Spanish heritage. That critique revolved around three fundamental values: liberty, modernity, and national authenticity. In the first instance, Spanish tradition was rejected because it was perceived as originating in a society accustomed to despotism and obscurantism. Even the Spanish language, according to Alberdi, should be dramatically transformed in the River Plate because its idioms and syntax were those of a language of despotism rather than of freedom (the paradigm of freedom, of course, was French).[17] The second reason for rejecting the Spanish heritage was the belief that the Revolution, by effecting a radical break with the ancien régime of the colonial era, had deliberately cast the River Plate headlong into a process of rapid modernization, the most salient (although not the only significant) feature of which was the adoption of a republican form of government. If Spain represented the rejection of science in favor of religion, undue commercial restrictions, absolute government, and social mores such as those relating to the role of women, all of which were now condemned as ineluctably archaic, then it would be necessary to uproot the remaining cultural elements received from Spain in order to place the national culture of the River Plate on new and very different foundations, whatever those might ultimately be. And finally, the third reason adduced for replacing or transforming the Spanish component in Argentine culture was that the new society was fundamentally American rather than European. What was Spanish was radically foreign. The new national culture had to take as its point of departure that which was authentically its own: its American origin.

Americanismo, in two distinct but connected modes, runs through Argentine discourse on the nation from the wars of independence to the beginning of the twentieth century, when a changed world panorama and the emergence of new ideological forces allowed a rival *hispanismo* to crystallize in the Argentine intellectual debate.[18] In the republican discourse of Rosas, as mentioned above, *americanismo* had become a central component during the 1840s. A longer-lasting and ultimately more complex version of *americanismo* was that which had emerged during the Revolution and which would become a central component in the arguments developed by Argentine romantic authors such as Alberdi, Juan María Gutiérrez, and Sarmiento against the Spanish cultural legacy. América and Spain were contrasted in this discourse in terms of the colonialist experience. Spanish colonialism had, according to this current of reasoning, distorted the authentically American elements in the cultural past of the new nations and had thereby prevented an authentically new, Creole culture from developing. What was Spanish was portrayed as antithetical to what was American in the culture of the Creoles. The subject of this nationalist and Americanist discourse was almost always, it should be emphasized, the Creole of European descent rather than the indigenous peoples of America or the equally "Creolized" descendants of Africans.

If Spain was rejected as a source and model for the new Argentine national identity, other possible sources and models were also rejected. As part of the repudiation of Spain, Argentina's cultural elites, unlike those of Peru, Colombia, and Central America, also dismissed the colonial past as something radically alien. Precisely because its authenticity had been subverted, the Creole experience during the three centuries of colonial rule was also included within that cultural conglomerate against which the romantic intellectuals of the New Generation claimed the Revolution to have been waged. Moreover, despite occasional attempts at recovery such as those of Juan María Gutiérrez, the pre-Columbian and indigenous heritage was also rejected out of hand, as were all the cultural attributes of the Quechua or Guaraní-speaking inhabitants of Argentina. The result was that the new Argentine nation came to be portrayed by a significant number of the writers of the nineteenth century as a nation without a past, rootless, even not yet fully formed. Perhaps the most powerful trope in elite discourse on the Argentine nation came to be that Argentina was a nation whose origin lay in the future rather than in the past.

This image of the Argentine nation came to be rendered more powerfully in the second half of the nineteenth century after the fall of Rosas and the completion of "national organization" created a new political, social, and cultural framework within which the projected construction of a nation seemed to be finally taking place. In a context of mass immigration, rapid urbanization, and the rapid growth of the national metropolis, Buenos Aires, the terms of the debate on the national identity took on a more concrete and decisive form.

Nowhere was this so evident as in the discussion on the fate of the Spanish language, which for better or worse continued to be the customary vehicle used by the inhabitants of Argentina to communicate with one another. At a time when the expansion of the reading public and of a commercially viable periodical press and printing industry had expanded the social range of impact of such debates and in the context of an increasingly complex print culture (marked by the emergence of a more plural readership, with a strong presence of elite women as well as Afro-Argentines, urban workers, immigrants belonging to non-Spanish linguistic communities, and rural gauchos and peons), the question of the national language took on a new urgency.

In the period between the 1860s and 1880s a series of events set the stage for the emergence of a debate on the status of the "Argentine" language that would continue to be sporadically reactivated until the middle of the twentieth century. The first event was the definitive consolidation of a strong literary current using the dialect of the Creole country dwellers, the gauchos, the crowning achievement of which was José Hernández's poem *El gaucho Martín Fierro* (1872). The existence of a growing corpus of *gauchesco* literature seemed to augur one alternative path toward the elaboration of a uniquely Argentine language, but the prejudice of Buenos Aires's cultural elites delayed the emergence of such a position until late in the nineteenth century, even while more and more immigrants became avid consumers of the prolific pulp fiction detailing in verse and prose the exploits of gaucho heroes and villains.[19] The other event that constituted the direct background to the debate that will be examined in greater detail below was the impact of mass immigration on the speech habits of the urban inhabitants of Argentina and especially on those of Buenos Aires.

Juan María Gutiérrez: The Politics of Language and the Real Academia de la Lengua Española

In 1873, as part of a new and more aggressive cultural policy directed toward its former colonies, the Real Academia de la Lengua Española, the institution charged with preparing the only officially sanctioned dictionary and grammars of the Spanish language in Spain and, more generally, with supervising the development and "purity" of that language, offered Juan María Gutiérrez, by then the most prestigious Argentine literary critic, membership in that corporation. The reason behind this decision had to do with Gutiérrez's prestigious career as a literary scholar and academic. A founding member of the Salón Literario of 1837 and leader of the New Generation, he had, over the next three decades, produced a sizeable body of literary studies centering chiefly on colonial and independence-era writers such as Sor Juana Inés de la Cruz, José Peralta Barnuevo, Pedro de Oña (whose work he discovered), the Cuban poet "Plácido,"

Juan Cruz Varela, and many others. He had also focused on certain aspects of pre-Columbian literature, as evinced in his studies on Netzahualcóyotl, the Quechua Ollantay, and contemporary oral Quechua-language poetry in Santiago del Estero. Moreover, he had compiled the first continent-wide anthology of Spanish American poetry, *América poética*; published the first history of higher education in the River Plate; participated in the Santa Fe Constitutional Convention of 1853, which framed Argentina's first successful, liberal, national constitution; served as foreign minister of the Argentine Confederation in the Urquiza presidency (1854–60); and presided over the University of Buenos Aires, where he was rector from 1861 to 1874. (In his capacity as rector he reestablished the Science Faculty, dismantled by Rosas in 1829, and promoted the formation of Argentina's first native crop of engineers.) Among contemporary Argentine intellectuals he was clearly the most obvious choice. However, Gutiérrez decided to publicly reject the appointment in 1876. In his letter of rejection he developed a series of arguments that tended to underline his long-standing critical stance toward the cultural tradition of Spain.

In that text Gutiérrez emphasized what seemed to him the irreconcilable contrast between two diametrically opposed national characters. Whereas the linguistic purism of the Spanish academicians directly expressed a conservative and xenophobic national tradition, the cosmopolitan and antipurist linguistic policy upheld by Gutiérrez expressed, in equally direct fashion, the modernizing and demographically mobile experience of the emerging Argentine nation. Moreover, if the national traditions were diametrically opposed, so too were the ideological underpinnings of each. According to Gutiérrez, the desire to establish fixed norms for Spanish linguistic usage stemmed from a reactionary, ultraconservative political culture, whereas the defense of a rule-free linguistic evolution expressed the radical liberalism that constituted the matrix of Argentine political identity.

In Argentina, according to Gutiérrez, the prevailing attitude toward linguistic usage was cosmopolitan and anarchic. Unlike Spain, hemmed in within its narrow borders by a rancid nationalism the central element of which was its opposition to all that was modern, "the cosmopolitan, universal spirit . . . has no exceptions among us." Argentina was a republic that welcomed people and ideas from all parts of Europe.

> From the beginning of this century, the form of government that we have given ourselves has thrown the doors of the country wide open to influences from all of Europe, and since then the foreign languages, ideas, and customs that they represent and bring with them have become naturalized citizens living among us. . . . The result of this commerce may be easily imagined. It has mixed the languages, so to speak, as it has the races. The blue eyes, white and rosy cheeks, and blonde hair typical of the heads

of the north of Europe may be observed mingling with the dark eyes, ebony hair, and black hue of the descendants of the meridional part of Spain. These differences in physical constitution, rather than altering the unity of patriotic sentiment, seem, through the operation of the generous laws of nature that are obeyed on the banks of the River Plate, to draw tighter and tighter the bonds of human fraternity, producing as a result a race privileged by its blood and its intelligence.[20]

The Argentine nation, precisely because of its cosmopolitan nature, was in the process of being transformed into something very different from its Spanish roots through the mixing of cultures, races, and languages. The vision of the "melting pot" operated as powerfully in the descriptions of Argentine nationality produced by Gutiérrez and his contemporaries as it did in North American writers of roughly the same epoch.

In regard to the issue of the language spoken in Argentina, Gutiérrez would argue that, at least in Buenos Aires, the effect of the "babel of tongues" was to make *porteños* and Argentines incapable even of *recognizing* linguistic purity. The emerging Argentine language was radically impure, and this was, according to Gutiérrez, its most positive aspect and the promise of its vigorous future. At the popular level, the mixing of languages and dialects was in the process of creating a new form of colloquial Spanish:

> In the streets of Buenos Aires the accents of all the Italian dialects may be heard, beside the Catalan, which was the language of the troubadours, the Galician, in which the wise king composed his "cantigas," the French of the north and of the Midi, the Welsh, the English of all the counties, and so on. These different sounds and modes of expression cosmopolitanize our hearing and render us incapable of even attempting to immobilize the national tongue in which our numerous periodicals are written, in which our laws are dictated and discussed, and that is the vehicle in which we *porteños* communicate with one another.[21]

That this was the concrete situation in Argentina was a direct result of the fundamentally liberal nature of modern Argentine republicanism. The thought of applying rules and grammatical constraints on an evolving language was unthinkable in a country where the people were sovereign; only in a monarchy of the Old World could such an endeavor seem reasonable.

A final strand of argument in Gutiérrez's letter of rejection was that Argentina's elite was better equipped for life in the modern world than that of Spain. Rather than feeling nostalgia for the linguistic usages of a fossilized past, Argentina's educated classes saw in language a purely utilitarian value:

> The men who among us pursue liberal careers, whether these pertain to politics or applied sciences, cannot, because of their manner of being, scale the centuries in search of models and purist [*castizo*] phrases in the ascetic writers and theological

publicists of a monarchy without counterweights. Practical men and, above all, of their own time, they read only books that teach them what they currently need to know and that the pages of tender Santa Teresa and her amorous companion, San Juan de la Cruz, do not teach them, nor do they read any book by those authors who form the infallible council in matters of linguistic purism [*lenguaje castizo*].[22]

It is probably no surprise that such an emphasis on the utilitarian and practical nature of modern Argentine culture, redolent of Alberdian sensibility, should appear in the writings of the intellectual who was, after all, the coauthor with Alberdi of Argentina's liberal national constitution of 1853.

Construction of a specifically Argentine identity through reference to a presumably antithetical Spanish identity was not a new endeavor in Gutiérrez's literary career. Most of his previous work as a literary historian had been concerned with the attempt to construct a specifically national literary tradition through a meticulous examination of the literary monuments of the colonial era and through the application of a method that sought to separate the specifically American elements (judged as authentic and literarily worthy) from the Spanish (judged as spurious and lacking in literary quality). Gutiérrez's vision of the colonial past was in this sense slightly different from that of most of his Argentine contemporaries, who rejected it in its totality. Gutiérrez believed that the Revolution had unveiled the deep historical roots of Spanish American literature; it had rendered visible what until then had been hidden through the operation of Spanish colonialism. Independence had handed over not only their government to the Spanish Americans but also their own history, colonized by Spaniards for over three centuries. Following a method that consisted of separating the authentically American content from the inauthentic Spanish incrustations present in each work, Gutiérrez undertook, from the 1840s onward, as mentioned above, a series of historicocritical studies of writers of the colonial past such as (in addition to those already mentioned) Juan Caviedes, Juan Baltazar Maziel, and Alonso de Ercilla. In all of these studies the crux of his critical effort lay in his attempt to distinguish the "positive American" from the "negative Spanish," to use the terms coined by Beatriz Sarlo.[23]

In the polemic provoked by the publication of Gutiérrez's letter to the Real Academia his arguments tended to synthesize and expand on that Americanist literary ideology. The position of Gutiérrez, whose pseudonym was *un porteño*, throws considerable light on the relationship joining the debate on the language to a more general conception of national identity. He sought to justify his antiacademicist posture on the basis of new theories concerning the origin and development of languages. In his second letter he invoked the authority of two of the most widely read romantic era linguists, Max Müller and Franz Bopp. Declaring his acceptance of their cartography of linguistic families, Gutiérrez indicated that the Spanish language belonged to the "Indo-Germanic" family. But, more important, he would emphasize what to many seemed the principal contribution of that early linguistic science: the recognition of the radical historicity of human languages and the direct relation of their historical transformations to the specific and unique historical experience of peoples (or races, as social Darwinists would have put it). Following this interpretation, it was not only the language of the *porteños*, of Argentines, that had resulted from changes and divergences from a common original trunk but also that of Spain. The language spoken in Spain could not have emerged had it not been for innumerable transformations experienced during its long history: "The language that we now speak, both Spaniards and their descendants, studied by Alderete, Covarrubias, and Mariana, turns out to be a mosaic to which the different races and nations that lived in the peninsula contributed their part, its words thus having Phoenician, Celtic, Gothic, Arabic, and so on, roots." Completing this observation with the emphatic statement that "no nation has created the language it speaks out of thin air, and the Spanish nation even less than any other," the *porteño* critic would go on to invoke the counterexample of the Latin language, whose purity, whose freedom from "corruption," was due exclusively to the fact that it was dead. Living languages, on the other hand, could not help but obey the general law of history, which establishes the necessity for progress, that is, for permanent modification. They had to submit to "the succession of the years, those irresistible revolutionaries."

This was the element of those linguistic theories that proved crucial to the second, explicitly nationalist, part of Gutiérrez's argument: if all languages evolved over time, if that change came from a racial and national cross-mixture (which Gutiérrez judged as entirely positive), then the peculiar form that a language assumed at any given historical moment would have to embody the national characteristics of the people who spoke it. Hence, if Argentina had already become a nation distinct from that of the Spaniards, its language would have to reflect that difference to an equal degree. This was the core of the nationalist argument developed in the letters published by Gutiérrez and later gathered into book form under the title *Cartas de un porteño*.[24] Two elements were stressed by Gutiérrez as specifically national: the free nature of the Argentine people and the cultural impact of immigration, which had made of the Argentines a cosmopolitan people par excellence.

The first national attribute identified by Gutiérrez was certainly not novel in the context of the historical discourse of the Generation of 1837. A leitmotif running through their writings and their private correspondence had been that Argentines were, as a people, less plagued by social inequality than were their neighbors or their European models, and they were more fierce in their defense of personal freedom (even when, as in the gaucho archetypes described by Sarmiento in *Facundo*, they were simply defending the right to reject all social restraints). When they came to write their respective histories of Argentina, both Bartolomé Mitre and Vicente Fidel López (the two most important nineteenth-century historians of Argentina) stressed freedom as a peculiar trait of the inhabitants of the River Plate. The former had argued that the rough conditions in Buenos Aires colonial society and the peculiar, antiaristocratic, and vaguely "democratic" sociability it had engendered had made personal liberty the value it most highly esteemed.[25] The latter had argued that a rough equality of property had prevented the emergence of a native Creole aristocracy such as those of neighboring Chile and Brazil.[26] Moreover, in the press of the post-Rosas era a national historical narrative had gradually emerged that portrayed the "Dictatorship" of 1835–52 as an anomaly, an unnatural moment in a history the central theme of which was the gradual perfection of liberal institutions. Hence, when Gutiérrez invoked this theme he was simply giving voice to one of the most widespread images of Argentine national identity, an image that fused, in a complex but resistant amalgam, the civic republican ideals of the second half of the nineteenth century with the cultural attributes that romantic historicists considered central to the definition of the unique specificity of individual nations. For the members of the Generation of 1837 and for most of their literate contemporaries in the River Plate, the nationalism that offered itself as a legitimate vehicle for defining Argentine identity was, above all else, a *civic nationalism*. This is why the apparent paradox contained in a *cosmopolitan* definition of *national* identity remained invisible to the politicians, writers, and educators of the period. In Americanist fashion Gutiérrez stressed the undeniable fact that Argentina had emerged as a nation with characteristics radically distinct from those of Spain: "Between the Americas and Spain there lies an ocean, but between the customs of one part and the other of the world there lies much more than an ocean."[27]

However, in the case of Argentina, that difference resided in the cosmopolitan character of the Argentine people. Gutiérrez declared that the essential difference separating Argentina from Spain and any other European country was that it was a country of immigrants; hence, its national identity had been constructed precisely through an amalgam of the cultural traits of the nations of the world. He described the Argentine situation thus:

> We, who are the citizens of a country of *immigration*, are affected by those customs and interests. In Paris everything is French; in Madrid everything is Spanish. To Buenos Aires *everything* has come, is coming, and, thank God, will continue to come from France, from Spain . . . , from all the civilized nations, and in that everything are encompassed, implicitly, the habits and modes of expression of the foreigners who settle and form a family in the Republic of Argentina. Our constitution does not

permit us to wall ourselves into our own [original] nationality, into those things that have nothing to do with real patriotism. She has made us a republic for ourselves, for our posterity and for all the inhabitants of the world who wish to inhabit Argentine soil.

If his earlier "literary Americanism" had prepared the path whereby Gutiérrez would come to espouse a form of linguistic nationalism in opposition to the purism and academicism of Spain and the Spaniards, this was a nationalism cast in the mold of Alberdian ideology, with its vision of a cosmopolitan destiny for a nation whose cultural inheritance—flawed as a result of Spanish colonialism— could not be harnessed into the service of any project of national foundation. Having repudiated the cultural heritage of the past, whether pre-Columbian, colonial, or Creole, the only national identity that could then be envisaged was that of the new culture and people expected to emerge out of the Argentine melting pot. In his arguments on the nature of the *porteño* or Argentine language that was in the process of being formed and on the relationship between that language and the specific national identity of Argentines, Gutiérrez elaborated a new strand of argument that would serve to enrich the cosmopolitan vision enunciated by other intellectuals of his generation, most notably, Alberdi, with his vision of the *pueblo-mundo*, the "world-nation."[28]

The Dilemma of Argentine Nationalism in the Nineteenth Century

Discourse on the subject of national identity is rarely, if ever, homogeneous, even in the smallest of nations. If the perpetuation of a national community over time is, as Ernest Renan so eloquently suggested, the product of a daily plebiscite, this is so in part because one of the constituent elements of national identity is, in fact, disagreement over the nature of that identity. As long as members of a national community continue to feel it more worth their while to seek to convince their fellow citizens of the inherent truth of their own interpretation of that identity than to attempt secession or authoritarian closure of the arena of debate, the plebiscitary mode, in Renan's sense, will continue to be active. In Argentina, after the construction of the rudimentary elements of a national state put an end to the era of civil war, discussion of the political nature of the new nation's identity came to be framed exclusively within the terms of that dissenting consensus that the plebiscitary mode implied. As regards the confrontation between opposing political understandings of the national project, it is true that the rivalry between provinces—and, above all, between the provinces of the interior and Buenos Aires—continued to exist, but it was now subordinated to a general acceptance of the legitimacy of the federal union. Despite the occasional uprising of isolated provinces with specific grievances, the politics of conciliation embodied in Juan Bautista Alberdi's 1853 constitution stood the test of time.[29] The political unity of the Argentine nation was no longer an object of debate.[30]

The cultural definition of the new national identity, however, continued to provoke intense and heated discussion, especially as the emerging profile of the new social order born of mass immigration—to which José Luis Romero applied the suggestively apt denomination the *sociedad aluvial*, the "floodwater society"—came to be seen as having established a new caesura, one that separated the future Argentina from the *criollo* society whose elites and masses had dominated the republic during four score years after independence.[31] The arguments in favor of a cosmopolitan definition of Argentine national identity, with its joint stress on the originality of American society vis-à-vis a traditionalist and ethnocentric Europe, and the positive value of a melting pot that would, in time, produce a culture and even a language, radically different from that of the *madre patria*, came to be increasingly contested both at the elite and the popular levels, albeit for different reasons in each case.

From the perspective of the governing Creole elite, whose patrician ethos was suffused with the civic values of the early years of the republic as well as with those of a self-conscious caste, the growing demographic tide of newcomers provoked first unease and then outright rejection. In the years after 1880, when immigration peaked, racist attitudes led many elite Argentines to deplore the national origin of many of the newcomers, considered as "inferior" as that of the South American polities themselves. The fact that Italian, Spanish, and eastern European peasants flocked to the shores of the River Plate in far greater numbers than skilled artisans, professionals, and even trained manual laborers from northern Europe contributed to a growing sense that the unintended consequence of Alberdian demographic engineering had been to re-create on Argentine soil the *classes dangereuses*, bearers of vice, unsound political and social ideas, and bafflingly exotic habits. A discourse began to crystallize, therefore, at almost the same time as Gutiérrez's polemic on the language and culture of Buenos Aires that stressed the importance of cultural homogenization, a process that was to be achieved through the expanding public school system and through the creation of an elaborate civic ritual that should operate as a vehicle for incorporating immigrants or their children into the established traditions of the republic.[32] This discourse, which stressed state action to foster national unity, was in its origin of liberal inspiration and was not necessarily incompatible with a certain—albeit considerably muted—respect for pluralism, especially if this was political rather than cultural.

In political-ideological terms this discourse, which would be implemented into policy gradually over the next few decades and most systematically during the period when the positivist historian and medical doctor, José María Ramos Mejía, presided over the Consejo Nacional de Educación, was compatible with positions such as those of Gutiérrez, at least in a very general sense, but its emphasis and its general structure of sentiment were entirely different. The spontaneity of unmediated cultural exchange should now be replaced, according to the defenders of this position, by state-directed channeling of such exchanges within a framework based explicitly on the superior hierarchy of the "native Argentine" republican tradition (and implicitly on that of the "native Argentine" cultural tradition).[33] A second alternative discourse would only emerge much later, although the elements it incorporated were already present in an unsystematic form in much of the literature and journalism of the last two decades of the nineteenth century: this was the Creole cultural nationalism that in its later manifestations would adopt an explicitly xenophobic stance, whether through a social Darwinist or *hispanista* (and "spiritualist") prism. In the writing of authors such as Eugenio Cambaceres, the most important naturalist novelist of Argentina whose works appeared in the 1870s and 1880s, and the pseudonymous "Julián Martel," author of *La bolsa* (1890), racist stereotypes were already in evidence, albeit in an unsystematic fashion.[34] And finally, although once again the full development of this counterdiscourse would only take place during the twentieth century, and especially after the beginning of Argentina's economic and political crisis in 1929–30, intellectuals from provincial elites defended an alternative view of the fundamental nature of Argentine national identity, stressing the Catholic and (in the case of many publicists from Tucumán, Salta, and Córdoba) Spanish heritage of Argentina.[35]

Embattled provincial elites in the interior, who saw in the simultaneous processes of economic modernization centered on Buenos Aires and the littoral, cultural change through the agency of immigration from Europe, and political subordination to the federal authorities in Buenos Aires so many forces eroding their traditional authority and social prestige, tended to challenge the cosmopolitan nationalist project through a defense of local traditions, established patterns of social deference, and the cultural centrality of Roman Catholicism. It should be noted, however, that in this case too what was being objected to was *cosmopolitan* nationalism, not civic nationalism per se (at least before the emergence of the essentialist nationalist discourse of the Nationalist movement of the 1930s): in the discourse of writers from the interior provinces, republican values were often represented as complementary rather than antithetical to the elements of their anticosmopolitan argument.

Equally significant in defining the field of discursive contestation and debate during the late nineteenth century is the fact that the social perspective of members of the cosmopolitan elite, even that of humane and nonracist writers such as Gutiérrez, could not help but have a restricted field of vision. In their case what most tended to fall by the wayside of the cosmopolitan ideal was the culture and lifestyle of the inhabitants of the countryside: the gauchos. In fact, as the ideological project of the Generation of 1837 had developed, what had become a constant leitmotif was the emphasis placed on the elites' "civilizing mission." Sarmiento's rhetorically charged trope of "civilization versus barbarism" permeated, at least implicitly, all the discursive formulations of the members of this generation and their political allies, even those that were, on the surface, least directly related to it. It was the transhumant populations of the pampas and, more generally, all the culturally marginal sectors (from an elite perspective) of Argentina's inhabitants—Afro-Argentines, indigenous peoples both within the area of Creole settlement and beyond its border, and the uneducated poor in general—who constituted the "barbarians" in need of civilizing.

In Gutiérrez's arguments on the fluid and transformative nature of the Argentine language it is significant that among the various sources of linguistic interaction that he mentions as exercising a positive, emancipatory role, the idiom of the Creole rural population is not included. In fact, Gutiérrez, who was the principal arbiter of Argentine literary taste from the 1850s until his death in 1878, disliked the *gauchesco* tradition of poetry. He considered it a subgenre of very dubious literary merit, and when called upon to comment on José Hernández's *Martín Fierro*—destined to become during the course of the twentieth century one of the symbols par excellence of Argentine national identity and a centerpiece of the Argentine literary canon—declared that it was not really literature at all. For him, if this anachronism may be permitted, it simply constituted, as did also Eduardo Gutiérrez's cycle of "villainous gaucho" novels initiated with *Juan Moreira*, a form of "pulp fiction."

Only very gradually, and partly through the agency of foreign literary critics and observers of Argentina, did the *gauchesco* tradition come to be identified as a significant marker of Argentine national identity. The *criollista* debate, which would eventually fuse with the second major polemic on the Argentine national language, was launched by the Spanish literary historian and polymath Marcelino Menéndez Pelayo.[36] His positive reception of *Martín Fierro* as a major work (a view seconded by Miguel de Unamuno only a few years later) would force Argentine intellectuals to reconsider that text and to reevaluate the *gauchesco* tradition in its entirety. Eventually, cultural *criollismo* would blend with the cosmopolitan ideal, as immigrants themselves came to identify with the heroes and villains of the burgeoning *gauchesco* literary tradition. As Adolfo Prieto has demonstrated so conclusively, the popular reading public for stories in prose or verse about gaucho outlaws and victims comprised, in the period from 1880 to 1910, a sizeable portion of the recent immigrants, whose reception of those literary types and the cultural lore surrounding them often produced syntheses between, for instance, Italian and gaucho popular traditions, as evinced in pantomimes and costumes during Carnival.

Cosmopolitan nationalism represented, therefore, but one among many discourses on the cultural identity of the Argentine nation. Closely tied to a liberal worldview, the image it projected of that nation was of one in the process of being forged: the cultural attributes of the new nation could not yet be precisely defined because its definitive formation—the expected result of a progressive interpretation of history—lay still in the future. Unlike the cosmopolitans and nationalists studied by Lilia Ana Bertoni, whose linguistic debates at the close of the nineteenth century tended to be framed in an either/or modality, Gutiérrez and the discursive tradition to which he gave rise, which would be continued in a slightly modified form by twentieth-century writers such as Jorge Luis Borges and Pedro Henríquez Ureña, posited the possibility of a nationalism the essence of which was the defense of a cosmopolitan destiny. As in other discursive formations developed in Latin America as part of the debates on national identity during the nineteenth and twentieth centuries such as Gilberto Freyre's "racial democracy" and José Vasconcelos's "cosmic race," the image of the melting pot was central to Argentine cosmopolitan nationalism.

The new cultural identity that would one day define Argentina as a distinctive nation could only be the product of a mixing of peoples and tongues. Potentially liberal and pluralist, the ultimate consequences of this discourse, which, as stressed above, was by no means the only nationalist trope in circulation during the last decades of the nineteenth century, were, however, determined by the character of Argentine republican values and the concept of citizenship to which it gave rise. Rather than contributing to a maintenance of the original ethnic and linguistic identities of the different peoples who inhabited Argentina, the force of state intervention, through the public school system and, after 1901, through the agency of universal male conscription into the armed forces, was toward cultural standardization.[37] This was so because the melting pot project can be developed in two different ways: as a spontaneous mixing of peoples and cultures—the position preferred by Alberdi and Gutiérrez—or as a state-guided fusion within the mold of an original "native" culture. In Argentina this second path was followed. Unlike Fernando Ortiz's recipe for Cuban cultural identity, expressed through the image of the *ajiaco*, a stew in which each of the component elements, rather than being dissolved in the course of cooking, maintains its original texture and identity, what prevailed in Argentina was a process of cultural uniformization the most salient expression of which was the virtual disappearance of ethnic neighborhoods in the major cities by the middle of the twentieth century.[38]

1. Domingo Faustino Sarmiento, *Conflicto y armonías de las razas en América*, vol. 1 (Buenos Aires, 1883), 1.

2. Useful recent studies are José Carlos Chiaramonte, *Ciudades, provincias, estados: Orígenes de la nacionalidad argentina* (Buenos Aires, 1998); Pilar González Bernaldo, *Civilidad y política* (Buenos Aires, 2002); Tulio Halperín Donghi, *Proyecto y construcción de una nación: Argentina 1846–1880* (1980; Buenos Aires, 1994). Classic arguments against *porteño* hegemony from the perspective of Santa Fe Province are Juan Álvarez's *Historia de Santa Fe* (1909), *Buenos Aires* (1910), and *Las guerras civiles argentinas* (1914).

3. During the Independence Wars the insurgents in Mexico had called the Spaniards *gachupines*; similarly, in South America and especially in the River Plate they were called *godos* (Goths).

4. On this issue the classic study is Angel Rosenblat, *Argentina: Historia de un nombre* (Buenos Aires, 1949).

5. Julio Schvartzman, *La batalla de los lenguajes (1830–1880)* (Buenos Aires, 2003); Angel Rama, *Los gauchi-políticos rioplatenses: Literatura y sociedad* (Buenos Aires, 1976).

6. The *federales* were defenders of a federal constitution whose political party was progressively taken over by Juan Manuel de Rosas after 1828 and made the instrument for his dictatorial rule (1829–32/1835–52) in all the provinces (and chiefly in the interests of Buenos Aires). On the political ideology and discourse of Rosas's regime see Jorge Myers, *Orden y virtud: El discurso republicano del régimen rosista* (Buenos Aires, 1995). On federalism itself in Argentina see the relevant chapters in Marcello Carmagnani, ed., *Federalismos latinoamericanos: México/Brasil/Argentina* (Mexico City, 1993). The *unitarios* were defenders of a centralist constitution whose ideological position, although they were just as inclined as Rosas and the *federales* to rule in an authoritarian manner, stemmed from the later Enlightenment and early forms of liberalism or protoliberalism. Although very little recent work has been done on the Unitarian Party per se, good intellectual and political biographies of some of its leaders may be found in Nancy Calvo, Roberto Di Stéfano, and Klaus Gallo, *Los curas de la revolución* (Buenos Aires, 2001). On the lingering power of provincial resistance to the center in Buenos Aires see Ariel de la Fuente, *The Children of Facundo* (Stanford, Calif., 1996); Jorge Lafforgue and Tulio Halperín Donghi, *Historias de caudillos argentinos* (Buenos Aires, 1999); Hilda Sábato and Alberto Lettieri, *Votos, voces y balas: Nuevas miradas sobre la historia política argentina, siglo XIX* (Buenos Aires, 2003). On state action in the later nineteenth century see Lilia Ana Bertoni's important recent book, *Patriotas, cosmopolitas y nacionalistas* (Buenos Aires, 2001).

7. And, in the case of some of its defenders, such as Sarmiento in his later works, Alberdi, and especially turn-of-the-century positivist essayists such as Carlos Octavio Bunge, European immigration was also meant to have a "eugenic" effect by gradually replacing African and indigenous racial attributes—deemed inferior in accordance with contemporary racist attitudes—with European ones. Recent studies on European immigration are Fernando Devoto, *Historia de la inmigración en la Argentina* (Buenos Aires, 2001); José Moya, *Spanish Immigration to Argentina 1850–1900* (Stanford, Calif., 1998).

8. On this topic see Adolfo Prieto, *El discurso criollista en la formación de la Argentina*

moderna (Buenos Aires, 1988); Ernesto Quesada et al., *En torno al criollismo: Textos y polémica* (Buenos Aires, 1983). On the "national language" issue see Mercedes I. Blanco de Margo, *Lenguaje e identidad: Actitudes lingüísticas en la Argentina 1800–1960* (Bahia Blanca, 1991).

9. On the construction of the Rosas régime see Myers, *Orden y virtud.* On the political system at the time see Marcela Ternavasio, *La revolución del voto* (Buenos Aires, 2001).

10. The central figures in this movement dominated the Argentine cultural scene from their return from exile in 1852 until the 1880s: Esteban Echeverría (1805–51), Juan Bautista Alberdi (1810–84), Juan María Gutiérrez (1809–78), Domingo Faustino Sarmiento (1811–88), Vicente Fidel López (1815–1904), Bartolomé Mitre (1821–1906), José Mármol (1807–82), Félix Frías (1816–81). To these should be added a significant number of writers from neighboring countries active in Argentine intellectual circles during the years of exile and after. The most comprehensive studies of this intellectual movement continue to be Donghi, *Proyecto y construcción de una nación*; and Natalio Botana, *La tradición republicana* (Buenos Aires, 1984).

11. "La poesía es la obra de la nación y no del poeta que la expresa; si es una faz, una expresión de la nación, el solo medio de agrandar esta expresión, es decir la poesía nacional, es agrandar la nación" (Juan Bautista Alberdi, "Del arte socialista," *El Iniciador* [1838–39], facsimile ed. [Buenos Aires, 1942], 181). [Poetry is the work of the nation and not of the poet who expresses it; if it is an aspect, an expression of the nation, then the only way to enlarge this expression, that is to say, national poetry, is to enlarge the nation.]

12. José Mármol, *Cantos del peregrino* (1847), numerous editions.

13. Alberdi then went on to declare: "Two chains tied us to Europe: a material one that was severed, an intelligent one that lives as yet. Our forefathers broke the first with their sword; we shall break the other through our thought [*el pensamiento*]. This new conquest should consummate our independence" (*Fragmento preliminar al estudio del derecho* [1837; Buenos Aires, 1984], 126).

14. Also known as the Asociación de Mayo and the Asociación de la Joven Argentina. A semiclandestine organization, its other sources of inspiration were the Carbonari movement and, closer to home, the recently instituted Masonic Lodges (González Bernaldo, *Civilidad y política*).

15. *Facundo* is Sarmiento's best-known work. Published in 1845, it is the first serious study of gaucho culture.

16. Lugones stated quite bluntly at the beginning of his essay on the retrieval of the cultural heritage of the gauchos that his stance was now possible thanks to the fact that the gaucho was no more (*El payador* [1913–16], numerous editions).

17. "Si la lengua no es otra cosa que una faz del pensamiento, la nuestra pide una armonía íntima con nuestro pensamiento americano, más simpático mil veces con el movimiento rápido y directo del pensamiento francés, que con los eternos contorneos del pensamiento español. . . . Decir que nuestra lengua, es la lengua española, es decir también que nuestra legislación, nuestras costumbres, no son nuestras, sino de España, esto es, que nuestra patria no tiene personalidad nacional, que nuestra patria no es una patria, que América no es América, sino que es España, de modo que no tener costum-

bres españolas es no tener las costumbres de nuestra nación. La lengua argentina no es pues la lengua española: es hija de la lengua española, como la nación argentina es hija de la nación española, sin ser por eso la nación española" (Alberdi, *Fragmento*, 153–54). [If language is nothing else but an aspect of thought, ours then demands an intimate harmony with our American thought, a thousand times more in tune with the rapid and direct movement of French thought, than with the eternal sidewindings of Spanish thought. . . . To say that our language is the Spanish language is also to say that our legislation, our customs, are not ours, but Spain's; that is, that our *patria* (native land, country) has no national personality, that our *patria* is not a *patria*, that America is not America, but rather that it is Spain: which is to say that to lack Spanish customs is to lack the customs of our nation. The Argentine language is not, therefore, the Spanish language; she is the daughter of the Spanish language, as the Argentine nation is the daughter of the Spanish nation, without being, on that account, the Spanish nation.]

18. Americanist discourse in Latin America (*americanismo*) assumed several different modes, although their central, constitutive core always revolved around the opposition between the "positive American" and the "negative European." In the independence era *americanismo* had been essentially a political mode of discourse, represented both in anti-Spaniard sentiment and in projects for a grand federation of Latin American states, such as those proposed by Simón Bolívar. In the 1830s and 1840s, as the River Plate was subjected to French and English blockades and military intervention, Juan Manuel de Rosas developed another version of political *americanismo* centered on what he termed the "American System": the Argentine Confederation, in its war with France and Great Britain, was defending (and leading) all the other American states in a struggle for continental freedom from Europe. Deeply imbued with "nativist" elements (such as a preference for Creole styles of dress rather than European or for local, River Plate cuisine), this discourse expired with the regime that had employed it. A much longer-lasting strand of Americanist discourse, centered on culture and, more especially, on literature, was "el americanismo literario," the earliest initiator of which happened to be Juan María Gutiérrez with the publication of *América poética*, the first anthology of Spanish American poetry, in Valparaíso in 1847. This strand stressed the cultural unity of Spanish or (later in the century) Latin America: a long line of essayists—from José Martí, to José Enrique Rodó, to Alfonso Reyes, to Pedro Henríquez Ureña, and beyond—would continue to reproduce and elaborate this *americanismo* well into the twentieth century, with the post-1959 anti-imperialist *americanismo* of the Cuban Revolution and its writers constituting a final twist to this line of argument.

19. See Prieto, *El discurso criollista*.

20. Ibid., 68–69.

21. Ibid., 69.

22. Ibid., 69–70.

23. Beatriz Sarlo, *Juan María Gutiérrez: Historiador y crítico de nuestra literatura* (Buenos Aires, 1967), 90–106.

24. The first edition was published by Ernesto Morales in 1940 on the basis of his compilation of the original newspaper articles. The title was also chosen by him.

25. "Todos estos elementos mancomunados y hasta cierto punto ponderados, con-

stituían una democracia rudimental, turbulenta por naturaleza y laboriosa por necesi-
dad, con instintos de independencia individual y de libertad comunal, a la vez que con
tendencia a la arbitrariedad, en que la fuerza y la opinión intervenían activamente, con
más eficacia que en el resto de la América" (Bartolomé Mitre, *Historia de Belgrano,
obras completas* [Buenos Aires, 1940], 6:15). [All these elements, held in common and
to a certain extent taken into account, constituted a rudimentary democracy, turbulent
by nature and laborious through necessity, with instincts of individual independence
and communal liberty, while at the same time with a tendency toward arbitrary rule,
in which force and opinion intervened actively, with more efficacy than in the rest of
America.]

26. See the first volume of his *Historia de la república argentina* (1881–83).

27. "Pero las imágenes, alusiones, modismos, juguetes de palabras, que pueden ser
muy agudas en Madrid, por ejemplo, pasan aquí desapercibidos o hacen bostezar. *La
Risa*, periódico chancista que se publicaba ahora años en aquella metrópoli, se reim-
primía en Valparaíso con el título *El Alegre*, por un impresor español, esperando pon-
erse rico. Pero ¿cuál sería su sorpresa cuando supo que las mujeres de Lima, le habían
cambiado el título y le llamaban *El Triste?*" (Juan María Gutiérrez, *Cartas de un porteño*
[Buenos Aires, 2003], 95–96). [But the images, allusions, turns of phrase, play of words,
which may be very witty in Madrid, for example, pass through here unnoticed or merely
eliciting a yawn. *La Risa* (Laughter), the jocular (humorous) periodical that was published, now many years ago, in that metropolis (Madrid), was published simultaneously
in Valparaíso, under the title *El Alegre* (The Joyful One), by a Spanish printer, in the hope
of obtaining riches. But what might not have been his surprise when he discovered that
the women of Lima had changed its title, calling it *El Triste* (The Sad One)?]

28. Juan B. Alberdi, *El crimen de la guerra* (1870; Buenos Aires, 1984).

29. Between 1852 and 1880 provincial rebellion and civil war continued to be endemic.
It was only after that date that the national authorities obtained complete supremacy
over the provincial governments.

30. One aspect of national identity in its political mode that I have preferred not
to discuss in this chapter is that of citizenship. The reason is that, in addition to other
relevant texts cited here, a comprehensive and insightful study of the problem of citizenship in post-1852 Argentina is readily available: see Hilda Sábato, *The Many and the Few:
Political Participation in Republican Buenos Aires* (Stanford, Calif., 2001).

31. José Luis Romero, *Las ideas políticas en Argentina* (Buenos Aires, 1946).

32. An ultimate irony, perhaps, concerning Gutiérrez's twentieth-century reception
is that one of his editors (and author of a panegyrical critical introduction) was Juan P.
Ramos, who, in addition to being a literary critic, was a violently xenophobic and anti-
democratic nationalist leader, the founder and supreme commander of Acción Nacionalista Argentina, one of the many paramilitary "leagues" that burgeoned during the 1930s.

33. See Lilia Ana Bertoni, *Patriotas, cosmopolitas y nacionalistas: La construcción de la
nacionalidad argentina a fines del siglo XIX* (Buenos Aires, 2001).

34. The following passage from *La bolsa*, a few pages after a paragraph whose description of immigrants began with the line "Filthy Turks," seems almost a direct reply
to Gutiérrez's *Cartas de un porteño*: "Promiscuidad de tipos y promiscuidad de idiomas.

Aquí los sonidos ásperos como escupitajos del alemán, mezclándose impíamente a las dulces notas de la lengua italiana; allí los acentos viriles del inglés haciendo dúo con los chisporroteos maliciosos de la terminología criolla; del otro lado las monerías y suavidades del francés, respondiendo al ceceo susurrante de la rancia pronunciación española" (Julián Martel, *La bolsa* [1891; Buenos Aires, 1981], 37). [Promiscuity of types and promiscuity of languages. Here we have the harsh accents of German, sounding like spit and mixing impiously with the sweet notes of the Italian language; there we have the virile accent of the Englishman singing a duo with the malicious crackling of "criollo" terminology; and on the other side the monkeying and suaveness of the French, responding to the murmuring lisp of the stale Spanish pronunciation.]

35. In the Nationalist movement of the 1930s and 1940s many central figures were of provincial origin: Carlos Ibarguren was from Salta, and the Irazusta brothers were from rural Entre Ríos. Their precursors were the liberal Ricardo Rojas, from Santiago del Estero, and the xenophobic Manuel Gálvez, from Santa Fe.

36. The *criollista* debate was triggered in 1900 by the publication of French scholar Lucien Abeille's *La lengua de los argentinos*, which predicted that the Spanish spoken in Argentina would soon evolve into a separate Argentine language.

37. "Todo conspiraba en aquel fin del siglo XIX y en la ciudad de Buenos Aires, contra los ideales de variedad cultural a la cual somos afectos en este nuevo fin de siglo. La escuela era una máquina de imposición de identidades, pero también extendía un pasaporte a condiciones mejores de existencia: entre la independencia cultural respecto del Estado y convertirse en servidor del proyecto cultural de ese mismo Estado, quedaban pocas posibilidades de elección." This quote, in reference to public education and the *maestra normal*, the state schoolteacher, is in Beatriz Sarlo, *La máquina cultural: Maestras, traductores y vanguardistas* (Buenos Aires, 1998). [Everything conspired in that nineteenth fin-de-siècle and in the city of Buenos Aires, against the ideals of cultural variety to which we are attached in this new fin-de-siècle. The school was a machine of imposition of identities, but also extended a passport to better conditions of existence: between (the alternative projects of) cultural independence with respect to the State and becoming a servant of the cultural project of that same State, few possibilities for choice remained.]

38. See Adrián Gorelik, *La grilla y el parque* (Buenos Aires, 1998); Adrián Gorelik, *Miradas sobre Buenos Aires* (Buenos Aires, 2004); Graciela Silvestri, *El color del río* (Buenos Aires, 2004). Gorelik stresses the positive aspects of urban homogenization achieved by the grid dividing the city into equal blocks and especially its leveling, socially democratizing consequences: cultural pluralism may have been sacrificed, but offsetting that loss was the gain represented by the attenuation of ostensible social differences.

Imagining *la raza argentina*

JEANE DELANEY

*I*n describing the conference for which these essays were prepared, Don Doyle and Marco Pamplona noted that, "in general, the American republics struggled to develop sources of unity in political rather than ethnic terms, in belief rather than blood, and in a shared destiny rather than a long past."[1] This observation about the volitional, constructed basis of New World identity would seem to find no better fit than in the case of Argentina. In contrast to Mexico and the Andean countries, where the survival of large indigenous populations has sometimes led elites to seek national unity by celebrating the supposedly unique qualities of their racially mixed populations, Argentina appears a poor candidate for such an enterprise. As is well known, the sparseness of their nation's indigenous population allowed nineteenth-century Argentine political leaders to expel or exterminate most of their territory's original inhabitants and thereby avoid having to incorporate native peoples into the national community. Another factor militating against any appeal to ethnicity as a source of Argentine unity was the view, uniformly embraced by nineteenth-century progressives, that theirs was a severely underpopulated country whose very viability depended on immigration from non-Spanish Europe. Given these circumstances, it would seem that, of all Latin Americans, Argentines would be the least likely to accept the romantic idea that nations arise naturally from primordial ethnic communities and instead to side with the constructionist view that nations are modern entities that must be created and shaped by conscious human efforts.

Reality, however, has proved more complicated. The rise of a new, nationalist discourse in early-twentieth-century Argentina had at its core the assumption that the peoples of each nation constitute a unique ethnic group or "race" whose members share underlying mental and emotional traits.[2] The most vocal and visible promoters of the idea of *la raza argentina* during this period were a loosely drawn group of young writers who have since become known as the cultural nationalists.[3] Based in Buenos Aires, these young writers saw themselves as the vanguard of a new cultural movement that would defend and define the putative racial values of the Argentine people during a period of excessive cosmopolitanism. The importance of these young intellectuals, however, should not be overestimated. Despite their vanguardist claims, the cultural nationalists proved influential precisely because they most forcefully articulated ideas that had already gained currency during this period, as growing numbers of intellectual and opinion makers concerned with national identity began to conflate nationality with ethnicity and to embrace the romantic notion that the Argentine people would ultimately form a unified *raza argentina*.

Romanticism and Nation in the Nineteenth Century

Romanticism, with its emphasis on national particularity and the supposedly unique inner qualities of national peoples, had long circulated in Argentina. To be sure, such ideas would have been alien to the members of Argentina's independence generation, who justified their break with Spain not in the name of a preexisting historico-cultural nation but for the purpose of establishing a new nation based on the principles of equality, liberty, and popular sovereignty.[4] This tendency to define the nation in political rather than ethnic or cultural terms continued throughout the despotic regime of Juan Manuel de Rosas (1829–52), whose classical republicanism stressed "civic virtue, subordination to the established order, and political unanimity."[5] It was in Rosas's enemies, the famous Argentine Generation of 1837, that the influence of romanticism can first be seen. As Jorge Myers has discussed in his contribution to this volume, the members of this generation blamed Argentina's failure to adopt liberal, representative political institutions on the negative cultural legacy of Spanish colonialism. Inspired by the ideas of Edgar Quinet, Jules Michelet, and Victor Cousin, all French interpreters of German romanticism, they sought to define a new Argentine identity vis-à-vis Spain. Whereas Spain was insular, obscurantist, and hierarchical, Argentina was a nation that prized liberty and was open to the world. Central to the efforts to eradicate the lingering effects of the Spanish legacy and to create a new Argentine identity was the plan to promote European immigration. By bringing "living pieces of English liberty and French culture" to Argentina, members of this generation believed, the native Creole culture would be transformed, and the values and habits necessary for a modern political and economic system would take root.[6]

Despite its importance, however, the influence of romanticism during this period should not be overestimated. As Myers has noted here and elsewhere, the romantic leanings of the Generation of 1837 were always tempered by the more dominant republican tradition that marked discussions of Argentine identity during the first half of the nineteenth century. Thus, in Myers's words, even when "the cultural attributes . . . [of Argentine identity] were stressed, these were almost always encompassed within or subordinated to the language of republicanism."[7]

The arrival of millions of European immigrants during the closing decades of the nineteenth century transformed the social and cultural terrain upon which discussions of Argentine identity would take place. Despite the fact that this had long been a goal of the Argentine state, when immigrants finally arrived in large numbers the response of the native elite was decidedly mixed. One reason for this ambivalence was the sheer volume of the influx. Between 1853 and 1916 over 2.5 million immigrants permanently settled in Argentina.[8] The impact in the areas of the Federal District of Buenos Aires was especially dramatic because large numbers of the newcomers settled there and formed the basis of the emerging urban working class. Indeed, it is estimated that in 1914 nearly 50 percent of the district's inhabitants were foreign-born.[9] Another source of concern for the Argentine elite was the nature of the immigrants themselves. Whereas nineteenth-century elites had hoped to attract skilled laborers and yeomen farmers from France and northern Europe, the immigrants who arrived during the closing decades of the century were of a different sort. Predominantly from the poorest sectors of Italy and Spain, these often uneducated newcomers provoked more disdain than admiration on the part of native Argentines.

By the end of the 1880s Argentine society, particularly in urban areas, had become highly diverse. In a matter of decades the cosmopolitanism celebrated by the Generation of 1837 as a mark of Argentina's distinctive, New World identity took on a threatening quality. The rising anti-immigrant sentiment took different forms, but this new xenophobia was tempered by the broadly held consensus that national prosperity remained dependent upon the continued influx of cheap labor. The question of Argentine identity was thus transformed from the nineteenth-century quest to establish a new national culture free from Spanish influence to one of how to forge a new nation from a heterogeneous people.

During the period 1880–1900 elite response to the question of nation building took two paths: one pointed to the constructivist vision of nationhood, the other looked toward the romanticized, primordialist view. The first response was a form of liberal nationalism and found its greatest expression in efforts to promote patriotic education. During the closing decades of the century politicians and educators alike lamented both the immigrants' lack of patriotic sentiment and what they saw as the country's growing loss of cohesion. Accordingly, they called upon the state to use the public school system to promote patriotic values in immigrant children. The emphasis on patriotic education continued through the 1890s and well into the new century. Of particular importance was the leadership of prominent positivist sociologist José María Ramos Mejía, who served as president of the influential Consejo Nacional de Educación from 1908 to 1912. During his tenure Ramos Mejía imposed a "civic liturgy" on primary schools that Tulio Halperin Donghi has described as "almost Japanese" in its intensity.[10] Under his energetic direction children were required to recite a pledge of allegiance, schools were urged to drop foreign texts in favor of ones authored by Argentines, and teachers were encouraged to organize frequent civic festivals. Evaluating the fruits of his efforts, Ramos Mejía noted approvingly that it was "the *pilluelo*, the half-Argentinized immigrant child, who applauds with greatest warmth the groups of [military] cadets" and who, on patriotic holidays, "marches with an enchanting gravity." It was this same child who "listens to the national hymn, sings, and recites it with a knitted brow and ardor that ranges on the comic."[11]

As disconcerting as Ramos Mejía's image may be to those who find all displays of patriotism troubling, it should be remembered that, at the very least, this was a nationalism that demanded from immigrants and their children only their loyalty to the state, not the abandonment of prior cultural or ethnic identities deemed un-Argentine. To be sure, no modern state is ever culturally neutral, and even the mildest forms of civic nationalism promote—or assume—some sort of shared national culture. But, as Rainer Bauböck argues, liberal nationalists understand national culture as a kind of "thin roof" under which cultural diversity survives within civil society.[12] Prominent intellectual Carlos Octavio Bunge, who, like Ramos Mejía, was an avid supporter of patriotic education, made clear his view of just how thin Argentina's cultural roof should be. According to Bunge, contemporary societies such as Argentina were unavoidably pluralistic, thus making it necessary "to seek social unity in something distinctive and superior to ethnic, linguistic, religious or geographic unity." This something, he continued, was the "unity of sentiment and the idea of the homeland [*patria*]."[13]

It is in the second response to massive immigration during this period that we see the influence of romanticism. For some Argentine political leaders the "unity of sentiment" sought by individuals such as Bunge was an insufficient basis for nationhood. They argued instead that national cohesion—and indeed the nation itself—required a deeper, more encompassing source of unity than that provided by liberal nationalism. Inspired by the ethnocultural nationalist currents sweeping Europe, these individuals believed that nations, by definition, were communities of culturally homogeneous peoples who were bound together by language, religion, shared historical memories, and common mental and emotional traits. This vision of nationhood comes through clearly in the 1894 parliamentary debates over immigrant-run private schools. Alarmed by the growing number of such schools, Deputy Indalecio Gómez introduced a bill to require that all instruction, both public and private, be carried out in

Spanish. The bill's supporters believed Argentina should remain a nation where all children were forced to learn a single, officially sanctioned language.

To be sure, the conviction that nations should be monolingual does not necessarily reflect an underlying belief in a romantic-style notion of nationhood. Individuals who imagine the nation in purely political terms can, with some justification, argue that exercising the rights and obligations of citizenship requires that citizens share a common language. But in the case of late-nineteenth-century Argentina it was clear that the desire for a common language was based not on pragmatic grounds but on the belief that a single language was essential to the maintenance of cultural homogeneity, itself a prerequisite for nationhood. In defending his proposal, for example, Gómez argued that preserving Spanish as the national language was important because language "throws its indissoluble bonds into the depths of the [individual] soul, where sentiment, ideas, and character come into being." Thus the inner being of an individual, he continued, "gets confused with the language, which is its outward form."[14] Deputy Marco Avellaneda also employed romantic reasoning when he explained his support for the bill. Language, he proclaimed, was "the basis of national unity" and was "that which is most essentially peculiar to the people, and the most exact manifestation of its character." Continuing, Avellaneda argued that language was something that was "inherited" and "perpetuated by the family," and it was the national language that "always conserves the consciousness of the nationality."[15] Striking a similar note, Deputy Lucas Ayarragaray expressed his support for the measure by arguing that language, "religion, race, [and] territory" were all essential to the creation of a moral unity that made nationality possible. Only after this moral unity was established could political unity be achieved, and then only through a process of slow and "ordered evolution."[16]

By the end of the nineteenth century, then, romantic-inspired notions of nationhood had clearly become part of the debates over Argentine identity but in a way that was strikingly different from before. In contrast to the members of the Generation of 1837 who drew from romantic, historicist notions of national particularity to define a uniquely cosmopolitan Argentine identity vis-à-vis Spain, these late-nineteenth-century political leaders marshaled romantic arguments to defend what they saw as an already formed nationality *against* a supposedly corrosive cosmopolitanism and to call for measures that would enforce a cultural and even ethnic homogeneity that they saw as the very basis of nationhood.

The romantic vision of the nation as ethnocultural community achieved greater currency after the turn of the century and, as Liliana Bertoni argues, gradually displaced—although did not eradicate—other visions of the nation that allowed for greater cultural diversity. The factors leading to this deepening romantic impulse were varied. Bertoni describes a combination of domestic political battles and the increasing influence of ethnolinguistic nationalism emanating from countries such as France and Italy. To these I would add the generalized prestige of positivism during the 1880–1900 period, which—at least in the Argentine context—encouraged intellectuals to focus on the unique qualities of their own society and to posit the existence of a unique national psychology.[17] Perhaps more important were the writings of the Spanish Generation of 1898, most notably, the works of Miguel de Unamuno and Angel Ganivet. These intellectuals, themselves deeply influenced by the romantic philosophy known as *krausismo*, were key initiators of *hispanismo*, an intellectual movement that swept Hispanic America at the turn of the century.[18] This movement promoted the essentialist notion that the peoples of Spanish descent were members of the same racial family and thus were endowed with common spiritual and mental qualities. Emerging during the final decades of the nineteenth century, *hispanismo* gained force after Spain's disastrous defeat by the United States and was popularized throughout Hispanic America by Uruguayan poet José Enrique Rodó's 1900 essay *Ariel*.

Imagining LA RAZA ARGENTINA

In any case, after the turn of the century romantic ideas about nationhood and the identification of nationality with putative ethnic qualities increasingly served as a conceptual filter through which leading intellectuals understood the challenges posed by immigration. In 1904, for example, poet Arturo O'Connor, who was closely associated with the cultural nationalists, warned that *la raza argentina* would soon disappear under the massive influx of immigrants.[19] Proclaiming that "race is nationality," he lamented that it was Argentina's "destiny" to be absorbed by the newcomers, thus giving birth to a "new nationality."[20] Novelist Manuel Gálvez, who is considered one of the key promoters of cultural nationalism, sounded a similar although somewhat less pessimistic note. Argentines, he believed, could resist the excessive cosmopolitanism produced by massive immigration by returning to their Spanish heritage. In his highly successful 1913 book, *El solar de la raza*, Gálvez described Spain as the "ancestral dwelling [*solar*] of the race" and proclaimed to his fellow Argentines that it was time to "feel ourselves [to be] Americans and, in the ultimate term, Spaniards, given that this is the race to which we belong."[21] In a similar vein, Manuel Carlés, founder of the right-wing Catholic Liga Patriótica Argentina, warned that immigrants were attempting to "alter the very essence [*entraña*] of the spirit of the tradition of the race" and thus threatened the foundation of Argentine nationality.[22]

But even with this deepened romantic impulse and the increasing fears that massive immigration threatened *la raza argentina*, the consensus that Argentina needed immigrant labor still held. In some cases, such as Germany, the paradox created by an ethnic understanding of nationhood and the need for workers has led to the creation of guest worker programs, whereby foreigners are understood to be temporary laborers who will eventually return to their native country. Until recently, even if these immigrants remain in the country for decades and have children born on German soil, they (and their offspring) were considered to be temporary residents. But because most Argentines continued to see their country as severely underpopulated, such an arrangement was undesirable. They wanted—and expected—immigration to continue and the immigrants themselves to stay. The way out of this dilemma was to adapt the ethnocultural understanding of nationhood in such a way as to incorporate rather than exclude the immigrant. How was this possible? The key lay in the view, widely accepted by even the most ardent nationalists, that in Argentina a new race was forming, one that would represent an amalgam of the Argentine Creoles and the immigrants, both present and future.

Representative of this position was well-known writer and critic Juan Mas y Pi. Writing in the prestigious literary review *Renacimiento*, Mas y Pi argued that although "Argentina has been, and continues to be, a country of great ethnic confusion . . . [comprised] of all races and castes," this heterogeneity would eventually pass. From this "confused conglomeration," he optimistically affirmed, " . . . a great race would inevitably emerge."[23] University of Buenos Aires professor Salvador Debenedetti expressed a similar view. According to Debenedetti, Argentines were currently witnessing the emergence of the "soul of the future race," which was slowly being shaped by the local "social medium and the environment." Already, he believed, there were "clear symptoms of a nationality defined or in the process of becoming defined."[24] Undoubtedly, the most colorful description of this supposed process of racial formation came from the pen of renowned poet Pedro B. Palacios, also known as Almafuerte:

> The future great soul . . . will appear . . . when the mind of the new race in gestation has formed, when the beautiful blonde beast that Nietzsche speaks of . . . has been formed, thanks to the fusion of the bloodlines, the atavisms, the degenerations, the histories, the diverse origins that now clash . . . and repel each other. . . . [The Argentine nation is a] frightful hurly-burly that will endure for . . . generations until it constitutes an organism [with a] clearly drawn body [and an] obvious, characteristic race.[25]

By around 1910 the trope of an emerging *raza argentina* came to dominate discourse about the future identity of the Argentine nation. But, like the idea of the cultural melting pot described by Myers that operated so powerfully during much of the nineteenth century, the concept of *la raza argentina* proved to be an empty screen upon which any number of images could be projected.

How individual intellectuals defined the emerging race and what qualities they privileged—shared descent, language, religion, personality traits—varied enormously. Just as important, how would this race form? Would it be a spontaneous process or one shaped by the native elite?

One version of *la raza argentina* put forth by some proponents of the new nationalism was that this *raza* at its core was Spanish and Catholic. For individuals such as the already mentioned Manuel Gálvez the emerging Argentine race was a variation of the Spanish race, which itself belonged to the greater Latin race. An ardent Catholic, Gálvez believed religion was an integral part of race and as such had played a central role in shaping the Latin character, imbuing it with a unique spirituality, warmth, and spontaneity.[26] (Conversely, the races of Protestant Europe were dull, predictable, and lacking an aesthetic sensibility.)[27] Given his vision of Argentina as a Hispanic Latin nation whose identity was intimately bound to Catholicism, it is not surprising that Gálvez believed immigrants from Latin countries were most desirable. Noting approvingly that the great majority of Argentina's immigrants came from Spain and Italy, Gálvez argued that these newcomers brought with them the "providential and invisible mission to conserve the qualities of *latinidad* in the mixture of peoples and to guarantee, in the amalgam of so many metals, [that] the pure gold of *latinidad* would endure."[28] Thus, despite the massive influx of immigrants from Europe, Argentina was, and would remain, a Latin and especially a Hispanic nation.

Gálvez's vision of the emerging Argentine race, whose character was preserved due to the sheer number of Latins entering the country, appeared to privilege heredity or common descent as the basis of nationality. Yet elsewhere he seemed to suggest that it was indeed possible for any immigrant to become a true Argentine. This occurred, he believed, through a mysterious process of transubstantiation when the foreigner "submerge[d]" his (or her) soul in the "vastness of the national soul, and his heart pulse[d] to the rhythm of the national sentiment."[29] Gálvez's deep friendship with fellow writer Alberto Gerchunoff, a Russian-born Jew, is also revealing. Lauding his friend as one of the great "attractions" of his generation and Gerchunoff's book, *Los gauchos judíos*, as "one of the most beautiful of our narrative literature," Gálvez seemed to believe, at least in some cases, that even foreign-born Jews could become real Argentines.[30]

Ricardo Rojas, who along with Gálvez is considered one of the most important proponents of cultural nationalism, had a more expansive vision of the emerging *raza argentina*. Whereas Gálvez defined the Argentine race as essentially Hispanic and Catholic, Rojas said little about religion and argued that Spain had provided only one element, albeit an important one, in the emerging Argentine race.[31] One of the few thinkers of the period to give even a token nod to the pre-Columbian past, Rojas believed the new Argentine race would result from the fertile coupling of both indigenous and European elements.[32] When describing how this felicitous blend of the foreign and the native would occur, Rojas's thought took on a decidedly mystical cast. According to Rojas, emanating from each nation's territory were spiritual forces that stamped the inhabitants with a particular set of mental characteristics and thus gave the nation its distinctive personality or character.[33] In Argentina, he argued, these telluric forces also served to transform or nationalize the millions of foreigners who continued to pour onto national shores. The interior, then, would serve as the "crucible" of the national race, "molding men into a race, and transforming this race until it was a true nationality."[34] Thus, while Rojas agreed that the current wave of immigrants had taxed the country's capacity to absorb or transform them, he continued to argue that the "cosmopolitan immigration" was a "key part of the ethnic development of our nationality."[35]

But despite Rojas's confident assessment of the molding power of the Argentine territory, he also believed that the state, counseled by intuitive intellectuals such as himself, should take an active role in shaping the character of this emerging race. A prominent advocate of patriotic education who received government funds to study European school curricula, Rojas used his report— unfairly, given past efforts—to blast what he saw as the traditional policy of blindly following foreign educational models.[36] Instead, he argued, the nation's schools should become the "hearth of citizenship" and be used to inculcate a patriotic spirit in all immigrant children.[37] Accordingly, Rojas advocated developing a new national school curriculum focusing on Argentine history, literature, geography, and the Spanish language. These proposals, of course, suggest a constructionist view of nationhood that seems at odds with Rojas's belief that the emerging *raza argentina* would be molded by the spiritual forces emanating from the national territory. He believed, however, that nationalistic educational policies would serve as a complement to these forces and would help the nation weather the current disruptions caused by massive immigration. "Our goal for now," Rojas argued, "is to create a community of national ideas" that will continue or complete the nationalization process that was already being realized by the "influence of the territory."[38]

Writer Eduardo Maglione, in two articles published in the prestigious literary review *Renacimiento* in late 1909, offered a very different vision of the emerging *raza argentina*.[39] Like many of his contemporaries, Maglione agreed that Argentina was currently witnessing a "fusion of the races" and that fusion would ultimately produce "the true Argentine race and nationality."[40] But in describing the content and character of this putative race he echoed the earlier, pre-1880 view that saw European immigration as a means of improving a defective Creole population. In terms reminiscent of those employed by the Generation of 1837 he contrasted the immigrants' superior intelligence and drive to the "turbulent and sterile indolence" of the Creoles.[41] In the current "contact, juxtaposition, and fusion of characters," Maglione maintained, those with the "most energy" and "greater vitality" would inevitably triumph.[42] Thus, he believed, it was only a matter of time before a new, superior race would emerge that would have little or nothing to do with the old.

In his account of the emerging *raza argentina* Maglione suggests a Darwinist-type struggle through which the fittest would survive. He believed, however, that forming the new nationality would entail more than a simple process of natural selection. It also required active human intervention. According to Maglione, "the need to give a soul to the variegated grouping of men and tendencies that is in the process of forming the Argentine race" was indisputable. Indeed, in his view the most pressing task facing the nation was to give "a uniform spirit to the clusters of individuals that are incorporating themselves on our soil."[43] But who would oversee this process? Maglione did not provide a direct answer, but he clearly believed it should *not* be elite intellectuals such as Rojas. In a direct reference to Rojas's *La restauración nacionalista* he blasted those who advocated a "national restoration" and whose ideas had begun "to have an ill effect on public instruction, military institutions, the national literature, and common sense." These individuals, whom he identified with the traditional landed elite, confused their class interests with those of the nation as a whole. "Behind all the sermons . . . regarding the baleful effects of cosmopolitanism," he wrote, " . . . exists the lament of a class that senses its privilege of exploitation is slipping away and feels itself without the power to conserve it."[44]

Language, Race, and Immigration

Disputes about the content of the emerging national race or personality and what role the immigrant should play were also evident in the ongoing preoccupation over language. As discussed earlier, during the 1890s Argentine political leaders had sought (unsuccessfully) to require that Spanish be the language of instruction in immigrant-run schools. Concern over this issue would remain, but after 1900 the major focus of the language controversy shifted. Now the question became, Was Argentine Spanish itself changing as a result of immigration, and, if so, was this a positive or negative development? Given romanticism's view of language as the manifestation of the inner soul or character of a people, this issue became a point of intense debate.

The impetus for this controversy was the growing popularity of two *jergas*, or jargons, both associated with the working-class immigrant population: *lunfardo*, an urban street slang with heavy Italian influence, and *cocoliche*, a kind of mixed Italian gaucho talk associated with *criollismo*, a term applied to an often hilarious type of theater and pulp fiction about rural life that was wildly popular among immigrants. The dilemma for those who came under the sway of romanticism, then, was obvious. Did *lunfardo* and/or *cocoliche* represent the beginning stages of a new, distinctive Argentine language? Or was Spanish, as spoken by the educated elite, the true national language?

Two publications, one appearing in 1900 and the other in 1902, set the terms of what was to become a decades-long debate over the language question. Those who embraced *criollismo* and believed that the hybrid speech it contained was the basis of a new, distinctively Argentine language found support in French linguist Luciano Abeille's *Idioma nacional de los argentinos*. A longtime resident of Argentina who was clearly steeped in the ethnocultural nationalism of the period, Abeille embraced both the concept of national races and the assumption that a nation's language was the expression of its unique racial soul. Consequently, it was impossible for different nations to share the same language. Arguing that "a nation that lacks its own language is incomplete," he believed it to be "as necessary to the nation to have its own language . . . as it is to have its own flag."[45] Continuing, Abeille argued, "In the Republic of Argentina a new race is forming. As a result, the Spanish language, or the language of the conquistadors of this country[,] has to evolve until a new language is formed." "To deny that the Argentine language is not evolving," he affirmed, was "to declare that the Argentine race will not reach its full development."[46] Indeed, according to Abeille, efforts to prevent the emergence of this new national language by teaching a pure, academic form of Spanish in the public schools would "warp [*viciar*] and falsify" the emerging Argentine language and, in doing so, would "perturb the national soul that is reflected in this language."[47]

Those Argentines who rejected Abeille's thesis and who saw immigrant-generated words and pronunciations as a source of linguistic contamination found their champion in elite intellectual Ernesto Quesada. One of the most prolific and well-respected scholars of his time, Quesada roundly rejected Abeille's argument that Argentina was developing a new, distinctive language and seemed especially incensed that the Frenchman saw the dialects or jargons associated with *criollismo* as the beginnings of this language. Can people really believe, Quesada asked sarcastically, that "these language corruptions produced by the everyday speech of the illiterate classes constitute that which is [most] characteristic of our country" and represent the Creole element of the Argentine way of thought?[48] Certainly, Quesada admitted, at times it was appropriate for educated writers to employ words from *cocoliche, lunfardo,* and gaucho speech, but "from there to convert these jargons into [a] national language or into the 'language of the Argentines,' as a certain French professor seeks to do, . . . is an immense distance."[49] Concluding his long essay, Quesada described language as "the depository of the spirit of the race, of its very genius [*genio*]." Thus it was the duty of literary men to protect Argentine Spanish from "the contamination and corruption [produced by the] intermixture of peoples and languages."

Given the cosmopolitanism of Argentine society, he concluded, it was essential that the "national tradition be maintained unscathed" and that the "purity and gallantry of our language" be preserved.[50]

The ensuing controversy over the language question was, in many ways, a proxy debate over the nature of the putative *raza argentina*. The conflicting views on how this supposed race would form and how much the immigrant contribution would affect its character were replayed in what would become a decades-long debate. Among those who believed that Argentine Spanish should be kept as pure as possible was author Miguel Toro y Gómez. In a 1918 article in a special issue of the literary review *Verbum* dedicated to the celebration of the Día de la Raza (Day of the Race, or Columbus Day) Toro y Gómez described the Spanish language as a "spiritual bond" between Spain and its former colonies that should be preserved at all costs.[51] Those individuals who had previously argued that Argentina was developing its own language from the "innumerable barbarisms, Gallicisms, and other excesses" brought by the tide of immigration were both ill informed and guilty of "sinning" against the nation.[52]

Manuel Gálvez, who, it will be recalled, believed the Argentine race to be fundamentally Spanish, also weighed in on behalf of the purists. In a 1927 survey on the language question sponsored by the progressive newspaper *Crítica* he impatiently dismissed the notion that Argentina would ever develop a distinctive language. "The enmity against pure Spanish," he contended, "is a defensive attitude stemming more from youthful ignorance than from true sentiment." Jargons like *lunfardo*, moreover, were destined to fade and thus would not have a permanent impact on Argentine Spanish.[53] Ricardo Rojas also rejected the notion that Argentines were developing a distinctive language and accused Abeille's theories of encouraging the "most barbaric and vain inclinations of a vulgar Creole patriotism."[54] Although he believed that Argentines inevitably would incorporate some new words and expressions in their speech, he also believed that any changes to the language must be the work of the educated elite rather than the popular classes. In a 1928 speech to the students of the Colegio de Buenos Aires he affirmed that Spanish was, and would always be, the "synthesis of our national personality and race [and part of] our collective memory of tradition and culture." It was therefore essential that educated individuals protect Argentine Spanish from contamination from below.[55]

There were, however, dissenting voices, as intellectuals throughout this period embraced the notion of a unique Argentine language. One of the first to defend Abeille's thesis was elite writer and folklore enthusiast Francisco Soto y Calvo, whose own work included *criollista*-inspired poetry. According to Soto y Calvo, up to this point Argentine writers had produced a "colorless" literature that "could just as well have been written in Paris as in Buenos Aires."[56] The problem, he believed, was that these writers had been indifferent to the sentiments and speech patterns of ordinary people. Only by liberating themselves from academic Spanish and by incorporating "*cocoliche* dialect" and "gaucho-esque norms" of speech that were "most genuinely Argentine" could Argentines produce an authentic national literature. This new literature, he argued, would be "cosmopolitan and strange, enchantingly splattered with [elements of] the gaucho and *cocoliche*, of Parisian elegance and Spanish lowlife, of just Saxon pride and Latin sickliness: in sum, chaos."[57]

Also supporting this position was a respondent to the above-mentioned *Crítica* survey, writing under the English pseudonym "Last Reason" and identified only as a master of Creole theater. Embracing the romantic view of language as the reflection of an underlying national character, "Last Reason" maintained that the formation of a distinctive language was central to the nation's emerging identity. Without this new language, the writer contended, "Buenos Aires would be merely a cosmopolitan, Europeanized city that lacked its own personality." What now seemed a crude slang, he believed, would form the basis of a new and ultimately rich national language. Attacking the elitism of "doctors" who worried about the vulgarity of this new language (here "Last Reason" specifically mentions Rojas), he proclaimed, writing in language laced with *lunfardo*,

[So you think] the language we use is barbaric and phonetically incorrect? I agree[:] . . . the kid is so ugly it's difficult to kiss him. Nonetheless, the baby is ours. . . . But take note: one day the kid will grow and be beautiful, he will be a man . . . [who will] one day enter into the history of nations through the front door, speaking in a loud voice a language that is beautiful, graphic, musical, and vibrant. . . . [T]his language will be the product of that rude and bastard dialect that today burns the lips of the doctors. . . . [T]omorrow it will be the powerful clarion that shouts to the decrepit and worm-eaten nations, the coming of a great and glorious nation.[58]

Elite playwright and novelist José Antonio Saldías also supported the notion of a new language. Responding to the *Crítica* survey, Saldías argued that such a language was becoming more and more necessary due to the permanent incorporation into everyday speech of expressions, words, and turns of phrase that were unacceptable to the Royal Academy. Driving this phenomenon, he argued, was the "composition of the new Argentine race," which had already emerged and was continuing to develop. Significantly, Saldías insisted that this new language would come from the people themselves, who needed "to express spontaneously and fully what [they] think." Calling those who resisted this development "prim and proper" and lacking in spontaneity, Saldías praised the new generation of "unquiet" writers who embraced this linguistic change and who battled against "rigid, established, and traditionally crystallized" norms. In the end, however, resistance to the new language was futile. "What does it matter," he proclaimed, "[if it receives] official sanction?" If the new words, phrases, and expressions became generally diffused among the people, the people themselves "have made it law."[59]

The defenders of Abeille's thesis represent an interesting twist to the early-twentieth-century debates over the Argentine language. Like the advocates of pure Spanish, they accepted the romantic ideal of the nation as a distinctive people evolving over time, marked by a common set of mental and emotional qualities and whose language somehow expressed or reflected the national soul. But clearly their vision of the Argentine race or nation had a more popular, proimmigrant tincture. In their view Argentine identity was still fluid and, like the new Argentine language, would spontaneously emerge from the unfettered interaction between natives and immigrants.

The spread of the romantic-inspired vision of the nation as a unique ethno-cultural community in early-twentieth-century Argentina established a conceptual framework that profoundly shaped how national elites confronted the challenges of massive immigration and the multicultural society it produced. But, somewhat paradoxically, the increasing acceptance of the idea of the Argentine people as a race-in-the-making failed to generate anything like a consensus among elites about the nature of this race. Instead, like nationalism itself, the idea of *la raza argentina* became—to borrow the words of Parsenjit Duara—"a site where very different views of the nation contest and negotiate with each other."[60] Although some of those who participated in the debates over the nature of the Argentine race and language believed that the character of this race—or at least its future form—had long been established, others saw its formation as a much more open-ended process. The differences between these two positions was important. Those who embraced the former believed that the immigrants should conform to some preexisting national identity that they, the native Argentines, would define. The latter, however, believed that the immigrant, whether consciously or unwittingly, would help shape the emerging national character.

But as significant as these differences were, it is important to remember that the conceptual parameters within which these debates occurred placed sharp limits on how these intellectuals imagined the future Argentine nation. Regardless of the differences between individuals such as Rojas and Maglione or Quesada and Saldías, all embraced the identification of nationality with ethnocultural traits and thus believed that the Argentine people eventually would, and should, form a unified homogeneous, culturally unified people. The triumph of this vision during the early decades of the twentieth century, while not complete, significantly weakened the competing ideal of the nation as primarily a political community whose identity rested not on the common ethnocultural traits of the population but on their shared beliefs and loyalties.[61]

In the end, what did it matter that this vision of the nation became so pervasive during this period in Argentine history? Do "imagined constructs" have, as Mark Thurner has argued in the case of Peru, "real historical consequences?"[62] The subsequent history of Argentina suggests that this indeed has been the case. One important consequence of this ideal of Argentina as a distinctive ethnocultural community was the corresponding pressure to achieve internal cultural uniformity. As Jorge Myers argues in his contribution to this volume, the elite drive to create a uniform, culturally homogeneous population was at least one reason behind the rapid erasure of the vibrant ethnic communities that were so prominent in turn-of-the-century Buenos Aires.

In addition to the loss of cultural diversity, another consequence was the weakening emphasis on the *political* component of Argentine identity. With the growing tendency to see presumed cultural and ethnic traits as the defining characteristics of Argentineness, Argentine identity became increasingly detached from the political principles, institutions, and practices enshrined in the Constitution of 1853. This devaluing of the political meant that increasing numbers of elites came to see the process of turning immigrants into Argentines as one of cultural and even ethnic transformation rather than as a legal process by which immigrants became naturalized citizens who were expected to participate in the political life of the nation. This privileging of the ethnocultural over the political is surely one of the reasons why, after 1890, few elites saw the immigrants' extraordinarily low naturalization rates (less than 2 percent) as problematic.

A final consequence of the early-twentieth-century belief in the existence of *la raza argentina* has been an enduring conviction among many Argentines that they are somehow intrinsically different from other peoples and that these differences have shaped their national history. Long after the term *raza argentina* fell into disuse, the tendency to believe in the existence of a "collective soul," Argentine psyche, or *ser nacional* (national being) that explains the nation's successes and failures has endured. This belief, in the words of historian Mariano Plotkin, has been behind Argentina's tendency to attribute the nation's many crises to "some essential dimension of the Argentine's collective psyche," a quest that he describes as part of a "long and utterly fruitless tradition."[63]

NOTES

I wish to thank the participants of the Vanderbilt University conference "Nationalism in the New World" and the anonymous reviewers of this volume for their suggestions. Thanks also go to Sandra McGee Deutsch for her helpful comments.

1. Don Doyle and Marco Pamplona, "Nationalism in the New World," excerpts from the NEH proposal for the Vanderbilt University conference.

2. The term "race" in this context clearly carried a meaning very different from that intended by Argentina's turn-of-the-century adherents of scientific racism, many of whom embraced the emerging field of eugenics. For promoters of the new nationalism who had come under the sway of romanticism, race was seen in cultural and historical rather than biological terms. Ricardo Rojas, for example, was explicit about this distinction, noting, "I use the term 'race' not in the sense used by materialist anthropologists but in the old, romantic sense [having to do with] collective personality, historical group, cultural consciousness" (*Silbarios de la decoración americana* [Buenos Aires, 1930], 151). This having been said, it is important to note that in some instances individuals moved freely between the two meanings of the term, seemingly unaware that they were doing so. For further discussion see Jeane DeLaney, "Imagining *El Ser Argentino*: Cultural Nationalism and Romantic Concepts of Nationhood in Early Twentieth-Century Argentina," *Journal of Latin American Studies* 34 (2002): esp. 644–46. Unless otherwise noted, in this chapter "race" will carry the meaning intended by these nationalists.

3. The core members of this intellectual movement consisted of Manuel Gálvez, Ricardo Rojas, Ricardo Olivera, Juan Pablo Echagüe, Emilio Becher, Atilio Chiappori, Mario Bravo, Ernesto Mario Barreda, Luis María Jordán, and Emilio Ortiz Grognet. For individual backgrounds see Manuel Gálvez, *Amigos y maestros de mi juventud*, vol. 1 of *Recuerdos de la vida literaria* (Buenos Aires, 1961), 35–75.

4. José Carlos Chiaramonte, *Formas de identidad en el Río de la Plata luego de 1810*, Boletín del Instituto de Historia Argentina y Americana Dr. E. Ravignani, 3rd series, no. 1, semester 1 (1989): 83.

5. See Jorge Myers's essay in this volume. For more extensive treatment see Myers's *Orden y virtud: El discurso republicano en el régimen rosista* (Quilmes, 1995).

6. Juan Bautista Alberdi, *Obras completas*, 3:88, cited in Susana Villavicencio, "Ciudadanos para una nación," in S. Villavicencio, ed., *Los contornos de la ciudadanía* (Buenos Aires, 2003), 27.

7. Myers, this volume.

8. Carl Solberg, *Immigration and Nationalism in Argentina and Chile, 1890–1914* (Austin, Tex., 1970), 35.

9. Adrián Jmelnizky, "Del proyecto inmigratorio argentino al modelo de absorción," in Villavicencio, *Los contornos*, 37.

10. Tulio Halperin Donghi, "Para qué la inmigración? Ideología y política inmigratoria y la aceleración del proceso modernizador: El caso argentino (1810–1914)," *Jahrbuch für Geschichte von Staat, Wirtschaft und Gesellschaft Lateinamerikas* 13 (1976): 479.

11. José María Ramos Mejía, *A martillo limpio* (Buenos Aires, 1959), 282–85, cited in Halperin, "Para qué?" 481.

12. Rainer Bauböck, "Cultural Citizenship, Minority Rights and Self-Government," in T. A. Aleinikoff and Douglas Klusmeyer, eds., *Citizenship Today: Global Perspectives and Practices* (Washington, D.C., 2001), 324.

13. Carlos Octavio Bunge, "La educación patriótica ante la sociología," *Monitor de la Educación Común*, 31 August 1908, 67–70, quoted in Carlos Escudé, *El fracaso del proyecto argentino* (Buenos Aires, 1990), 38. I should note that here my view of patriotic education as part of a program of liberal, civic nationalism differs from that of Lilia Ana Bertoni,

who, in her highly nuanced study of this period, sees in these policies an essentialist understanding of nationhood and the intent to create a single, homogeneous national culture (*Patriotas, cosmopolitas y nacionalistas: La construcción de la nacionalidad argentina a fines del siglo XIX* [Buenos Aires, 2001], 315). Relevant to this issue is her discussion of the case of a Señor Urdapilleta, who, despite his electoral victory, was not allowed to take a seat in Congress because he held dual citizenship (130–33). According to Bertoni, congressional efforts to reject Urdapilleta's credentials reflected a "defensive and essentialist" view of nationality. I would argue, however, this was not necessarily the case. In their arguments against allowing Urdapilleta to take his seat his opponents objected not to the fact that he was born in Uruguay but that he refused to renounce his Uruguayan citizenship. In other words, what seemed to be driving Urdapilleta's detractors was not the essentialist idea that one's nationality is an integral and inherent part of one's personality but that political leaders should not have divided loyalties.

14. Congreso Nacional, Cámara de Diputados, September 1896, quoted in Bertoni, *Patriotas*, 200.

15. Ibid., 194.

16. Ibid., 193.

17. For more discussion see DeLaney, "Imagining *El Ser Argentino*," esp. 643–47.

18. The importance of the Generation of 1898 and of *krausismo* in understanding the deepening romantic tendencies of the early twentieth century is developed in my paper, "Argentine Cultural Nationalism: Tracing the German Connection," delivered at the International Congress of Americanists, Santiago, Chile, July 2003.

19. Elements of the following discussion have appeared in an earlier form in my article "National Identity, Nationhood, and Immigration in Argentina: 1900–1930," *Stanford Humanities Review* 5, no. 2 (1997): 116–45.

20. Arturo Reynal O'Connor, *Ideas* (July 1904): 259.

21. Manuel Gálvez, *El solar de la raza* (1913; Buenos Aires, 1936), 37. Between 1913 and 1943 *El solar* went through eight editions and was favorably reviewed in the leading literary magazines of the period. According to Gálvez, its publication generated a "downpour of [congratulatory] letters" (*En el mundo de los seres ficticios*, vol. 2 of *Recuerdos de la vida literaria* [Buenos Aires, 1961], 15).

22. Manuel Carlés, inaugural address, *Liga Patriótica Argentina: Primer Congreso de Trabajadores* (pamphlet) (Buenos Aires, 1920), 5.

23. Juan Mas y Pi, "El arte en la Argentina," *Renacimiento* (January 1911): 307.

24. Salvador Debenedetti, "Sobre la formación de una raza argentina," *Revista de Filosofía*, year 1, semester 2 (1915): 416–17.

25. Almafuerte (Pedro B. Palacios), "Discurso a la juventud," *Hebe*, no. 1 (1918): 18.

26. Manuel Gálvez, *El diario de Gabriel Quiroga* (Buenos Aires, 1910), 67.

27. See, for example, Gálvez's comments on the Swiss in *El solar*, 56.

28. Ibid., 58–59.

29. Gálvez, *El diario*, 68.

30. Gálvez, *Amigos y maestros de mi juventud*, 44, 46. It should be noted that Gálvez could at times be quite hostile to immigrants.

31. Indeed, Rojas at times was extremely critical of Spanish traditions. See, for exam-

ple, his complaints about Spanish influences on Argentine culture and economic organization in *Eurindia*, 2nd ed., vol. 4 of *Obras completas* (Buenos Aires, 1924), 197.

32. Ibid., 170. The idea that the Argentine nation was formed by the blending of European and indigenous elements was the central theme of Rojas's widely read book *Eurindia*. It should be noted, however, that this was not an attempt to integrate what was left of Argentina's indigenous population into the national community. For Rojas, actual living Indians were irrelevant.

33. Ibid., 161, 169.

34. Ricardo Rojas, *Los gauchescos*, 2nd ed., vol. 9 of *Obras completas* (Buenos Aires, 1924), 74, 58.

35. Rojas, *Eurindia*, 134.

36. The report, published in book form in 1909 under the title *La restauración nacionalista*, had virtually nothing to do with European education. Received with great enthusiasm, it continues to be viewed as one of the most influential nationalist tracts of the period.

37. Ricardo Rojas, *La restauración nacionalista*, 3rd ed. (1909; Buenos Aires, 1971), 135, 48.

38. Ibid., 136.

39. The first article, entitled "El espíritu nacional y el cosmopolitismo," appeared in *Renacimiento* (October 1909); the second was published under the title "Cosmopolitanismo y espíritu nacional" and appeared in November 1909. The timing and content of these articles indicate that they were intended to be a direct response to Ricardo Rojas's *Restauración nacionalista*, which had appeared earlier that year.

40. Eduardo Maglione, "Cosmopolitismo y espíritu nacional," *Renacimiento* (November 1909): 328–29.

41. Ibid., 326.

42. Ibid. In Maglione, of course, the blending of romantic and scientific notions of race is evident.

43. Ibid., 327.

44. Ibid., 324.

45. Luciano Abeille, *Idioma nacional de los argentinos* (Paris, 1900), 2, 5. The copy of Abeille's book I consulted is located in the personal library of Ricardo Rojas and was heavily underlined.

46. Ibid., 35, 37 (quotations underlined in Rojas's copy).

47. Ibid., 424.

48. Ernesto Quesada, "El criollismo," *Estudios* (June–July 1902): 319.

49. Ibid.

50. Ibid., 452–53.

51. Until 1917 this day was known as the Day of Discovery. The change to Day of the Race reflects just how pervasive this romantic notion of race had become in Argentina.

52. Miguel de Toro y Gómez, "Nuestra lengua: Vínculo espiritual de la raza," *Verbum* 12, no. 46 (1918): 30.

53. Manuel Gálvez, response to *Crítica* opinion survey "Llegaremos a tener un idioma propio?" *Crítica*, 20 June 1927.

54. Rojas, *Los gauchescos*, 867–68.

55. Ricardo Rojas, *Alocución dirigido a los bachilleres del Colegio Nacional de Buenos Aires* (pamphlet) (Buenos Aires, 1928), 13, 16–17, located in the Museo Ricardo Rojas.

56. Francisco Soto y Calvo, "De la falta de carácter en la literatura argentina," *Estudios* 2, no. 4 (1903): 273, 300.

57. Ibid., 267.

58. "Last Reason," response to *Crítica* opinion survey "Llegaremos a tener un idioma propio?" *Crítica*, 16 June 1927.

59. José Antonio Saldías, response to *Crítica* opinion survey "Llegaremos a tener un idioma propio?" *Crítica*, 12 June 1927.

60. Parsenjit Duara, "Historicizing National Identity, or Who Imagines What and When," in Geoff Eley and Ronald Suny, eds., *Becoming National* (New York, 1996), 152.

61. The most important advocate of the idea of Argentina as a civic community during this period was the Argentine Socialist Party. Founded in 1894, the party adopted a reformist rather than a revolutionary program. While advocating the eventual socialization of the Argentine economy, the leaders of the party were committed democrats and believed that socialism could be achieved in Argentina through the legislative process. Deeply critical of the new nationalist currents of the period, they criticized as "mystical" the very idea that nations were "rigorously delimited entities," with distinctive personalities and destinies (Juan B. Justo, quoted in Adolfo Dickmann, "El socialismo y el principio de nacionalidad," in his *Nacionalismo y socialismo* [Buenos Aires, 1933], 29). For the socialists the nation was above all a political association: membership into the national community had nothing to do with an individual's ethnic characteristics, language, or even length of residence in Argentina but rather with his or her willingness to participate in the political system and contribute to the general well-being and greatness of the nation. This identification of citizenship and Argentineness, and the volitional nature of nationality, comes through clearly in socialist leader Augusto Bunge's argument that the naturalized citizen who is loyal to his or her adoptive nation was more completely Argentine than the corrupt, native-born politician who stole from the public till or the "decadent society matron whose only concern was to spend her husband's fortune on Parisian fashions" (*El ideal argentino y el socialismo* [Buenos Aires, 1918], 53).

62. Mark Thurner, *From Two Republics to One Divided: Contradictions of Postcolonial Nationmaking in Andean Peru* (Durham, N.C., 1997), 6.

63. Mariano Plotkin, "Mental Health and the Argentine Crisis," epilogue to Mariano Plotkin, ed., *Argentina on the Couch: Psychiatry, State and Society, 1880 to the Present* (Albuquerque, N.M., 2003), 226.

The *regeneración de la raza* in Colombia

HAYLEY FROYSLAND

*C*olombia's history has been shaped by its spatial fragmentation, which has found expression in economic atomization and cultural differentiation."[1] This statement constitutes one of the opening lines of a recent synthesis of Colombian history by Frank Safford and Marco Palacios entitled *Colombia: Fragmented Land, Divided Society.* More than most Latin American countries, Colombia is known for its extreme fragmentation, largely a result of geography. In particular, three majestic Andes mountain ranges traverse the Colombian countryside. The Andes of Colombia have historically made communication and transportation between regions more difficult and costly than in other Latin American countries. They have served as obstacles to economic development and national unity. Sufficiently isolated from other regions and having diverse political and economic interests, Colombians characteristically formed regional identities and rivalries. These persisted even after independence from Spain was achieved in 1819, thus complicating the formation of a nation-state.

Though a centralist constitution was adopted in 1821 that united Gran Colombia (present-day Venezuela, Colombia, Panama, and Ecuador) under the leadership of Simón Bolívar, regional disputes ultimately resulted in the dissolution of this larger entity in 1830 and made the task of constructing and defining Colombia as a nation particularly troublesome. Whereas Brazil, for example, was united under a monarchy in 1822, notwithstanding regional differences, regional identification in Colombia was so strong that people in some southern regions and Panama, in particular, considered secession. Nonetheless, Colombia was formed as a nation. The debate óver the form of government, centralist or federalist, and the precise distribution of power, however, would remain paramount throughout the nineteenth century. The centralist tendency of the early years as a nation was followed by the implementation of an extremely federalist constitution in 1863 in the midst of the midcentury period of Liberal reforms typical throughout Latin America. The result in Colombia was a remarkably weak central government that allowed for considerable regional autonomy.

Not surprisingly, regional studies dominate Colombian historiography. Indeed, some scholars today wonder if Colombia has yet formed a national identity. The historian Jaime Jaramillo Uribe, for example, declares that the "project of [forming] a nation-state is still just that: a project."[2] Noting a general lack of a "proper spirit of nationalism" in Colombia, historian David Bushnell, in *The Making of Modern Colombia: A Nation in Spite of Itself*, professes that, "indeed, hyperbolic nationalism is not common in Colombia; and the national character, if such a thing can be said to exist, is a composite of sometimes contradictory traits." He continues, though, and states that, "for better or worse, Colombia does exist as a nation in the world today" despite having been "torn by social, cultural, political, and regional antagonisms."[3]

"Antagonisms," a "divided society"—these words are commonly used to describe Colombian history. The scholarship on Colombia is, in fact, dominated by studies of conflict and violence. Indeed, contrasts and economic, social, and cultural disparities have been quite pronounced. This is perhaps especially so after 1880, during the era of "progress and poverty." While the export trade and related sectors of the economy expanded and many elites prospered, misery and poverty prevailed for the majority. Influenced by positivism and scientific racism, most Colombian elites equated this abounding misery with the "degeneration" of the Colombian race. As will be demonstrated in this essay, they associated moral ills with physical illnesses and the health of the nation. Though the range of particular concerns varied from country to country, the views of Colombian elites were certainly not unique. Brazilian physicians worried about the connection between disease, the large Afro-Brazilian population, and racial degeneration.[4] Middle-class individuals and groups in the United States were particularly concerned about immigrant groups. Argentina, unlike Colombia, experienced a wave of immigration from Europe. As discussed elsewhere in this volume, the immigrant population was a primary cause of concern among Argentine nationalists who worried about cultural contamination. Among the growing body of literature linking public health, gender, race, and nation, Donna Guy discusses in particular the perceived threat of immigrant prostitutes to the Argentine nation.[5] Since Colombia had no large immigrant population, it was the poor, mixed-race masses in general that prompted concern among Colombian elites. Around them they viewed not only social and cultural contrasts but degeneration and decadence, epitomized by vagrancy, alcoholism, poor hygiene, prostitution, and the spread of diseases.

This is hardly the image of the community that Colombian elites were beginning to "imagine," to use Benedict Anderson's terminology.[6] Despite a supposed lack of a sense of Colombian nationalism, Colombian elites did imagine a national community and attempt to form a fraternal spirit and a national identity during the late nineteenth century, thus exemplifying a strong correlation between nationalism and social and economic transformation.[7] It was under the leadership of President Rafael Núñez and the ideologue and vice president Miguel Antonio Caro, who also served as president from 1894 to 1898, that a sense of nationalism developed as part of the nation-building project. Núñez, Caro, and their Nationalist Party dominated the political life of the country from 1884 to 1900, a period known as "La Regeneración," the Regeneration, so named for the Núñez slogan, "Regeneration or Catastrophe." Though the Regeneration ended at the turn of the century, its conservative outlook and policies persisted until the Liberal Party gained power in 1930.

By the 1880s a more conservative outlook had been consolidated in Colombia as many political and intellectual elites began to question liberalism and the faith placed in the individual.[8] The elites of the Conservative and new Nationalist parties especially, but many members of the Liberal Party as well, believed that leaders of the Liberal reform period had been too hasty to reject Catholicism and some Spanish traditions that were an integral part of the Colombian character. When Rafael Núñez took office in 1884 for a second presidential term that initiated the Regeneration, he set into motion his program to repair a society damaged from a blind faith in individual liberty and private enterprise. The extreme federalism and laissez-faire policies of the preceding Liberal period had resulted in a weak central government and political instability.

Though many Liberals had previously modified their laissez-faire stance and taken steps favoring a stronger state, it was Núñez and his followers who, with the Constitution of 1886, created a centralist and more powerful national government. For the first time, a national anthem and a coat of arms were adopted as symbols of the nation. To build the nation, the Constitution of 1886 expanded the national government's role in the economy. Under the new constitution, public health expressly became a national responsibility, and a Central Board of Health was created in 1888. The constitution also increased the role of the national government in the supervision of education. The Nationalist governments that instituted the Regeneration also accorded the Catholic Church an influential role in society. Religion and the Catholic Church were deemed essential to moral and social order. Thus, the "regeneration" of the Colombian race and nation required a modification of political and economic policies and more. It required moral edification.

Morality became a central issue. Political, intellectual, ecclesiastical, and medical elites became increasingly concerned not only about regional fragmentation and Liberal economic policies but also about the *degeneración de la raza*. Degeneration and the prevailing poverty were linked to immorality, and the *gente decente*, the respectable people of white, European descent, were troubled by what they perceived as the disintegration of morality and the loss of a sense of community in the face of modernity. Colombia was in need of a *regeneración de la raza.*

While historians have studied the array of economic, political, and administrative reforms implemented during the Regeneration, only rarely have they examined the Regeneration's social mission. A social and moral reformation was critical, and this essay offers a fresh look at the Regeneration period and beyond by approaching the question of nation building and the formation of national character through an analysis of the social, moral, and medical dimensions of these processes. It explores the medical, racial, moral, and gendered discourse on poverty, class, citizenship, and nation formation, all of which were intertwined. In the "degenerate" society of Colombia the obstacles to progress and a positive national image were embodied in the image of the prostitute, the vagrant, and the ill and were defined using a set of moral, medical, and gendered criteria, as they had been with regard to immigrants in the United States and immigrants and prostitutes in Argentina. Such criteria were used to delineate the immoral and unhealthy behavior of those who deviated from prescribed norms and thus threatened the nation as well as to establish the roles required of individuals and families in order to achieve national stability and progress.

Thus, the image of the ideal "citizen" and the renewed Colombian nation was constructed on the basis of class- and gender-specific notions, whereby moral and healthy individuals and their stable families constituted the basic cells required for the proper functioning of the social organism that was the nation. It is further argued, then, that public health, charity, and moral instruction were paramount in the quest to improve the Colombian race and form the common culture and common values that are so often deemed essential to the formation of a national identity.[9] The "moral question" prevailed more in Colombia than in other nations principally because of the unique and continued strength of the Catholic Church and its strong alliance with the Conservative Party as well as the concomitant intensity of the belief in hierarchy and the perception of society as a social organism.

By conceptualizing poverty, class, and citizenship in social and moral terms, whereby a "citizen" is a constituent of a collective, hierarchical whole in which each contributes according to his or her station, as did various Colombian elites, this essay also posits a slight adaptation of Anderson's conception of the nation. Anderson defines the nation as a "*community*, because, regardless of the actual inequality and exploitation that may prevail in each, the nation is always conceived as a deep, horizontal comradeship."[10] Instead, Colombian elites viewed the poor as foul smelling and despicable and held for them a general distaste, hardly a horizontal comradeship. Yet in this deeply religious, moral, and hierarchical society the elites also felt compassion for the poor and possessed an altruistic desire to save lives and uplift and incorporate the degenerate poor into the national community. Through public health, charity, and moral reform they would impart the "proper" moral conduct and physical soundness that were required in order for individuals to contribute as healthy, useful, and productive citizens of an organic society. Thus, the poor would be incorporated, at a still unequal level, because of the responsibility felt on the part of members of the elite to guide and care for their social inferiors in the community and nation they were obliged to share. Social inferiors were not to participate as effective, "political" citizens. Their superiors, or patrons, would exercise that role, which they embraced as part of their duty to serve the common good. Tantamount to the nation-building process and the creation of a sense of nationalism, then, was the need to create harmony, not conflict between groups. Through public health reforms, charity, and moral instruction a hierarchical, harmonious social order was to be maintained in a time of rapid social and economic change. By this means would an organic community and national cohesion be attained.

Racial and National Degeneration

Though Núñez, the Nationalists, and most elite individuals did not abandon Liberal principles, they feared excessive liberty and "immorality" among the working classes, members of which were also potential carriers of deadly diseases. In fact, most elites believed that physical illnesses were virtually indistinguishable from *enfermedades morales* (moral illnesses), all of which resulted in the degeneration of the Colombian race. Colombians lived in a personal and relational world that was based on racial and social inequality and brought together through paternalism and reciprocity. The elites adhered to this organic approach to society as well as the scientific racism of positivism as they examined the social and moral condition of the national character.[11] They viewed their society as a degenerating social organism, plagued with physical and moral illnesses. They spoke of a decaying Colombian race, whereby the term *raza* (race) was used to refer to the population as a whole, a collective character rather than a particular racial group. It was a *raza mestiza*, a truly mixed race, formed from white Europeans, indigenous American groups, and black slaves from Africa. Indeed, there were far fewer "pure" Indians who survived conquest and the subsequent depopulation in Colombia than in regions such as Mexico, Guatemala, and Peru, where larger and more advanced pre-Columbian civilizations had existed. There were also fewer slaves in Colombia than in countries such as Brazil and Cuba, whose economies were based on plantation labor. The vast majority of the Colombian population was of mixed race, and it was the majority of this population whom the elites, who considered themselves white even if in reality they were products of miscegenation, perceived as degenerate.

Colombian elites, most of whom had white, European ancestry, believed in the existence of natural inequalities. By virtue of their "purity of blood" as well as their culture and higher education, which were viewed as racial attributes, they believed they possessed qualities superior to those of the indigenous and mixed race. In 1861 José María Samper, for instance, defined Colombian society as one formed by a "stratification" whose "strata" were "the numerous and varied races and castes, resulting from very complicated crossings." The "white race," he declared, "predominated" due to its "intelligence and moral faculties."[12] The poor, mixed, mestizo race, on the other hand, was a *raza degenerada*, a degenerate race, a *raza desgraciada*, an unfortunate, disagreeable, and disgraced race. Indigenous people and mestizos were characterized by many elites as *indolente* (indolent), *malicioso* (malicious), *estúpido* (stupid). They were "intellectually deficient," "barbaric," "uncultured," "immoral," "alcoholic," "disorderly," "disdainful," and dishonorable, not to be trusted.[13]

Race, class, morality, and poverty, then, were intimately linked. Class was principally a cultural concept in Colombia from the middle of the nineteenth century to at least the third decade of the twentieth century. The world of the elite was divided into moral categories, and the elites expressed anxiety about the immoral poor, often referred to as *indios* because of the connection between race and class. They differentiated the contaminated from the cleansed, the honorable from the unprincipled, the slothful from the diligent, the virtuous from the licentious, and the worthy from the unworthy.

The use of moral criteria to distinguish the *gente decente* from *el pueblo*, the lower classes or rabble, was intimately connected to the elites' view of poverty and the physical illnesses that increasingly ravaged the poor. Influenced by Enlightenment thought and reflecting views then espoused in Europe and the United States, Colombian elites, beginning in the late eighteenth century, underwent an ideological shift from traditional Catholic notions regarding the poor and charity. Throughout most of the colonial period, all paupers were viewed as God's poor who possessed the right to receive alms. By the late nineteenth century many elites understood poverty to be more nearly the result of the failure of individuals to lead their lives as they should, in a responsible and honorable fashion, than as a social condition caused by a dearth of material resources at the disposal of many. Though their ideas were not as "scientific" and systematically executed as in Europe and the United States, particularly during the Progressive Era, Colombian elites began to distinguish the "deserving" from the "undeserving," largely based on a work ethic. The "worthy" were the shame-faced poor who were honorable and too proud to beg, and the "unworthy" were those whose poverty and physical sicknesses stemmed only from personal and moral failings.[14] For example, in 1897 Raimundo Ordoñez, a priest, asserted his conviction that "a certain class of people live in a state of poverty because they loathe work and find it degrading." This "vandalism engenders all sorts of vices and disorder."[15] The achievement of *civilización* required, above all, not *desarrollo económico* (economic development) but *moralidad* (morality). The achievement of "civilization" required work rather than habits of indolence, sloth, and extravagant spending, and work was conceived of as a moral and religious virtue.

Ordoñez was especially critical of what he viewed as the many immoral parents who, instead of fulfilling their duty to maintain stable families, merely "bequeathed to society" a *progenie degenerada* (degenerate progeny).[16] As in other Latin American countries, family was often used as a metaphor for the nation.[17] Conservative ex-president Mariano Ospina believed that impoverished families produced the "impoverishment of the nation" and "degraded the national character."[18] In Colombia, then, the social question and the question of nation building were moral questions that centered on the formation of ideal families. They were questions of national character, which depended on individual character, and individual character was measured by moral worth.

What most troubled Ospina and many other elites was the widespread habit among families to spend beyond their means. He denounced those whose spending did not correspond to their position on the social ladder and attributed it to their *vanidad* (vanity), *debilidad de carácter* (weakness of character), *infatuación* (infatuation), *ociosidad* (idleness), and *egoismo* (selfishness): "One should clothe, feed, shelter, and entertain oneself in a manner appropriate to one's class." The *pueblo ignorante* (ignorant populace) was the most "inept of judges in this matter and others, as it regarded luxury as excessive spending, without considering whether he who spends has the resources or not."[19] The "habits, caprices, and weaknesses" of mothers were especially to blame for this *llaga social corrosiva* (corrosive social affliction), since mothers were not fulfilling their duty to be prudent in the management of domestic economies and to instill good habits in their children.

Attributing the habit of excessive spending to a lack of moral and religious education on the part of those who practiced it, Ospina believed the cure for this *enfermedad moral* was the inculcation of "good," "Catholic" morals and habits. Clearly elucidating the idea that the family and the nation were intimately connected, he regarded the family as the primary cell of society and believed that moral education was essential to achieve happiness and prosperity within families, which would produce a corresponding regeneration of society. An ordered society depended on ordered families. Critical of the curriculum in schools, where Liberals had allowed the instruction of the doctrines of Bentham and other "immoral" European philosophies, Ospina called upon clerics to impart moral education from the pulpit. Such instruction was to be directed especially to mothers, whose duty it was to pass along such habits as order, love, and prudent spending to their children.[20] Accordingly, families would be up-lifted, society saved, and progress assured. The home thus became a primary space in which moral reform efforts were directed and mothers were to exercise a principal role.

The role of women was central to definitions of the ideal national community. Gendered notions shaped the vision of the roles both men and women were to exercise, but the female, especially she who diverged from the ideal and thus constituted a threat, was perhaps the object of most concern. Men were to con-tribute to family and nation as honorable workers and responsible fathers who provided for their families. Those who engaged in vices such as alcoholism and gambling were deemed obstacles to family and national stability, as resources were squandered and immoral traits were bequeathed to future generations. However, women who deviated from the ideal role as mother and moral author-ity in the private domain of the home caused more alarm. Though prostitution was both a male and female problem, reformers, charitable elites, and medical doctors began to regard prostitution as both a moral and medical problem and directed their reforms primarily at women.

The problem of prostitution must be analyzed in the context of perceived no-tions of family, citizenship, and nation formation.[21] Though prostitution had always existed, the conception of prostitution began to be reconfigured as the discourse was medicalized so that prostitution and the spread of venereal dis-eases could be regarded as perilous to society. By the 1880s an ideological climate had emerged whereby Colombian elites were increasingly amenable to a more favorable embrace of scientific investigation and state involvement in public health. A new generation of public health physicians, *higienistas*, was more ap-prised of modern scientific and medical advances, including the germ theory. Just as economic trade with the North Atlantic world was expanding, so too was the exchange of ideas. More frequently, elites were reading the political, philo-sophical, and medical treatises published in Western Europe and the United States and traveling abroad to be educated in France, England, and the United States. Medical professionals and scientists also founded the Colombian Society of Medicine and Natural Sciences, which had connections with the Smithsonian Institution in Washington, D.C.[22]

Increasingly convinced of the utility of modern scientific notions and influ-enced by the positivist school of thought, social Darwinism, and Lamarckian concepts, many medical practitioners and other elites clamored for the initia-tion of well-organized health and public works projects and reforms based on sound scientific principles. Their studies and recommendations increasingly fo-cused on the environmental causes of disease, yet "immoral" habits were still linked to disease. Adapting scientific theories of race and racial degeneration from European thought and applying them to Colombia and its people, this new generation of *higienistas* began to see the connection between the health of each individual and the health of the nation. Indeed, as Josué Gómez, a medical doctor, proclaimed, "The birth of the science of hygiene" was due to an increased knowledge of infectious diseases, a "well-developed spirit of humanity that day by day placed greater value on human life and general well-being," and "perfect comprehension of the economic fact that national health is national wealth."[23]

Since venereal diseases spread through prostitution and thus weakened bodies, national health and prosperity were endangered. The scope of syphilis in Bogotá, for example, was so far-reaching that doctors José María Lombana Barreneche and Martín Camacho estimated that over 70 percent of the city's youth had been infected by 1909.[24] In 1890 Dr. Gabriel Castañeda emphatically recommended government support of efforts to treat syphilitic patients by arguing the following: "Syphilis is a disease that threatens all of society, and its victims represent a notable loss for the country and its future. It is the youth who . . . contract the disease most frequently. These young people, reduced to weakness and impotence, will bear scarce and valetudinarian descendants, who represent losses for the nation, as the latter requires individuals who are vigorous and suitable for labor."[25]

The peril posed by prostitutes was conceived of not only in medical terms but in moral terms as well. Prostitutes failed to conform to the newly interpreted ideal of women's proper role in society, since they did not carry out the domestic and civilizing duties conferred upon women. They existed in the street, the symbolic and literal antithesis of the home. Though a double standard existed, and men were rarely chastised for engaging the services of prostitutes, men who did so also threatened the family unit, the stabilizing force in society. The Liberal-minded law student Juan Ceballos in 1892 noted that not only did these men neglect the duties they were to perform within their own families, they produced illegitimate descendants (many of whom were abandoned).[26] Thus, the family ideal and the stability of society were endangered, especially since these children often became wards of the state.

Prostitution became a focal point of efforts of the Regeneration governments of the 1890s to reorder and moralize society. A new, professionalized police force was created in 1891 under the direction of José María Marcelino Gilibert, who was contracted from France. The police force was enlarged from fifty to four hundred agents, all of whom were to have a robust physical constitution and be of sound moral character. The mission of the new force was to maintain public security, order, and morality as well as to assist in the duty of maintaining public health. A Division of Security composed of undercover police was established for the purpose of controlling and regulating vice, vagrants, and "suspicious and dangerous people." As part of this campaign to regulate public spaces, customs, and morality in the interests of the nation, agents were to clandestinely enter hotels and secret houses of gambling and prostitution, from where they would record the names and activities of people suspected of engaging in illegal vices. In addition, they closely supervised the activities of beggars and street children. The information recorded was archived in police stations throughout the city and used to pursue vagrants, prostitutes, and other offenders of public morality and order.[27]

These measures were used in an attempt to control the behavior of these "dangerous degenerates" and the space in which they acted. The reorganization of the police force involved the creation of a division that would serve at the disposition of the Central Board of Health. Agents in this division were entrusted with the surveillance and detention of prostitutes and those afflicted with contagious illnesses, who were forcibly subjected to isolation or medical examinations and treatment. The specific focus on removing prostitutes found in the vicinity of schools and other public spaces where public morality might be offended (and children corrupted) demonstrates the desire of the state to impose moral convictions when authorities perceived a threat to the common good. The ultimate goal, then, was national progress, not merely for those at the top of the social scale but for the entire social organism.

Although Colombian *higienistas* began to focus more on bodies and the environment beginning in the late 1880s with the rise of the germ theory and the public health movement throughout the Western world, they still believed that physical ills were intimately connected to moral ills. In expressly racist terminology Gómez contended in 1898 that the indigenous race was "shrinking in stature and weight, and this relates directly to the Indians' incapacity to work, habitual state of stupor and indifference, and intellectual poverty." Indians, "whose dark eyes had a malicious and suspicious look," were "visibly decaying; their energy, will, and firmness of character have disappeared."[28] Though he did attribute the recurrence of disease in part to the high cost of living and the lack of access to water, ultimately he viewed the poor as responsible for their own misery and disease.

The pessimism of the elites might have been exacerbated by the European degeneration theories they were reading. The latter saw in race mixture the ultimate loss of "white" qualities and the subsequent retrogression of the race, rendering the countries of mixed races incapable of democratic political organization and progress. Yet Colombian elites adapted such theories and possessed a ray of hope that the race might be improved.[29] Optimism among elites was often grounded in the Lamarckian conviction that acquired traits could be transmitted from generation to generation. Just as negative traits such as an inclination toward crime, indolence, drinking, and uncleanliness could be transmitted, so too could positive traits, including honor, hard work, sobriety, and cleanliness.

Yet the elites lacked faith in the poor. They were considered to be dirty and to prefer a life in the streets as opposed to honorable behavior that would serve to support themselves and their families. Obsessed with the physical appearance and odors emanating from the poor, Gómez declared that throughout the streets could be observed people who were "full of vile insects" and from whom emanated "an unbearable odor." This class of rabble, declared Gómez, engaged in gambling, drinking, and sloth. These people constituted "the soul of the population," as they provided soldiers and workers and served as parents to new generations. The soul of the population was dying. Speaking of Bogotá, Gómez proclaimed that "the center of the city resembles a veritable cemetery of the living . . . that announces to visitors that it is a true place of death."[30]

Perceiving the poor as they did, the elite could possess nothing but a lack of confidence in the poor who roamed the streets. The latter could not be trusted to engage in honorable work or to raise healthy, virtuous children. Members of the elite postulated that certainly the poor, as inferior beings, could never achieve the same level of culture, education, and civilization as the superior elite. Equality was not possible. Poverty, a moral condition, would always exist, but the poor could be improved.

Despite a generalized belief in degeneration, reformers believed that individuals could be educated and uplifted, but only to a certain level. They would need to be guided. The inculcation of good moral habits, then, was essential to the creation of the "imagined" community and national progress, which was understood not fundamentally in economic terms but as the antithesis of degeneration. The focus on morality in a personal, hierarchical society must be emphasized in the Colombian case, in contrast to the Protestant outlook of reformers in the United States during the Progressive Era. Imbued with Catholicism, sentiments of abnegation, and patriotism, the elites felt that they had a duty to guide, care for, and incorporate the poor, despite or because of this general aversion. They were driven by fear and disgust, by a paternalistic concern for those less fortunate, and by a dream of order, harmony, and national progress.

Regeneration and the Vision of a Hierarchical, Fraternal, National Community

The need to create a moral, national character was paramount during the Regeneration period. To do so, the Nationalist Party not only fortified the power of the police but strengthened the power and influence of the Church and declared Catholicism the official religion of the country. The Church and the Conservative press and elites steadfastly clamored for a *regeneración de la raza*.[31] The Conservative *La Caridad*, for instance, declared the need for "moral and social regeneration" through religion.[32] Religion began to be viewed as fundamental to the political, economic, and social order, all of which depended on moral character. For example, in 1892 Núñez declared that religion was "the basis of internal order, of moral order."[33] Tradition, faith, and religion were to exercise a paramount role in government in order to maintain social unity.[34] Caro criticized a speech made by Liberal Felipe Pérez in which the latter measured progress in material terms by railroads, telegraphs, and schools. Indeed, Caro affirmed, the latter constituted the "movement of cultured nations"; however, "the great necessity of those nations is to better accommodate its customs and institutions to the Christian spirit. What worth do telegraphs and railroads have without education? With telegraphs, railroads, and schools but without religion a nation heads unfailingly to barbarity."[35]

Many members of the Liberal Party, traditionally recognized for their anticlericalism, likewise extolled religion and morality as fundamental to the formation and advancement of society. Ricardo Becerra, for instance, pronounced that "Colombian liberalism, far from being hostile to the true religious spirit, draws inspiration from it and seeks its protection."[36] In his 1896 essay "Libertad y orden" the famous Liberal intellectual Miguel Samper professed, "Moral progress cannot consist, according to our beliefs, save in the more and more faithful, more and more extended practice of the precepts and maxims of Christianity."[37]

Among those precepts were a belief in natural inequality and the favorable view of a hierarchical social order. Miguel Samper is recognized in the historiography on Colombia for his continued adherence to classical economic liberalism.[38] In the political and social realms, however, he did not embrace universal suffrage and equality. Like most of his Liberal and Conservative counterparts, he believed in the existence of natural inequalities and differentiation based on individual talent and faculties, personal experience, and tradition.[39] The Conservative Caro, a chief exponent of the belief in natural inequalities, affirmed, "Christian doctrine assumes inequality," and "the inequality of conditions is necessary in society, in all societies" or there "would not be harmony" or progress.[40]

The principal challenge, then, was to secure a social and moral order in which each contributed according to his or her station. The late-nineteenth-century Colombian elite, led by Núñez and Caro, sought balance between individual rights and the common good, between liberty and order. The *gente culta* viewed society as hierarchical and organic, and they searched for a national community based on what I have deemed individual collectivism, individual action, and independence accompanied by a responsibility to contribute to the collectivity. They continued to champion a respect for individual rights to property, free trade, and, most of all, self-reliance. However, what concerned the elite was an excessive individualism characterized by selfishness, greed, and slothfulness.

Individuals were viewed as parts of the collectivity who possessed a duty to contribute to the social organism.

Thus, the elite had a vision of a nation based on individual collectivism in which a spirit of association prevailed. By this means would be formed a community, not a socialist community but a collectivity of individuals who labored independently to obtain property and resources to support themselves, their families, and the common good. Indeed, individual initiative was stressed, yet the elite sought to evade selfishness and an individualism run amok. Individual initiative was to be accompanied by a duty to contribute to the collective whole. Those who failed to do so not only neglected to contribute to the nation but constituted a burden on society.

The *gente superior* possessed a duty as individuals to paternalistically guide and assist their inferiors in the community and nation they were obliged to share. The language used in an 1893 *Colombia Cristiana* article encouraging the *clases superiores* to provide moral guidance to their inferiors exemplifies the importance placed on the national community. The elites should provide guidance to the poor in order to support "the dignity of the society in which they live, the society of which they form a part."[41] The Regeneration Nationalists, as well as intellectual and ecclesiastical elites, then, sought to direct the lives of the poor from the street to the home, the former a symbol of danger and immorality and the latter a bastion of stability and virtue. They would do so through the media, the pulpit, and the schools, most of which were administered by the Church and in which Catholic instruction was required. They also embraced private charity and public health campaigns in an attempt to incorporate the *degenerados* into the national community.

As a moral question in a personal and hierarchical society, the remedy for the perceived degeneration and for the social question involved the abnegation of a disinterested elite who felt it their duty as part of an organic community to serve the poor and the nation through moral instruction, public health campaigns, and the exercise of charity. They did so not merely out of a self-interested desire to achieve "social control" and maintain their dominant position, as posited by much of the scholarship on charity and moral reform, but *para el bien común* (for the common good).[42]

The underlying disdain for sloth and the belief that social organization was based on reciprocity, whereby an individual should contribute to the collective whole according to his or her station, shaped the preference for private charity rather than other alternatives, such as a system of social welfare administered by the state, as a prescription to alleviate the ills of society. Furthermore and foremost, late-nineteenth-century Colombian elites were wary of the state and the administration of social assistance by impersonal bureaucrats, for they lived in a hierarchical, relational universe in which they felt it their patriotic and Christian duty to paternalistically help those with whom they held personal, patron-client-type bonds.

Responsibility, sacrifice, disinterest, and patriotism were the values embraced by the elite as they served the poor and their country.[43] José María Samper avowed in 1881 that the "profound passion" that had always "stirred my soul" was "that of achieving a high glory, founded principally on the virtue of patriotism, exalted even to sacrifice, which is the supreme philanthropy of the Christian."[44]

Though the federal government did not institute a system of social welfare, it sought to cooperate with the Church, *higienistas*, and private individuals in the establishment of charitable institutions and the coordination of public health activities. Science, medicine, and hygiene became instruments of progress that were used to improve the health of individuals and, especially, the collectivity. As such, public health and charitable institutions were based primarily on the notion of the utility of individuals to the nation rather than on a sense of social justice.[45]

After 1880 a burgeoning class of *higienistas* adopted the role of emissaries between the state and society as they medicalized the discourse on race, citizenship, and nation. As exemplified by the discussion of prostitution and syphilis, this new generation of medical doctors began to see the connection between the health of each individual and the health of the nation. They embarked on campaigns to improve the sanitary conditions of the city, eradicate illnesses, and reform habits that were deemed antithetical to progress. They attempted to avert racial degeneration by scientifically improving the Colombian race.

Science was linked to charity. Medical doctors indeed carved a space for themselves in a changing economic and social environment and became a powerful, professionalized elite.[46] Doctors may have been driven in part by the desire for power, yet they clearly conceived of their role as charitable and patriotic. Medical doctors believed they were, in a sense, "saviors" of the nation contributing to the quest to populate the nation with healthy, productive individuals, improve the race, and define national character. Gómez professed that providing instruction on hygiene was "working for the nation, raising the physical level of man, awakening the human spirit to intellectual toil, and making productive capital out of every man. . . . [I]t is, finally, to make men of character, lift the soul of the country."[47]

Though fragmentation in the organization of public health remained a problem, the Regeneration governments provided a space in which medical elites could begin to consolidate public health as a national responsibility. In the realm of social assistance and moral reform the Regeneration leaders primarily called on the Church and the charity of private individuals. Charitable institutions were viewed as essential to the nation-building process, and elites embraced charitable activity as a duty.[48] During the Regeneration several private charitable institutions were created, administered, and supported primarily by religious orders and various elite individuals, Conservative and Liberal alike, while the state made modest financial contributions.[49] Pope Leo XIII's 1891 encyclical, *Rerum Novarum*, gave added impulse to the trend, but the convictions were not novel, and the process was already under way. In his encyclical the pope called attention to the working classes of the world and sought to counter socialism by urging the formation of Catholic associations to protect the working classes. In Colombia the pope's words resonated. *El Correo Nacional* proclaimed in 1892 that "the arduous industrial conflicts, and the frightening problems that proletarianism is implanting throughout the world, will not be resolved by economists; the solution to those problems . . . will descend from the Vatican, with the assistance and through the ministry of innumerable Catholic associations that are in possession of the sovereign formula for all social equations: charity."[50]

The charitable impulse continued in the Conservative era that followed the Regeneration governments and lasted until 1930. Over a hundred mutual aid societies and charitable associations and institutions were created in Bogotá, a city of scarcely three hundred thousand by 1930.[51] In their charitable endeavors elites displayed the fulfillment of their civic and religious obligations to the national community.

Women were particularly active in charitable activity. Considered as moral authorities, elite women were often called upon or took the initiative themselves to form charitable institutions, as charitable activities were increasingly viewed as acceptable within the women's sphere, a symbolic extension of family to the public realm. Through charitable activity women exercised their patriotic and social duty to assist the poor. This important mission of women prompted some elites, mostly Liberals, to deem the education of women as imperative. The education they received would coincide with their social status. They argued that higher education should be available to women of the upper social strata and, given widespread opposition, defended their position not merely on the basis of women's individual rights but on the basis of their duties to the nation. Though he considered it blasphemous to believe women should not be granted the right to an education for their own edification, Rafael Merchán proclaimed that if women were not "worthy of education themselves, then they are worthy of it as a gift to man." Citing the scientific knowledge of the day, he stated that moral and intellectual as well as physical traits were hereditary; thus it was imperative to educate women in order to ensure that morality and intellect were passed to future generations so that national development could be achieved.[52]

By participating in charitable endeavors and arguing for expanded education, women were themselves helping to define the national character and the duties of motherhood. In order for women of the lower classes to be capable of fulfilling their role in society as mothers and as workers, they needed to be prepared to live independently. Priscila de Núñez, Dolores T. de Aguiar, and Mercedes C. de Aldana wrote to Congress, declaring, "Women, honorable Representatives, are called by civilization to accomplish great destinies in society. As a mother, she forms the heart of man and inculcates him with his first ideas, good or bad. If we want to form a nation of men who are free, honorable, laborious, and devoted to progress and civilization, we should begin by uplifting the woman, educating her, and teaching her the law of work that will grant her independence and well-being."[53]

The charitable efforts of women were often directed toward other women, especially those in danger of "falling" into a life of vice and to mothers unable to care for their children. For example, Ana V. de Carrasquilla and Josefina Rivas Groot were part of a "select group of ladies" on the Board of the Domestic Protectorate, created in 1916. It provided women with temporary shelter, recreation, and "classes for actual life," that of domestic service in the homes of their social superiors. In conjunction with a religious order that operated the shelter on a daily basis, the *damas distinguidas* (distinguished ladies) of Bogotá intended to ensure the moral formation as well as the economic betterment of young girls. They would thus form "women useful for the family, for society, and for the Nation."[54] Self-interest was also apparent, as they also assured themselves of a pool of well-trained servants.

The women of Bogotá's high society also sought to protect the servant class (and elite families) by serving on the board of the House of Mary for the Relief of Servants, founded by Salesian clergymen. The house, founded in 1924, was designed to give shelter to young female migrants who came to the city in search of work, thus protecting them from "the dangers contained within the city." The shelter would "save them from a life that would lead to the loss of their moral and material health" not only by keeping them from the dangers of the streets but by providing assistance in case of illness.[55] Such institutions would also prevent prostitution and the spread of disease.[56] They were contrived to prevent the numerous disease-carrying servants from entering the homes of the upper classes. The female board members declared that servants were "a grave danger that threatens society." Appealing to Congress for a subsidy, the board members asserted that the House of Mary lends "immense benefits . . . to society and to hygiene" by "saving our homes from all forms of contagion."[57]

Charity empowered the women of Bogotá's high society. It allowed women to gain organizational, administrative, and financial experience as well as authority in society when most other avenues were closed to them, thus serving as a means by which other doors might be opened to them. Furthermore, women took pride in their charitable activities, felt useful, and believed they were fulfilling a patriotic duty.

Charitable institutions served to reproduce the hierarchical order of society. However, elites did not engage in charitable activity to achieve social control in a repressive manner as a means by which to maintain their domination. Their efforts were infused with paternalism and a contempt for the poor who lay outside the realms of civility, yet they were also well intentioned and rooted in a genuine humanitarian desire to uplift and incorporate the poor. They believed it their noble duty, as educated and cultured elites, to participate in charitable activities in order to serve the nation and contribute to the common good. They viewed society as an organic whole in which each person was part of a collectivity and was to contribute according to his or her social position.

It was during the Regeneration that Colombian elites embarked on a project to create a national consciousness, and charity and morality were essential to their vision. The historian James O. Morris has stated that consensus is "fundamentally a human value involving attitudes and relationships among people."[58] It was attitudes about morality and personal relationships based on reciprocity and hierarchy that would achieve consensus in Colombia. Through charity as well as health and moral reforms the elite sought a reformation involving "moral and corporal hygiene" in order to teach honorable behavior and create healthy bodies that were requisites for social citizenship and national progress.[59] They sought to form healthy, moral, and industrious citizens that would divert Colombia from the path of barbarity and degeneration to that of civilization and progress.

Charity and reform served to reproduce the hierarchical order of society. Charity is inherently hierarchical, and in Colombia it served to perpetuate gender and class inequalities.[60] However, the elite did not engage in a project of social control. They did not see a problem of control but one of degeneration. The elites in Bogotá were deeply pessimistic about the Colombian *raza*. Yet in their Catholic, moral, and personal world they sought to incorporate the poor. Scholars of Latin America have generally chided the elites for their failure to "modernize." However, in some ways the elites of Colombia were struggling against modernization. They were desirous of national progress, but progress in their eyes was more moral than material. Therefore, they elected to retain a hierarchical society based on personal bonds and reciprocity. In the face of liberalism they feared the tendency toward division, fragmentation, and an atomistic society. Indeed, Safford and Palacios asserted that nationalism during the Regeneration had an "anticapitalist tint."[61] Instead, Colombian elites sought what I have called individual collectivism. Individual freedoms were to be accompanied by responsibilities. These included the responsibility to be self-reliant as well as to contribute to the common good. One was not to be a burden on society but should participate in the community.

Until the 1930s Bogotá was still a society based primarily on traditional, hierarchical, and personal relationships. The elites felt a sense of obligation to the poor, whom they hoped would serve them with obedience and respect. As industrial activity expanded and society became increasingly complex as economic and material concerns became more prevalent, the personal basis of society began to wane. Perhaps the elites began to wonder whether the poor might no longer be worth their efforts or worthy of their compassion. By 1946 the elites who served in the public realm for the common good were losing their sense of responsibility and duty as the nation erupted into "La Violencia."[62] Subsequently, the history of the nation was characterized by violence and conflict and by fragmentation and social division, causing people to wonder whether or not Colombians today have a true sense of nationalism and national identity. This is not the Colombia envisioned during the Regeneration. In their charitable endeavors from 1884 to 1930 Colombian elites desired to incorporate the poor into the imagined community. They sought to create the fraternity and the common values and obligations that would bind the community together. Through them they could paternalistically create a consensus of values, preserve hierarchy, and maintain a moral and cohesive social organism that would ensure progress for the nation. A general harmony between social classes, church and state, and Liberals and Conservatives indeed prevailed during the period from 1904 to 1930. It seems that the exercise of charity may have contributed to that harmony.

NOTES

1. Frank Safford and Marco Palacios, *Colombia: Fragmented Land, Divided Society* (Oxford, 2002), ix.

2. Comment of Jaime Jaramillo Uribe in a roundtable discussion entitled "Regiones y nación en el siglo XIX," the proceedings of which are published in *Aspectos polémicos de la historia colombiana del siglo XIX* (Bogotá, 1983).

3. David Bushnell, *The Making of Modern Colombia: A Nation in Spite of Itself* (Berkeley, 1993), viii. On the development and scope of Colombian nationalism see Hans-Joachim König, *En el camino hacia la nación: Nacionalismo en el proceso de formación del estado y de la nación de la Nueva Granada, 1750 a 1856* (Santafé de Bogotá, 1988).

4. See, for example, Dain Borges, "'Puffy, Ugly, Slothful and Inert': Degeneration in Brazilian Social Thought, 1880–1940," *Journal of Latin American Studies* 25, no. 2 (May 1993): 235–56.

5. Donna Guy, *Sex and Danger in Buenos Aires: Prostitution, Family, and Nation in Argentina* (Lincoln, Neb., 1991). For the case of Mexico see, for example, Katherine Bliss,

Compromised Positions: Prostitution, Public Health, and Gender Politics in Revolutionary Mexico City (University Park, Pa., 2002).

6. Benedict Anderson, *Imagined Communities: Reflections on the Origin and Spread of Nationalism* (London, 1991), 6.

7. See König, *En el camino hacia la nación*, 28–31, 36–37, for a discussion of the "crisis model of political development," in which concerns about integration and participation become particularly pronounced in the process of modernization and result in a surge of nationalism.

8. For a synthesis of the "crisis of liberalism" see Jaime Jaramillo Uribe, *El pensamiento colombiano en el siglo XIX* (Bogotá, 1996), chaps. 15–19. See also, for example, Miguel Antonio Caro, *Escritos políticos*, ed. Carlos Valderrama Andrade (Bogotá, 1990).

9. Some of the arguments and analysis presented here are elaborated on in Hayley Froysland, "*Para el bien común*: Charity, Health, and Moral Order in Bogotá, Colombia, 1850–1936," Ph.D. dissertation, University of Virginia, 2002.

10. Anderson, *Imagined Communities*, 7.

11. Martin Stabb provides an analysis of essays that reflect the adherence to "social organicism" and the embrace of positivism's scientific and racist approach to political and social problems in other Spanish American countries (*In Quest of Identity: Patterns in the Spanish American Essay of Ideas, 1890–1960* [Chapel Hill, N.C., 1967], chap. 1). See also Nancy Stepan, "*The Hour of Eugenics*": *Race, Gender, and Nation in Latin America* (Ithaca, N.Y., 1991); Eduardo A. Zimmerman, "Racial Ideas and Social Reform: Argentina, 1890–1916," *Hispanic American Historical Review* 72, no. 1 (February 1992): 23–46; Borges, "Puffy, Ugly, Slothful and Inert."

12. José María Samper, *Ensayo sobre las revoluciones políticas y la condición social de las repúblicas colombianas (hispano-americanas)* (Bogotá, 1969), 99, 100.

13. For detailed descriptions of the elites' perceptions of the physical characteristics and moral habits of the indigenous population see, for example, Rufino Cuervo, *Documentos oficiales para la historia y la estadística de la Nueva Granada* (Bogotá, 1843); Manuel Uribe Angel, *Geografía y compendio histórico del estado de Antioquia en Colombia* (Paris, 1895); Samper, *Ensayo sobre las revoluciones políticas*; José María Cordovez Moure, *Reminiscencias: Santafé y Bogotá*, 6th ed., vol. 10 (Bogotá, 1942), 157–59, 175–78; and José Domingo Ospina C., *Informe del ministro de gobierno al Congreso de 1890* (Bogotá, 1890), 13.

14. For a discussion of perceptions of the poor and poverty in Europe and the United States see, for example, Gertrude Himmelfarb, *Poverty and Compassion: The Moral Imagination of the Late Victorians* (New York, 1991); Walter I. Trattner, *From Poor Law to Welfare State: A History of Social Welfare in America* (New York, 1984); Paul Boyer, *Urban Masses and Moral Order in America, 1820–1920* (Cambridge, Mass., 1978); and Lori Ginzberg, *Women and the Work of Benevolence: Morality, Politics, and Class in the Nineteenth-Century United States* (New Haven, Conn., 1990). For more on the ideological shift regarding the poor and poverty in Colombia see Froysland, "*Para el bien común*," chap. 3, esp. 119–34.

15. Pbro. Raimundo Ordoñez Y., *Los ricos de nuestros días y la limosna* (Bogotá, 1897), 25.

16. Pbro. Raimundo Ordoñez Y., "No desesperemos," *Colombia Cristiana*, 15 April 1894, 106.

17. See, for example, Guy, *Sex and Danger.*

18. Mariano Ospina, "Conversaciones familiares sobre cuestiones sociales: El lujo," *Repertorio Colombiano* (August 1878).

19. Ibid., 146, 151, 152, 155, 157, 147.

20. Ibid., 151–58.

21. The connection between prostitutes, family, and nation has been analyzed in other Latin American countries in the following accounts: William French, "Prostitutes and Guardian Angels: Women, Work, and the Family in Porfirian Mexico," *Hispanic American Historical Review* (November 1992); Guy, *Sex and Danger*; and Teresita Martínez-Vergne, *Shaping the Discourse on Space: Charity and Its Wards in Nineteenth-Century San Juan, Puerto Rico* (Austin, Tex., 1999).

22. Pedro Ibañez, *Papel Periódico Ilustrado*, 21 September 1884, 47.

23. Josué Gómez, *Las epidemias de Bogotá* (Bogotá, 1898), 86.

24. "Memorial sobre creación de una Junta Central de Higiene," *Repertorio de Medicina y Cirugía*, 15 October 1909, in Roberto de Zubiría C. and Luis A. Santos V., eds., *José María Lombana Barreneche: Ensayo preliminar* (Bogotá, n.d.), 33. See also Adriano Páez to Ramón Gómez, 5 December 1878, in *Revista de los Establecimientos de Beneficencia*, 20 February 1879.

25. Dr. Gabriel Castañeda, médico del servicio de sifilíticas, Hospital de San Juan de Dios, to Carlos Michelsen U., Síndico del Hospital de San Juan de Dios, 1 May 1890, in "Informe del Síndico del Hospital de San Juan de Dios," 10 May 1890, in Bernardino Medina, *Informe del presidente de la Junta General de Beneficencia dirigido al gobernador del departamento* (Bogotá, 1890), 45.

26. Juan Ceballos, *Beneficencia pública* (Bogotá, 1892), 11–12.

27. On the new police force see Carlos Holguín, *Informe del ministro de gobierno al Congreso Constitucional de 1892* (Bogotá, 1892), xliv–xlviii; Gonzalo Mallarino-Constans, "Contrato celebrado entre Gonzalo Mallarino, encargado de negocios de Colombia en París, y M. Constans, ministro del interior de la República francesa," in "Documentos," in ibid., 120–21; Holguín, "Decreto número 1000 de 1891," 5 November 1891, in "Documentos," in ibid., 122–24; José María Gilibert and Pedro M. Corena, "Informes del director y subdirector de la policía nacional," 10 July 1892, in "Documentos," in ibid., 152–63; and Fabio Puyo Vasco, ed., *Historia de Bogotá: Siglo XIX*, vol. 3 (Bogotá, 1988), 124. Interestingly, these police stations were targeted during a riot in 1893. For more information on the riot see David Sowell, "The 1893 *Bogotazo*: Artisans and Public Violence in Late Nineteenth Century Bogotá," *Journal of Latin American Studies* (May 1989); and Froysland, "*Para el bien común*," 209–15.

28. Gómez, *Las epidemias de Bogotá*, 63.

29. Uribe Angel, *Geografía y compendio histórico*, 462, 467, 469, 471. On the rejection of European theories of race mixture in Brazil see Borges, "Puffy, Ugly, Slothful and Inert."

30. Gómez, *Las epidemias de Bogotá*, 6, 7.

31. See, for example, "No desesperemos," *Colombia Cristiana*, 15 April 1894, 106.

32. "El Progreso," *La Caridad*, 15 July 1869, 39.

33. Rafael Núñez quoted in Helen Delpar, *Red against Blue: The Liberal Party in Colombian Politics* (University, Ala., 1981), 78.

34. Jaramillo Uribe, *El pensamiento colombiano*, 292–93, 299–302.

35. Miguel Antonio Caro, "El monstruo inaugural," in *Escritos políticos*, 87.

36. Ricardo Becerra quoted in Delpar, *Red against Blue*, 68–69.

37. Miguel Samper, "Libertad y orden," in José María Samper Brush and Luis Samper Sordo, eds., *Escritos político-económicos* (Bogotá, 1925), 2:300.

38. See, for example, Delpar, *Red against Blue*, 72.

39. Jaramillo Uribe, *El pensamiento colombiano*, 286–89; Samper, "Libertad y orden."

40. Miguel Antonio Caro, "La lucha," in *Escritos políticos*, 247–48.

41. Aisthesis, "Moralidad," *Colombia Cristiana*, 22 October 1893, 342.

42. See, for example, Michel Foucault, *Madness and Civilization: A History of Insanity in the Age of Reason*, trans. Richard Howard (New York, 1965); Michel Foucault, *Discipline and Punish: The Birth of the Prison*, trans. Alan Sheridan (New York, 1979); Frances R. Piven and Richard A. Cloward, *Regulating the Poor: The Functions of Public Welfare* (New York, 1971); and David Rothman, *The Discovery of the Asylum: Social Order and Disorder in the New Republic* (Boston, 1971).

43. "El Progreso," *La Caridad*, 15 July 1869, 39.

44. José María Samper, *Historia de una alma* (Bogotá, 1946), 1:7.

45. Zimmerman, "Racial Ideas and Social Reform," 38.

46. Diana Obregón has argued that doctors engaged in the study of leprosy in Colombia exaggerated the number of and threat posed by lepers in order to serve their own interests of attaining the status of a powerful group. See Diana Obregón, "Del árbol maldito a 'enfermedad curable': Los médicos y la construcción de la lepra en Colombia, 1884–1939," in Marcos Cueto, ed., *Salud, cultura y sociedad en América Latina: Nuevas perspectivas históricas* (Lima, 1996).

47. Gómez, *Las epidemias de Bogotá*, 91.

48. It is worth noting that in the United States it was primarily middle-class reformers, many of whom were professionals, who were responsible for the administration of more scientific social assistance, a significant contrast from the Colombian situation.

49. On the charitable institutions established see Froysland, "*Para el bien común*," chap. 6.

50. Quoted in Mario Aguilera Peña, *Insurgencia urbana en Bogotá* (Bogotá, 1997), 231.

51. See Froysland, "*Para el bien común*," chap. 7 and appendix.

52. Rafael Merchán, *La educación de la mujer* (Bogotá, 1894), 22–23.

53. Priscila de Núñez, Dolores T. de Aguiar, and Mercedes C. de Aldana to congressional representatives, 27 March 1884, *La Abeja*, 1 April 1884, 188–89.

54. Members of the boards of the Círculo Obrero de la Sagrada Familia y Protectorado Doméstico to members of Congress, 24 July 1928, Archivo del Congreso, Cámara, Proyectos, vol. 1 (1928), fols. 105–6.

55. Leonor de Francisco de Huertas et al. to the president of the House of Representatives, 8 October 1927, Archivo del Congreso, Cámara, Proyectos de Ley, vol. 5 (1927), fols. 34r–34v. The letter was signed by numerous female board members and patrons of

the Casa and included women from some of Bogotá's most prominent families, many of whom were related.

56. "Memorial de Padre Jorge Herrán," 12 August 1928 (accompanying "Proyecto de Ley"), 1928, Archivo del Congreso, Cámara, Proyectos, vol. 3 (1928), fols. 70v–71r.

57. Huertas et al., fols. 34r–34v. Sandra Lauderdale Graham discusses servants as carriers of contagion for the case of Rio de Janeiro in *House and Street: The Domestic World of Servants and Masters in Nineteenth-Century Rio de Janeiro* (Austin, Tex., 1988), chap. 5. See also Dain Borges, *The Family in Bahia, Brazil* (Stanford, Calif., 1992), chap. 3. The fear of servants as carriers of contagion was of paramount importance in motivating elite women to participate in such organizations targeted at domestic servants. René de la Pedraja Tomán mentions their moralizing aims in a brief discussion of servant organizations but does not relate them to health and hygiene. The women of the Casa de María Auxiliadora themselves, for example, declared that the shelter was a "social" issue and also one of "hygiene" in the letter from Huertas et al., fol. 35r. See Pedraja Tomán, "Women in Colombian Organizations: A Study in Changing Gender Roles, 1900–1940," *Journal of Women's History* (Spring 1990): 113–15.

58. James O. Morris, *Elites, Intellectuals, and Consensus: A Study on the Social Question and the Industrial Relations System in Chile* (Ithaca, N.Y., 1966), 54.

59. "Los Niños Desamparados," *Cromos*, 4 April 1936.

60. Teresita Martínez-Vergne refers to the inherently hierarchical nature of charity and *beneficencia* (*Shaping the Discourse on Space*, esp. 66, 68–69, 134, 137, 144, 152–55).

61. Safford and Palacios, *Colombia*, 247.

62. Herbert Braun, *The Assassination of Gaitán: Public Life and Urban Violence in Colombia* (Madison, Wisc., 1985).

Revolution and Imagined Communities in Mexico, 1810–1821

ERIC VAN YOUNG

*R*evolutions, especially when they give birth to new nations, eventually generate their own mythologies. New ruling groups need to make these large-scale social and political upheavals seem natural, heroic, legitimate, and just, common people to make sense out of their experiences of internal war, social dislocation, and death. Postrevolutionary social institutions and practices—schools, most obviously, but also the mobilization of armies, the creation of public art, ceremonial occasions, symbolic expressions such as flags, the discourse of the political class, and so forth—collaborate to set the stamp of inevitability on the violent disappearance of the old regime and the emergence of the new. A pantheon of prescient heroes must be sanctified. Great public convulsions inscribed in chaotic events, collective action, blood, and words are then reproduced generation after generation by the guardians of the public memory, including politicians, historians, teachers, writers, and artists. Especially since the emergence of modern revolutionary nationalism in the late-eighteenth-century Atlantic world, these social and political inversions have become tied to the fate of the great invented tribes we call nation-states.

But while revolutionary mythologies create social memory of a certain sort, they may also blur or efface it altogether, so that the act of creative remembering implies selective forgetting as well. Political roads not taken are erased from the maps of officialist history, dissenting voices from the time silenced, and inconvenient social groups airbrushed out of the picture or their actions reconfigured to conform to a neater, idealized scenario. Thus the teleology of revolution explains how and why the existing postrevolutionary reality came to be the only one possible and did not follow some other course. Even the critical social science study of revolutionary upheaval by historians and other scholars after the fact may be pressed into the service of what can be called "outcomism." This would take the form, for example, of the apparently reasonable proposition that because almost all of the Spanish American colonies had become independent nation-states by the third decade of the nineteenth century, the winning of independence and the establishment of republican regimes in its wake were therefore the necessary outcome of the struggles against Spanish dominion. It would follow from this that all social groups swept up in the struggle, apart from those defenders of the Spanish regime overtly opposed to independence, were striving for that result. Such an interpretation of the widespread violence in Spanish America between about 1808 and 1825 fits well with the romance of nationalism as it has emerged over the last two centuries in the West and has even been seen (e.g., by Benedict Anderson, on whom more is to follow) as explaining how nationalism became so deeply embedded in world history more generally since the time of the French Revolution or so. The revolutions that pave the way for new nations are likely to be extremely complex events, however, in which different groups of people, to say nothing of individuals, engage in collective political violence for different reasons, nation making not necessarily foremost among them. This simple idea stands behind the analysis offered here of the process of Mexican independence.

The Anderson Thesis and Mexican Independence

The decade of insurgency in New Spain (as Mexico was known during the colonial era) that resulted in the colony's independence from Spain in 1821 was punctuated by hundreds of attacks by rebels and reputed rebels on peninsular-born Spaniards. These occurred primarily in rural areas, but there were also some famous urban incidents of violence specifically visited upon European Spaniards. One of these took place in Guadalajara in the early winter of 1810–11, when as many as a thousand men, all civilians, were taken to the outskirts of the city by night and slaughtered over the course of about a month.[1] What was the meaning of such sanguinary incidents and, more generally, of the widespread victimization of European-born Spaniards in Mexico during the insurgent decade 1810–21? Can we detect in such episodes signs of even an embryonic Mexican nationalism, embodied in violence directed at ethnically, culturally, and politically marked Others who stood outside the Mexican nation and threatened it? If we cannot detect nationalism in such incidents, then where can we? Or were the Guadalajara killings and other incidents simply urban jacqueries?

As a probative exercise testing for the presence of national consciousness among the population of Mexico as a whole or even among that subset of the colonial population that can be identified as actively participating in the insurgency, this is, admittedly, a somewhat crude formulation. Yet the crudeness of the test is justified by the scarcity of the historical evidence as to just what popular sentiments and political consciousness actually were.[2] The conventional wisdom with regard to Mexican independence developed through generations of quite meticulous historical scholarship is that when independence from Spain came in 1821, and with it the creation of the Mexican nation, it was the outcome of a cross-class and cross-ethnic alliance cemented together with at least a rudimentary nationalist ideology. Furthermore, in this triumphalist narrative the independence movement was represented iconically by the Virgin of Guadalupe, whose invocation bespoke the intense religiosity of Mexican society across ethnic, class, and regional divisions, lending the insurgency its strongly providentialist character. The avatars of this epochal event were the great (and for the most part martyred) Creole and mestizo heroes of the independence struggle, either clerical insurgents such as Miguel Hidalgo, Mariano Matamoros, and José María Morelos or military men such as Ignacio Allende, Juan Aldama, Agustín de Iturbide, Vicente Guerrero, and others.[3] How valid is this interpretive framework, however, and where did the locus of nationalist sentiment actually lie?

To put this in a slightly different way and apply Anderson's now famous formulation, did most common Mexicans of the 1810–21 period "imagine" a community called Mexico, a national entity beyond the reach of their own accustomed horizons of political reference and the apprehension of their own personal experience, which they found "emotionally plausible" and in whose name they might sacrifice themselves or at least show up on time for a battle?[4] An affirmative answer to this question requires us to assume that the discourse of the Creole/mestizo directorate of the insurgency as it evolved over this decade may be taken as a proxy for popular political thinking and, furthermore, that the concrete outcomes of the struggle—the severing of New Spain from the Spanish transatlantic monarchy, the creation of a new nation called Mexico, and the eventual establishment of a republican form of government—were the goals of all or most of its participants. While there is some evidence that such a widespread subaltern conception of politics, with its underlying nationalist sensibility, had developed in Mexico by the middle decades of the nineteenth century, there is little support for the view that it had come to exist by 1810, or that even by the close of the following decade such a consciousness had been forged among large groups of common people by the personal experience of civil conflict.[5]

One of the great unanswered questions about the history of Mexico after about 1800 or so is when and how widely a sense of national identity did come to stamp the thinking of common Mexicans and how it jostled against other forms of identity—of class, ethnicity, gender, localism, and so forth. If scholars like Florencia Mallon and Peter Guardino are correct, then something in public life changed considerably in Mexico between independence and the Reform of the 1850s, although where the facilitators of those changes are to be looked for is not yet clear, whether in the proliferation of newspapers, the increased accessibility of public schooling, the induction of men into militia units during the endemic internecine political violence, the thickening and extension of market relationships, or other factors. To return to the era of independence, while the thinking of the directorate of the anticolonial insurgency can with some adjustment be enfolded within the broad rubric of an "Atlantic revolutionary/nationalist tradition," popular political thinking, for the most part, cannot.[6] A very basic question about the Mexican independence movement, therefore, is, Who was imagining a community, and what sort of community was it?

Over the two decades since its initial publication Anderson's widely influential book *Imagined Communities* has gained attention for its comparative reach, its historical depth, and the intellectual leverage it has provided scholars in a number of fields for dealing with the etiology and character of nationalism, a force still shaping the modern world even while it is often said to be growing moribund in the face of advancing globalization. For historians of the Latin American independence movements, especially, accustomed to having their objects of study relegated to the periphery in studies of Atlantic nationalism, revolutionary typologies, and state-building processes (Don Doyle and Marco Pamplona have noted this benign neglect in their introductory essay), Anderson's urbane and penetrating essay can be both enlightening and comforting. It not only attempts to provide a broad framework for much of what they seek to explain, but it also imports to the very center of modern nationalism, as its foundational moment, the Spanish American independence process (with roughly contemporaneous events in the Anglo-American colonies and Brazil).[7] The only problem with Anderson's analysis of the Spanish American independence process, and in this case specifically of Mexican independence, is that his argument does not fit the facts or fits them only very imperfectly. One of his major errors stems from the assumption that elite political discourse among the group he calls the "creole pioneers" is a close proxy for subaltern views of politics and that if one plausibly interprets the former, the work of interpreting the latter is done, ipso facto. This assumption apparently springs in turn from an implicit theoretical proposition about the relationship of elites to masses in revolutionary settings: that leaders, nominal though their leadership may prove in the long run, nonetheless speak for their followers in the short run and in so speaking mold their followers' thinking while at the same time "representing" them in both senses of the word.[8]

What difference does the reincorporation of the colonial "masses" on their own ideological terms make?[9] The most important difference is to enable us to distinguish in Mexican (and Latin American) independence between the development of a "nationalist movement," the program of a very reduced segment of the population, and nationalism itself, in the sense of a virtually universal affective and cognitive identification with the nation-in-becoming. And this makes a large difference, in turn, in how we view long-term outcomes in political life. But is it fair to hold Anderson to account for constructing an etiology of nationalism for the entire Mexican population when he has so clearly limited himself to the "creole pioneers" and left the other 95 percent or so of Mexicans (and other Latin Americans) in ideological limbo? Ultimately, I think it is fair, because he claims to be describing the birth of a new subjectivity in which people will die for the imagined community that is the nation. If this is so, they must be shown to have imbibed the ideas that supposedly motivated them to move in that direction, even over a long haul. What is at stake here is the answer to whether and when ordinary Mexicans developed a national consciousness in the sense of having a common political and cultural identification not only with the state and its mythology represented as the embodiments of the nation but also laterally, with each other. If such a nationalist sensibility arrived on the scene later (in the latter decades of the nineteenth century, say, or even as late as the years following the Revolution of 1910–20), it becomes somewhat easier to explain the endemic political violence of the century 1820–1920 as the struggle to build an imagined community congruent with the reach of the state and the national territory, to replace strong regional structures with strong class structures, and to reduce or at least smooth out ethnic relations within the country.

There are a number of grounds on which we may criticize Benedict Anderson's treatment of the Spanish American independence movements while still granting that his ideas have greater applicability to other cases. One such reservation arises from Anderson's suggestion of a successional relationship between religion and nationalism as the binding cultural medium among Mexicans and in the history of other emergent national polities, whereas it makes more sense to see them as concurrent and even organically related.[10] As Claudio Lomnitz has noted, however, "Spanish nationalism was . . . based on the national appropriation of the true faith" and its intervention in the New World on forms of religious militancy, so that religion and the genesis of nationalism were interlocked in the Spanish world.[11] More important, however, than the problem of religion in the lack of fit between Anderson's model and the Mexican case is the issue of the social and cultural horizontality Anderson deems essential to the formation of national consciousness. His argument suggests that most elite, literate Mexicans were at the outset of the independence movements already able to think sideways, as it were, imagining a community in which the greatest single common denominator of the members (we may call them citizens at some risk of anachronism) was Mexicanness. Anderson does not seem to mean by this that ethnic, class, regional, and other distinctions had disappeared or been substantially attenuated, leaving a socially and culturally isotropic population, but only that by this time Mexicanness had trumped other markers of identity or was well on its way to doing so. The Mexican nation, in other words, already existed in embryo in the modern sense of the term before its formal constitution as a nation-state and therefore required only a trigger and a sort of technical change in status to bring it forth.

Anderson devotes considerable space in his chapter on Latin America to explaining what the mechanisms of this intellectual integration were. He dismisses the divergence of metropolitan and colonial economic interests, the influence of the Enlightenment, and the advent of liberalism as streams that irrigated the roots of nationalism, emphasizing instead "pilgrim creole functionaries and provincial creole printmen [as playing] the decisive historic role."[12] Anderson adduces as the prime mover of Mexican independence the putative split along social and political lines between Creoles and peninsular Spaniards. Among essential facilitating variables he emphasizes two factors. One of these is the habit of bureaucratic pilgrimages, that is, the geographical and career mobility of colonial functionaries beyond their places of birth, which allowed them to conceive of a "nation." The second is the presence of print media (Anderson's famous "print-capitalism") in the colonial setting, especially the newspapers that produced and diffused, in black and white and all in a common language, knowledge of a wider world and political events and the idea of a potential Mexico waiting to emerge from the chrysalis of colonial New Spain.[13] Between these forces, the nationalist project they fostered, and the mass of the colonial population there was clearly a social disjunction, however, that Anderson himself handles in a rather gingerly fashion, acknowledging the "social thinness" of the Latin American independence movements and the fact that fear of lower-class political mobilizations on the part of Creole elites was a "key factor" in the movements in Venezuela, Mexico, and Peru.[14] When we perceive the slippage between Anderson's framework and the historical facts, however, we begin to see Anderson's model as plausible only if it is situated socially within fairly restricted boundaries. These wider claims shatter when they are stretched to embrace Mexican society as a whole.

Let me turn from this abbreviated and abstract discussion of Anderson's model of the imagined community to the concrete characteristics of the Mexican independence movement to begin to illustrate how, in essence, a nation-state could be formed in the absence of the *generalized* nationalist consciousness Anderson sees as its necessary antecedent. But since a negative proof by itself is not ultimately very interesting, I will also suggest in passing an alternative interpretation of how to resolve the apparent contradiction here, the creation of a nation in the absence of widespread nationalism. The gist of this interpretation of the Mexican independence struggle is that it encompassed at least two separate movements that touched at many points but that can be joined under the conventional rubric of the cross-class, cross-ethnic alliance only at risk of erasing the history of popular insurgency. One of these movements was a nationalist or protonationalist Creole and mestizo project linked to the Atlantic revolutionary/nationalist tradition (although it harbored atavistic elements), which can more or less be accommodated under the imagined community rubric and the heirs of which survived to celebrate the providential deliverance of Mexico, form the new nation, and write its history. Let us pause here for a moment, then, to sketch some of the basic elements of creole nationalism, less by way of seeking a coherent project at its heart than by way of explaining what popular political sensibility was *not*.[15]

A Detour: Creole Patriotism or Nationalism?

The burgeoning nationalism that undergirded Creole projects for independence from Spain was not necessarily linked to the republicanism that pervaded much of the Atlantic world. Indeed, an important subset of Mexican thinkers and statesmen, right through the mid-nineteenth century, advocated monarchy constrained within constitutional forms and at least limited popular representation.[16] A preference for monarchy was the rule within the ranks of the autonomist thinkers before the actual outbreak of the rebellion in 1810. Miguel Hidalgo initially espoused the candidacy of King Ferdinand VII of Spain to be monarch of New Spain, provided his legitimacy could be proved uncompromised, while monarchical projects were frequently proposed by other Creole thinkers as well. Because of the unsettled situation in Spain the issue remained murky until Ferdinand's restoration in 1814.[17] Royalist thinkers and propagandists on both sides of the Atlantic also stressed the religious underpinnings of the Spanish Bourbon monarchy and the king's authority, attempting constantly to hammer this home to the "humble portion of the people" and even stressing the Iberian tradition of quasi-mystical, messianic kingship. Even so, royalist propaganda appeals to these principles of social authority had about them a corporatist, secular, and peculiarly bloodless quality that may have represented the authors' thinking but that were based on a fundamental misapprehension of what the popular classes believed and how they believed it.[18] In this light the continuing discussion of the possibility of inviting King Ferdinand to rule the colony appears more natural, his wide popular acclamation as a messianic figure less bizarre, and the short-lived Mexican Empire (1822–23) of Agustín de Iturbide less cynical and idiosyncratic.[19] On the whole, however, it seems fair to say that, more than monarchy or republicanism or the instrumentalities of state making, what engaged the attention of Creole thinkers most centrally was the concrete issue of political autonomy and behind it the larger question of Mexican nationhood.

Nor was radicalism, whether within a monarchical or a republican framework, a notable characteristic of Mexican political thought. The rebel Act of Independence of 1813, the constitution that took shape the following year, and the loose program associated with them were anything but Jacobin. There is some controversy among modern scholars as to the liberal content of these documents, some claiming that they were essentially quite conservative, others that they followed closely the lines of the French revolutionary constitution of 1793.[20] What we see in the 1814 Constitution of Apatzingán is an insistence on political autonomy from Spain, popular sovereignty, representative forms, separation of powers, an established and exclusive Catholic Church, and so forth. Although there is some scholarly difference of opinion as to whether this charter, which never took effect, exercised an important influence on subsequent Mexican constitution writing or was a complete nullity, it did represent an initial effort to tie into Atlantic world state making.[21]

More interesting from the perspective of comparing elite Creole political worldviews with popular ones and these in turn with an Atlantic revolutionary tradition is the question of emerging Mexican nationhood and its place in the respective thinking of the two Mexican groups. In the thinking of elite Creole ideologues the concept of nationhood occupied the central place that loyalty to the natal community and messianically tinged mystical kingship were to occupy in the thinking of the popular rural masses of the country, as we shall see. The belief in the historical role of the nation-state surely constituted one important point of convergence between Mexican Creole insurgents and the greater Atlantic revolutionary thinking within which their ideas were in part formed, although it was almost entirely absent from popular political ideas and forms of group identification, as was any preoccupation with state making.[22] In Creole thinking the idea of the nation emerged most clearly in propositions about popular sovereignty and state legitimacy, initially during the period of the 1808–10 political crisis in the Spanish Empire triggered by Napoleon's interference in Iberian politics. In 1808 the Creole-dominated city council (*ayuntamiento*) of Mexico City argued in the face of the crisis of the imperial monarchy that the coerced abdications of Spanish monarchs Charles IV and his son Ferdinand VII were null because they were acts of usurpation. Furthermore, the imposition of Joseph Bonaparte as king of Spain was, in the words of the *ayuntamiento*, "contrary to the rights of the nation to which no one can give a king if it is not . . . by the universal consent of the people."[23]

A contractualist view of monarchical authority and the idea of immanent popular sovereignty associated with it can be traced back in Spanish political thinking to the sixteenth-century writers Francisco de Vitoria and Francisco Suárez. These ideas were reinforced and elaborated in the eighteenth century in the writing of natural-law theorist Samuel Pufendorf and others and were espoused strongly in Mexico by a number of Creole patriots (among them Fray Servando Teresa de Mier), becoming in their hands an explicit doctrine of national self-determination later echoed in various pronouncements by Father José María Morelos and in the official discourse of the nation. This rather abstract idea was buttressed in the Mexican case by the notion that Mexico was not, in fact, a *new* nation at all but an ancient one whose rightful monarchs had been usurped and subjugated illegitimately. Thus the 1813 Mexican declaration of independence specified that the country was to "recover the exercise of its usurped sovereignty."[24] As with constitutional forms, however, there is little if any evidence to indicate that Creole ideas about nationhood, popular sovereignty, emerging Mexicanness, and citizenship resonated in any but the dullest register with popular concepts of personal or community identity.

The Creole patriotism whose origins David Brading has traced so interestingly and that began developing toward a genuine nationalism in the decades after independence was a very different ideology from the localist rural and indigenous worldview often linked to messianic expectation and mystical kingship. In fact, Creole patriotism was undergirded by certain racist ideas regarding the indigenous peoples of New Spain and their "degraded" condition at the close of the colonial period, even while many Creole thinkers attempted to appropriate a noble (pre-Columbian) indigenous past for purposes of nation building. Creole ambivalence about indigenous Mexicans originated in the attempt of Creole ideologues to distance themselves from the stain of race mixture (*mestizaje*) and the prevailing negative pseudoscientific ideas about the nature of man in the New World, concepts elaborated and popularized by European writers of the time such as the comte de Buffon, Abbé Raynal, Cornelius de Pauw, and William Robertson.[25] Creole thinking of the independence era was shot through with an attempt to create a Mexican nation, even if not yet with coherent nationalist imagery. The locus of community for most Creole autonomist thinkers was in the nation, and the struggle by them and their ideological heirs throughout the next 150 years was to invent a coherent ideology and a state structure congruent with their community of sentiment.

The second movement, largely airbrushed out of modern historical accounts, its goals hardly ever articulated and producing no coherent program, embraced much of the humble and rural population of the country in a struggle to preserve the "habitus" and autonomy of village life as well as forms of individual and group identity in which ethnicity, locality, and religious sensibility were tightly interwoven.[26] While the object of the second struggle may not have been hostile to a nationalist sensibility or project, it was at best indifferent to it. The two tendencies were not isolated from each other ideologically, militarily, or socially, although what I choose to emphasize for present purposes is their difference. I will look briefly at four indicators of the relationship of the Mexican popular sectors in the independence struggle, especially country people, to the tendencies of the Atlantic revolutionary/nationalist project: (1) literacy and the likely reach of print-capitalism; (2) the social geography of insurgency; (3) the choreography of village uprising between 1810 and 1821; and (4) the phenomena of messianism and naive monarchism. What we will have at the end of this treatment is an overall pattern suggesting the difference between the imagined community of an Atlantic revolutionary/nationalist tradition and the lived community of rural Mexico at the transition from colony to nation-state. In the end the difference was one between two communities imagined in different ways.

Social and Cultural Characteristics of the Mexican Insurgency

Literacy and the Social Reach of Print-Capitalism

If the simultaneous communion represented by newspaper, book, and pamphlet reading in a common language (in this case, Spanish), which Anderson associates with the advent of capitalism, is essential to the forging of nationalist sensibility, the basic questions to ask with regard to the nature of Mexican independence as a nation-building project are, Who was reading newspapers and/or books? What was the social and spatial reach of such information (which is not necessarily the same thing)?

The literacy rate in New Spain around 1810, at a guess, could not have been much higher than 10 percent overall, with much of the literate population compressed spatially into the cities and socially into the upper reaches of the social hierarchy, so that rural literacy must have been considerably lower.[27] In the area of Oaxaca, in the heavily indigenous southeastern part of the country, for example, reading and writing were limited to indigenous nobles and notaries throughout the colonial period. Even the ability to sign one's name was limited among indigenous *cabildo* (town council) members in Cuernavaca during the late eighteenth century.[28] Keen to make an Andersonian argument (without citing Anderson, as far as I can tell) that a "modern revolutionary movement" in Spanish America (and, presumably, the nationalist sensibility that preceded and accompanied it) required a relatively high degree of literacy and a significant development of printing, the late François-Xavier Guerra implied, though he provided no proof, that literacy levels were quite high in late colonial New Spain, although his case is much the strongest for urban areas.[29] By way of comparison, around the time of the French Revolution estimates of male literacy in the western part of France (excluding Normandy) ranged from something under 40 percent to less than 10 percent, with the large gap between urban and rural rates putting the latter down toward the 10 percent figure. Perhaps a more apt comparison of Mexican literacy rates would be with Russia in the 1860s, when rural literacy stood at about 6 percent, only to rise to around 20 percent by 1900 or so. The striking contrast, not surprisingly, is that between Mexico and New England, which had achieved a male literacy rate of no less than 90 percent by 1790 or so and where the imagined community model works much better on all counts.[30] These literacy estimates do suggest, at a minimum, that the situation with regard to the "imagining" of Mexico on the basis of a burgeoning nationalist mind-set common to both the Creole elite and the mass of common people was not as sanguine as Anderson or even Guerra have painted it. And as for the indigenous peoples who made up nearly two-thirds of the Mexican population at the end of the colonial period, not only was literacy rare, but rural schools were notoriously indifferent or bad in quality, and rates of monolingual Indian-language speech were still quite elevated.

The Social Geography of Insurgency

When common people took up arms during the period 1810–21, what did they actually do? And is their behavior consonant with the idea that they were imagining a community whose outlines corresponded to a notional Mexican nation-state? A close look at the historical record reveals that collective political violence in large parts of the country reflected anything but a nationalist sensibility.

Several lines of evidence suggest strongly that not only did popular and elite rebels have in mind substantially different and even mutually contradictory agendas when they took up arms against the Spanish colonial regime but also that much of the accepted wisdom about the social composition of the insurgent movement is mistaken. In ethnocultural terms the popular component of the independence movement has been characterized by most historians primarily as mestizo and secondarily as Creole (i.e., Mexican-born white). Such people rebelled, it is asserted, out of a combination of motives: disenchantment with the late Bourbon dynasty arising out of the crisis of political legitimacy associated with Napoleon's meddling in Spanish politics, resentment against exclusion from political office and the rupture of a tacit colonial compact arising from intraimperial political and fiscal reforms (these issues figure in Anderson's account of Spanish American independence), blocked upward social mobility, a burgeoning nationalist sentiment (Anderson's star player), and a wide variety of economic grievances. Such factors certainly played a part in the origins and process of Mexican independence in a complex tapestry of causation, but they do not by themselves account very well for *popular* insurgency.

My own research on this question indicates that throughout its life, but most especially in its early phases (up to 1814 or so), the popular sector of the insurgent movement was in the main identifiably indigenous as opposed to mestizo in its makeup. Some 55 percent of accused rebels were Indian, 25 percent Spanish (overwhelmingly Creole), 15 percent mestizo, and 5 percent mulatto or black.[31] This corresponds fairly closely to the generally accepted overall ethnic makeup of New Spain at the end of the colonial period, when the population was comprised of about 60 percent Indians, 18 percent whites, and about 22 percent people of mixed ethnicity.[32] Some well-substantiated conclusions from my data on insurgents extend to other variables such as age, marital status, occupation, place of origin, and so forth. To summarize here, the modal rebel of the period turns out to have been a married Indian farmer or rural laborer—a peasant, it is fair to say—about thirty years old (almost elderly by the standards of the time), probably the head of a nuclear family, and most likely captured within sixty miles or so of his house, a two- or three-day trip by foot. One of the most telling of these variables was the distance between home and place of capture, and here there were significant differences among ethnic groups. The clearest of these was between Indians and Spaniards, the former about four times more likely than the latter to be captured within a short distance (say, three hours or so by foot) of their homes. Indians, laborers and farmers, and married men tended generally to stay closest to home, while Spaniards, small merchants and muleteers, and single men wandered farthest afield. The most likely interpretation of this, in my view, hinges on differences in mentality among the groups in question. The most important of these in the present context was a metaphorical political horizon defining the effective limits of people's action in collectivities. Indian peasants, who made up the largest group among the insurgents, were profoundly localocentric in their worldview, and their actions tended to be constrained by the political and affective references characteristic of their mentality, in contrast to the wider-ranging mixed-blood and Spanish groups. There would appear to be a spatial gradient, therefore, corresponding closely to an ethnic one that reflected not the importance of race per se in stimulating or damping collective action but the largely unarticulated views of different groups as to what constituted the appropriate community of reference for such action. Nor can popular political participation during the insurgent decade be reduced to a reflex of economic grievances, since across the Mexican colony similar forms of popular collective action often arose within very different economic environments, while similar economic conditions saw quite different political responses, even within a single community. The ideas and habits of mind of common country people mediated their perception of their material circumstances or even overrode them, producing here an endemic state of unrest, there prolonged passivity.

Consonant with the social geography of popular insurgency just sketched was the behavior of country people in their pueblos in large parts of New Spain once the rebellion had actually begun. Although it was enfolded with myriad other manifestations of rebellion and resistance, the highly localized village riot was one of the prime forms in which humble people acted out their ideas about The Good. It had enjoyed a long history as part of the repertoire of political tools with which they confronted power and attempted to reestablish the equilibrium of rural life when they felt it to be disturbed. In the decade 1810–21 the civil and military authorities of New Spain, and generally unsympathetic observers of the insurgency, often employed vivid metaphors in describing collective political violence of just this kind in the countryside and the rapidity with which it could spread. The most frequently invoked images were those of epidemic, cancer, and fire.[33] If we think in terms of the fire metaphor, on a colony-wide scale the insurgency did not so much ignite the dry tinder of local grievance as grow to subsume smaller conflagrations already burning for some time or reignite blazes only recently extinguished but still smoldering. A local history of long-standing grievance and conflict, intracommunity rivalry and factionalism, and intimate, face-to-face social relations among contending parties most often lay behind the apparently spontaneous eruption of political violence.[34] Where no precedent for political riot existed, widespread public passivity was likely to result, which explains at least in part the relative calm prevailing in the cities of New Spain between 1810 and 1821.[35] Contrary to the fire and epidemic images invoked by many observers, however, many villages tended to *implode* and close in on themselves when they were struck by riot during the insurgency rather than *explode* like infected buboes to contaminate neighboring communities, as the authorities feared they might. The collective mental template for this was the localocentrism to which I have already alluded: the tendency of villagers to see the social and political horizon as extending only as far as the view from their pueblo church tower.

In the heated political atmosphere of the years around 1810 it should therefore come as no surprise that the violent manifestation of local loyalties should emerge even more clearly as a form of political expression. It has often been noted that rural disturbances before 1810 tended for the most part to remain localized, very infrequently coalescing into broader insurrection, which was also true of the independence period proper. As to forms of collective violence, the organization of many village uprisings both before and after 1810 resembled nothing less than rural soviets, or perhaps free communes along Fourierist lines. These cases consisted of short-lived attempts by rural communities apparently to cut their political and other bonds with the outside world and govern themselves in utopian independence. Occasionally, we see in such episodes hints of attacks on local systems of privilege and property, such as occurred in the village rising at Chicontepec in the Huasteca highlands to the northeast of Mexico City in May 1811. Here the evidence of an insurgent program points to the local land-holding structure as the most specific item of grievance, although the explicit expression of agrarian conflict is surprisingly rare in insurgency-era incidents of rural disturbance, much less attacks on landowners or attempts to seize and re-distribute landed property.[36] Local agrarianism was occasionally accompanied by actual or threatened violence directed against non-Indian racial groups and by a highly amplified, almost obsessive concern with local political legitimacy and authority. As a manifestation of the localocentric identity and worldview of peasant communities, we see this village utopianism prefigured in incidents before the outbreak of the independence movement as well as in movements of the 1810–21 period; what changed was the context.

One fairly vivid example of the pueblo-as-soviet during the insurgency is that of the village of San Lorenzo Ixtacoyotla in the district of Zacualtipan near Metztitlán and not far from Chicontepec, also to the northeast of Mexico City, taken by force of royalist arms on 15 November 1811. Although the defenders of the pueblo had virtually no firearms, they had held it as an avowedly insur-gent "commune" for some two months. The major leadership came not from outsiders but from the Indian governor of the pueblo and the local insurgent leaders Luis Vite and Vicente Acosta, both Indians. Other villages in the area were known to the rebels as "cantons," although their action in concert was vir-tually nonexistent. Local roads connecting the insurgent village with other ar-eas were cut not only for tactical reasons but to underline, whether consciously or not, the autochthonous nature of the uprising. Acosta enjoined the village rebels not to believe in or acknowledge the authority of King Ferdinand VII (this was rather unusual), while Vite convinced them that the royalist troops oper-ating in the region "came killing everyone because, since they were *gachupines* [European-born Spaniards], they did not like the local men [*los hijos del pueblo*, literally, the sons of the pueblo] because they are Indians." It was also widely believed by village insurgents in the area that the *gachupines* and other non-Indian locals were allied against the Indian villagers, "and if the non-Indians help the *gachupines*, we have no other support than our Lady of Guadalupe."[37] So we have in many such cases what looks to be the embryonic stage of an in-sular village utopia, substantially cut off from other such communes, acting to expropriate property from non-Indians, and following at least to some degree an ideology of American religious legitimation, ethnic exclusion, and rejection of the colonial state from the top down. What we might call the internal chore-ography of these village uprisings—their interior logic, the patterns of move-ment of their participants, and the sites of public action—also reflects this same localocentrism, that is, a marked tendency to turn inward to protect community integrity instead of turning outward to alter the external political world.

Messianism and Naive Monarchism

A final facet of popular political thinking and behavior worth exploring also points away from an imagined national community, demonstrating forcefully the way localism, ethnicity, religious sensibility, and political ideas were inextricably knotted together for common people. This is the dramatic strain of messianic expectation to be found in subaltern ideas about rebellion, which can be linked to what I have been calling the localocentrism of rural Mexican popular political culture. While ideologues among the elite Creole directorate of the rebels were beginning to struggle with the knotty problems of nationhood, political legitimacy, the nature of the Mexican state, and the question of inclusionary or exclusionary citizenship, the expression of popular insurgent ideas was taking a different course. Fragmentary but powerful evidence points in the direction of a widespread, subterranean messianic expectation focused on the figure of King Ferdinand VII, forced by Napoleon to abdicate the Spanish throne in 1808 and replaced by Napoleon's brother, Joseph Bonaparte. It is fair to say that for several reasons popular beliefs in the redemptive powers of the Spanish king or his surrogates were of a messianic type rather than simply a charismatic pact between absent king and colonial subjects. First, the king himself was never actually present in New Spain, so if his leadership can be seen as charismatic, it was not because it grew out of direct personal contact with a public but was instead of an institutionalized, mythic sort. Second, the person of the Spanish king was clearly held by popular insurgents to possess at least limited magical abilities; if he was not precisely a *roi thaumaturge*, he nevertheless bore the mark of the supernatural.[38] Third, there are elements of chiliastic thinking both in preinsurgency indigenous uprisings and in the long-term cultural etiology of insurgency-era royal messianism, or at least the belief in the return of some sort of religio-cultural hero.

A list of Ferdinand sightings during the years after 1810 would excessively extend this essay, so I will cite just one or two representative instances. Of a group of young Indian men and women from Celaya captured in November 1810 and accused of insurgent activities, for example, all but two clearly believed they were following the orders of the legitimate king of Spain, who was physically present in Mexico, riding about the countryside in a mysterious black coach, and who had himself commanded Father Hidalgo to take up arms against the Spanish colonial authorities. Furthermore, through their village *gobernador* (chief magistrate) the king had enjoined them to kill the viceroy and all other European-born Spaniards and divide their property amongst the poor. Another captured rebel was reported to have said that "a person is coming in a veiled coach, and when people come to see him, they kneel down and go away very happy."[39] The king was masked; he was invisible; he was traveling alone in a closed coach; he was with Father Hidalgo or Ignacio Allende, the priest's lieutenant; he was working in concert with the Virgin of Guadalupe to destroy the Spanish armies. Knowing the depth of these beliefs among the common people, some rebel leaders even feared that word of King Ferdinand's restoration to the Spanish throne in 1814 at the close of the Peninsular War might undermine the loyalty of their Indian followers, so they sought to suppress the news.[40]

Interestingly enough, there were candidates other than King Ferdinand VII (or "El Deseado," the Desired One, as he was known) to whom messianic expectation came to be attached. It is widely believed that the objects of messianic veneration by the indigenous masses of the country were the priests who led the rebellion in its early phases, most especially Miguel Hidalgo and José María Morelos. Apart from a very few scattered references to the imminent return of Hidalgo and Morelos at the head of avenging armies even after their widely publicized deaths at the hands of the royalists, however, there is very little evidence of the sort of apotheosis ("spontaneous canonization," as Jacques Lafaye has called it) of these popular leaders undergone in more recent times by such figures as Emiliano Zapata, Pancho Villa, and Che Guevara.[41] A more widely venerated figure in the messianic mold, or at least one more widely spoken of, was Ignacio Allende, the wealthy Creole militia officer from the central Mexican town of San Miguel el Grande, Hidalgo's coconspirator and the priest's second-in-command during the initial short-lived 1810–11 rebellion. Allende was thought to be in the company of King Ferdinand; he was often singled out over Father Hidalgo as the paramount leader of the insurgency; his name appeared in seditious verses and in people's prayers; and he was believed by some to have been sent by God to scourge the *gachupines*.[42] In one instance, in the rough and isolated further reaches of the sierra of Metztitlán to the northeast of Mexico City—while Allende's capture was being denied at almost the exact moment he was being executed by the royalists in Chihuahua, in the north of the colony—he was being acclaimed as a popular candidate for king. One rebel had declared: "And now he [Allende] is going to obtain the crown of Mexico, and in a few days we will fall at his feet and kiss his feet and hands, because he is going to be our Catholic king [*nuestro católico*]."[43]

Popular messianic longings had not just arisen with the eruption of Miguel Hidalgo's revolt, and in the very first years of the nineteenth century rumors of conspiracy, foreign invasion, Indian saviors and kings, and massive rural uprising ricocheted around the countryside of New Spain. For example, at least two Indian pseudomessiahs were reported to have appeared, one in the area of Durango and another near Tepic toward the west coast.[44] We may even speak legitimately of a long tradition of such collective manifestations beginning immediately after the conquest and stretching through the eighteenth century, with something of a hiatus after about the early 1760s.[45] Nor did this spate of messianic, quasi-messianic, and cryptomessianic popular expressions arise out of a historical or cultural vacuum. It had its own cultural antecedents— preconditions necessary but not sufficient for the rapid deployment and activation of such ideas at the end of the colonial period. Among other elements, the Christian contribution to this belief system, introduced to Mesoamerican peoples through the centuries-long evangelization project of the colonizers, consisted in the connection in Western religious/eschatological thought of the millennium with a cyclical closure or recurrence in time, an idea complex too well known to require extended comment here.[46] Christian eschatology resonated strongly with an indigenous intellectual and religious tradition of cyclical cosmogony. Intertwined with this cyclical view of time there existed a strong mythicohistorical tradition of man-gods and messianic prophecy, stretching back through the Mesoamerican Classic era and embodied most strikingly in the figure of Quetzalcoatl, the Plumed Serpent deity. Such beliefs would have predisposed large segments of the colony's rural masses during times of stress to form the highly charged relationship with a single charismatic figure typical of messianism.

There were yet other important elements in the alchemy of messianic belief. Among the most important of these was the existence and wide recognition among the colonial rural masses of a protective, patriarchal tradition of monarchical government at whose center stood the quasi-thaumaturgical figure of the Spanish king himself. Such associations would have contributed powerfully to popular veneration of the monarch, especially among the Indians, who so often sheltered under his protective patriarchal mantle and made of his figure a preeminent candidate for messianic expectation.[47] Furthermore, a widespread survival of elements of pre-Christian native religious belief characterized the Mexican countryside and with them a tradition of popular piety, an often problematic and even antagonistic relationship between indigenous parishioners and their (for the most part white) curates, and a notably imperfect application of schooling and other enculturative mechanisms, as I have suggested above.[48] These conditions created a cultural milieu in many heavily indigenous parts of the country in which heterodox popular religious sensibilities might flourish and with them a disposition not only to see political issues in religious terms, at the very center of celebratory life and community identity, but also to look at the Spanish king or his surrogates as messianic figures situated in a very particular relationship to rural communities. Thus the elements of a village millennium were readily at hand, especially for Indian peasants: a messiah (the Spanish king or his stand-ins) and a millennial space (the embattled village itself). But these were truncated utopias in which the millenarian program consisted in the stubborn survival of the community itself rather than any well-articulated set of objectives, much less the creation of a new nation.

By contrast, elite insurgent ideology disputed the legitimacy and authority of the imperial monarchical structure and sought to replace it with a national mythology and ideology cobbled together from the particularisms salvaged from the proximate levels of the colonial structure (market and regional organization, economic institutions, the legal regimen, etc.), the very components the country people sought to keep at arm's length or in some cases to dismantle. The meaning of rural popular culture for the dynamics of rebellion, therefore, is that Indians, particularly among popular rebel groups, at least in the heartland of New Spain, tended to erase from their political cosmology the very middle-level structures represented in Creole thinking by the concept of a nation. This difference in the cognitive map and worldview of Mexicans represented a discontinuity between popular and elite cultures that no political ideology, program, or national mythology could easily bridge. The closing of this gap during the nineteenth and early twentieth centuries was finally effected by forms of civic ritual, widespread public schooling, the increased physical and information mobility afforded Mexicans by the railroad and other technologies, and—yes—the greater reach of print and other communications media.

In closing, let me revisit briefly the killings by rebels of European Spaniards that recurred with regularity throughout the 1810–21 period, exemplified most spectacularly by a few large-scale episodes such as the Guadalajara massacres of 1810–11 but also embracing numerous more ad hoc sorts of murders by common people, including indigenous villagers, in small towns and along country roads. It would be a mistake, surely, to assert that there was absolutely no element of nationalist impulse at work in the killings of such people in the many instances documented especially in the earliest months of the independence struggle. But under royalist interrogation months later, facing their own deaths, in their allusions to the Guadalajara episode in particular, neither Miguel Hidalgo nor Ignacio Allende, nominally commanding insurgent forces in the city, claimed to see in the killings anything other than the bloodthirsty propensities of their Indian followers. In fact, there was probably a mix of motives involved in this and other incidents: revenge, a desire to appropriate the property of the victims, and a sentiment on the part of the insurgent leadership that since their bridges to the regime had been burned from the earliest days of the rebellion they might as well make the breach irreparable. As with many such moments in the course of this or that epic political struggle, we simply do not know enough about the microhistory of the events themselves—who exactly did what and said what—to reach any definitive conclusions. But what I have been illustrating in this essay is that insofar as common men swept up in the rebellion were concerned, particularly those from rural peasant villages, they are extremely unlikely to have had the ideological or experiential template to see such killings as an expression of nationalist sensibility. In fact, the victimization of Europeans during this period was more typically a displacement of aggression away from Spaniards (i.e., whites) in general and onto peninsular Spaniards in particular as a psychologically and socially more efficient way for subaltern people of color, primarily indigenous villagers, to locate a cultural "Other" whose destruction might expiate the wrongs of the colonial order in which their communities were politically embedded. In essence, this was to be seen as a form of scapegoating.[49]

However we may choose to explain such episodes during the insurgency in New Spain, it is difficult to find evidence to support Anderson's interpretation of Mexican independence as an expression of nationalist sensibility nourished by the political, social, and economic split between native-born colonial Spaniards and peninsulars, by the sense of a larger potential polity instilled through bureaucratic pilgrimages within the Spanish Empire, or by the advent of print-capitalism. The only way to sustain such an interpretation is to situate nationalism as an ideological and state-building project almost exclusively in the relatively shallow stratum of Creole insurgent leaders, intellectuals, and churchmen, leaving out of the narrative most of the other six million or so Mexicans who came to make up the new nation after 1821, albeit through mediated forms of citizenship. This might explain the basis for later nationalist mythologizing, but it does not explain adequately how the Mexican nation itself came into existence, nor does it help to account for the troubled political history of the country well into the nineteenth century.

NOTES

1. The classic account of the Guadalajara massacre, still indispensable albeit darkly colored by its author's highly conservative bias, is Lucas Alamán, *Historia de Méjico*, vol. 2 (Mexico City, 1968); for modern reconstructions see José Ramírez Flores, *El gobierno insurgente en Guadalajara, 1810–1811* (Guadalajara, 1969), 107–10; and Eric Van Young, "El sociópata: Agustín Marroquín," in Felipe Castro Gutiérrez, Virginia Guedea, and José Luis Mirafuentes, eds., *Organización y liderazgo en los movimientos populares novohispanos* (Mexico City, 1992), 243–44. For a somewhat tainted first-person account see the judicial confession of Ignacio Allende, Father Miguel Hidalgo's most famous lieutenant, in Archivo General de la Nación (Mexico) (hereafter AGN), Historia, vol. 584, expediente 3, 1811.

2. So as not to dilate excessively on definitional issues, let me suggest very briefly what I take nationalism to mean. Nationalism I understand to signify identification with and loyalty to a more or less extensive political community based upon some limited form

of membership, sovereignty, and typically (although by no means exclusively) focused upon a territory and a coterminous state.

3. Among major modern works, Ernesto de la Torre Villar, *La independencia mexicana*, 3 vols. (Mexico City, 1982); Luis Villoro, *El proceso ideológico de la revolución de independencia* (Mexico City, 1983); and Hugh M. Hamill Jr., *The Hidalgo Revolt: Prelude to Mexican Independence* (Westport, Conn., 1981) adhere more or less to this interpretation.

4. Benedict Anderson, *Imagined Communities: Reflections on the Origin and Spread of Nationalism*, rev. ed. (London, 1991).

5. For some closely reasoned work in support of growing peasant political consciousness and national identification in the decades following independence see Peter F. Guardino, *Peasants, Politics, and the Formation of Mexico's National State: Guerrero, 1800–1857* (Stanford, Calif., 1996); and Florencia E. Mallon, *Peasant and Nation: The Making of Postcolonial Mexico and Peru* (Berkeley, Calif., 1994).

6. For a more detailed discussion of the contrast between elite and popular political thinking see, among other articles of my own, Eric Van Young, "The Raw and the Cooked: Popular and Elite Ideology in Mexico, 1800–1821," in Mark D. Szuchman, ed., *The Middle Period in Latin American History: Values and Attitudes in the 18th–19th Centuries* (Boulder, Colo., 1989), 75–102; Van Young, " 'To Throw Off a Tyrannical Government': Atlantic Revolutionary Traditions and Popular Insurgency in Mexico," in Michael A. Morrison and Melinda S. Zook, eds., *Revolutionary Currents: Nation-Building in the Transatlantic World, 1688–1821* (New York, 2004), 127–71; and for the distinctly religious cast of popular insurgent discourse see Van Young, "Popular Religion and the Politics of Insurgency in Mexico, 1810–1821," in Austen Ivereigh, ed., *The Politics of Religion in Nineteenth-Century Europe and Latin America* (London, 2000), 74–114.

7. Given the power and even elegance of Anderson's general argument, it is surprising that his work is not cited more often in the literature on the independence movements and subsequent nation and state building in Spanish America. Although the presence or absence of some discussion of Anderson should obviously not be adduced as a proof of anything much, it is telling that, given his vindicative value for historians of Latin American independence, he is so often neglected. Claudio Lomnitz, in *Deep Mexico, Silent Mexico: An Anthropology of Nationalism* (Minneapolis, 2001), refers to the reception of Anderson's ideas among Latin Americanist historians and anthropologists as "slothful" (4), although he ascribes this in part to the fact that Anderson's account of Latin American independence is "incorrect in a number of particulars" despite its theoretical suggestiveness.

8. To be fair to Anderson, when his book was first published two decades ago there was little in the Anglophone historiography dealing with the social history of the movements themselves (apart from Hugh Hamill's masterful study of the Hidalgo rebellion, not heavily social in emphasis). Thus, at least to judge by his footnotes, Anderson needed to rely heavily on works of a fairly traditional political cast, primarily by John Lynch and Gerhard Masur.

9. I am referring here to nationalism as an "ideology" rather than the "hegemonic, commonsensical, and tacitly shared cultural construct" that Anderson seems to think

it (per Lomnitz, *Deep Mexico, Silent Mexico*, 3), because although hegemony and commonsensicality may be its end state (i.e., it became naturalized), that condition seems to have been an artifact of state action after independence.

10. This argument is developed at length in Claudio Lomnitz's essay "Nationalism as a Practical System: Benedict Anderson's Theory of Nationalism from the Vantage Point of Spanish America," in ibid., 3–34.

11. Ibid., 14.

12. Anderson, *Imagined Communities*, 65.

13. Anderson performs some curious sleight-of-hand in his discussion of the arrival of print-capitalism in Spanish America (61 ff.). He uses the figure of printer Benjamin Franklin as an all-weather colonial exemplar, along with some statistics on the existence of newspapers in the northern Anglo-American colonies and some speculations on the proliferation of print media in the late eighteenth century, all to suggest what was occurring in Spanish America, for which he provides little or no direct evidence.

14. Anderson, *Imagined Communities*, 49, 48.

15. The following few paragraphs are drawn largely from Eric Van Young, " 'To Throw Off a Tyrannical Government.' "

16. John Murrin, among other historians, reminds us that when the American revolutionaries repudiated King George III definitively, no monarchist project was seriously discussed after 1776 ("1776: The Countercyclical Revolution," in Morrison and Zook, *Revolutionary Currents*, 65–90). For the tensions among mass politics, citizenship, and the question of authority in an urban setting in the early republican period in Mexico see Richard A. Warren, *Vagrants and Citizens: Politics and the Masses in Mexico City from Colony to Republic* (Wilmington, Del., 2001).

17. On Hidalgo's political ideas see Alfonso Ruiz García, *Ideario de Hidalgo* (Mexico City, 1955); and on the republicward drift of insurgent political projects during the early years of the insurgency see Gabriela Soto Laveaga, "Breaking the Silence: Murmurs of a 'National' Identity in the Mexican Insurgent Press, 1810–1813," paper presented at the joint meetings of the Rocky Mountain Conference on Latin American Studies and the Pacific Coast Council on Latin American Studies, San Diego, February 1997.

18. For a masterful treatment of the propaganda issue see Hugh M. Hamill Jr., "Royalist Propaganda and 'La porción humilde del pueblo' during Mexican Independence," *Americas* 36 (1980): 423–44. On the Iberian tradition of Sebastianism and mystical kingship see Mary Elizabeth Brooks, *A King for Portugal: The Madrigal Conspiracy, 1594–1595* (Madison, Wisc., 1964); and Richard Kagan, *Lucrecia's Dreams: Politics and Prophecy in Sixteenth-Century Spain* (Berkeley, Calif., 1990).

19. On politics and ideology in the immediate postindependence period see Timothy Anna, *The Mexican Empire of Iturbide* (Lincoln, Neb., 1990) and *Forging Mexico, 1821–1835* (Lincoln, Neb., 1998); and also Jaime E. Rodríguez O., ed., *Mexico in the Age of Democratic Revolutions, 1750–1850* (Boulder, Colo., 1994).

20. The former position would be occupied by David A. Brading, *The Origins of Mexican Nationalism* (Cambridge, 1985), the latter by José Miranda, *Las ideas políticas mexicanas* (Mexico City, 1978).

21. For a recent anthology of scholarly essays exploring briefly the influence of this

document, the transcendent influence of the Spanish liberal Constitution of Cádiz of 1812, and the trajectory of liberalism in Mexico see Jaime E. Rodríguez O., ed., *The Divine Charter: Constitutionalism and Liberalism in Nineteenth-Century Mexico* (Lanham, Md., 2005).

22. As William H. Sewell Jr. makes clear in his essay "The French Revolution and the Emergence of the Nation Form," in Morrison and Zook, *Revolutionary Currents*, 91–126, after 1789 the locus of sovereignty passed from the French monarchy to the (revolutionary) French nation, making of it not only an *affective* but *effective* community. In Mexico an analogous process produced a truncated outcome: a (partially) *effective* community but little in the way of an *affective* one, and even that socially localized to a high degree.

23. Luis Villoro, *El proceso ideológico de la revolución de independencia* (Mexico City, 1986), 44–45; Enrique Florescano, *Memory, Myth, and Time in Mexico: From the Aztecs to Independence* (Austin, Tex., 1994), chaps. 4 and 5.

24. Florescano, *Memory, Myth, and Time*, 226.

25. On Creole patriotism see Brading, *The Origins of Mexican Nationalism;* and David A. Brading, *The First America: The Spanish Monarchy, Creole Patriots, and the Liberal State, 1492–1867* (Cambridge, 1991); and on Brading's work on Mexican nationalism in greater historiographical detail see Eric Van Young, "Brading's Century: Some Reflections on David A. Brading's Work and the Historiography of Mexico, 1750–1850," in Susan Deans-Smith and Eric Van Young, eds., *Mexican Soundings: Essays in Honour of David A. Brading* (London, forthcoming). On European writing of the eighteenth century about the New World see Jorge Cañizares-Esguerra, *How to Write the History of the New World: Historiographies, Epistemologies, and Identities in the Eighteenth-Century Atlantic World* (Stanford, Calif., 2001).

26. The concept of "habitus," of course, is drawn from the work of Pierre Bourdieu, *Distinction: A Social Critique of the Judgement of Taste*, trans. Richard Nice (Cambridge, Mass., 1984).

27. Much of this discussion of literacy rates, schooling, language policy, and so on, follows closely chapter 18 of my book *The Other Rebellion: Popular Violence, Ideology, and the Struggle for Mexican Independence, 1810–1821* (Stanford, Calif., 2001), and my essay "In the Gloomy Caverns of Paganism: Popular Culture, Insurgency, and Nation-Building in Mexico, 1800–1821," in Christon I. Archer, ed., *The Birth of Modern Mexico, 1780–1824* (Wilmington, Del., 2003), 41–66.

28. Kevin Terraciano, *The Mixtecs of Colonial Oaxaca: Ñudzahui History, Sixteenth through Eighteenth Centuries* (Stanford, Calif., 2001), 54; and on Cuernavaca see Robert Haskett, *Indigenous Rulers: An Ethnohistory of Town Government in Colonial Cuernavaca* (Albuquerque, N.M., 1991), 132–43.

29. François-Xavier Guerra, *Modernidad e independencias: Ensayos sobre las revoluciones hispánicas* (Mexico City, 1993), 275–85.

30. For France see Timothy Tackett, "The West in France in 1789: The Religious Factor in the Origins of the Counterrevolution," in T. C. W. Blanning, ed., *The Rise and Fall of the French Revolution* (Chicago, 1996), 343; for Russia see Jeffrey Brooks, *When Russia Learned to Read: Literacy and Popular Literature, 1861–1917* (Princeton, N.J., 1985), 4, and Robert Edelman, *Proletarian Peasants: The Revolution of 1905 in Russia's South-*

west (Ithaca, N.Y., 1987), 39; and for New England see Kenneth A. Lockridge, *Literacy in Colonial New England: An Inquiry into the Social Context of Literacy in the Early Modern West* (New York, 1974).

31. For a detailed discussion of these estimates and the data set upon which they are based see Van Young, *The Other Rebellion*, chap. 2 and app. A.

32. For an overview discussion of the Mexican population at the close of the colonial period see Eric Van Young, *La crisis del orden colonial: Estructura agraria y rebeliones populares en la Nueva España, 1750–1821* (Mexico City, 1992), chap. 2.

33. For some examples see the following: fire: AGN, Criminal, vol. 229, no expediente no., fols. 263r–413v, 1810; cancer: AGN, Operaciones de Guerra, vol. 146, fols. 20r–21v, Venegas to Cruz, Mexico City, 3 January 1811; pestilence: AGN, Infidencias, vol. 24, expediente 6, fols. 157r–92r, 1811; Epidemias, vol. 8, expediente 9, fols. 113r–20r, Cuernavaca, 1814; Epidemias, vol. 8, expediente 7, fols. 49r–108r, Mexico City, 1813.

34. See, for example, Eric Van Young, "De tempestades y teteras: Crisis imperial y conflicto local en México a principios del siglo XIX," in Leticia Reina and Elisa Servin, eds., *Crisis, reforma y revolución. México: Historias de fin de siglo* (Mexico City, 2002), 161–208; and Michael T. Ducey, *A Nation of Villages: Riot and Rebellion in the Mexican Huasteca, 1750–1850* (Tucson, Ariz., 2004).

35. See Eric Van Young, "Islands in the Storm: Quiet Cities and Violent Countrysides in the Mexican Independence Era," *Past and Present* (February 1988): 120–56.

36. AGN, Historia, vol. 411, expediente 14, fols. 84r–116v, 1811; Infidencias, vol. 17, expedientes 7–11, fols. 137r–307r, 1811. The one concrete proposal talked of in the village was the division of privately held land amongst the Indian householders and the setting aside of some goods to support the insurgent forces of Ignacio Allende, Father Miguel Hidalgo's lieutenant.

37. AGN, Criminal, vol. 251, expedientes 1, 10, 11, respectively, fols. 1r–12v, 309r–19v, and 320r–29v, 1812.

38. Marc Bloch, *The Royal Touch: Monarchy and Miracles in France and England*, trans. J. E. Anderson (New York, 1989).

39. Celaya: AGN, Criminal, vol. 134, expediente 3, fols. 36r–50r, 1810; veiled coach: AGN, Criminal, vol. 454, no expediente no., n.p., 1811; and for a number of other examples see Van Young, *The Other Rebellion*, chap. 18.

40. For example, University of Texas at Austin, Benson Latin American Collection, Hernández y Dávalos Collection, 1.212, 1815; and on one particularly fascinating episode see Christon I. Archer, "The Indian Insurgents of Mezcala Island on the Lake Chapala Front, 1812–1816," in Susan Schroeder, ed., *The "Pax Colonial" and Native Resistance in New Spain* (Lincoln, Neb., 1998), 84–128, 158–65.

41. For the messianic veneration supposedly attached to Hidalgo and Morelos see Jacques Lafaye, *Mesías, cruzadas, utopías: El judeo-cristianismo en las sociedades ibéricas* (Mexico City, 1984), 87–88; and the same author's classic study, *Quetzalcoatl and Guadalupe: The Formation of Mexican National Consciousness, 1531–1813*, trans. Benjamin Keen (Chicago, 1976), 28.

42. With King Ferdinand: AGN, Criminal, vol. 194, expediente 1, fols. 1r–13r, 1811; paramount leader: AGN, Criminal, vol. 2, expediente 21, n.p., 1811; seditious verses and

prayers: AGN, Operaciones de Guerra, vol. 9, no expediente no., fols. 133r–34r, 41r–v, 1817; Infidencias, vol. 2, expediente 8, fols. 154r–62v, 1810; Infidencias, vol. 2, expediente 4, fols. 100r–116v, 1811; Inquisición, vol. 1416, expediente 11, fols. 173r–78v, 1811.

43. AGN, Criminal, vol. 163, expediente 18, fols. 307r–20r, 1811.

44. For the Durango incident see Eric Van Young, "Millennium on the Northern Marches: The Mad Messiah of Durango and Popular Rebellion in Mexico, 1800–1815," *Comparative Studies in Society and History* 28 (1986): 385–413; and for the Tepic incident, involving the shadowy figure of El Indio Mariano, see Felipe Castro Gutiérrez, "La rebelión del Indio Mariano (Nayarit, 1801)," *Estudios de Historia Novohispana* 10 (1991): 347–67.

45. For an interesting and exceedingly suggestive treatment of four such figures and their followers see Serge Gruzinski, *Man-Gods of the Mexican Highlands: Indian Power and Colonial Society, 1520–1820*, trans. Eileen Corrigan (Stanford, Calif., 1989).

46. This was arguably a deeply embedded concept among Mesoamerican peoples, and its apparent survival in popular thinking well into the nineteenth century accords ill with the advent of the notion of "empty time" that Benedict Anderson sees as a necessary element for the growth of a nationalist sensibility, a concept he adapted from Karl Benjamin.

47. For example, although under colonial law and practice indigenous people were diminished subjects occupying for some purposes the position of legal minors, by that very fact they fell under the particular protection of the monarchy and, in colonial Mexico, at least, even had a special court devoted to their legal needs, the Juzgado General de Indios, in whose use indigenous people early became very adept; see Woodrow W. Borah, *Justice by Insurance: The General Indian Court of Colonial Mexico and the Legal Aides of the Half-Real* (Berkeley, Calif., 1983).

48. On late colonial curates, their careers, and their complex relations with their (especially Indian) parishioners see William B. Taylor, *Magistrates of the Sacred: Priests and Parishioners in Eighteenth-Century Mexico* (Stanford, Calif., 1996); and Van Young, *The Other Rebellion*, 201–24.

49. For a detailed discussion of this "splitting" hypothesis (i.e., of good king from bad European Spaniards) and the scapegoating that underlay it see Van Young, *The Other Rebellion*, throughout but esp. chap. 18.

European Travelers and the Writing of the Brazilian Nation

WILMA PERES COSTA

*I*n Spanish American and Portuguese American nations the process of building national identities had distinctive features compared to the European historical experience. In the case of Brazil, some specific sources of identity arose both from the colonial experience and from the disruption of its colonial relationship to Portugal. It is useful to recall that, unlike European nations, where the strategy for building national identity involved recalling myths and traditions of a remote past, in Brazil and other American nations independence meant a complex balance of allegiance and rupture with metropolises that were sources of political and cultural identity. This situation involved a very complicated process of keeping some assets, destroying others, and, at the same time, reconstructing new bonds with the European world and the world system of nation-states. In order to achieve this, Brazil, like other new American nations, would have to take into account references that were at once distinct from those of the former colonial powers as well as still linked to Europe and acceptable to European standards. Even if their behavior often seemed paradoxical and contradictory, the elites who led the independence movements did not aim to separate entirely from Europe; they wanted to share the benefits of modernity and capitalism that could only be realized within the European Atlantic world.

In Brazil's case we must also consider that the idea of a Brazilian territorial and political unity resulting from a "friendly divorce" with Portugal and of the wisdom of a moderate monarchy is a myth created by conservative historiography, one that is being consistently challenged by recent research.[1] Historians have shown that the crisis of the Iberian colonial system produced political collective identities corresponding at the same time to local and regional allegiances and to forces coming from the liberal revolution in Portugal. These movements lived together inside a Brazilian territory centered around Prince

Dom Pedro. Different lines of force—some centered in Portugal, others in Brazil, still others in its provinces—changed the outline of different territorial imaginings. The segment of elites who successfully rallied around unity, monarchy, and the political center in Rio de Janeiro had to carve a sense of national identity surpassing both the centrifugal forces of disparate regional identities and those coming from profound social and racial heterogeneity. Part of their achievement came from their ability to manage a very complex and volatile international environment within which they legitimated their goals.

The Metamorphosis of a Nation

Since the middle of the eighteenth century the idea of "nation" itself had been transformed, acquiring new meanings and recycling old ones. The path has been described as a transition between ethnocultural and civic contents of the idea of nation, but we must bear in mind that both contents were bound to cohabit, often in veiled or outright conflict, throughout the century in old and new nation-states.[2] Mirroring the changes in the new balance of power established by the Congress of Vienna in 1815, another innovation was to affect European states: the establishment of a hierarchical disposition among nations that allowed the most powerful ones to arbitrate the destiny of the less powerful, enabling them to grant or deny the political autonomy of ancient nationalities and control the acceptance of new candidates to the select group of nation-states.[3] Among these powers, Britain, France, and the Holy Alliance (Prussia, Austria, and Russia) would compete with different instruments to influence the destiny of the new American nation-states. If Britain enjoyed the greatest commercial influence over the political choices of Latin American elites after independence, France managed to compensate its diminished economic prowess by trying to exert its cultural hegemony in the New World.

This essay deals with the question of building national identities in the New World by looking at European geographical exploration and scientific missions in Brazil. These missions brought travelers and scholars eager to unveil a part of the world thus far little known to them. We will consider how these scientific explorations became an important tool in changing the meanings of words such as "nation," "civilization," and, later on, "colonization" itself. Coinciding with these changing meanings, American nations sought to see themselves reflected in the mirror of Europe. In Brazil and elsewhere they ascribed to these "traveling scholars" a major role in the building of the international image of the countries of the New World.[4]

Travel writing was a "two-way mirror" in the identity-otherness game between nations of the two worlds, as others have stressed. We will see also that images of the country came to influence not only how the country was judged by

European standards but also how Brazilian elites saw themselves. This exchange shaped one of the most distinctive traces of Brazilian culture in the nineteenth century: the need to be mirrored by Europe and the vulnerability Brazilians felt before this external evaluation. Much of Brazilian writing in this period assumed a foreign point of view, as if the writer looked at his fellow countrymen through the eyes of a passionate but distant scientific traveler trying to bring civilization to a wild and resistant primitive world.[5]

We profit here from the suggestions brought by the recent work on the contacts between the Old and New World in the nineteenth century and from a somewhat heretical reading of Benedict Anderson's idea of pilgrimage.[6] This may help us explore some important aspects of the role played by French travel writing in the forging of a favorable image of the emergent Brazilian nationality, an image that was to endure in the Brazilian national imagination.

Travels as Pilgrims: The Construction of a Fractured World

Anderson sees nations arising from a deliberate process of *manufacture* and *creation.* One of the most intriguing aspects of this approach is the emphasis it places on the role of intellectuals as craftsmen who devise collective imaginaries. The craft of the intellectual is thus associated with the definition of the territory and the creation of political centers, an idea expressed by the metaphor of *pilgrimage.* The emphasis Anderson put on the role of the press as a paramount creator of the imaginary community is well known, as is the criticism his arguments aroused in Latin America, where literate culture was shared by very few. We borrow here the idea of pilgrimage from Anderson, using it as metaphor to ponder the role played by traveling scholars and the extensive narratives they wrote on the landscape, society, and institutions of the New World. Therefore, the meaning of pilgrimage is both enlarged and twisted. It is enlarged because it is not confined to the territorial and cultural formation of a unique nation but is envisaged as a game in which traveling around the world became an essential means of professional (and political) reconnaissance and national pride for scholars and men of science. It is twisted because it designates not a shared experience but the image of a fractured world.

In each of the "worlds" the routes of pilgrimage matched the movement of traveling in different ways. In Europe the prototype of the nineteenth-century traveler was increasingly that of a professional: one traveled for one's country in the service of the Academy of Sciences or the Geographical Society, that is, as part of an official mission. But accounts written by the traveling scholar were not necessarily restricted to official readers. As a result of the development of journalism, the growing autonomy of university structures, and the multiplication of scientific associations, travel accounts found a growing audience in the educated public. The experience of traveling could result in a specialization or a career in scientific journalism, university teaching, governmental offices, or diplomacy. This route traversed the New World, but its final destination was located in the European capitals.

Another route brought many European scholars to the New World, where they settled down, temporarily or permanently, attracted by the opportunities offered by the emergence of new nations, which opened themselves to the knowledge of the Old World. Within this New World setting their learning was overvalued precisely because so few were capable of dealing with the new cultural and scientific standards. Scientific traveling and travel writing helped to situate intellectual (and political) careers in Europe, linked as they were to the European public and European institutions. How did these scientists come to evaluate the Brazilian economic and political potential to become a viable nation? These scientists helped to create a hierarchical view of nations that by itself indicated the significance of comparison, contention, and rivalry between and within these two worlds (Europe and America) in the construction of the legitimacy and sovereignty of the new nations.

Inside Brazil, however, around the mid-nineteenth century a new route was opened as native and immigrant Brazilian intellectuals engaged in a dialogue with the illustrated travel accounts. This dialogue was established in a field of action firmly controlled by the monarchy and its institutions, to which the main pilgrimage routes inevitably led due to the scarcity of readers and the limited cultural market. The path to an intellectual career led always to the monarchy and its court throughout the nineteenth century. Beginning in the 1830s, this was underscored by state-sponsored institutions such as the Sociedade Auxiliadora da Indústria Nacional (Society for the Support of National Industry) and the Instituto Histórico e Geográfico Brasileiro (Brazilian Institute for History and Geography). These institutions were in constant communication with their European counterparts, providing central channels for the flow of foreign ideas and places where they could be filtered, selected, and criticized.[7] In these institutions both native and nationalized intellectuals found a route of pilgrimage to their own careers while helping build Brazilian identity.

Some Dimensions of a Polyvalent Mirror

The dialogue with European views on the landscape, institutions, and customs of the New World was not peculiar to Brazil. Confronting Alexander von Humboldt's narratives and views had been an important part of defining national identity for many Hispanic American countries, mainly Mexico and Cuba. Likewise, Alexis de Tocqueville's views had sparked lively debate in North American intellectual circles. For American nations, North and South, the European mirror was an important part of self-identification.

However, in Brazil it seems that the dialogue with foreign views was not only more intense but also more lasting in its effects on Brazilian literature, historiography, and social thinking. In fact, when Brazil was born as an independent political entity in 1822, it already had many histories, the most influential being written by a foreigner, the erudite English poet Robert Southey in 1810. Southey did not come to Brazil to write its history, and his research was based extensively on British and Portuguese sources. Years later, in 1840, at its fifty-first meeting, the Brazilian Historical and Geographical Institute sponsored a contest to choose the best proposal for a history of Brazil. The winner was a famous German man of science, Karl Friedrich Philip von Martius, participant of the intellectual entourage of Humboldt who had traveled extensively in Brazil between 1817 and 1820. His winning project never came to light, but in 1858 Francisco Adolpho de Varnhagen published the first volume of his *Historia geral do Brasil,* which became a major milestone in Brazilian historiography. The book was cast as a dialogue with Martius's project and included a debate that expressed the views of most of the travelers who had visited Brazil during the first half of the nineteenth century. Varnhagen himself was the son of a military official of German origin, a specialist in mineralogy who came to Brazil with the migration of the Portuguese court in 1808. He spent most of his life in Europe, where he was a member of some of the most important scientific associations. Because he made an impassioned defense of Portuguese sources against some foreign (mainly French) views, his work received bitter criticism during the meetings of the Société de géographie de Paris, where it was extensively debated.[8]

The most enduring ties of Brazilian intellectual elites in the nineteenth century were to France and French culture. The links to the French network of intellectuals went largely through Ferdinand Denis (1798–1890), a man of letters who traveled in Brazil between 1816 and 1822. Though he never returned to Brazil, he built a successful intellectual career dedicated largely to Brazilian matters. He brought to light many historical documents that became fundamentally important to Brazilian historiography on the colonial period, such as the first Portuguese description of Brazil in the sixteenth century—the Pero Vaz de Caminha letter. He also stressed the importance of Brazilian historians and intellectuals using European travel narratives of the nineteenth century for their understanding of Brazil.

Denis, this Brazilianist avant la lettre, wrote many books on Brazil aimed at the general public in France. One of them, in Portuguese translation, was officially adopted in Brazilian high schools during the nineteenth century. Denis is also well known for his role in urging young Brazilian novelists to explore romantic themes in the culture of the Indians, an idea inspired by the great French romantic René de Chateaubriand. From his prestigious position as librarian of the Sainte Geneviève Library in Paris, Denis guided Brazilian intellectuals from abroad and received and counseled Brazilian travelers in France, not least among them Dom Pedro II, the emperor of Brazil.[9]

To add some light to this French connection and its significance we must consider the special features of Brazil as a field for travel and a subject for travel writing. Everyone who has dealt with the subject mentions that Portuguese American territory was closed to foreign (i.e., non-Portuguese) travelers until the migration of the Portuguese court in 1808. The oft-cited example of this political attitude was the denial of permission to Humboldt to explore the Amazonian region under Portuguese jurisdiction during his celebrated travels on the American continent between 1804 and 1808. After the arrival of the court the country was opened to foreign travelers and researchers, a change that is commonly interpreted as the natural consequence of the opening of Brazilian ports to foreign trade in 1808. Less familiar, however, is the point that, in spite of being connected in geopolitical terms, these decisions to open trade and open the country to travelers pointed in different directions. The opening of Brazilian ports to foreign trade would primarily benefit the British, while the opening to foreign scientific missions envisaged a broader group of countries: France and the countries of the Holy Alliance. This choice suggests a well-defined diplomatic strategy to establish a counterweight to British influence. After 1816, when Brazil was elevated in status as part of a united kingdom with Portugal, foreign missions were not only welcomed but invited in a concerted plan of binding international alliances. The scientists now needed official permits, passports, and connections to facilitate their work. They were, in a word, treated as official guests.

This geopolitical strategy becomes apparent simply by listing the main official cultural missions received in Brazil between 1815 and 1822. All of them came either from France or from countries of the Holy Alliance. British travelers were many, but most were linked to private businesses and religion. Among the main scientific and cultural missions was the French Artistic Mission of 1815, which brought a group of distinguished painters, sculptors, and artisans to establish the Academy of Fine Arts in Rio de Janeiro. The artists included the family of painter Nicolau Taunay, the painter Auguste Debret, and the architect Grandjean de Montigny. Part of the group, including the Taunay family, remained in Brazil and built an extensive network within Brazilian political and cultural life. Among their circle were Felix Taunay, preceptor of the young emperor Dom Pedro (the future Dom Pedro II), and his son Alfredo Taunay, one of the most important Brazilian novelists of the second half of the nineteenth century.[10] The main scientific missions of the period included the ethnographic expedition of the Bavarian Maximilian, Prinz zu Wied from 1815 to 1817, the Austro-Bavarian group of scientists who followed Princess Leopoldina on the occasion of her marriage to Prince Dom Pedro (the future Dom Pedro I) in 1817, the huge and partially unsuccessful expedition sponsored by the Russian czar and led by Baron Georg Heinrich von Langsdorff in 1821, and an extensive scientific expedition led by the French botanist Auguste de Saint-Hilaire between 1816 and 1822, to which we will turn below.

Unlikely Borders

In Brazil the different meanings that cohabited in the idea of nation—either in its ethnocultural or civic dimensions—acquired special features because they had to coexist within a country with vast populations of African slaves and Amerindians. Their presence in many ways challenged the intellectuals' ideas of the "modern" nation Brazil aspired to become.

Modern Brazilian social thinkers have been pointing out that this sharp heterogeneity was important in attributing a special role to *territory* in compounding differences among Brazilian regional elites. The "one and indivisible territory" became a substitute for an unlikely "united and indivisible nation." This was one more powerful gathering element pointing to monarchy because it meant looking at the territory of Portuguese America as a legacy rather than as the result of construction.[11]

Nevertheless, even at this level Brazilian elites operated within an ambitious and contradictory objective. The projected borders of their territorial imaginary were delimited by the basins of the Amazon and the Río de la Plata in an attempt to establish an unlikely continuous natural border. Most of the extension of this imaginary border was under dispute either by other countries within the South American continent (the western border) or by European powers (the northern border), since a considerable portion of the vast territory was to be found in a region disputed by England, the Netherlands, and France (the Guianas). At the time of independence only a small portion of this territorial claim was undisputed: the region of the Guaporé River on the western border. This region was a subject of great interest for European scientific travelers, because they hoped to find there a point where a link between the two main fluvial systems of South America could be established. All the remaining part of the western border was under dispute by neighboring countries and intertwined with volatile European interests. Most of the territories under dispute were inhabited by indigenous peoples.

Brazil's other border, the *invisible border*, incorporated the African coastline and the control of the Atlantic slave trade. This "frontier" was subject to violent contestation by Great Britain and became officially illegal under the treaty whereby Brazil agreed to put a halt to the slave trade by 1831. (Brazil did not outlaw the slave trade until 1850.)[12] Slavery, the slave trade, and the relations between the white and black populations were unavoidable subjects in the narratives of scientific travelers, as was their interest in the variety of indigenous customs associated with their geographic explorations. That is the main reason why the writings of visiting scientists were always scrutinized carefully by the emperor's aides and were often subjected to comment, praise, criticism, or even damning silence. In many ways, these travelers' narratives were to become fundamental in establishing the possibilities of nationhood.

Convergences in the Route

The impulse to travel fostered most of France's cultural production during the nineteenth century. It brought together the main sources of intellectual output of the period—the romantic impulse and scientific knowledge. The French intellectual of the nineteenth century was almost always a traveler, from Chateaubriand's and Lamartine's search for exotic landscapes to Tocqueville's methodical investigations of the institutions of other peoples. The persistent efforts of geographical societies to map the earth were based on the concentrated efforts of naturalists, geographers, ethnographers, and artists. Besides this, the attraction of Parisian cultural life for scholars all over Europe made the city and French publications a sort of Mecca for the circulation of travel reports of various nations, a phenomenon that was also stimulated by the widespread knowledge of the French language among the cultivated classes of the whole world.

Among the points of convergence that marked the development of closer relations between Brazil and France in the first half of the nineteenth century stand defense of monarchy and the opposition to English pressure to end the slave trade. The defense of monarchic legitimacy led French foreign policy to elect support for the sole New World monarchy as one of its priorities, thus seeking to compensate in the political field for the unquestionable economic primacy of Great Britain. This interest, pervasive in French politics until 1848, was especially important in the 1820s, when it was feared that republicanism, defeated by the Restoration and the reactionary policies of the Holy Alliance, could once again set fire to Europe, this time originating in the Americas.

Ever since the 1791 revolution in Haiti, the conservative powers in France had become extremely careful regarding "hasty" decisions involving slavery, particularly in countries with vast numbers of African slaves. Furthermore, with the Restoration, France started to reactivate the slave trade to its American colonies, which then underwent a period of great prosperity. France's slave trade continued to be active until the 1830s, when the Orleanist monarchy decided to collaborate with Great Britain in repressing it. Collaboration with its historic rival, Britain, was, however, extremely unpopular, even among the fiercest detractors of the slave trade and slavery. For all these reasons, it was always easier to find shelter in French public opinion by criticizing English actions and alleged abuses in the repression of the Atlantic slave trade.[13]

Certain points of overt or potential dissent also permeated relations between France and Brazil in the nineteenth century. The first of these was what would lead French explorers and geographers to concentrate their interest on the possibilities for communication between the Amazon and the Río de la Plata. The second point was related, and it stemmed from the rivalry between England and France in the La Plata region and, at the northern extreme of the Brazilian frontier, from the boundary dispute with French Guiana, which claimed all the land to the mouth of the Amazon, incorporating the current Brazilian state of Amapá.

It is because France was both a key cultural reference and a strategic political ally that French intellectuals played a special role in mirroring Brazilian efforts in nation building. Images of the country produced during this period would be influential not only in the way the country was judged by European standards but also in shaping how Brazilian elites saw themselves. The "French mirror" therefore reflected an important image back to the Brazilian elite engaged in nation building during the first half of the nineteenth century.

The changing context in both sides of the mirror failed to generate an unequivocal view of Brazil; on the contrary, it came to produce a kaleidoscope of images.[14] Many of the most important of these images were conceived and circulated between 1819 and 1850 in an important journal devoted to travel reports, the *Nouvelles Annales des Voyages, de la Géographie et de l'Histoire, ou Recueil des Relations Originales Inédites, Communiquées par des Voyageurs Français et Étrangers.*

The *Nouvelles Annales des Voyages* published and reviewed travel narratives for a broad reading public. It was edited by two prestigious French geographers, J. B. Eyriès and Conrad Malte-Brun, connected to the group that had formed the Société de géographie de Paris in 1821. The journal tried to cater to the increasing interest in narratives of travel not only for the cultivated reader but also for the general public by publishing information about travels to distant lands, abridged narratives, and critical analyses of narratives. Very strict in its criteria for accepting material, the *Nouvelles Annales des Voyages* intended to create a sort of reference for the production of travel reports, privileging scientific objectivity and establishing rules for observing and publicizing results.

In addition were numerous travel accounts published in the *Revue des Deux Mondes*, which was the most important French journal for traveling, culture, and politics in the nineteenth century and remains widely read to this day. The

Revue first appeared in 1829, finding many readers among the cultivated classes in Brazil.[15]

The Initial Period: Translating Brazil into French

In 1819, the first year of the *Nouvelles Annales des Voyages*, the journal published a small article by the scientist Wilhelm Ludwig von Eschwedge, a German mineralogist who lived in Brazil from 1810 to 1821 at the service of Dom João VI. This article, translated from the original German, stressed the importance of opening Brazilian territory to foreign scientists and praised the leading role Germans had taken in traversing the inhospitable hinterland. National pride clearly lent strength to the text; as Eschwedge put it, "Nothing can deprive Germans who travel through this kingdom from the honor of being the first to draw its natural history." Despite the scientific enthusiasm, the author seemed to believe that the task facing European scientists would be especially strenuous, since "a narrative of travels in Brazil can only be extremely dry. . . . [A]t the end of a full day there is nothing to insert in one's diary; one day goes by equal to the preceding day, without any finding of objects that might give indications concerning the tastes or the activities of the inhabitants." He believed that anyone who traveled a few miles from the coastline would be able to imagine all of Brazil. A monotonous landscape, a monotonous people, with no "artwork" that might impress the traveler; nor were the fields covered with flowers, as in Europe. The people Eschwedge encountered were not able to converse on a level that might interest a cultivated European. They spoke only of their crops, their land, and their cattle. Most of the inhabitants he considered "idlers," a category he subdivided into "useful idlers" and "dangerous idlers." The first could render good service to the traveler, but care had to be taken with the dangerous idlers, for they committed murders, gave false testimony for payment, and killed the horses. They were, in short, the "scum of the earth." There followed a number of sensible and useful remarks for the benefit of his fellow travelers: never travel on foot, ensure the aid of a good guide, take care with food, watch out for poisonous snakes. He even gave advice on how to hold a parasol while riding so as not to hamper one's ability to write. At the close of the article came his main piece of advice: Brazilians were highly sensitive, and, although they were polite toward foreigners, they did not appreciate them. Therefore, the traveler should at all costs avoid criticizing the habits and institutions of the country. "There is no nation which appreciates less any form of criticism than the Portuguese, especially when such criticism is offered by a foreigner. Nor is there any other nation on which criticism produces less effect."[16]

Subsequent developments were to dismiss the remarks of the mineralogist baron. At the very time of his writing a surge of interest in Brazil came into

being, an interest that was not limited to its potential natural and material resources but extended to the peculiarities of its heterogeneous population and,
as of 1822, to its possibilities in aspiring to the status of the "concert of civilized
nations." Nor would the travelers in their reports refrain from criticizing the
new country, its habits, and its institutions. On the contrary: the farther we
move in time from the "disinterested" scientific discourse, the more space is
devoted to economic and geopolitical comments.

The unavoidable distance between the actual travels and the publication of
narratives in French reviews gave rise to certain noteworthy phenomena. The
results of the intense movement of scientific travel fostered by Dom João VI between 1815 and 1822 would reach the public after independence (1822), mostly
during the 1830s, when the Brazilian monarchical and unitary project was challenged by a series of regional uprisings and Rio de Janeiro's government was
under mounting British pressure to curtail the slave trade.

A second phenomenon worth mentioning is that, between 1819 and 1829,
none of the reports concerning Brazil published or reviewed by the journal were
written by French travelers. The information about Brazil was gleaned from
German and English travelers, information that the journal attempted to use in
order to develop its own point of view by means of critical analyses, commentaries, and syntheses.

In this first decade of the journal Brazil was mentioned twenty-one times in
texts of differing lengths. Between 1819 and 1829 the approach of the journal was
characterized by an interest in geography and ethnography. The major passages
referred to the trips of Maximilian, Prinz zu Wied, Johan Baptist von Spix and
Martius, Johann Natterer, Langsdorff, and Saint-Hilaire. The journal's interest
in political events was expressed in a discreet and metaphorical way, though it
was markedly conservative. Thus, Eschwedge's recommendations were echoed
in the critical commentaries concerning the publication of the report of Maximilian's travels. The report of the prince was praised because he was very reserved in expressing his opinions: "He describes with truth the scenes of the
beautiful and majestic nature of the tropical region: he relates, with paramount
recognition, all the services that were paid to him; he does not allow himself
digressions that are not related to his subject. In summary, he keeps within the
limits that should never be trespassed by the author of a traveler's report."[17]

The first departure from this attitude appeared in 1826, when the independence of South American nations was admitted for the first time in the *Nouvelles
Annales des Voyages*. It comes from the critical analysis of the report written by
the secretary for the British Legation in Rio de Janeiro. Extensive excerpts of
this report were published, followed by comments by an unidentified reviewer
(probably one of the editors of the journal). According to the British official,

"the condition in which the provinces of South America were to be found before gave no grounds for any hopes of a peaceful transformation into a better state of social organization: this exception in the annals of human history was given only to the United States of North America, where evangelical religion prepared the population to enjoy political liberty."[18]

In the part referring to Rio de Janeiro, the French reviewer pitied the English narrative for its lack of literary beauty and did not avoid "completing" it with lengthy comments that emphasized the contrast between the beauty of nature and the shock resulting from the close encounter with slavery, a common theme that had become obligatory in describing an impression of Rio de Janeiro after Humboldt's famous narrative of his arrival in Cuba.[19] From the point of view of its natural beauties Brazil was described as offering a "charming theme for the paintbrushes of travelers." Its mountains were "covered up to the top with majestic forests whose sides conceal diamonds, topazes, and the most precious of metals," in its plains "all products of the vegetal kingdom grow freely[, and] in all aspects Brazil is the country that has been most favored by nature."[20] These opening remarks introduced the contrast, since "all these unique advantages were in one way or another lost by its inhabitants for so long that, while a colony of Portugal, Brazil remained paralyzed by the shackles which the metropolis imposed on it." There followed a condemnation of the continuity of the African slave trade (more than thirty thousand slaves entered the country every year), which could not be tolerated "save by those who are utterly deprived of energy, themselves slaves to habit and idleness."[21]

The same repertoire of images could still be found in 1830 in an anonymous article entitled "Souvenirs du Brésil," which presented a sort of summary of the travel literature of preceding decades. The texts opened with the standard statement that, "as a rule, travelers agree there is nothing quite as charming as the sea-view of Rio de Janeiro. . . . The fields that spread out behind the city are crowned with lush hillocks, magnificently covered by woods, specked with convents and residences, while the harbor is in constant movement thanks to the many vessels that come from all parts of the world. . . . Generally, the air is balmy, the sky pure, and every breeze from land brings with it, over the tranquil waves, the delicious aroma of limes and oranges." This impression, however, could not be long-lasting, because "one is soon to be disappointed, when placing one's feet on land, since in all parts one will find a multitude of Negroes and mulattoes. The mien of these unhappy, seminaked, and brutalized unfortunate beings painfully distresses the European traveler, accustomed as he is to cleanliness in clothing and politeness in manners." There followed a long description of the Valongo slave market summarizing information extracted from British and German travelers.[22]

Saint-Hilaire, the View That Approximates

The absence of a French authority on Brazil who could write in the journal before 1829 was purely circumstantial: the major French traveler during the time of Dom João VI's stay in Brazil, the naturalist Auguste de Saint-Hilaire (1779–1853), who had remained in Brazil from 1816 to 1822, was forced to put off publication of his reports due to ill health. The reports did not come to light until the 1830s and 1840s. Arriving in Brazil together with the first French diplomatic representation after the Congress of Vienna, Saint-Hilaire traveled concurrently with Spix and Martius and the Prinz zu Wied. He was a specialist in botany, and the recognition he received from his trip to Brazil led to his admission to the French Academy of Sciences in 1830, his appointment as professor on the Faculty of Sciences in Paris, and his membership in the Institute of France. He became one of the leading authorities on Brazil and was frequently invited to write about Brazil in specialized journals. [23]

The presence of Auguste de Saint-Hilaire's writings in the pages of the journal from 1829 marks a departure from the type of travel literature that had prevailed until then, especially in the view of his adopted Brazil. Between 1829 and 1849 Brazil was constantly present in the *Nouvelles Annales des Voyages* through passages selected from the travel narratives by Saint-Hilaire and by very favorable comments on it by the journal's reviewers. Over these two decades Saint-Hilaire appeared at least sixteen times in the *Nouvelles Annales des Voyages*, including announcements related to his travels and scientific presentations, excerpts from his writings, and reviews of his publications and articles. His presence, side by side with Ferdinand Denis (and, at times, jointly with Denis), was important to the composition of Brazil's image in the world at the time. Saint-Hilaire's impact on this image was enhanced by his willingness to break away from the then-dominant stereotypes of Brazil advanced by earlier writers.

In the extracts of his works published in the *Nouvelles Annales des Voyages* Saint-Hilaire usually selected passages that allowed readers to see the diversity of Brazilian nature as well as of its human types. Taken as a whole, their most outstanding feature is their silence on slavery. We may only suppose that this omission was a deliberate choice made by Saint-Hilaire as author rather than one made by the journal and that it was his selection of topics, regions, and approaches that emphasized the diversity of Brazilian nature as a background for the cultural and ethnic diversity of its populations. Unlike the old descriptions of Rio de Janeiro, which built on the dichotomy of the splendor of nature versus the degradation brought about by slavery, Saint-Hilaire's writings allowed a presentation of human types described in short ethnographic fragments collected from diverse regions within Brazil. He emphasized the miscegenation of different Amerindian groups and their mixing with the white and black population.

In 1829 the *Nouvelles Annales des Voyages* offered readers their first glimpse of Saint-Hilaire's travels, a small piece on Brazil's human types that described the indigenous populations of Minas Gerais. Saint-Hilaire described a community originally erected by adventurers in search of gold that, at the time of his visit, had a population largely made up of various Amerindian peoples. In contrast with previously published ethnographic reports the Amerindians of Saint-Hilaire were presented as people less separate from whites, with much emphasis on their biological blending and social contact with whites and blacks and among themselves. One of these Amerindians, wrote Saint-Hilaire, "had the lower part of his face much narrower than the upper part, a rather slim body as compared with the Coroados, a smaller head, and a nose not as flat. He actually resembled very much two Caiapós . . . whom I had the opportunity of meeting at Ubá." There also two youngsters "who, regarding their appearance, were as different as that one from the other inhabitants of Santo Antonio. These two youngsters . . . did not appear to bear any trait belonging to the Amerindian race, but I found something closer to the traits and the color of the mulattoes. This resemblance can be explained by the former relations between Malalis and escaping black slaves, as well as by the fact that the captain's grandmother was a black woman, the same who . . . rules the village."[24]

Saint-Hilaire's sharp eye for individual differences and his sensitivity to half-tones are recurrent features in his travel accounts. This distinguished him from the distant outlook of the naturalists who always looked for what was typical, characteristic, or exemplary. Saint-Hilaire was fascinated by various forms of miscegenation and by cultural and religious syncretism. For example, he informed readers that members of the Amerindian group described above spoke their own language but could communicate perfectly in Portuguese, just as they were baptized into the Catholic faith while at the same time continuing to hold on to their traditional beliefs and superstitions. In their manner of dress (cheap cotton pants and shirts hanging loose) "they resemble poor Portuguese people."[25]

In this constant exercise of identity and otherness the "lens of approximation" also seemed to mediate the contact between the traveler's background and the populations under observation. Saint-Hilaire actually points out that "the Pinhami looked very much like . . . our French peasants who maintain the appearance of simplicity that we always hope to find in the countryside."[26] The approximation of people's appearance also was expressed in descriptions that at once established critical distance from the people depicted and engaged readers in a feeling of humanitarian and philanthropic protection: "These good fellows are shy," he wrote, "extremely sweet, and one can get anything from them, cherishing them as small children. The taste for being cherished is not peculiar to this village and actually testifies to their inferiority. Whatever it may mean, the

Portuguese, either white or mulatto, appear to treat Amerindians very kindly and live among them in a very good understanding."[27]

In 1831, when the first critical review of Saint-Hilaire's works was published, the *Nouvelles Annales des Voyages* reported the triumphant reception Saint-Hilaire received from the Academy of Sciences when he presented the results of his works to them. His triumph was shared by the journal, which now counted on a trustworthy expert on Brazil to offer to its readers. His ability to paint human types was especially praised, with one example being his description of a plantation owner: he "has a fine bearing, which proves that he eats well and works little. When he is among his inferiors and even among his peers, he stands up straight, keeps his head up, and speaks with the strong and imperious tone of one who is used to commanding a large number of slaves." Such pride and grandeur are sadly contrasted with the physical bearing of the Indians and mixed-race peoples, "a kind of stupid timidity that betrays the idea they have of their own inferiority. This group . . . shocked me more than I had expected and inspired in me a feeling of pity and humiliation."[28]

In 1834 Saint-Hilaire returned to the pages of the *Nouvelles Annales des Voyages*, this time through the critical review of the second volume of his work. The journal chose to focus again on the Amerindian. In this instance the reviewer cited extracts in which the traveler speaks of the effects of the appropriation of land on the Amerindians: "M. Saint-Hilaire regards the Amerindian race to be destined to disappear from Brazil and probably from other regions of America." The reviewer used Saint-Hilaire's own text to point out, in an as yet very incipient form but one nevertheless worthy of note, a topic that would begin to draw growing attention from that moment. "In dealing with the first two volumes written by Saint-Hilaire, we have seen that, in the province of Minas Gerais, the Portuguese made war against the Amerindians, but that men with deep human feelings have managed, through the perseverance of good treatment, to tame the rebellious character of these savages. We find further comforting examples of this in the coastal regions." Following this review is a detailed description of the work of a Frenchman, M. Mallière, who advocated the pacification of the Amerindians of Minas Gerais.[29]

During this period Saint-Hilaire's writings frequently promote this idea of the Brazilians as a people in formation who needed to be protected by a wise state and king and also to be helped by European commerce, knowledge, and skills. The appropriation of empty lands and their improvements by European science is a constant theme in his writing. The journal's (not Saint-Hilaire's) comment is noteworthy, because its concerns about the disappearance of Amerindians and about the need for protecting them, as well as the model for protection proposed by Mallière, illustrate the link between this ethnography and

French interests in the South American frontier concerning the dispute over a large portion of territory in French Guiana.

An example of this can be seen in some articles published by French travelers in the 1840s both in the *Nouvelles Annales des Voyages* and in the *Revue des Deux Mondes*. The most blatant version of the linkage between a protective attitude toward the Indians and territorial ambition in Guyana appeared in 1844 in a long article signed by M. L. Chavagnes, comte de Suzannet. The article made a critical assessment of Brazil's problems surrounding African slaves and Indians and raised serious doubts about the future of the nation and the monarchy. In this context the focus on the slave trade and the inhuman treatment of Amerindians barely disguised French interest in the disputed territory of Amapá.[30] Entire sections of this article appeared also in a review in the *Nouvelles Annales de Voyage* in 1847 by the same author. In these extracts the matter of the frontiers of Guyana is dealt with primarily in the context of Anglo-French rivalry: "England and France are face to face on the banks of the Amazon, and . . . the invasive action of English policy can give rise to grievous complications. To this issue of boundaries another matter . . . is related: the fight of Amerindians against Brazilian authorities. If a European power were to extend its influence to these savage peoples, I believe that the cause of civilization would be, as from that moment, victorious in this country."[31]

As we shall see, Saint-Hilaire's work provided an important counterpoint by avoiding the "sensitive frontier" and offering, as a substitute, a geopolitical outlook that helped defend the monarchy and "center" the geographical and territorial imaginary of Brazil.

The *Revue des Deux Mondes*: A Political Intervention

In 1831 Saint-Hilaire made what was clearly a political rather than scientific intervention in an article published in the *Revue des Deux Mondes*. The article is of special interest not only for its approach but also because it was preceded by a long introduction written by Ferdinand Denis, an intellectual of utmost importance for the building up of the "French mirror" in Brazil. Denis had been a traveler in Brazil himself (1816–19) and was reputed to be a specialist in Brazilian culture and politics. In this article Denis, who had been a contemporary of Saint-Hilaire at the time of his stay in Brazil as well as a pioneering Brazilianist, ascribed to Saint-Hilaire's work a transcendent significance. He placed it within the long tradition of French interest in Brazil and in doing so underscored a French sponsorship of the Brazilian nation.

Following Denis's introduction, Saint-Hilaire's article dealt with a topic altogether different from the extracts that had been appearing in the *Nouvelles*

Annales des Voyages. It contained a sharp political analysis and covered the time from the "Brazilian revolutions" during the reign of Dom João VI to the recent abdication of Dom Pedro I and built an impressive discourse in defense of the Brazilian monarchy as the only means of ensuring the future of the nation. Saint-Hilaire's starting point was an overview of the present situation of Brazil, emphasizing the contrast between the country's potential and the heavy legacy it had received from the colonial past:

> The colonial system tended not only to impoverish Brazil but had an even more hateful objective: to ensure its lack of unity. By sowing the seeds of division among its provinces, the metropolis hoped to maintain for a longer period of time the superiority of forces it required to wield its tyranny. Each captaincy had its satrap, a small army, and a small treasury. . . . There was no common center in Brazil: the land resembled a huge circle whose radii would converge far away from the circumference.[32]

Based on this evaluation of the colonial era, Saint-Hilaire emphasized the importance of the transfer of the Portuguese court to Brazil in 1808 and assessed positively Dom João's political vision, his administrative work, and the enlightened character of his ministers. Brazilians experienced the return of the king to Portugal with sadness and frustration, he wrote, especially because, at the same time, the revolution in Portugal further encouraged disunion and rivalry among the captaincies of the South American territory. Thus, Saint-Hilaire helped to consolidate an enduring interpretation in Brazilian historiography according to which the participation of Crown Prince Dom Pedro in the process of claiming independence ensured the unification of the nation against the disruptive forces that were still active and, in fact, sustained by the metropolitan Cortes.

For Saint-Hilaire, however, Dom Pedro's career in Brazil had come to an end, and his abdication meant a major breach with the Portuguese past. The Brazilian nation's challenge was to overcome the disintegration of the Portuguese Empire by building a monarchy that would be at once legitimate and authentically American. This seemed to be the sole guarantee of unity. Saint-Hilaire's prose was powerful, especially when depicting the whole destiny of Brazil lying in the hands of a child. (Young Prince Dom Pedro was only five years old when his father left him in Brazil.) This boy alone "keeps the provinces of this vast empire united; and his existence poses a barrier against the ambitious who surge from all places moved by a mediocrity matched only by their gigantic resolve."[33] The unifying power of monarchy appears here not as an element of tradition but as an object of reinvention, the sole possibility for monarchy to take root in America:

> A European cannot rule over America, but he is Brazilian; the bright blue of the tropical skies has touched his first sights; it was under the shade of the virgin woods that

his first steps were guided; he will never pine for the palaces of Lisbon nor for the tasty fruits of the Douro. . . . Alone among Brazilians, this child binds together past and present. . . . Let us hope that all Brazilians who honor the name of their fatherland may gather around young Pedro, those who love liberty with all their heart and do not wish to see it put to loss by a pack of ravenous and abject tyrants.[34]

Monarchy alone, Saint-Hilaire seemed to argue, could prevent Brazil's disunity, particularly the secession of the La Plata republics, where decentralized power threatened dissolution. By warning against the republican tendencies and centripetal forces present in the Brazilian political scene and in Spanish American examples of political fragmentation, Saint-Hilaire stressed that the absence of a strong central state authority would lead to chaos because "each town, each village intended to 'establish its own fatherland,' despicable commanders armed themselves on all sides, the population was dispersed or annihilated, ranches were destroyed, territories the size of entire provinces are now nothing but weeds, and, on plains where numerous cattle grazed, there are now packs of wild dogs, deer, ostriches, and ferocious jaguars."[35]

It is impossible to overrate the importance of Saint-Hilaire's 1831 intervention. He expressed himself in passionate language that differed markedly from his usual restrained and scholarly tone, and his article came at a time when Brazilian regional elites were very keen on the idea of federation following the abdication of the first emperor the same year the article appeared. It was also in 1831 that Brazil accorded with Britain to put an end to the slave trade. From here on the British would regard the slave trade as smuggling and would harass slave traders on the high seas and even on Brazilian shores. At the same time, after the 1830 revolution the French monarchy tended to converge toward the British opposition to the slave trade. In 1832, still in the *Revue des Deux Mondes*, Theodore Lacordaire published an article in which appears the cruelest description of the slave trade depicted in the *Revue des Deux Mondes* throughout the whole period.[36]

Centering the Territory

The mounting aggressiveness in the "audit of the nation" in the *Revue des Deux Mondes* that was echoed in the *Nouvelles Annales des Voyages* came about at a time when there was mounting pressure for the ending of the slave trade, the negotiations of a new tariff were in process, and the Guyana question grew in bitterness. This state of things rendered all the more meaningful the continuous appearances of Saint-Hilaire's extracts and comments in the *Nouvelles Annales des Voyages* during this turbulent period. The most noteworthy aspect of such selections is the fact that, in the extracts published in the 1840s, attention was drawn away from the disputed west border, where the two main fluvial systems of South America communicate, thus inverting the meaning of the geopolitical discussion. Most articles and comments dealt with the fluvial systems that run from the center of the territory and allowed territorial integration. Thus, in 1842, for example, he described in great detail the source and course of the San Francisco River, drawing attention to the role played by this river in the integration of the territory. At the same time, he underlined the importance of the province of Minas Gerais as the watershed of the northern and southern hydrographical systems of the country.[37]

Saint-Hilaire's last appearance in the journal, in 1849, is a sort of grand finale, for there we find a critical evaluation of his works as a whole. This text emphasized the strategic importance of his trip, which took six years, covered 2,500 leagues, and made known the various regions of Brazil, their geography, vegetation, arts, and articles of trade. During the trip Saint-Hilaire fixed the boundaries of Brazil's territory, in each stage collecting, describing, and then returning to Rio de Janeiro to organize the collected material. "Thus, this long trip is completed, which will provide the centuries to come with the knowledge of the original condition of places which have a calling for a bright destiny."[38]

The brighter destiny was reserved for the province of Goiás. This region, whose initial settlement was triggered by the discovery of gold, was depicted in a state of abandon and decadence, owing to the exhaustion of the gold mines. The province would, nevertheless, be called to a brighter future because, according to Saint-Hilaire, it stood as the geopolitical center of Brazil. Brazilian geographers should focus their attention on the province of Goiás, he insisted, for it is here that the Amazon and La Plata fluvial systems could be integrated. This observation drew an internal network of communication by means of internal rivers as a means of integration, free of frontier contestations. A few leagues away from Vila Boa, in Goiás, Saint-Hilaire located the point of contact for the two major fluvial systems of the continent: "This is a point . . . called to establish communication, by water and almost without interruption, between two ports, Montevidéu and Pará. . . . It also allows for communication with Mato Grosso, Paraguay, Entre Ríos, and the former mission territory of Uruguay."[39] Saint-Hilaire for the first time determined the place where the present national capital, Brasília, would be located more than a century later.

Avoiding slavery, stressing racial blending, emphasizing the centripetal effect of a monarchical regime, centering the territory—with all these achievements to his credit it is impossible to exaggerate the importance of Auguste de Saint-Hilaire as one of the most important interlocutors of the original Brazilian nationalism. His reports, filtered by their circulation in France between 1830 and 1850, appeared regularly in difficult moments for the political consolidation of the Brazilian Empire. Brazil's legitimacy as a sovereign member of the international system of nation-states was rendered difficult by both internal and external forces. By carefully avoiding the disputed issues, both the visible (the matter of the La Plata region) and the invisible (slavery and the slave trade), Saint-Hilaire perceived the possibility of a Brazilian nation in spite of all the frailties it had to cope with in the first half of the nineteenth century. He stressed the importance of the Brazilian monarchy for unifying a country otherwise fragmented by regional dissent and external territorial disputes. Most of all, he threw light on the effort of Brazilian elites in reinventing monarchy, giving it American roots. In doing so he laid down a lasting reference on which Brazilian intellectuals could build their own cognitive map for imagining their nation. It expresses vividly the selective internalization of the foreign mirror that was essential to the building of Brazilian nationalism.

NOTES

This text is a preliminary result of research supported by a postdoctorate scholarship granted by the Coordenação de Aperfeiçoamento do Pessoal do Ensino Superior (CAPES).

1. For the origins of this persistent myth see João Manuel de Oliveira Lima, *O movimento de Independência, 1821–1822* (São Paulo, 1922) and *The Evolution of Brazil Compared with That of Spanish and Anglo-Saxon America* (New York, 1966). For recent research on the subject of Brazilian independence and national identity see István Jancsó and João Paulo Pimenta, "Peças de um mosaico: Apontamentos para o estudo da unidade nacional brasileira," in Carlos Guilherme Mota, ed., *Viagem incompleta: A experiência brasileira (1500–2000). Formação: Histórias* (São Paulo, 2000); Márcia Regina Berbel, *A nação como artefato: Deputados do Brasil nas Cortes portuguesas, 1821–1822* (São Paulo, 1999); Miriam Dolhnikoff, "Construindo o Brasil: Unidade nacional e pacto federativo nos projetos das elites (1820–1842)," Ph.D. dissertation, FFLCH-USP, 2000.

2. See François-Xavier Guerra, *Modernidad e independencias* (Mexico City, 1993).

3. Eric Hobsbawm, *The Age of Revolution: Europe, 1789–1848* (London, 1962), chap. 5.

4. Among others, I have been inspired by M. L. Pratt, *Imperial Eyes: Travel Writing and Transculturation* (London, 1992); Pagden, *European Encounters with the New World: From Renaissance to Romanticism* (New Haven, Conn., 1993); Tzvetan Todorov, *On Human Diversity: Nationalism, Racism, and Exoticism in French Thought* (Cambridge, Mass., 1994).

5. See Flora Sussekind, *O Brasil não é longe daqui. O Narrador. A Viagem* (São Paulo, 1990); and Mario Carelli Carelli, *Cultures croisées histoire des échanges culturels entre la France et le Brésil de la découverte aux temps modernes* (Paris, 1993).

6. Major references are Anthony D. Smith, *National Identity* (London, 1991); Benedict Anderson, *Imagined Communities: Reflections on the Origins and Spread of Nationalism* (London, 1993); E. Gellner, *Nations and Nationalism* (Oxford, 1983); Eric Hobsbawm, *Nations and Nationalisms since 1780: Program, Myth, Reality* (London, 1990). See the overall picture in Gil Delannoi and P. A. Taguieff, *Teorías del nacionalismo* (Barcelona, 1993).

7. For the Instituto Histórico e Geográfico see Manoel I. S. Guimarães, "Nação e civilização nos trópicos: O I.H.G.B. e o projeto de uma história nacional," in *Estudos históricos* (Rio de Janeiro, 1988), 1:5–27.

8. For an extensive analysis of this debate see Arno Wehling, *Estado, história, memória: Varnhagen e a construção da identidade nacional* (Rio de Janeiro, 1999); and Temistocles Correa Cezar, "L'écriture de l'histoire au Brésil, au XIXe siècle. Essai sur une rhétorique de la nationalité: Le cas Varnhagen," Ph.D. dissertation, École des Hautes Études en Sciences Sociales, 2002.

9. On the major role of Ferdinand Denis in Brazilian cultural life see Maria Helena Rouanet, *Eternamente em berço esplêndido—a fundação de, uma literatura nacional* (São Paulo, 1991).

10. See Affonso Taunay, *A missão artística de 1816* (Rio de Janeiro, 1956).

11. See Demetrio Magnoli, *O corpo da pátria: Imaginação geográfica e política externa no Brasil (1808–1912)* (São Paulo, 1997); and Antonio Carlos Robert de Moraes, *Bases da formação territorial do Brasil* (São Paulo, 2000).

12. Luiz Felipe de Alencastro, "La traite négrière et l'unité nationale brésilienne," *Revue Française d'Histoire d'Autre-Mer* (Paris), nos. 244–45 (1979).

13. Robin Blackburn, *The Overthrow of Colonial Slavery, 1776–1848* (London, 1988); Philippe Darriulat, *Les patriotes: La gauche républicaine et la nation (1830–1870)* (Paris, 2001).

14. For an overall treatment see Janine Potelet, *Le Brésil vu par les voyageurs et les marins français (1816–1840)* (Paris, 1993); and also Lorelay Brilhante Kury, *Histoire naturelle et voyages scientifiques (1780–1830)* (Paris, n.d.).

15. For the *Revue* and his reception in Brazil see Gabriel Broglie, *Histoire politique de la Revue des Deux Mondes de 1829 à 1879* (Paris, 1979); and Luis Dantas, "A presença e a imagem do Brasil na Revue des Deux Mondes no século XIX," in *Imagens recíprocas do Brasil e da França (Projeto France-Brésil)* (Paris, 1991).

16. Baron von Eschwedge, "Observations sur la manière de voyager dans l'intérieur du Brésil, et tableau de cette partie du pays, traduits de l'allemand," *Nouvelles Annales des Voyages, de la Géographie et de l'Histoire, ou Recueil des Relations Originales Inédites, Communiquées par des Voyageurs Français et Étrangers (NAV)* 1, no. 3 (1819): 21, 99, 118.

17. "Voyage au Brésil pendant les années 1815, 1816 et 1817; par S. A. S. le prince Maximilien de Wied-Neuwied," *NAV* 1, no. 18 (1823): 88–89.

18. "Voyages dans l'Amérique méridionale pendant les années 1819, 1820, 1821; état présent de Beunos Ayres et Chili, par Alexandre Claudecleugh" (review), *NAV* 1, no. 31 (1826): 225–26.

19. Alexander von Humboldt, "Essai politique sur l'île de Cuba," in *Voyage aux régions équinoxiales du Nouveau Continent fait in 1799, 1800, 1801, 1803 et 1804* (Paris, 1825), 348–60.

20. "Voyages dans l'Amérique méridionale," 229.

21. Ibid., 231.

22. "Souvenirs du Brésil," *NAV*, 2nd series, 46, no. 16 (1830): 199–200.

23. For a recent work on Auguste de Saint-Hilaire see Kury, *Histoire naturelle*; and "Auguste de Saint-Hilaire, viajante exemplar," *Revista Intellectus* 2, no. 3 (2003): 1–11.

24. Auguste de Saint-Hilaire, "Les Indiens de Passanha, fragment inédit par M. Auguste de St. Hilaire, correspondant de l'Institut," *NAV*, 2nd series, 44, no. 14 (1829): 70.

25. Ibid., 74.

26. Ibid., 76.

27. Ibid., 73.

28. "Voyage dans les provinces de Rio de Janeiro et de Minas Geraes, par Auguste de Saint-Hilaire" (review), *NAV*, 2nd series, 50 (1831): 89–93.

29. "Voyage dans le district des Diamans et sur le littoral du Brésil, suivi de notes sur quelques plantes caractéristiques, et d'un précis de l'histoire des révolutions de l'empire brésilien, depuis le commencement du règne de Jean VI jusqu'à l'abdication de don Pedro; par M. Auguste de Saint-Hilaire" (review), *NAV* 1, no. 63 (1834): 88.

30. M. L. Chavagnes, "Le Brésil en 1844.—Sa Situation morale, politique, commerciale et financière.—La société brésilienne," *Revue des Deux Mondes*, n.s. 7 (1844): 66–107.

31. "Souvenirs de voyages. Les provinces du Caucase. L'empire du Brésil. Par M. le comte de Suzannet" (review), *NAV* 1, no. 116 (1847): 348.

32. Auguste de Saint-Hilaire, "Tableau des dernières révolutions du Brésil," *Revue des Deux Mondes* 1–2 (1831): 345.

33. Ibid., 347.

34. Ibid., 348.

35. Ibid., 349.

36. Theodore Lacordaire, "Um Souvenir du Brésil," *Revue des Deux Mondes* 8, no. 6 (1832): 645–72.

37. Auguste de Saint-Hilaire, "M. Aug. de Saint-Hilaire. Les sources du Rio de S. Francisco," *NAV* 95 (1842): 171–87; Auguste de Saint-Hilaire, "Observations sur les diviseurs des eaux de plusieurs des grandes rivières de l'Amérique du Sud, et les noms qu'il convient de leur appliquer. Par M. Aug. de Saint-Hilaire membre de l'Institut," *NAV* 1, no. 116 (1847): 341–55.

38. "Voyage aux sources du Rio de São Francisco et dans la Province de Goyaz, Paris, Arthur Betrand, 1847" (review), *NAV* 1, no. 121 (1849): 90–91.

39. Ibid., 98.

Caudillo Nationalism in Bolivia

HEATHER THIESSEN-REILY

On a clear August morning in 1850 the recently elected constitutional president of Bolivia, Manuel Isidoro Belzú, led a procession up Sumaj Urqu, the mountain that rises above the city of Potosí. With this act of ascension, Belzú reenacted an earlier ascent of the mountain while firmly claiming his own place in Bolivian history. The historical importance of Sumaj Urqu, or Cerro Rico, had been recognized and its symbolism appropriated in 1825 when Simón Bolívar climbed to its top to mark Bolivia's liberation from Spain. Bolívar's act, as Tristan Platt has argued, not only symbolically liberated Potosí from Spanish rule but also was interpreted by the indigenous population as a "restoration of divine intercession in defense of their lands and productivity." As a result, "the virgin of the mountain of Potosí, as Pachamama, earth-mother, would provide the legitimacy the new republic needed in Indian eyes."[1] It is clear in Belzú's later ascent that he, who had seized power in 1848 and served two years as Bolivia's provisional president, sought to reinforce the political legitimacy he gained through the May 1850 election with a similarly profound and deeper-rooted legitimacy.[2] At this historic place Belzú not only sought to connect himself with the republic's struggle for nationhood but also reached into Bolivia's colonial and pre-Columbian pasts in an attempt to create a tradition that would promote a sense of national identity based on inclusion rather than exclusion.

Eric Hobsbawm has identified three types of "invented traditions" used to promote national identity: first, those acts that establish or symbolize social cohesion or membership of real or artificial communities; second, those that establish or legitimize institutions, status, or relations of authority; and finally, those that aim to socialize by inculcating beliefs, value systems, and conventions of behavior.[3] Such inventions may also include symbolic materials or means of spreading state legitimacy that inculcate national unity. The role of the more traditional of such symbols (flags, anthems, and other heraldic sources) has been long considered, but we can also identify the process of national identity construction in such varied sources as state rituals, currency, public architecture, civic festivals, and even burial monuments. Such "invented traditions" are created by governments and individuals in the pursuit of political legitimacy, national unity, and a collective national identity.

For Belzú to achieve any success in creating a collective national identity for Bolivia he had to appeal across social and cultural lines. As a result, his project marked an attempted departure from those defined and directed by the Bolivian elite. His attempts at national construction embraced elements of modernity and tradition, and his use of the state to shape the direction and nature of the Bolivian nation was as much a response to demands from the popular classes as an institutional demand from above. As Luis Roniger and Mario Sznajder have observed, in "societies with cleavages, strong pressures existed to develop formulae that allowed the different groups to co-exist under the same political institutions."[4] Nineteenth-century Bolivia was clearly a society with deep cleavages based upon ethnicity and class, and as such any attempt to develop institutions or symbols that could transcend or at least minimize those divisions would require more than demagogic rhetoric.

It was during Belzú's presidency that Bolivia adopted or finalized the three most powerful symbols of national identity: the national flag, the national anthem, and the national emblem. Through these three symbols "an independent country proclaims its identity and sovereignty, and as such they command instantaneous respect and loyalty. In themselves they reflect the entire background, thought and culture of a nation."[5] But before they can project national identity outward, they must gain internal allegiance. Belzú recognized the importance of creating symbols that could attract a common allegiance among Bolivia's population. A flag, a coat of arms, and a national anthem would be represented in the same fashion to the entire population.

In 1854 a presidential decree mandated the proper presentation of the national flag in public buildings and specified that a second flag with the national coat of arms on a backdrop of one of the three national flag colors should be displayed with the national flag. For example, educational institutions were assigned a flag depicting the condor on a yellow backdrop; government buildings were assigned one with a green background; and citizens could fly one upon a bright red background.[6] The invention of ceremonies and state rituals around these symbols reinforced state authority and was used to inculcate further social cohesion among groups within the nation.

The presence of a national flag in public and private buildings can be a powerful reminder of the nation; however, it can also project a sense of passivity if the flag is not being used in a ceremony or celebration. If a flag is not rippling in the wind or being waved at a public ceremony, it hangs listless in government buildings and classrooms. Thus, in itself, a flag may not be enough to remind people on a daily basis of their connection with the nation. Such representations are made all the more powerful if they are associated with some form of national oration. In a presidential order dated 27 March 1852 copies of the new national anthem of Bolivia were distributed in schools throughout the country.[7] The words of Dr. Ignacio de Sanjines were set to the music of Benedetto Vincenti. The national anthem was published widely in local newspapers throughout the year, often in the papers' regular sections entitled "Poesía nacional."

The images invoked in the national anthem were meant to inspire and elicit a sense of national pride and belonging. The lyrics established a new creation belief for the young nation, one to which, it was hoped, all citizens could connect. The anthem referred to the new national flag; identified the nation's founder hero, Bolívar, since he personified the nation; and described the glorious struggle that resulted in freedom for the country. Another powerful series of images in the anthem are the constant references to Bolivia's natural resources and environment. In a country where the vast majority of the population had a deep connection to the land and where survival depended on adapting to the harsh environment, such images were potent messages. Through the expansion of public instruction, Belzú provided the anthem and its message an audience. The invention of such ceremonies and state rituals around these symbols reinforced state authority and were used to inculcate further social cohesion among groups within the nation. Such "emotionally and symbolically charged signs of club membership" would not only unite Bolivians under the same symbols but would also come to represent state power and identity. As such, Belzú oversaw the creation of these new heraldic symbols of nationhood.[8]

Heraldic symbols are powerful images of national identity, but it is not only with flags or anthems that a sense of national consciousness can be constructed. Lynn Hunt argues that languages, phrases, and even individual words can be used to create a sense of national community because they do not "just reflect social and political reality; they were instruments for transforming reality."[9] We also see this attempt to transform Bolivian social reality and to inculcate a sense of equality when Belzú's government abolished traditional titles, decreeing that all Bolivians should be addressed by the title of *ciudadano* (citizen).[10] The idea that all were citizens of the republic without consideration of ethnicity or social rank was a conscious attempt to promote a sense not only of equality among the population but of shared identity "to establish or symbolize social cohesion or the membership of groups in real or artificial communities."[11] While it would take more than a simple word to transcend the ethnic, linguistic, and racial divides in Bolivian society, the message of this decree was clear: the government of Belzú considered all Bolivians citizens of the republic and as such part of the *patria*. But this act and the new nation's symbols of flag and anthem would not be enough to convince the majority of the Bolivian population of a common allegiance, let alone be accessible to them all. To create an inclusionary national identity Belzú could not solely rely on new symbolic inventions. He would have to reach back and connect with Bolivia's multiple pasts.

The task of creating a collective and inclusionary national identity was daunting if not foolhardy. Bolívar and Antonio José de Sucre, Bolivia's first president, had failed and met with miserable ends. Former Bolivian president Andrés Santa Cruz had abandoned it in favor of reestablishing the Bourbon viceroyalty of Peru, albeit in the form of the Peru-Bolivian Confederation. The Creole elite of the country were taken aback by the audacity of a man such as Belzú to undertake and redefine a project they had long considered their own. National construction was a prerogative of elite control. The idea that someone from outside their class and, even worse, from below it could envision a national project was problematic and threatened the majority of the Bolivian elites' control over the postindependence political project. In the opinion of the elite nationalism was equated with modernity, and from their perspective Indians, artisans, and caudillos were opposed to modernity in all its forms and thus were barriers to creating a national identity. To reinforce this marginalization, Bolivian elites rested their concept of the nation upon a narrowly defined aristocratic sovereignty.

While members of Bolivia's Creole elite may have considered themselves modern, when they were faced with the challenge of Belzú's nationalist project based on popular sovereignty their actions actually reinforced those traditional barriers against the creation of the nation, giving proof to Victor Alba's conclusion that "Latin American society is a traditional one: it is a society opposed to being transformed into a nation. The Latin American States are not nation-states but oligarchies: true nationalism would end the oligarchy's existence."[12] It would be up to a caudillo to invent, invoke, and imagine methods to promote inclusion in the Bolivian nation.

It is appropriate to return to the highly symbolic act of this alternative path, Belzú's ascent of Sumaj Urqu.

The mountain of Sumaj Urqu towers over the city of Potosí; the little hill of Huayna Potosí lies at its feet. The power and significance of these two geological features long predated their colonial importance, as they had been present in the symbolic rituals of the indigenous peoples of the region for thousands of years. Appearing in songs and legends, the two mountains, large and small, were sacred sources of inspiration and worship for the indigenous population. With the arrival of the Spanish and the discovery of the rich veins of silver coursing through them, the mountains became not only a source of wealth but also proof of divine Providence and fortune.

In one of the most famous paintings of the colonial era Sumaj Urqu has been transformed into the Virgin Mary. Entitled *La Virgen del cerro* and painted by an anonymous artist during the eighteenth century, the painting shows the Virgin encompassed by Sumaj Urqu and being crowned by the archangels, with the pope and the king paying homage at her feet below Huayna Potosí.[13] The religious symbolism of the mountain in this painting was transferred from the Indian earth mother, Pachamama, to the Spanish Catholic Holy Mother, not only reinforcing the mountain's potent appeal across ethnic and religious divides but symbolically legitimizing the authority and power of the colonial administration and the Spanish.[14] The Spanish thus not only occupied the physical landscape but appropriated the spiritual and cultural landscape as well.

At the onset of the republican era the physical ascent of the mountain by Bolívar was clearly an attempt not only to legitimize the new republican government but also to link it to the cyclical notion of Andean time in the indigenous imagination. Belzú's ascent twenty-five years after Bolívar's climb was also the recognition of the cultural significance of the mountain and the invocation of historical legitimacy that would allow Belzú's government to again transcend ethnic and religious divisions. As Sarah Radcliffe and Sallie Westwood have argued, "Place as a defining marker of the national experience and, therefore, of the lived experience and understanding of a national identity is not intended to imply inert geography and the notion of region, but the political, economic, cultural and social dynamics of place."[15] Sumaj Urqu was (and is) more than a mountain: it lives and breathes the history of the people and, more than any other place in Bolivia, defines the country's past in all the aforementioned dynamics.[16]

Bolívar could not have chosen a more powerful place to symbolize the defeat of the colonial era and the onset of the new age of republicanism, and Belzú could not have picked a more powerful and symbolic ritual to reenact than Bolívar's ascent of Sumaj Urqu. Whether we view such acts with a jaded eye or not, the appropriation of places sacred to indigenous populations and dominant in a country's historical memory reflects a recognition on the part of men like Bolívar and Belzú of the multiethnic and polytheistic nature of their country's societies. Belzú's election earlier in the year had given him political legitimacy among elements of the Creole and mestizo populations, but the climb up Sumaj Urqu in 1850 was a direct message to Bolivia's indigenous population, a clear indication that he recognized their cultural and political importance in Bolivia's past and would continue to do so in his plans for Bolivia's future as a nation.

The recognition of the indigenous population and the active cultivation of their support in a project of national construction was a rare attempt in nineteenth-century Latin America. Nation building was generally considered a project for the intellectual and political elites of the new republics. Benedict Anderson's *Imagined Communities* posits the argument that the emergence of "print-capitalism" was crucial in the creation and consolidation of national identities in Latin America and elsewhere. The printed word in popular and elite form provided the distribution and inculcation of a common body of knowledge as well as the interpretation of that knowledge, resulting in a sense of an "imagined community" of the nation among the small, albeit increasing, literate population. While this process indeed occurred in Bolivia among the elite and was encouraged by the educational policies of Belzú among the lower classes, the large indigenous population, most of whom were illiterate in Spanish, could not have shared in this common body of knowledge and thus remained outside of the elite's process of national construction. Despite the rhetoric of citizenship and the Creole notion of a common people in pursuit of independence and nationhood, the indigenous and mixed-race peoples of the continent were largely "unimagined" in the national community. But while "unimagined" by the elite, this did not mean Indians or mestizos were without hope within the new republic. Belzú was the first political leader who truly attempted to expand the process of national construction to incorporate popular sovereignty and who tried to reject the narrow and controlled aristocratic sovereignty of the Bolivian elite.

It is clear that Belzú's administration invented or created elements of nationalism that were then used to promote his vision for Bolivia's future. The promotion of literacy and the use of an active print media as well as the expansion of public instruction all figured prominently among Belzú's methods.[17] But to tell the whole story of Bolivia's national construction we need to expand our understanding of the nationalist project and its accompanying characteristics. Using the categories of Hobsbawm and Platt, we can see that Belzú employed a number of nonliterate means to promote the concept of nationhood among the general population. And it was this attempt on his part to "imagine" Indian and mestizo, peasant and artisan not just as recipients of an elite-defined national identity but as active participants in defining that identity that engendered the wrath of the Bolivian elite. For what Belzú did or at least threatened to do was essentially to hijack the elite's nationalist project and open it to popular interpretation and participation, with potentially radical results.[18]

Belzú's ascent of Sumaj Urqu can be interpreted as one of a number of means he employed not only to gain political legitimacy among the popular classes but to show them that they, in this case the indigenous population, would indeed be imagined in his nation-building project. Anderson's interpretation of national construction thus falls short when applied to Belzú's project. As Anthony Smith has argued, Anderson's reliance upon the printed media and therefore the literate population in national construction fails to consider the impact and importance of the "traditional media of song, dance, ritual object, costume, artwork" as well as "landscapes, monuments, buildings, tombstones, the more durable elements of collective cultures, which provided their historical environment" and also facilitated the incorporation of the popular classes into the nation and their participation in the process of national construction.[19] And while Smith and Hobsbawm do not agree completely concerning the process of national construction and identity, Hobsbawm's "historical continuity" reinforces Smith's consideration of the importance of nonwritten sources and means in the construction or imagination of the nation. Hobsbawm observed, "Sometimes new traditions can be grafted on to old ones, and sometimes they can be devised by 'borrowing from the well-supplied warehouses of official ritual, symbolism and moral exhortation . . . creating an ancient past beyond effective historical continuity, either by semi-fiction or by forgery."[20] By 1850 the ascent of Potosí's mountain had become a "defining marker of the national experience," with deep roots in the Bolivian psyche both indigenous and Creole.[21] Belzú's decision to re-create Bolívar's epic climb of the mountain of Potosí connected him symbolically not only to the indigenous past of the country but to the new republican era as well.

We should not be surprised that Belzú, a man rejected by much of the Bolivian elite, should attempt a nationalist project. As Anthony Smith reminds us, "the idea that nationalism is a product of 'marginal men' or uprooted individuals caught between tradition and westernization is not an original one," and he cites the works of political theorists Hugh Trevor-Roper, Thomas Hodgkin, Hans Kohn, and Elie Kedouri in his argument.[22] We must recognize that national construction cannot simply be left as the preserve of educated elites fearful of the lower classes. While Anderson forced scholars to expand their understanding and approach to nationalism, in this instance he seems more reflective of traditional interpretations of culture and power in Latin America, his imagined community no more than a modified culture "controlled by elites who socialize new generations and emergent groups into its principles and practices."[23]

Belzú's approach to developing a collective identity among Bolivia's disparate population groups challenges traditional notions of state formation in Latin America. Mark Berger's assessment of the existing literature on postcolonial state formation in Latin America found it dominated by an elite-directed Eurocentric approach much in the same vein as Anderson suggested. While many of the works are critical of the elite, they dismiss the role of the lower classes in any of these national construction projects in favor of elite-directed modernization projects that are at best moderated by the resistance of the lower classes.[24] Until recently, studies of the role of subaltern or indigenous groups characterized them as exploited on all fronts during both the colonial and republican eras, marginalized and excluded from the process of national construction.[25] Belzú's attempt to create an inclusionary national identity created openings for the lower and indigenous classes to interpret and define the nation for themselves. It is the envisioning and opening of this process that set Belzú apart from but also at odds with the majority of the Bolivian political elite.

Contemporaries, nineteenth-century writers, and even scholars today have reduced Belzú's national project to acts of demagoguery and meaningless symbols to empower himself over all others. For them and the majority of the Bolivian elite, Belzú and his policies reflected nothing more than a "pathetic fallacy," a false relationship stemming from "disorientation and religious fervor," which results in an "emotional link between leaders and led, which satisfies the leader's will to power, fostering the 'pathetic fallacy,' namely that there is no difference between them and those who[m] they rule."[26] If the Bolivian elites could promote the "pathetic fallacy" and reduce Belzú to nothing more than a barbaric caudillo, then they could reduce those who followed him to nothing more than a mass of easily manipulated and superstitious people who lacked free will and intelligence.

It has also been posited that, despite his humble mestizo origins, once Belzú rose to the presidency he became part of the political elite, whether he faced opposition from within that class or not. And indeed, it is clear that his national project was transmitted to the population in a top-down manner, albeit with a populist character. But when considering Belzú's nation-building project, we must consider both "official" and "popular" nationalisms in the creation and imagination of the nation.[27] Radcliffe and Westwood concluded in their study of modern-day Ecuador that "the distinction between 'official' and 'popular' does not signal a binary opposition but a complex articulation which both supports and fractures the nation."[28] While Belzú clearly hoped his actions would result in the development of a collective identity for the nation, the reality of class and social relations of the time ensured not only that his actions would fracture the nation but that he himself would have to employ language and actions that would undermine the unifying intent of his program. Still, his attempts at inculcating a sense of loyalty to and identification with his government and vision for the nation among the population revealed a complex layering of motives and methods as well as numerous audiences. To dismiss the attempts and actions of Belzú as simply hollow invented traditions with little or no meaning "does scant justice to the complex ways in which these and other ceremonies were reconstructed and reinterpreted. . . . It is hard to believe that most people would willingly . . . be duped by propaganda and ritual over a long period, unless that ritual and propaganda expressed and amplified pre-existing popular sentiments."[29] As a result, Belzú's national project was based upon a balance between the forces of tradition and modernity as expressed through both concrete and symbolic action.

The failure to imagine the unlettered classes as active participants in the project of national construction has been a long-standing oversight in Bolivian politics and history, as the Creole elite consistently discounted the role of the masses in the conceptualization of the nation and in its notions of citizenship and political participation. Historically, the Bolivian elite presented the indigenous population as an obstacle to nation building, one that had to be modified or removed. The early years of most Latin American republics were dominated by a small Eurocentric elite who pursued a limited project of nationhood. But in Bolivia's case, members of the elite dismissed or ignored the massive ethnic majority, which had its own ideas about the significance of independence.[30] As Belzú was victimized by elite vilification and negation, the indigenous population was again defined as a "problem" to be suppressed and whose voice fell on deaf ears.

At best, the attitudes of the elite toward the indigenous population were paternalistic. Marta Irurozqui has made a forceful argument concerning the role of the indigenous population in the elite's conception of the nation. She argued that the elites used the cliché of "racial war" to deny the indigenous population access to participating in the national project. Any attempt by members of the indigenous population to claim their rights as citizens or for justice and equality could be easily dismissed or completely ignored, for at the time the common perception was that Indians rebelled because they were barbaric savages and hated Europeans, not because they had legitimate grievances or because they acted out of a desire for national integration and assimilation. The elites "did not want Bolivia to be perceived as an 'Indian nation,'" and thus any attempt to integrate the Indians had to take the form of either assimilation or eradication.[31]

For Bolivia's heterogeneous population to experience national inclusion, elite intransigence and hostility would have to be overcome. Traditionally, Spanish elites had treated the indigenous population with disdain and contempt, condemning them to eternal infancy within a heavily patriarchal system of governance. During the republican era the Bolivian elites were not much better, continuing to approach the Indian question with a mixture of paternalism, fear, and loathing. Such attitudes were not lost on the indigenous population in Bolivia. Over time, the Indians made sense of what they had learned within this system by translating it into their own codes; in practice, this meant questioning the attitudes of the elite and the rhetoric that derived from the notion that the Indians were ignorant individuals who had to be kept away from state institutions and whose participation in a politically representative system must be limited.[32] Rejecting the notion that Bolivia's Indian communities were completely powerless and marginalized in the nineteenth century, Erick Langer and Robert Jackson argued that they actually formed one of the most powerful entities in nineteenth-century Bolivia, even more so than the Catholic Church.[33] Belzú recognized within these communities a powerful support base and employed numerous methods to attract their support while sympathetically identifying with their concerns.

Belzú rejected the elite notion that the indigenous population was incapable of incorporation into Bolivia's body politic. Even if he was unsuccessful in restructuring Bolivian society in a truly revolutionary way, his rhetoric and nascent support for indigenous issues recognized their importance for Bolivia's economy. This intent to include all Bolivians in the new nation was reiterated in 1850 in the ministerial report of Belzú's minister of public instruction and culture, José Agustín de la Tapia, when he announced the government's intent to eradicate the odious racial distinctions of "Spaniard, mestizo, Indian, black, slave, etc.," used in determining religious fees on the grounds that such categories were contrary to the concept of a single nationality, to democracy, and to all good reason.[34] Bolivia's citizenry would suffer no official distinctions based on race or ethnicity on the threshold of the cemetery, and Belzú hoped that one day the population would experience the unity of the term *boliviano* at the cradle as well as at the grave.

Belzú also held out the promise of adulthood for the Indians through citizenship in the nation. This desire would culminate in the Resolution of 22 December 1855 under the Belcista-dominated Córdova government, which officially stated that all Bolivians, including *indígenas contribuyentes* (Indians who paid tribute taxes to the state), were guaranteed civil and political rights under the law.[35] Above all else, this illustrates what was at stake beneath the symbolic representations of the nation and Belzú's populist appeal. This issue is at the heart of the conflict between Belzú's inclusionary national project and the traditional elite's more exclusionary model. For the elite, Belzú's inclusionary national project contained the possibility that via citizenship in the nation the lower classes, divided by class and ethnicity, could actually conceive of the nation "as the family and locality writ large" and thus not only identify with the nation but make claims upon it.[36]

While the 1855 resolution would seem a radical step toward incorporation of the indigenous population into Bolivia's body politic, recent historiography surmises that the indigenous population was deeply divided over the benefits of citizenship and illustrated an ambiguity toward it due to the issue of tribute. Bolívar had abolished tribute on the grounds that it separated the indigenous communities from the rest of the population, but, as Tristan Platt argued, it was tribute payments that essentially gave the indigenous population not only their identity but also grounds for preserving their communal lands. As the nineteenth century wore on, citizenship was linked to land, an association that would not change until the Bolivian Revolution in 1952.

On the surface it appears that the continuation of the tributary system countered the new spirit of republicanism and liberty associated with independence and seemed to undermine full incorporation of the Indians into the nation. Indeed, the continuance of the tributary system after independence raised the question whether the Indians constituted a separate collective within the actual state. According to the Creole elite, since the Indian communities' corporate nature was coupled with a separate ethnic identity, the Indians presented a problem for the constitution of a homogeneous nation.[37] But it would seem this confusion over the definition of citizenship and the integration of the Indians into the new republic was a one-sided discussion. Marta Irurozqui argued that as early as 1829 the Indian population saw themselves as citizens of the new nation due to their fiscal obligations to the state and the Church. The Indians' understanding of their relationship with the state, colonial or republican, was that their tribute payments ensured government recognition of their land rights based on the age-old system of reciprocity, and that was all they needed to claim citizenship. At the time, taxation systems were based upon the idea that ownership of private property, particularly land, not wealth or production, bestowed citizenship.[38] As long as the Indians met their tribute obligations they believed the state would recognize their landownership, which gave them the basis to claim full citizenship. Thus if a government's actions undermined their ownership of land, such as President José Ballivián's attempt during the 1840s to renegotiate the reciprocal pact by reassigning landownership to the state, their citizenship would be in jeopardy. The Indians very clearly understood that the key to citizenship in the new republic lay in their ability to protect their communal lands. Indian political activity manifested itself in rebellions or land occupations, as "a medium through which the Indians discovered their capacity for social and national growth" began with the "land question which first articulated their national political demands."[39] Such action on the part of the indigenous population in Bolivia clearly undermines the notion that the masses were simply passive at worst, reactive at best to elite actions, "participating little in 'national life,' lacking awareness of, or a commitment to, a Bolivian nation."[40] This behavior also challenges the notion, posited by Eric Hobsbawm, that the popular classes are simply protonationalist and that their passivity prevents them from participating in a nationalist project. Anthony Smith urged scholars to take into consideration the influence of indigenous traditions and beliefs, which often translate into the "passion and fervor of mass followings for nationalist movements, and the frequent willingness on the part of the unlettered and poor to make great sacrifices" in pursuit of nationalist aims.[41] Belzú's recognition of the important economic role the indigenous peoples played in the maintenance of the nation through the payment of tribute was reflected symbolically in the ascent of Sumaj Urqu as well as in legislative action.

As president, Belzú reversed Ballivián's attack on Indian lands. His support of the tributary system was seen by the Indian communities as a continued recognition and protection of their communal landholding system. The Indians interpreted Belzú's willingness to act on their complaints, ease their financial burdens, and turn a blind eye to new land occupations as a recognition of their position in Bolivian society, reinforcing their perceived status as citizens of the nation. Thus ethnicity was not the stumbling block for inclusion in the nation. Economic issues in the form of landownership were, in fact, paramount in defining citizenship in nineteenth-century Bolivia. Under the Belzú administration the indigenous peoples found their claims as citizens of the republic recognized, and as such they were included in the process of national construction. When Belzú's government redefined tribute as a tax without increasing the financial burden on Indian communities, it appeared that concern on the part of Belzú's government over the inclusion of the Indians into the nation had been solved with a semantic sleight of hand. From the Indian perspective, paying tribute was equated with citizenship. By referring to tribute as tax, the government could incorporate the Indians intellectually as well as economically into the republic: Indians paid tribute and citizens paid taxes, so if tribute was a tax, then, ipso facto, Indians were citizens. Indian support of Belzú and his political project of national construction stemmed from a clear understanding of his government's support of their interests.

A simple coin or two will suffice to illustrate this understanding of Belzú's political message by the indigenous population. Coinage was much more than a means of financial exchange for the indigenous peoples of the Andes, even more so in Bolivia than in other countries due to the profound domination of Potosí's silver production. Coinage not only functioned in a practical sense but took on political meaning as "the most effective means available to the state for ensuring an audience for its symbolic rhetoric in remote parts of the countryside where the most persistent reminder of the change of regime would be the means of circulation that passed from hand to hand."[42] Basically, with a large illiterate rural population, the awareness of important national symbols or political events such as a change of government would come from seeing a new face on a new coin. New coins were minted and circulated throughout the republic in recognition and celebration of changes in government and as a means to mark and legitimize a president's power and position. Such coins were more important among the general population than among the elite to transmit such political information.[43]

Belzú seemed to understand this process, as he became one of Bolivia's most prolific issuers of coinage. But while it has been argued that Belzú issued coins with images to fund a debased currency economy or simply to reinforce the caudillistic nature of his regime, perhaps we should consider another reason for issuing so much coinage.[44] Clearly, there were financial reasons for increasing coin production and circulation, but could Belzú have recognized that silver coinage in Bolivia had become endowed with "profound religious connotations by the Andean imagination" due in part to its origin in Sumaj Urqu, the powerful religious symbol and location for the indigenous population long before the Spanish set up their mint? If "every instrument of production and circulation, every relationship in the structure of hierarchy and power, was . . . surrounded with ritual invocations of divine protection, designed to ensure the prosperous completion of a new round in the ongoing process of social and cosmic reproduction," then something as simple as a coin takes on a much greater meaning in the relationship between the governing and the governed (figure 1).[45]

Belzú's prolific minting of small-denomination coins could have been an attempt to communicate not only his power but his political message, and Belzú's image on proclamation coinage, like the coins themselves, came to represent something more than money (figure 2).[46] The Creole elite attempted to control and direct their imagined community of criollo nationhood through the "control of pen and ink, expanding literacy and liberal enlightenment to primarily mestizo towns, islands of relative 'civilization' which exercised their delegated authority over a surrounding sea of Indian communities."[47] Belzú also promoted education and literacy to the lower classes, but he also sought more immediate and tangible methods of transmitting his project of nationhood. His project was transmitted through the small silver coins passed hand to hand among the indigenous population. These coins were valued not only as money and a means of communication but also as a connection to a sacred place. Belzú, by placing not only his image on these coins but also those images symbolic of the nation, not only reinforced his connection with the indigenous population but perhaps hoped to transform that personal allegiance into support for his vision of nationhood for Bolivia.[48]

Heraldic symbols, coinage, and ritual were used by Belzú to promote his legitimacy and authority as president. But while many have suggested that his use of these methods was simply in the pursuit of a demagogue's personal power, these critics fail to consider the larger meaning behind these symbols. Invented or invoked, imagined or imbued, these symbols and Belzú's actions should be considered to be more about inculcating the idea of the nation among an expanded citizenry than about personal ambition. Belzú sought to connect to the indigenous population by tapping into traditional belief systems and practices to uphold or recast customs and traditions. He attempted to open up doors to the popular classes to allow their participation in his alternative vision of the Bolivian nation. Ultimately, many of Belzú's policies won him not only the support of the indigenous population but also the enmity of the elite. Combining elements of populism with sympathetic political and economic policies, Belzú cultivated the indigenous communities into a powerful and threatening force within his conceptualization of the Bolivian nation. Throughout his presidency

Figure 1. Coin: Belzú and the commemorative chapel.

Figure 2. Coin: Belzú on one side, Hercules on the other.

Manuel Isidoro Belzú tried to create opportunities for the indigenous and popular classes to become active participants in and interpreters of Bolivia's emerging national identity. By invoking the power of place, acknowledging Andean religious consciousness, tradition, and ceremony, creating new national symbols, and employing other nonliterate means of communication, Belzú sought to expand the concept of who belonged in the nation. His subaltern supporters should be seen not as dupes or impediments but as crucial participants in an expanded definition of the modern Bolivian nation. In addition, this analysis should raise serious questions about the role of the caudillo as an important participant in the imagining of the nation in Latin America and as a figure who empowered the subaltern to engage in political discourse in an attempt to claim a role in the process of national construction.

1. Tristan Platt, "Simón Bolívar, the Sun of Justice and the Amerindian Virgin: Andean Conceptions of the Patria in Nineteenth Century Potosi," *Journal of Latin American Studies* 25, no. 1 (February 1993), electronic collection: A13700399, Cambridge University Press, unpaginated.

2. Belzú won the presidential election earlier that year in May with 5,935 votes and was sworn in as constitutional president on 15 August 1850. See A. Morales, *Los primeros cien años de la República de Bolivia: Tomo 1, 1825–1860* (La Paz, 1925), 408. Belzú has most often been associated with the artisan class and policies of economic protectionism. These issues are examined in my work "Puertas muy altas para gente tan baja: Manuel Isidoro Belzú and the Pursuit of the Modern Bolivian Nation, 1848–1855," Ph.D. dissertation, Tulane University, 2002. I propose in this chapter to push beyond the limitations of the traditional historiography to explore Belzú's national vision and his attempts to reach a wider constituency within the Bolivian popular classes. Although his attempts to promote a more inclusive national project were frustrated, his vision challenged the elite's hegemonic versions of nationalism and nation building in nineteenth-century Latin America.

3. Eric Hobsbawm, "Introduction: Inventing Traditions," in E. Hobsbawm and T. Ranger, eds., *The Invention of Tradition* (Cambridge, 2000), 9.

4. Luis Roniger and Mario Sznajder, *Constructing Collective Identities and Shaping Public Spheres: Latin American Paths* (Brighton, 1998), 3.

5. Official Indian government commentary as quoted in R. Firth, *Symbols, Public and Private* (London, 1973), 341.

6. Decree, 27 June 1854, in *Anuario 1853–1854: Coleción official de leyes, decretos, órdenes y resoluciones supremas que se han expedido para el regimen de la República de Bolivia* (Sucre, 1865), 16:266.

7. Order, 27 March 1852, in *Anuario 1851–1853: Coleción official de leyes, decretos, órdenes y resoluciones supremas que se han expedido para el regimen de la República de Bolivia* (Sucre, 1865), 15:102.

8. Ortiz Mesa also refers to Belzú's government designating a national flower, but I have not found any reference to such an act in government records ("Poder y sociedad en los Andes: Manuel Isidoro Belzú, un caudillo popular, Bolivia 1848–1855," *Anuario Colombiano de Historia Social y de la Cultura* 22 [1995]: 88).

9. Lynn Hunt, "Politics, Culture and Class," in *The New Cultural History* (Berkeley, Calif., 1989), 17.

10. See, for example, decree, 10 May 1853, in *Anuario 1851–1853*, 15:302. This decree is in keeping with an earlier decree of the provisional government of Velasco that abolished "las ceremonias oficiales de corte y besamanos, conceptuados como envilecedoras de la dignidad del hombre" (Morales, *Primer centenario de Bolivia*, 1:383).

11. Hobsbawm, "Introduction," 9.

12. Victor Alba, *Nationalists without Nations* (New York, 1968).

13. Today this painting hangs in the Museo de la Casa de Moneda in Potosí.

14. Platt, "Simón Bolívar."

15. Sarah Radcliffe and Sallie Westwood, *Remaking the Nation: Place, Identity and Politics in Latin America* (London, 1996), 3.

16. The mountain's vast reserves of silver brought great wealth to the Spaniards but also took a devastating toll on the Indians and Africans who worked the mines and mint. Peter Bakewell suggests that the exact mortality rate can never be accurately calculated but explores the often brutal conditions above and below ground in the mines of colonial Potosí in *Miners of the Red Mountain* (Albuquerque, N.M., 1984), 137–78.

17. Thiessen-Reily, "Puertas muy altas," chaps. 5, 6.

18. It is not surprising Belzú was able to imagine the marginalized of Bolivia as active participants, as his own life could attest a rise from the underclass to a public political life. Born to a poor mestizo family, at a very young age Belzú ran away to join the republican forces during the wars of independence and, like many of his mixed-race caudillo counterparts, parlayed a military career into a presidency.

19. Anthony Smith, *Nationalism and Modernism*, 3rd ed. (London, 2000), 139.

20. Hobsbawm, "Introduction," 7.

21. Eric Hobsbawm identified such behavior as a method of "invented tradition . . . which automatically implies continuity with the past," and while "the historical past into which the new tradition is inserted need not be lengthy, stretching back into the assumed mists of time . . . the peculiarity of 'invented' traditions is that the continuity with it is largely the form of reference to old situations, or which establish their own past by quasi-obligatory repetition" ("Introduction," 1–2). In this case, Belzú's attempt clearly does reach "back into the assumed mists of time" and as such does reference a deeply entrenched historical memory.

22. Smith, *Nationalism and Modernism*, 106. This interpretation is also reinforced in John Lynch, *Caudillos in Spanish America 1800–1850* (Oxford, 1992), in which Lynch characterizes the caudillo as a transitional figure between tradition and modernity, colony and republic.

23. Daniel Levine, "Constructing Culture and Power," in Daniel Levine, ed., *Constructing Culture and Power in Latin America* (Ann Arbor, Mich., 1993), 4.

24. Mark Berger praises Peter Guardino's work *Peasants, Politics and the Formation of Mexico's National State; Guerrero 1800–1857,* as Guardino argues that state formation cannot be viewed as a simple process of the state being unilaterally imposed on existing societal groups ("Specter of Colonialism: Building Postcolonial States and Making Modern Nations in the Americas," *Latin American Research Review* 35, no. 1 [2000]: 151–71).

25. Exceptions to such studies include David Nugent's *Modernity at the Edge of Empire: State, Individual, and Nation in the Northern Peruvian Andes, 1885–1935* (Stanford, Calif., 1997); Mark Thurner, "'Republicanos' and 'la comunidad de Peruanos': Unimagined Political Communities in Postcolonial Andean Peru," *Journal of Latin American Studies* (May 1995); and Charles Walker, *Smoldering Ashes: Cuzco and the Creation of Republican Peru 1780–1840* (Durham, N.C., 1999).

26. Elie Kedourie as quoted in Smith, *Nationalism and Modernism*, 131. Belzú often invoked his humble upbringing and mixed-race heritage in public orations, but it was not a fallacy. He did rise out of the masses and shared their frustrations and aspirations throughout his life.

27. William Rowe and Vivian Schelling criticized Anderson for his failure to consider popular elements in his analysis of Latin American nationalism. For Anderson, national construction remained a preserve of the elite and those who controlled the printed page. Rowe and Schelling argued that participation of popular groups in independence "depended not on literacy but on oral transmission and iconography; and the fact that popular identity did not and does not necessarily correspond with the nation and its boundaries as state but may involve other allegiances of a regional, ethnic or class nature" (*Memory and Modernity: Popular Culture in Latin America* [London, 1994], 25).

28. Radcliffe and Westwood, *Remaking the Nation,* 2.

29. Smith, *Nationalism and Modernism,* 130.

30. Platt, "Simón Bolívar."

31. Marta Irurozqui, "The Sound of the Pututos: Politicisation and Indigenous Rebellions in Bolivia 1826–1921," *Journal of Latin American Studies* (February 2000): 100.

32. Ibid., 86.

33. Erick Langer and Robert Jackson, "Liberalism and the Land Question in Bolivia, 1825–1920," in Robert Jackson, ed., *Liberals, the Church and Indian Peasants: Corporate Lands and the Challenge of Reform in Nineteenth Century Spanish America* (Albuquerque, N.M., 1997), 187.

34. José Agustín de la Tapia, Ministerio de Instrucción Pública y Culto, *Exposoción de que presente el ministro de estado en los departamentos del culto e instrucción pública a las cámaras legislativas de la república boliviano en 1850* (Sucre, 1850).

35. Resolution, 22 December 1855, in Flores Moncayo, *Legislación boliviana del indio: Recopiliación de resoluciones, órdenes, decretos, leyes, decretos supremos y otras disposiciones legales 1825–1953* (La Paz, 1953), 164.

36. Smith, *Nationalism and Modernism,* 130.

37. Ibid., 90.

38. Ibid., 88.

39. Ibid., 86.

40. Brian Loveman, *The Constitution of Tyranny: Regimes of Exception in Spanish America* (Pittsburgh, Pa., 1993), 234.

41. Smith, *Nationalism and Modernism,* 127–29.

42. Platt, "Simón Bolívar."

43. George Lill, "Caudillismo as Demonstrated by Bolivian Propaganda Coinage," in Saul Needleman, ed., *Perspectives in Numismatics* (Chicago, 1986), http://www.ece.iit .edu/~prh/coins/PiN/cdb.html, paragraph 9.

44. Ibid. The debased currency (*moneda feble*) issue is also explored in Thiessen-Reily, "Puertas muy altas."

45. Platt, "Simón Bolívar."

46. Richard G. Doty explored the connection of the issuance of proclamation medal and monies on the part of new national leaders in Latin America to gain a sense of legitimacy for themselves and the nation in his work "Nationhood through Numismatics: Latin American Proclamation Pieces," in William L. Bischoff, ed., *The Coinage of El Perú,* Coinage of the Americas Conference, Proceedings, no. 5 (New York, 1989).

47. Ibid.

48. Upon his seizure of power in 1849, the Potosí mint issued two one-sol coins. One expressed gratitude to Manuel Isidoro Belzú, presumably for freeing Bolivia from the grip of tyranny, and the second was inscribed to Belzú. It was flanked by laurel branches on one side, and upon the other side was an image of a crossed sword and branch and caduceus underneath a liberty cap behind two clasped hands. In 1851 Belzú's government issued a one-sol coin with the image of an open book upon which was inscribed "Bolivian Constitution" across its pages. The image was ringed by the words "sworn in on the 28th of October of 1851."

Slavery, Citizenship, and National Identity in Brazil and the U.S. South

BARBARA WEINSTEIN

*A*mong the many provocative insights in Benedict Anderson's *Imagined Communities* was his audacious transposition of the course and chronology of nation making, identifying the "Creole Pioneers" of the New World rather than the old kingdoms of Europe as the earliest modern nations.[1] This interpretive claim highlighted the crucial role of the colonial experience in the construction of the modern concept of nationhood. Oddly, what has received less attention from scholars studying the history of the nation is the fact that every single one of the New World nations that emerged from these "old empires" included within its population a substantial number of persons subjected to the bonds of chattel slavery. Thus, those with a voice in the public sphere of these emerging nations had to consider from the outset the status of these enslaved persons and the very institution of slavery as part and parcel of the process of postcolonial nation building. It seems reasonable to assume, therefore, that slavery as a political question occupied an important place in that process.

What I propose to do in this essay is to begin to redress this relative neglect in the historiography by approaching the decline of slavery in the Americas as a process intricately linked to nation formation and the question of national identity. In only one historical case were the architects of national identity able to construct, in tandem, a potent nationalism and a strong proslavery argument. Elsewhere in the hemisphere the rise of nation-states seems to have been a powerful force in undermining the institution of slavery.[2] Imagined bonds of horizontal solidarity, citizenship, and cultural homogeneity made the bondage of slavery at the very least an awkward presence and at the very worst a serious threat to the survival of the modern nation. To be sure, historians have long acknowledged that the first era of independence movements in the former Spanish American colonies—informed by liberal republican ideologies—also set in motion a process of abolition in those nations similar to the wave of slave emancipations that occurred in the northern states of the newly independent

United States.[3] But the tendency has been to treat slavery in those contexts as a marginal concern and its abolition as a relatively "automatic" aftereffect of revolution, since these regions or nations had never been full-blown slave societies.[4]

By the same token, scholars have identified Brazil and the U.S. South as major exceptions to this pattern of postcolonial emancipation.[5] (The persistence of slavery in Cuba and Puerto Rico lies outside the scope of this discussion, since they remained colonies of Spain until the very end of the nineteenth century.) The standard explanation for these exceptions has been simple and straightforward: the elites in these two societies simply had too much of a social and economic stake in slave property to embrace abolition and therefore had to reinterpret liberalism and/or republicanism in such a way as to accommodate their class interests. This implies that there is no particularly compelling relationship between the national question and the slavery question, since anticolonial movements only led to slave emancipation where slavery was a supposedly inconsequential aspect of the socioeconomic order. Where slave labor was a crucial element of that order, it managed to survive the birth of the nation intact. However, this commonsense view of antislavery trends—or the absence of them—in the postcolonial Americas underestimates the considerable stake that Spanish American or Northern U.S. elites had in chattel slavery.[6] It also greatly overstates the ease with which the Brazilian and U.S. Southern elites adapted the framework of modern nationhood and their respective postcolonial political structures to the reality of a slaveholding society.[7]

Historians have seen Brazil in particular as exceptional because of a singularly compelling datum: it was, by a matter of decades, the last independent nation in the New World to abolish slavery. This would seem at first glance to indicate an especially fierce resistance to abolitionist ideas and a profound commitment to the institution of slavery on the part of Brazilian elites (and perhaps some nonelites). Yet if we broaden the scope of our inquiry to include not just the actual political process of abolition—which, in a nondemocratic system such as that of imperial Brazil, could be delayed or prolonged even in the face of growing antislavery sentiment—but also the shifting meanings of and changing discourses about slavery, Brazil starts to seem less exceptional. Indeed, it is my contention that, from the time of independence, Brazilians from a wide range of social backgrounds and racial categories viewed slavery as a doomed institution and defended it, if at all, as a necessary but temporary evil whose continued existence and/or expansion were incompatible with the construction of a modern nation.[8] In this sense it is the U.S. South, and the U.S. South alone, that can be categorized as an exception to the otherwise historically inverse relationship between nation building and proslavery sentiment. We could go even further and argue that, in the case of the antebellum South, proslavery ideology played a central role in the construction of horizontal solidarities (among whites) that Anderson regards as crucial to the imagined national community.[9]

In drawing this contrast between Brazil and the U.S. South my purpose is not to engage in a search for definitive causes and explanations, as was the case with much of the comparative slavery literature.[10] Instead, I see myself as concerned with "origins" rather than causes, following the well-known distinction drawn by Roger Chartier (writing with reference to the origins of the French Revolution):

> It is now less important to know whether the event was already present in the ideas that announced it, prefigured it, or demanded it than it is to recognize changes in belief and sensibility that would render such a rapid and profound destruction of the old political and social order decipherable and acceptable. In this sense, attributing "cultural origins" to the French Revolution does not by any means establish the Revolution's causes; rather, it pinpoints certain of the conditions that made it possible because it was conceivable.[11]

This is the approach, *mutatis mutandis*, that guides my comparison of proslavery ideology in Brazil and the U.S. South. Particularly in regard to the former, I am asking why, after more than three centuries in which slavery was an absolutely normative and largely unquestioned aspect of Brazilian society and economy, does it become possible to imagine Brazil without slavery in the nineteenth century? Why are interests, norms, and values being redefined so that the end of slavery does not imply a potentially catastrophic upheaval for Brazilian society?[12] Why is slavery increasingly seen as a source of weakness and an obstacle to progress for the new Brazilian nation? Why is the meaning (or meanings) of enslavement changing in nineteenth-century Brazil? And what do these changes imply for the capacity of different groups (including the growing population of freedpersons) to negotiate their place in the political order? Conversely, in the U.S. South, why did national identity formation transform the public perception of slavery *not* into that of a doomed institution but instead into one that was ever more central to the meaning of Southern identity?[13]

My claim that attitudes about slavery, even among slaveholding elites, took very different trajectories in Brazil and the U.S. South in the process of nation building goes against the grain of an argument that has been widely embraced in the more recent comparative slavery literature. In *Slavery and Human Progress* David Brion Davis argued that "until 1887, when the slaves took matters into their own hands, the Paulista fazendeiros were as hostile as Mississippi planters to the most moderate antislavery proposals."[14] This homogenization of the slaveholding classes and its concomitant erasure of actors other than masters and slaves is understandably appealing to scholars wishing to emphasize the agency of the enslaved in the process of emancipation and eager to reject older comparative approaches that essentialized differences between Brazilian and Southern slave societies.[15] Yet in the very same paragraph where he equates Paulista *fazendeiros* (coffee planters) with Mississippi planters, Davis readily admits that, "unlike American planters of the Old [U.S.] Southwest, [the Paulistas] were not ideologically committed to slavery as a permanent system," apparently regarding this as a trifling qualification.[16] My point is that it is not trifling, or it is only so if we conclude that mentalities and meanings are irrelevant to historical investigation or historical actions.

Moreover, the distinctions that I propose to draw between Brazilian slavocrats and Southern planters cannot be reduced to a question of liberal versus republican ideological influences, since I do not regard these ideologies as foundational or as independent variables but rather as widely available idioms of political discourse. Nor do I think they can be reduced to the differences between a "genuine" republic (i.e., the United States, North and South) and a constitutional monarchy with very limited popular participation.[17] Nor can they be reduced to a question of timing.[18] Instead, I would argue that for much of the nineteenth century Brazilian slaveholders or their spokesmen adopted a very different set of justifications for slavery predicated on the assumption that slavery would not and should not constitute a permanent feature of the emerging Brazilian nation—something that sets the political culture of the Brazilian slaveholding class sharply apart from that of the antebellum Southern planters in the United States. And the explanation for this divergence, I contend, cannot be divorced from the process of nation building.

Slavery: Positive Good or Necessary Evil?

In his classic work of comparative slavery, *The World the Slaveholders Made*, Eugene Genovese cited as an important distinction between Southern U.S. planters and Brazilian slaveholders the absence of what has been called a "positive-good" proslavery argument among the latter.[19] A few years after reading Genovese's provocative study I had occasion to read the 1826 slave trade debates in the Brazilian Chamber of Deputies. Among the most startling aspects of these debates was the almost complete consensus on the evils of the slave trade as well as widespread commentary on the evils of slavery itself (indeed, many of the speakers slipped in the course of their speeches from referring to the slave trade to referring to slavery). Even those speakers vigorously defending the slave trade and slavery did so on purely pragmatic/materialist grounds. At no point did anyone offer any sort of moral or philosophical defense of the slave trade and slavery.

Instead, Raymundo José da Cunha Matos, secretary in perpetuity of the Sociedade Auxiliadora da Indústria Nacional (a planters association), protested that the impending abolition of the slave trade would "cause enormous harm to national commerce," would "destroy agriculture, the vital foundation of our people's existence," would be "a cruel blow to state revenues," and would be "premature." To be sure, these were all serious concerns for the Brazilian elites, but they were not the basis for a permanent commitment to a slave-based economic and social order or a compelling moral vision for an emerging Brazilian nation. Moreover, Cunha Matos felt obliged to preface these objections with the following statement: "I am in no way proposing to defend the justice and eternal convenience of the commerce in slaves for the Brazilian Empire: I would not fall into the unpardonable absurdity of supporting in today's world and in the midst of the top-ranking intellects of the Brazilian nation a doctrine that is repugnant to the enlightened men of this century and that contradicts generally accepted philanthropic principles."[20] Cunha Matos is referring to the slave trade, not slavery, but it is impossible to read this description of the trade and its fundamental incompatibility with enlightenment and progress without hearing implications for slavery itself. And this from one of the few avid defenders of the slave trade in the Chamber of Deputies.

Of course, such attitudes did not imply that these deputies (with a few interesting exceptions) were contemplating the abolition of slavery anytime in the near future—after all, the imperial minister, José Bonifácio, had recently been forced into exile partly for pressing the issue of abolition.[21] And it might be argued that the 1820s were an unusual decade that reflected the liberalizing impulses of a recently independent nation (analogous to the brief period following U.S. independence, when Southern slaveholders expressed relatively liberal views about slavery).[22] Just a decade later, in response to widespread political turbulence and social unrest, there was a marked conservative turn in Brazilian politics that, together with the coffee boom that began in the 1840s, served to harden the (limited) defense of slavery. Thus, for example, Bernardo Pereira de Vasconcelos went from being a liberal, mildly anti-slave-trade deputy to a deeply conservative and vocal apologist for slavery.[23]

Yet even in the midst of this conservative turn, proslavery advocates resorted to what seem, in comparative terms, to be "weak" arguments. Pereira de Vasconcelos and his ilk drew on pragmatic pretexts that defended slavery, not as itself a moral or salutary element of Brazilian society but as crucial, at least for the near future, to Brazil's participation in the world market and to the maintenance of the country's precarious social order. Much has also been written about the slaveholders' use of liberal notions of property to defend their ownership of slaves, but this has to be regarded as an even weaker argument given the contemporaneous abolition of slave property in the resolutely liberal British Empire and the widespread acknowledgment that property rights were not absolute.[24] The private property argument was a strong basis on which to claim indemnification but a shaky basis for defending slavery as a permanent or enduring institution. Finally, while it is well known that intense British pressure bore most of the responsibility for the effective termination of the slave trade in 1850, it should still be noted that no Brazilian deputy attempted to mount a moral defense of the slave trade (or slavery itself) in the debates that led to the passage of the Queiróz Law.[25] From the mid-nineteenth century on the major arguments expressed to support slavery in Brazil "aimed not to defend the institution as a positive good but to extend its life."[26] As Genovese argued, in Brazil "slavery was defended as economically necessary and traditionally sanctioned, but no one argued with any discernible conviction that it was a good thing in itself or the proper condition of the laboring classes." Or as Emilia Viotti da Costa categorically declared, "Contrary to what happened in the United States, no one dared to make an outright doctrinaire defense of [Brazilian] slavery in the second half of the nineteenth century."[27]

The difference between these "weak" justifications and the strong arguments expressed by Southern U.S. slaveholders from the 1820s on is difficult to exaggerate. Far from basing their defense of slave ownership on liberal notions of property rights or a forecast of economic collapse, the Southerners rested their claims on the immorality of free-market capitalism and the inhumanity of a labor system in which relations between employer and employee were mediated solely by the profit motive.[28] Slavery, in contrast (argued the Southern slavocrats), assured propertyless dependents of a master's protection and created a harmonious relationship between capital and labor. And, of course, it protected the purity of the white race (though, as Genovese and William Freehling have noted, the logical extension of the Southerners' argument would mean subjecting propertyless whites to paternalist authority as well).[29] To take just one of the many apposite quotes from the writings and speeches of John C. Calhoun: "I hold that in the present state of civilization, where two races of different origin . . . are brought together, the relation now existing in the slaveholding States between the two is, instead of an evil, a good—a positive good. . . . There is and always has been in an advanced stage of wealth and civilization, a conflict between labor and capital. The condition of society in the South exempts us from the disorders and dangers resulting from this conflict."[30]

In a similar vein James Hammond, a prominent politician and planter in South Carolina, favorably compared the status of slaves in the South with that of free laborers in the North: "The difference between us is that our slaves are hired for life and well compensated. . . . Yours are hired by the day, not cared for, and scantily compensated. . . . Why, you meet more beggars in one day, in any single street of the city of New York, than you would meet in a lifetime in the whole South."[31] The planter, politician, and poet William J. Grayson expressed similar ideas in the lyrical lines of his widely read poem "The Hireling and the Slave," and George Frederick Holmes, in a predictably vitriolic review of *Uncle Tom's Cabin*, denounced the author—and abolitionists in general—for attempting to substitute "the real thralldom of free labor for the imaginary hardships of slavery."[32] In short, the proslavery ideologues of the Old South were publicists, not apologists, for slavery and crafted notions of race and status that created a permanent place for slavery in their emerging nation.

It is not that Brazilian slaveholders and politicians were immune to concerns about the new forms of poverty or social conflict that a fully capitalist society might entail. But such concerns were usually manifested in calls for a very gradual and orderly transition to free labor rather than in claims that slavery was the best possible foundation for the construction of the Brazilian nation.[33] There were, to be sure, the occasional partial exceptions. As late as 1870 Peixoto de Brito published a tract that portrayed slavery as a "beneficent tutelage" and argued that the slave "knows nothing of the bitterness of misery and begging."[34] Similarly, during the slavery debates in the Brazilian parliament one deputy declared himself a "slavocrat to the core" and suggested that "slavery ought to be maintained for the love of the slaves themselves." Yet the very same deputy also admitted that "no one reputes slavery to be a good and virtuous institution," while another leading proslavery politician publicly declared slavery "a cancer" on Brazilian society.[35] In Brazil, unlike the U.S. South, even slavery's most vigorous defenders rarely managed to express their support for the institution in unambiguous terms.

In our postmodern age, when most scholars take language very seriously, it makes sense to consider more carefully the origins and the implications of these discursive differences. Furthermore, I think it is possible to demonstrate that these differences had implications for political and legal practices that even the conventional social historian would regard as worthy of study. For example, in contrast to the U.S. South, there was never any significant effort in Brazil to restrict or roll back the process of manumission; indeed, Hebe M. Mattos argues that the rate of manumissions actually accelerated in most regions of Brazil in the half century before abolition; by midcentury free people of color had become the single largest category of the Brazilian population.[36] Whereas free blacks increasingly signified a potential challenge to the political order in the South as well as an implicit criticism of slavery, manumission was perfectly compatible with a defense of slavery as a "necessary evil," not to mention the claim that there was no great urgency to abolish Brazilian slavery because of its humane character.[37] Brazilian and Southern planters might coincide in their claims that slavery in their societies was a benevolent and civilizing force, but only in the Brazilian case could opportunity for manumission be identified as evidence to that effect. In contrast, the positive-good argument implied that it would be dangerous and inhumane to grant a slave his or her freedom.

The "weak" defense of slavery also created a political climate in which experiments with sharecropping and other nonslave labor arrangements could be applauded in Brazil rather than denounced for encouraging abolitionist sentiment, as in the South. Senator Nicolau Vergueiro's efforts to substitute immigrant workers for slaves on his coffee estates in São Paulo in the 1840s might have proved unsuccessful, but they were generally met with abundant praise and public subsidies.[38] The failure of these efforts probably reinforced the "necessary evil" argument, as planters concluded that free immigrant laborers were less adaptable to the plantation work routine than slaves, but they did not foreclose all discussion of alternative sources and forms of labor or undermine the growing consensus that free labor, *properly conceived*, would be more productive than slave labor and a better foundation for the nation's welfare.[39]

As for the origins of these discursive differences, I would argue that a major constitutive element of Brazilian discourse about the future of slavery would be the appeal of and anxiety about modernity among Brazilian elites (and nonelites) and the strong association between slavery and backwardness in the Brazilian cultural milieu from the early nineteenth century on. Brazilian politicians, essayists, and even popular leaders in the first half of the nineteenth century already characterized their homeland as "lagging" in terms of technology, culture, wealth, and power when compared to those societies where mechanization and industrialization were advancing productivity, efficiency, and national prestige. This close and persistent association between the ideology of progress and free labor, reinforced by Brazil's own apparent stagnation and repeated subjection to Britain's will, made it extremely difficult for the defenders of slavery to find a position from which to construct positive arguments for building a nation on the basis of slave labor.

In a very insightful study of debates over citizenship and the problem of slavery in the Brazilian Constituent Assembly of 1823, Kirsten Schultz discusses three explicit critiques of slavery prepared by leading statesmen-intellectuals for presentation in the assembly. Each author, along with the routine denunciations of the evils and horrors of slavery, detailed its economic liabilities as well. According to Maciel da Costa, slavery was part of an old colonial system that would foster an agricultural economy dependent upon foreign demand, while Silva Lisboa warned that the continued existence of slavery would mean prolonged reliance on primitive methods of production.[40] Though such ideas can be explained partly as a response to the agricultural depression of the 1820s, the essential concepts informing these critiques continued to circulate in Brazilian society even after coffee had rescued the agrarian economy from its doldrums.

A full discussion of this issue is beyond the scope of this essay. There are many possible factors to explain why nineteenth-century Brazilian elites tended to regard their society as lagging behind, including the preponderance of nonwhites in the population, the noncompetitiveness of certain economic sectors, widespread notions about the degenerative effects of tropical climates, derisive views of the former metropolis (Portugal), on the one hand, and Brazil's rapid subordination to British commercial and informal political hegemony, on the other. In any case, this sense of "backwardness" and the consequently strong association of free labor with progress made it difficult and perhaps impossible to construct a vision of their nation's future in which slavery constituted a permanent (and positively good) feature of Brazilian life.[41] And, as we will see, the presence of people of mixed race even within the ranks of the powerful and prestigious formed an impediment to the use of racial difference as a strong justification for enslavement.

As the flip side of this thesis, I am contending, by implication, that the positive-good argument was an important defensive element of emergent Southern (U.S.) nationalism. It both fortified the Southern planter class with an anticapitalist worldview that shielded it from mounting abolitionist criticism and increasingly hegemonic liberal notions of progress and made them more confident in their appeals to nonslaveholding whites. Southern planters, politicians, and intellectuals also had the luxury of constructing an antimodern (and anti-Northern) discourse even as they enjoyed the technological, financial, military, political, and commercial resources created by a rapidly modernizing (conjoined) nation.[42] It has become a commonplace to explain the Southerners' extreme proslavery sentiment as a response to intensifying attacks from abolitionist Northerners. The contiguous presence of a modernizing, free-labor society supposedly made it all the more pressing for the Southern planter class to erect a strong defense of slavery. But we could argue, taking a different tack, that the South's association with the North (indeed, their common national boundaries until the outbreak of the Civil War) also enabled the formation of an aggressive proslavery worldview by masking or minimizing certain "backward" features of other slave-plantation societies.[43] This unusual set of circumstances made it possible for white Southerners to imagine a national community that had slave ownership as one of its foundational characteristics.

Not that Southerners could completely dismiss the problem of uneven development, but they deployed various discursive strategies to neutralize the negative implications of the diverging economic prospects of North and South. A good example is the following excerpt from an 1837 speech that Calhoun delivered to the U.S. Senate in which he contended that, despite living side by side with African slaves, "the white or European race [in the South] has not degenerated":

> It has kept pace with its brethren in other sections of the Union where slavery does not exist. It is odious to make comparison; but I appeal to all sides whether the South

is not equal in virtue, intelligence, patriotism, courage, disinterestedness, and all the high qualities which adorn our nature. I ask whether we have not contributed our full share of talents and political wisdom in forming and sustaining this political fabric; and whether we have not constantly inclined most strongly to the side of liberty, and been the first to see and first to resist the encroachments of power. *In one thing only are we inferior—the arts of gain; we acknowledge that we are less wealthy than the Northern section of this Union.*[44]

It proved far more difficult for Brazilian elites to dismiss the yawning and continually widening material and technological gap between their agrarian economy and the emerging industrial economies to their north and east or to claim cultural or political superiority as an alternative marker of superiority.[45] As William Freehling observed in an intriguing comparative essay, "Latin American slaveholders [compared to U.S. Southerners] lacked illusions about their worldwide economic power."

It should also be acknowledged that the "necessary evil" argument was far from unknown in the antebellum Southern context, even after 1830. Freehling, in the essay cited above, remarks that "Lower South slaveholders came to call slavery a probably perpetual blessing, while Border South masters persistently called the institution a hopefully temporary evil."[46] Making the positive-good argument the hegemonic discourse in the Old South—with its intraregional diversity—required a great deal of ideological work, including an intensified racism and the complete exclusion of all conflicting views from public life. Indeed, the point of Freehling's essay is to argue that it was precisely the softening of proslavery sentiment around the edges—that is, in the border regions—that produced a sense of crisis among the most diehard slavocrats following Lincoln's election and pushed them to raise the stakes and prematurely induce the birth of a new nation. The planters of South Carolina understood that a weak defense of slavery could prove no defense at all in the face of rising international antislavery sentiment.[47]

In the late 1860s, as Brazil began to consider concrete measures for the gradual abolition of slavery, Senator José Tomaz Nabuco de Araújo inquired of his colleagues in the Brazilian parliament, "How can Brazil, isolated and the only one of its kind on the globe, resist the pressure of the entire world?" Yet another senator declared, "The eyes of the world are upon us, judging us barbarians, savages."[48] Two more decades would pass until Brazil finally and definitively abolished slavery, but these statements vividly illuminate the failure of the Brazilian elites to construct an alternative national identity that would allow for a vigorous defense of human bondage. Unlike the antebellum Southern planters, the Brazilian elites could not "resist the pressure of the entire world," either discursively or politically. Indeed, by the 1860s slavery in Brazil was so thoroughly identified with backwardness that a leading senator could invert the usual association of slaves with barbarity and rhetorically label the slaveholders barbarians.

Race, National Identity, and the Defense of Slavery

Thus far I have focused mainly on the way in which concerns about building a modern nation and the association of slavery with backwardness produced a relatively weak defense of slavery in Brazil when compared with the antebellum U.S. South. But there is, of course, also the issue of race. Although numerous scholars have demonstrated that the Southern planters' positive-good proslavery argument could easily overflow racial boundaries and take on class implications as well, it still seems evident that a rigid construction of racial difference—especially in a white man's republic—was crucial to the articulation of proslavery discourse and the construction of a protonational (white) Southern identity.[49]

Comparing racial attitudes in the United States and Brazil has become a slightly perilous exercise. In recent decades the many scholarly works debunking Brazil's "myth of racial democracy" have been highly critical of comparisons between the United States and Brazil that serve to conceal the magnitude of racism in Brazilian society.[50] Despite the merits of these arguments, they should not move historians to efface what were genuinely dramatic differences between North American and Brazilian defenses of slavery with regard to race. I hardly need to provide quotations to substantiate the claim that Southern slaveholders used every imaginable racist argument, including separate creation, to insist on the inferiority of dark-skinned peoples and their suitability for enslavement.[51] In contrast, no matter what the private views of white, privileged Brazilians, skin color could never be publicly deployed as a major and deliberate justification for enslavement. It is not just that a massive segment of Brazil's free population could be classified as *pardo* or *prêto* (loosely, brown or black), but people of color also numbered among the minority of Brazilians who wielded political and economic power and participated in the upper levels of the political process. In recent works on politics under the empire historians have contended that the presence of prominent mulattos (or, to use the term more common at the time, *pardos*) in the Brazilian imperial political system made a racialized defense of slavery virtually impossible.[52] And while some prominent *pardo* politicians energetically distanced themselves from their non-European origins, others, particularly military officers, retained links to highly politicized collectivities of soldiers and urban dwellers of African descent in the decades following independence. These popular "constituencies" gave these politicians' denunciations of racist legislative initiatives considerably more force than they might otherwise have had.

More politically tenable in Brazil was a proslavery discourse that identified slaves as *Africans*—a group that could be defined as outsiders from a non-Christian culture and in need of civilizing. As Hendrik Kraay astutely notes, while discussing rising anti-Portuguese sentiment during the conflicts over independence, "less often explicit, but nevertheless very real was the anti-African sentiment that demarcated the other side of the Brazilian nation."[53] This position outside the boundaries of the national community was most evident in the realm of political status (broadly defined), as Africans were not automatically eligible, upon manumission, for citizenship in the new nation.

Using Brazilian versus African birth as the dividing line between potential citizens and quasi-permanent outsiders obviated the need for any explicit reference to color, but it raised other issues with respect to the "viability" of the new nation. For one, it created the unwelcome prospect of an alien population embedded within the nation whose various means of resistance and rebellion formed an ongoing threat to national strength and stability. Schultz notes that the same antislavery treatises cited above that critiqued slavery's deleterious effect on the nation's economic future devoted even more space to the negative *political* consequences of continued reliance on (African) slave labor. José Bonifácio put it most vividly when he denounced the "commerce in human flesh" as "the cancer that gnaws at the entrails of Brazil." Similarly, Silva Lisboa worried that it "prevented the formation of a homogeneous and compact nation," and Maciel da Costa claimed that "the indefinite multiplication of a heterogeneous population" posed an "imminent and inevitable threat [to the] security of the state." Such heterogeneity, José Bonifácio noted, was hardly regarded as a problem under colonial rule; indeed, Portuguese imperial interests "wanted [us to be] . . . a mixed and heterogeneous people, without nationality, and without brotherhood, so as to better enslave us."[54] In other words, it was the very condition of nationhood—and the perceived imperative of cultural homogeneity—that made these questions of vital concern.

In the same vein, under colonial rule—when all residents of the Portuguese Empire were subjects or vassals of the Crown—there was little need for debate over the civil status of different social and ethnic groups. But the construction of an independent nation (even one with a monarchy) raised the question of citizenship and who would qualify for it. (It is worth noting, in this context, that questions of suffrage and citizenship rights in the United States were largely left to the individual states until after the Civil War.)[55] This, in fact, could be divided into two questions: Who was to be considered Brazilian? Among those categorized as Brazilian, who would enjoy the rights of citizenship? The latter question could also be parsed into even more specific queries about the degree of citizenship permitted, since the Brazilian Constitution of 1824 created categories of nonactive and active citizens (with the latter having the right not only to vote but also to be electors and to hold elected office). Schultz, in her essay, carefully traces the arguments and decisions that emerged from the 1823 Constituent Assembly and that, with respect to the rights of Brazilians of color, identified Brazilian versus African birth as the crucial dividing line. Color or African *descent* were not, in and of themselves, relevant categories for the determination of either civil status or political rights. Thus, a man born free (in Brazil), even though his parents might both have been slaves of African birth, enjoyed active citizenship rights if he could meet the designated property requirements. More troubling was the question of *escravos forros* or *libertos*—men of color who had been born into slavery and attained their freedom. Even in this case the constitution favored full citizenship rights if the *liberto* were Brazilian-born. In contrast, the *liberto* of African birth (by no means a negligible segment of the population) would not be considered a "Brazilian" prior to his manumission and did not automatically achieve that status upon acquiring his liberty. The African-born *liberto* could be naturalized as a Brazilian but, even so, could only enjoy the political rights of the nonactive citizen.[56]

Given elite anxieties about the "dangerous classes of color," it is hardly surprising that white politicians mounted concerted attempts to roll back the rights achieved by freedpersons in the 1824 Constitution. But even such campaigns exploited distinctions between those people of color *born into slavery* and those *born free* rather than skin color or degree of African descent. Thus in the early 1830s the Brazilian Chamber of Deputies voted to exclude *libertos* from the ranks of National Guard officers over the fierce objections of Antonio Rebouças—the distinguished *pardo* deputy from Bahia—and other Liberals in the chamber. Lamenting this decision, the newspaper *O Brasileiro Pardo* commented in 1833 that "we *pardos*, as a result of the exclusion of *libertos* from the National Guard, find ourselves reduced to not being able to belong to it [the Guard] except for those among us who were born free." This restriction, as Keila Grinberg argues in her fine study of Rebouças's career, reflected the increasing conservatism of politicians who had previously supported a more liberal interpretation of the *liberto*'s status.[57] Yet this restriction did not go into effect without a struggle, and the continued reliance on the juridical status of enslavement rather than on "innate" qualities associated with color or African descent to forge discriminatory laws clearly indicated the limits of a racial defense of slavery or a racialized conception of citizenship.

This is not to suggest that "white" Brazilians did not exhibit racist attitudes toward blacks, whether in social practice or in print. Certainly, the distinction between "Brazilian-born" and "African-born" relied on a construction of the

African's "barbarism" that cannot be disentangled from notions of black inferiority or dangerousness. Not surprisingly, in nineteenth-century Brazil the term *prêto* was most readily applied to the African-born and in certain contexts became synonymous with "slave." Thus, during the prolonged process of abolition, freedpersons of whatever color often denied that they were *prêto*.[58] What I *am* saying is that a particular type of racist discourse, one that defined race according to skin color or the slightest degree of African descent, could not be mobilized either in the political arena or in the broader public sphere to justify the institution of slavery in Brazil.

Many historians have argued, as Freehling does, that "the racial argument for *black* slavery was more necessary in a white men's republic," that is, the United States, a claim that has a certain compelling logic to it.[59] But too much emphasis on the relationship between republicanism and racial exclusion can mislead us into concluding that the less formally democratic character of the Brazilian imperial political system somehow made the racist argument less *necessary*. What this erases is the considerable effort by politicians such as Rebouças and other Liberal deputies to limit the legislative ratification of white supremacy. And it overlooks the efforts of nonwhite military officers as well as more popular groups of *libertos* and free people of color (many of them veterans of the proindependence struggles) to make it undesirable—even unthinkable—for the white elites to base their defense of slavery on racial premises.[60] To be sure, the other side of this coin was the relatively accommodating attitude of these groups (especially *pardos*) toward the institution of slavery; in other words, a defense of the rights of *libertos* or of blacks to serve as army officers should not be automatically equated with abolitionist sentiment.[61] At the same time, points of tension and contradiction inevitably arose: when Rebouças took up the cause of *libertos*, he then had to consider whether slaves who were in the process of accumulating property to purchase their freedom should enjoy legal protections normally restricted to those classified as "Brazilians."[62] And that question became even more complicated, legally and culturally, if the slave in question were Brazilian-born.

Historians of Brazilian abolition have widely assumed that the effective closing of the African slave trade in 1850 sounded the death knell for Brazilian slavery due to the low rate of reproduction among Brazilian slaves.[63] Recent research, however, suggests another reason for 1850 being "the beginning of the end" for Brazilian slavery in addition to this long-term demographic forecast. The end of the slave trade not only threatened a labor shortage but also produced the inevitable "Creolization" of the slave population, a process that deprived slavery's defenders of their only politically "legitimate" basis for justifying continued enslavement (i.e., African versus Brazilian). And a number of historians, beginning with Warren Dean, have insisted that it also meant the formation of a slave population ever more aware of and insistent on their rights as Brazilians and even as future Brazilian citizens.[64]

In contrast, the "Creolization" of the U.S. slave population, which was well under way by the time of independence, posed no dilemma for the construction of proslavery arguments. Slavery's defenders in the United States (North and South) increasingly relied on a nineteenth-century notion of race as a fixed, inherent, biological classification, rather than the more culturally inflected "African," to designate a permanently subordinate population that might become more "civilized" and Christian through the experience of New World enslavement but could never rise to the level of the white race. The racial barriers erected in the U.S. South were meant to be not only impermeable but immutable as well.

My intent in this essay has been to argue that it is hardly coincidental that the New World simultaneously witnessed, in the hundred years stretching from the 1780s to the 1880s, the near universal rise of the nation-state and nationalism and the total abolition of chattel slavery. Rather than being parallel processes with wholly separate logics, discourses about the nation and about slavery were mutually constitutive. Thus a key factor in altering the meaning of slavery for many Brazilians (whether slave or free, propertyless or propertied) was the emergence of the modern nation-state, an entity widely imagined in a way that made it incompatible with the institution of slavery.

To be sure, slavery and the nation were not inherently or automatically antithetical. To claim this would be to revert to a structuralist approach divorced from the particular historical circumstances of the New World's new nations. It would also mean dismissing the considerable human effort invested by slaves, freedpersons, and white abolitionists in every instance of slave emancipation. But what I am suggesting is that it took a great deal of ideological work and a set of particularly "propitious" circumstances to make proslavery and nationalist discourses compatible. In that regard, the Southern planters and their minions, despite their leisured lifestyle, were the workhorses of ideological labor. Enjoying political, economic, and demographic conditions unparalleled in other New World slave societies, the antebellum Southerners were uniquely successful in crafting a national imaginary that legitimated slavery (among whites) as a permanent institution. To do this required both a thoroughgoing critique of industrial capitalism and a system of white supremacy that was singularly rigid in its definition of race. In its capacity to "accomplish" this the emerging Confederate nation was genuinely exceptional.[65]

Again, elsewhere in the Americas the rise of nation-states seems to have been a significant factor in undermining slavery (and we might say the same about the nation and serfdom in Europe).[66] The presence of a large population of enslaved persons posed a serious challenge to any project for a culturally homo-geneous national identity or a politically safe and secure nation. Few slave own-ers could forget that the first nation to declare itself independent after the United States was born of a massive slave rebellion against attempts by slaveholders to separate from France while maintaining the slave plantation economy intact.[67] It is not surprising, then, that when a segment of the Cuban planter class, some eighty years later, took up the anticolonial crusade, they understood that this struggle could not be separated from the process of abolition.[68] Returning to Chartier's distinction between origins and causes, the rise of the nation was not the "cause" of the abolition of slavery, but it created a context in which proslav-ery arguments (and the disciplinary power that gave them force) became ever more difficult to sustain.

It is beyond the scope of this essay to explore in detail the ramifications of these differences for national or regional identities in the aftermath of aboli-tion. Moreover, the traumatic impact of the Civil War on the United States, North and South, makes all postemancipation comparisons between the former Confederacy and Brazil highly problematic. Still, there are a few implications that might be drawn, at least tentatively, from the foregoing discussion of race, modernity, and nation. One is an evident, and unsurprising, similarity in the national/regional memory of slavery in Brazil and the U.S. South: the construc-tion of a historical and literary corpus that portrayed chattel slavery as a hu-mane and benevolent institution.[69] But here the similarities end, especially since some of the writings that have been most responsible for this view of Brazilian slavery as benign also fueled what has become known as "the myth of racial democracy"—the idea that Brazil is a country free of racism and racial strife.[70] It is, of course, quite remarkable that a nation where slavery lasted longer than any other in the hemisphere could incorporate "racial democracy" as a central element of its national identity. I would contend that part of what made this questionable claim plausible was the *absence* of an explicitly racist proslavery argument in nineteenth-century Brazil combined with a narrative of abolition that portrayed the process as consensual and nonconflictive. The contrast with the U.S. South could not be more manifest: no matter how much "Lost Cause" writers endeavored to romanticize or idealize the master-slave relationship, the ongoing racial segregation and the rise of Jim Crow made a discourse of "racial democracy" the very last claim one would expect from the pens or mouths of white Southerners (or black Southerners, for that matter).[71]

Just as earlier differences in racial rhetoric produced contrasting discourses about race relations in the U.S. South and Brazil, so did the divergent attitudes about modernity, progress, and slave labor. Particularly if we compare the post-bellum plantation South to the leading plantation economy of postemancipa-tion Brazil, the São Paulo coffee zone, the contrasts are once again striking and illuminating. The Southern planters, far from expelling the former slaves from their estates, made every effort to retain as many elements of the slave regime as possible—only the remarkable struggles of the freedpersons themselves limited the extent to which postbellum labor relations could be characterized as slavery except in name.[72] The "Negro worker" was seen by whites as entirely suited to the role of plantation laborer and as crucial to the renewed prosperity of the plantation South. Thus, there was no large-scale effort to supplant the former slaves with new sources of cheap manual labor.[73]

The scenario in postemancipation São Paulo was dramatically different.[74] The coffee planters, drawing on abundant state-level revenues from export taxes, rapidly replaced their former slave laborers with European immigrant families whose passage to Brazil had been subsidized with public monies. Not only did the Paulista elite distance itself from its slave-owning past by literally whitening its labor force, but its spokesmen also insisted that the coffee planters, with their modern and progressive attitudes, had always been reluctant slave-holders, eager for the day when available alternatives would free them from their dependence upon a backward institution such as slavery. Meanwhile, freedpersons found themselves excluded from most regular forms of employment and forced to occupy ever more marginal positions within the Paulista economy and society.[75] As Alfredo Bosi has aptly noted, the "consensual" narrative of Brazilian abolition allowed the master "to liberate himself from the slave" and enabled the "expulsion of the Black from *modern* Brazil."[76]

The irony of this contrast is that the rigidly racist Southerners made every effort to immobilize the black population and keep the ex-slaves on the white-owned plantations, while the less flagrantly racist Paulistas eagerly whitened their workforce and excluded Afro-Paulistas from any meaningful role in the region's history. The tragedy of this contrast is that, despite the dramatically different outcomes, people of African descent found themselves with few options and few rights in both of these postemancipation societies. Indeed, what we might conclude from this brief discussion of implications is that, even though New World slavery could not long survive the rise of the modern nation, the national bodies of those former slave societies would bear its scars well into the twentieth century and perhaps beyond.

NOTES

My thanks to the participants in the Vanderbilt conference "Nationalism in the New World," particularly Marco Antonio Pamplona, for their comments and suggestions, which have been very helpful for revising this essay. Above all, I am indebted to Rachel N. Klein for reading the essay, pointing out various inconsistencies in the argument, and indicating places where I have missed some crucial issue in the historiography of the antebellum South. I hope she has saved me from embarrassing myself too much, but if any errors or gaps remain, the fault is entirely my own.

1. Benedict Anderson, *Imagined Communities: Reflections on the Origins and Spread of Nationalism,* rev. ed. (London, 1992), 47–65. In this edition Anderson actually renamed his chapter on New World nations "Creole Pioneers" instead of the original "Old Empires, New Nations" because he felt that readers had missed the analytical significance of this chapter in the original edition.

2. For an excellent comparative discussion of emancipation in Europe and the Americas see Steven Hahn, "Class and State in Postemancipation Societies: Southern Planters in Comparative Perspective," *American Historical Review* 95, no. 1 (1990): 75–98. Hahn argues that emancipation in the United States—everywhere a complicated and contested ordeal—should be seen as one continuous process, beginning with New England and extending through the end of the Civil War.

3. A major study that barely acknowledges the issue of abolition is Gordon Wood, *The Radicalism of the American Revolution* (New York, 1993). On the Latin American independence wars see John Lynch, *The Spanish American Revolutions, 1808–1826* (New York, 1973).

4. Here I would cite the very useful distinction drawn by Ira Berlin between "slave societies" and "societies with slaves" (*Many Thousands Gone: The First Two Centuries of Slavery in North America* [Cambridge, Mass., 1998], 8).

5. Obviously, the U.S. South was not, until 1860, a nation in any formal sense, but one assumption in this essay is that white Southerners, throughout the decades preceding the Civil War, were imagining a regional cum national identity. On the relationship between regions, protonations, and nations see Celia Applegate, "A Europe of Regions," *American Historical Review* 104, no. 4 (October 1999): 1157–82; Barbara Weinstein, "Racializing Regional Difference: São Paulo vs. Brazil, 1932," in N. Appelbaum, A. Macpherson, and K. Rosemblatt, eds., *Race and Nation in Modern Latin America* (Chapel Hill, N.C., 2003), 237–62.

6. On the contested process of emancipation in Colombia and its ongoing implications for national politics see James E. Sanders, " 'Citizens of a Free People': Popular Liberalism and Race in Nineteenth-Century Southwestern Colombia," *Hispanic American Historical Review* 84, no. 2 (May 2004); on gradual slave emancipation in the northern United States see Joanne Pope Melish, *Disowning Slavery: Gradual Emancipation and Race in New England, 1780–1860* (Ithaca, N.Y., 1998).

7. Rachel N. Klein has persuasively argued for the compatibility of slavery and republicanism among South Carolina planters, the most vocal proslavery cohort, in *Unification of a Slave State: The Rise of the Planter Class in the South Carolina Backcountry, 1760–1808* (Chapel Hill, N.C., 1990), esp. chap. 5. I thoroughly agree with this; my point is only that the process of nation building raised challenges not *easily* addressed by Southern republican discourse, especially with its strong antifederalist tendencies. See also Stephanie McCurry, "The Two Faces of Republicanism: Gender and Proslavery Politics in Antebellum South Carolina," *Journal of American History* 78 (March 1992): 1245–64.

8. This is not to imply that Brazilians, wealthy or poor, declined to own slaves following independence. But I think this "acceptance" of slavery as a part of everyday life

coexisted increasingly uneasily with a critique of slavery that emerged in the context of modern nation building and in struggles over citizenship rights, though the hierarchical and nondemocratic features of the imperial political system dampened the impact of such struggles. On smallholding slave owners see Hebe M. Mattos [de Castro], *Ao sul da história: Lavradores pobres na crise do trabalho escravo* (São Paulo, 1987).

9. Proslavery ideologues were already exploring the "national" implications of the ideological divide over slavery well before the Civil War. See, for instance, the statements made by the South Carolina planter-politician James Henry Hammond in 1845 in Drew Gilpin Faust, ed., *The Ideology of Slavery: Proslavery Thought in the Antebellum South, 1830–1860* (Baton Rouge, La., 1981), 176.

10. An example of this sort of search for (mono)causality through comparative analysis is Anthony W. Marx, *Making Race and Nation: A Comparison of South Africa, the United States and Brazil* (Cambridge, 1998). For a penetrating critique of the comparative method as applied to race relations in Brazil and the United States see Micol Seigel, "Beyond Compare: Comparative Method after the Transnational Turn," *Radical History Review* 91 (Winter 2005).

11. Roger Chartier, *The Cultural Origins of the French Revolution* (Durham, N.C., 1991), 2.

12. It is important to note that there were widespread fears among elites (and probably among less privileged groups as well) of social unrest as abolition drew near. See Célia M. Marinho de Azevedo, *Onda negra, mêdo branco: O negro no imaginário das elites, século XIX* (Rio de Janeiro, 1987).

13. Here I am endorsing Drew Gilpin Faust's argument that the defeat of the Confederacy does not imply a failure to construct a viable national identity. Moreover, she cites slavery as a principal element, if not *the* principal element, of that identity (*The Creation of Confederate Nationalism: Ideology and Identity in the Civil War South* [Baton Rouge, La., 1988], 1–7).

14. David Brion Davis, *Slavery and Human Progress* (Oxford, 1984), 292.

15. The many fine studies of slave emancipation in Brazil that foreground slave agency include Sidney Chalhoub, *Visões da liberdade* (São Paulo, 1990); Hebe M. Mattos [de Castro], *As cores do silêncio: Os significados da liberdade no sudeste escravista* (Rio de Janeiro, 1995); Maria Helena Machado, *O plano e o pânico: Os movimentos sociais na década da abolição* (São Paulo, 1994); and Eduardo Silva, *As camélias do leblon e a abolição da escravatura: Uma investigação de história cultural* (São Paulo, 2003).

16. Davis, *Slavery and Human Progress*, 292.

17. Edmund S. Morgan has cogently argued that race-based slavery made republicanism possible for Virginia's plantation society (*American Slavery, American Freedom: The Ordeal of Colonial Virginia* [New York, 1975]). We might then conclude, as the flip side of his argument, that in Brazil's hierarchical, largely nondemocratic society, where webs of patronage presumably insured popular quiescence, elites did not *need* to bother to construct a hegemonic ideology based on race or proslavery arguments. But I think we can appreciate the wisdom of Morgan's historical interpretation of colonial Virginia without assuming that its converse could formulaically explain postcolonial Brazil. It should also be kept in mind that Brazil was the site of many forms of elite and popular insurgency

during the first two decades following independence and that the stable, nondemocratic society associated with imperial Brazil is more a product of the period from the 1840s on.

18. According to Teresa Meade, "the victory of the North in the U.S. Civil War was a powerful sign that slavery's days were numbered" (*A Brief History of Brazil* [New York, 2003], 85). This was certainly the case, but I am arguing that well before the South lost the Civil War Brazilian politicians and citizens generally were adopting a very different view of slavery's "future" from that of the antebellum Southerners.

19. Eugene D. Genovese, *The World the Slaveholders Made* (New York, 1969), 91. Genovese half-heartedly offered Catholicism—with its supposed position on slavery as fundamentally sinful—as a possible explanation for this difference, an ahistorical argument that cannot explain shifting views over time.

20. Brasil (Governo), *Anais da câmara dos deputados*, 3 July 1827, 21.

21. See Viotti da Costa, "José Bonifácio de Andrada e Silva: A Brazilian Founding Father," in *The Brazilian Empire: Myths and Histories* (Chicago, 1985), 24–52.

22. On liberalism in this era see Viotti da Costa, "Liberalism," in ibid., 53–77; and Roderick Barman, *Brazil: The Forging of a Nation, 1798–1852* (Stanford, Calif., 1988). For a critical discussion of "conditional antislavery" sentiment (conditional on the removal of blacks from U.S. territory) in the age of the American Revolution see William Freehling, "The Founding Fathers, Conditional Antislavery, and the Nonradicalism of the American Revolution," in *The Reintegration of American History: Slavery and the Civil War* (Oxford, 1994), 12–33.

23. On this conservative turn in Brazilian politics see Ilmar Rohloff de Mattos, *O tempo saquarema* (São Paulo, 1987).

24. Alfredo Bosi, "A escravidão entre dois liberalismos," in *Dialética da colonização* (São Paulo, 1992), 194–245.

25. The classic study is Leslie Bethell, *The Abolition of the Brazilian Slave Trade: Britain, Brazil and the Slave Trade Question, 1807–1869* (Cambridge, 1970). Again, the slave trade and slavery are not easily separable issues in Brazil for a variety of reasons. Maria Stella Bresciani observes that, in the state-of-the-province speeches delivered by the presidents of São Paulo from 1850 to 1858, slavery "shifted from being an accepted and practiced labor arrangement to a condemned and practiced one" ("Liberalismo: Ideologia e controle social," Ph.D. dissertation, University of São Paulo, 1976, 1:123).

26. Robert Brent Toplin, *The Abolition of Slavery in Brazil* (New York, 1975), 131. Toplin's chapter on "The Defense of Slavery" (131–44) echoes many of the points I raise here, but he insists that the Rio Branco (Free Womb) Law of 1871 was the event that derailed the formulation of a positive-good argument in Brazil, whereas my contention is that at no point in the nineteenth century were the political climate and conditions in Brazil conducive to such an argument.

27. Genovese, *The World the Slaveholders Made*, 131; Viotti da Costa, "Masters and Slaves," in *The Brazilian Empire*, 163.

28. On the proslavery argument generally see Drew Gilpin Faust, "Introduction," in Faust, *The Ideology of Slavery*, 1–20.

29. This is the central argument in Genovese's essay on George Fitzhugh in *The World*

the Slaveholders Made; see also Freehling, "Unlimited Paternalism's Problems: The Transforming Moment on My Road Toward Understanding Disunion," in *Reintegration of American History*, 105–37.

30. Eric L. McKitrick, ed., *Slavery Defended: The Views of the Old South* (Englewood Cliffs, N.J., 1963), 13–14. This is from Calhoun's "Speech on the Reception of Abolition Petitions," 6 February 1837.

31. Ibid., 123.

32. Ibid., 57–68, 101.

33. Da Costa, "Masters and Slaves," 163.

34. Cited in Viotti da Costa, *Da senzala à colônia* (São Paulo, 1966), 349–50.

35. Toplin, *The Abolition of Slavery*, 132.

36. Hebe Maria Mattos, *Escravidão e cidadania no Brasil monárquico* (Rio de Janeiro, 2000), 12–13. Moreover, as Keila Grinberg has shown, the different politics of manumission cannot be reduced to Iberian versus Anglo-Saxon legal traditions ("Freedom Suits and Civil Law in Brazil and the United States," *Slavery & Abolition* [December 2001]: 66–82).

37. On deteriorating conditions for free blacks in the antebellum South see Ira Berlin, *Slaves without Masters* (New York, 1974).

38. In his 1852 state-of-the-province speech to the São Paulo provincial assembly Nabuco d'Araújo claimed that several other wealthy planters were interested in following Vergueiro's example. He also urged the imperial government to forbid the use of slave labor in agricultural settlements (*Discurso com que . . . Senhor Doutor José Thomaz Nabuco d'Araújo, presidente da província de São Paulo, abrio a Assembléa legislativa provincial no dia 1 de maio 1852*).

39. For differing views of these experiments with free labor see Warren Dean, *Rio Claro: A Brazilian Plantation System, 1820–1920* (Stanford, Calif., 1976), 106, and Viotti da Costa, "Sharecroppers and Plantation Owners: An Experiment with Free Labor," in *The Brazilian Empire*, 94–124.

40. Kirsten Schultz, "Brazilian Independence, Citizenship, and the Problem of Slavery: The Assembléia Constituinte of 1823," paper presented at the symposium "Revolution, Independence and the New Nations of Latin America," Irvine, Calif., 23–24 March 2003, 11–12. My thanks to Dr. Schultz for allowing me to cite this unpublished work.

41. On the association between progress and free labor see Iraci Galvão Salles, *Trabalho, progresso e a sociedade civilizada* (São Paulo, 1986). For a wide-ranging discussion of slavery and modernity see Rafael de Bivar Marquese, *Feitores do corpo, missionários da mente: Senhores, letrados e controle dos escravos nas Américas, 1660–1860* (São Paulo, 2004). Viotti da Costa observes that these early critiques of slavery were concerned not with the slave as a human being but with the problem of slavery from the perspective of the dominant class (*Da senzala à colônia*, 340). I have put the term "backwardness" in quotes because the notion of *atraso* only gradually emerged over the course of the nineteenth century; in the earlier decades of the century it referred to the persistence of colonial traits.

42. This is why slave plantation agriculture in the U.S. South could feature some "modern capitalist" production methods even while the regional ruling class was con-

structing a radical critique of capitalism and free labor. There is a vast literature on whether relations of production in the antebellum South were "essentially" noncapitalist or capitalist, with Eugene Genovese being the standard-bearer for the noncapitalist argument; see his *The Political Economy of Slavery: Studies in the Economy and Society of the Slave South* (New York, 1965). The latter produced a wave of studies seeking to demonstrate that Southern plantations were capitalist after all. See, for example, Mark M. Smith, *Mastered by the Clock: Time, Slavery, and Freedom in the American South* (Chapel Hill, N.C., 1997). It no longer seems useful to pose the question in this either/or way. What we can observe is the incapacity of a slave plantation society—even one that has adopted modern technology and production methods—to keep pace with the productivity and wealth creation of an industrializing capitalist (free-labor) society.

43. On the relative modernity of U.S. Southern agriculture see Richard Graham, "Slavery and Economic Development: Brazil and the United States South in the 19th Century," *Comparative Studies in Society and History* 23, no. 4 (1981): 620–55. On the Southern planters' somewhat illusory sense of their economic power see William Freehling, "The Divided South, Democracy's Limitations, and the Causes of the Peculiarly North American Civil War," in *The Reintegration of American History*, 178–79.

44. John C. Calhoun, "Speech on the Reception of Abolition Petitions," U.S. Senate, 6 February 1837, reproduced in McKitrick, *Slavery Defended*, 12–16, emphasis added.

45. On the widening gap in the GDP between the nineteenth-century United States and Mexico and Brazil see John Coatsworth, "Obstacles to Economic Growth in Nineteenth-Century Mexico," *American Historical Review* (February 1978): 80–100.

46. Freehling, "The Divided South," 183.

47. Ibid., 196.

48. Cited in Toplin, *The Abolition of Slavery*, 42.

49. See note 32.

50. For recent critiques of the "myth" of racial democracy see George Reid Andrews, *Blacks and Whites in São Paulo, Brazil, 1888–1988* (Madison, Wisc., 1991); and Michael G. Hanchard, *Orpheus and Power* (Princeton, N.J., 1994).

51. The best introduction to proslavery writings is Faust, *The Ideology of Slavery*.

52. Mattos, *Escravidão e cidadania*; Keila Grinberg, *O fiador dos brasileiros: Cidadania, escravidão e direito civil no tempo de Antonio Pereira Rebouças* (Rio de Janeiro, 2002). According to Mattos, referring to the political situation in Brazil during the 1830s, "from the point of view of slave-owning interests, the construction of any racialized justification for the continuance of the institution of slavery had shown itself to be simply explosive" (*Escravidão e cidadania*, 22–23). The introduction of racial discrimination into legal codes also harked back to colonial prohibitions related to "blood stain" (*mancha de sangue*), widely despised as a relic of unenlightened Portuguese rule.

53. Hendrik Kraay, *Race, State, and Armed Forces in Independence-Era Brazil: Bahia, 1790s–1840s* (Stanford, Calif., 2001), 114.

54. Schultz, "Brazilian Independence," 12–15.

55. On the far from universal manhood suffrage in the United States in the antebellum era see Alexander Keyssar, *The Right to Vote: The Contested History of Democracy in the United States* (New York, 2000).

56. Schultz, "Brazilian Independence," 12–15. Brazilian law drew a distinction between civil rights, which all free and freedpersons enjoyed, male and, with some restrictions, female, and political rights, which were only enjoyed by free males with designated "qualities."

57. Grinberg, *O fiador dos brasileiros*, 115.

58. Mattos, *As cores do silêncio*.

59. Freehling, "The Divided South," 191.

60. For a solid discussion of agitation by men of color in the army and militia following independence see Kraay, *Race, State, and Armed Forces*, esp. chap. 5.

61. Mattos, *Escravidão e cidadania*, 30. More radical citizens of color also found themselves outside the boundaries of "civilized" politics if they allied with fugitive slaves or other "outcast" sectors of society. See, for example, Matthias Röhrig Assunção, "Elite Politics and Popular Rebellion in the Construction of Post-Colonial Order: The Case of Maranhão, Brazil (1820–1841)," *Journal of Latin American Studies* 31 (1999): 1–38.

62. Grinberg, *O fiador dos brasileiros*, 119. Defending the legal rights of *libertos* could place the *libertos'* champions in some uncomfortable positions. Thus the liberal and antislavery deputy from Bahia, Montezuma, found himself obliged to argue that Indians and slaves were legally "things" in order to argue for the rights of *libertos* as Brazilians (109).

63. Seymour Drescher, "Brazilian Abolition in Comparative Perspective," *Hispanic American Historical Review* 68, no. 3 (1988): 429–60.

64. Dean, *Rio Claro*, chap. 5. I am using "Creolization" here strictly to refer to the rising proportion of Brazilian-born slaves rather than a cultural process per se.

65. There were other factors related to states' rights and gender that are not discussed in this essay but that contributed significantly to the appeal of Southern national identity and the proslavery argument, especially among white nonslaveholders. See, for example, Stephanie McCurry, *Masters of Small Worlds: Yeoman Households, Gender Relations, and the Political Culture of the Antebellum South Carolina Low Country* (New York, 1995).

66. For a comparative discussion of the abolition of slavery in the Americas and serfdom in Europe see Hahn, "Class and State."

67. Carolyn E. Fick, *The Making of Haiti* (Knoxville, Tenn., 1990), 76–88.

68. On anticolonialism and antislavery in Cuba see Ada Ferrer, *Insurgent Cuba: Race, Nation, and Revolution, 1868–1898* (Chapel Hill, N.C., 1999), 15–89.

69. On white Southerners' romanticization of slavery after the Civil War see David W. Blight, *Race and Reunion: The Civil War in American Memory* (Cambridge, Mass., 2001), 258–60. The classic "nostalgic" view of slavery in colonial Brazil is Gilberto Freyre, *The Masters and the Slaves* (New York, 1956). Freyre's classic work was first published (in Brazil) in 1934.

70. Again, Freyre, *The Masters and the Slaves*, is the crucial text, but there were many others in this vein.

71. On the "Lost Cause" historiography of slavery and the Civil War see Blight, *Race and Reunion*, 255–99.

72. See the essay by Rebecca Scott on Louisiana and Cuba in F. Cooper, T. Holt, and

R. Scott, eds., *Beyond Slavery: Explorations of Race, Labor, and Citizenship in Postemancipation Societies* (Chapel Hill, N.C., 2000), 61–106.

73. Ibid.

74. The Paulista coffee zones were exceptional in their ability to rapidly replace ex-slaves with immigrant workers, but planters in many other former slave societies made similar efforts. For the Cuban case see Rebecca J. Scott, *Slave Emancipation in Cuba: The Transition to Free Labor, 1860–1899* (Princeton, N.J., 1985).

75. On the fate of the freedpersons following abolition in São Paulo see Kim D. Butler, *Freedoms Given, Freedoms Won: Afro-Brazilians in Post-Abolition São Paulo and Salvador* (New Brunswick, N.J., 1998); and George Reid Andrews, *Blacks and Whites in São Paulo, Brazil, 1888–1988* (Madison, Wisc., 1991). Andrews makes a compelling argument for the agency of freedpersons, contending that planter preferences for immigrants were not based exclusively on race but on the willingness of immigrant families (in contrast to the former slaves) to put the whole household into the fields. Still, the planters showed little reluctance with respect to the transformation of their workforce.

76. Bosi, "Sob o signo de cam," in *Dialética da colonização* (São Paulo, 1992), 246–72.

Race and Nation in the United States, Mexico, and Cuba, 1880–1940

GARY GERSTLE

*T*his essay examines the ways in which racial identities and ideologies shaped the construction of nationhood in the United States, Mexico, and Cuba in the late nineteenth and early twentieth centuries. These years were formative ones for each of these three societies, with Mexico undergoing modernization and revolution, Cuba achieving slave emancipation and national independence, and the United States struggling with postbellum reunification, industrialization, and empire. In the United States nationhood depended equally on the contradictory but coexisting ideologies of civic and racial nationalism. Mexico and Cuba are often thought to have incubated alternative conceptions of nationhood, especially in regard to race, yet systematic comparisons of the nationalist projects in Mexico and Cuba with that in the United States are hard to find. I provide such a comparison in this essay, being careful to treat these three countries not simply as discrete entities but as neighbors unequally endowed with power and enmeshed in each other's affairs. Thus I explore both the similarities in nationalist discourses circulating through the three societies and the particular conceptions of race and nation that, owing to divergent historical experiences and asymmetric power relations, emerged in each.

In the United States the concept of civic nationalism signified a desire to construct a polity and a people on an egalitarian and democratic foundation. Civic nationalists argued that the United States should open itself and be prepared to grant equal rights to all individuals, irrespective of race, religion, gender, ethnicity, or political creed, who were willing to declare their loyalty to America and obey its laws. Racial nationalism in the United States, by contrast, expressed a sense of peoplehood grounded in common blood and skin color and an inherited fitness for self-government. At the turn of the twentieth century racial nationalism in the United States was as potent a force as civic nationalism and shaped the country's nationhood in profound ways. Mexican and Cuban nationalists understood well the vigorous racial basis of U.S. nationhood in part because of their proximity to the United States and their intimate knowledge of its internal affairs and in part because they experienced firsthand how the United States used racial nationalism as a justification for extending its imperial reach into their own countries: the "racially inferior" peoples of Latin America, Theodore Roosevelt and other U.S. imperialists often insisted, were simply not "fit" to govern themselves.

In order to refute this imperial argument and legitimate the central role played by nonwhites in their nations' struggles for independence and justice, Mexican and Cuban nationalists each developed an ideology that repudiated North American conceptions of race as a marker of their nationhood: *mestizaje* in Mexico, "racelessness" in Cuba. These ideologies were notable accomplishments given the pressure, both political and cultural, that the United States was able to exert on both countries. I explore the origins and evolution of these two nationalist ideologies in this essay. I also note, however, the difficulties that both Mexican and Cuban nationalists experienced in freeing themselves from their own racial nationalist impulses. These difficulties suggest how tough it was, even for the most progressive and anti-imperialist nationalists in the Western Hemisphere, to transcend ethnically and racially based notions of national belonging.

The United States, 1880–1940: The Resurgence of Racial Nationalism

Civic and racial nationalism mutually constituted the ideological foundation of the U.S. nation at its very origins. The Declaration of Independence and in particular its statement that "all men are created equal" embodied the country's civic nationalist creed, revealing America's aspiration to become a nation for all kinds of individuals irrespective of their caste, religion, nationality, race, or politics. The openness of U.S. society went hand in hand with the nation's commitment to equal rights and democratic government: empowered as citizens and protected by the rule of law, the American people would rule. The centrality and appeal of this civic creed quickly made this new nation a beacon to other peoples in the world seeking freedom and equality, especially those in western Europe and Iberian America.

But the United States was also a slaveholders' republic. Slave owners played key roles in the 1776 revolution against Britain and in drafting the 1789 Constitution, which endorsed slavery and apportioned congressional delegates to ensure that slave owners would exercise disproportionate power in national affairs. In 1790 the first U.S. Congress passed a law limiting naturalization to "free white persons," thereby creating a racial test for citizenship that would remain in force for more than 160 years. From the very beginning, in other words, the United States propagated a racial nationalism that conceived of the country in racial terms, as a home for white people, which, in the eighteenth century, meant those of European origin and descent. As the case of Thomas Jefferson exemplifies, many of those who fashioned America's universalist and democratic political creed were also the architects of its racial nationalism—a paradox that has been one of the most fascinating and enduring in U.S. history.[1]

The North's victory over the slaveholding South in the Civil War (1861–65) offered the United States an opportunity to uproot its racial nationalist tradition and to reorganize the republic solely around its civic creed. Indeed, the abolition of slavery, the passage of the 14th Amendment (outlawing discrimination based on race, creed, or color), and the wide-ranging efforts to empower freedmen and women in the years between 1863 and 1877 constituted a second American revolution—Reconstruction—every bit as fundamental as the first. But this revolution, unlike the first one, failed. Propertied Southern whites who had lost their political power regained it after 1877. Though these elites could not restore slavery, they did fashion a system of peonage that held rural blacks in economic semiservitude and an ideology of Jim Crow that ensured African American segregation and subordination in politics and culture. White Southerners stripped blacks of basic citizenship rights—to vote, hold elective offices, and sit on juries—while denying them access to any space, public or private, defined as white: schools, parks, restaurants, stores, theaters, churches, railroad cars, and bathrooms. Through this system of apartheid white Southerners revived America's tradition of racial nationalism for a new century and mocked black claims to be equal or full participants in the American nation.[2]

An invigorated tradition of racial nationalism also influenced U.S. attitudes toward the country's indigenous population. In the second half of the nineteenth century Indians were subjected to a system of apartheid different from Jim Crow, this one organized around ever-shrinking reservations into which the surviving populations of Native Americans, those who had not been killed in the Indian wars nor had succumbed to illness, had been confined. The Dawes Severalty Act (1887) nominally attempted to promote the assimilation of Indians into the (white) American nation by giving individual Indians the opportunity to withdraw from tribal control, cultivate their own plots of land, and transform themselves into that great hero of Euro-American life, the yeoman farmer. That the U.S. Congress would even consider a policy that might lead to the assimilation and integration of Indians into white America so soon after it had repudiated Reconstruction (1877) suggests that Indians possessed a higher stature in America than did blacks. Indeed, many white Americans developed a romantic attachment to Indians that they rarely displayed toward African Americans, admiring the former for their alleged ferocity as warriors, for their "simplicity," "purity," and "noble savagery," and for their supposed freedom from the contaminating effects of civilization.[3]

The history of the Dawes Act demonstrates, however, that such romance rarely led white Americans to treat Indians as their equals or to ensure that Indians would be given the assistance necessary to allow them to become full participants in the American nation. Most Indians who took possession of individual lands under the Dawes Act either failed as farmers or quickly lost their property to white speculators. After the law had operated for two decades, Indians found themselves on smaller reservations that had been stripped of their best land. They sank into a kind of poverty that mocked purported efforts to include them in American bounty or American dreams. And to the extent to which public and private agencies persisted in their integrative campaigns, these campaigns often degenerated into ugly attempts at coercive assimilation, as in the case of white educators who forcibly removed Indian children from their families and placed them in special Indian schools hundreds, even thousands, of miles away. If Indians had a higher stature than blacks in the U.S. nationalist imagination, it did nothing to improve the condition of Indian life in the United States in the first thirty years of the twentieth century.[4]

The late-nineteenth-century subordination and marginalization of blacks and Indians are developments that U.S. historians have known about for a long time. But, for an equally long period of time, their significance for understanding the development or "progress" of the U.S. nation was minimized or rationalized by reference to the "backward" nature of the South and the "primitive" nature of the West. In the early twentieth century America's social and political weight seemed to be gravitating to its industrial-urban cores in the Northeast and Midwest and on the West Coast. Here conditions of political equality prevailed; here a reform-minded liberalism intent on reducing economic inequities and righting social wrongs gained vigor; here hundreds of thousands of immigrants (and sometimes as many as a million), many of them impoverished and unwanted in their homelands, arrived every year and were greeted with respect and opportunity. Here, in the words of the political thinker and *New Republic* founder Herbert Croly, a new nation, inclusive and progressive, was taking shape. Croly, indeed, called for a "new nationalism" that was both demographically inclusive and reformist in its efforts to tame capitalist excess. Theodore Roosevelt became this new nationalism's most famous tribune, making it a robust expression of the civic nationalist creed.[5]

In the view of progressives such as Croly and Roosevelt and many of the key historians at work in the middle decades of the twentieth century, themselves partisans of this Progressive (and then New Deal) tradition, the new urban-industrial nation would realize America's democratic ideals. As this new civic nation deepened democratic practice and spread economic opportunity through the social order, the South would be modernized and see its apartheid abolished and the West would be civilized, its Indians given a better deal. But the ease with which Progressive thinkers and liberal historians pushed the South and West to the periphery or treated both regions as belonging to America's flawed past rather than to its bright future always rested on a series of evasions about the role of the West and South in shaping modern America and about the ways in which Croly's new nation had implicated itself in sustaining racialized discourses of national belonging. Nothing illustrates this better than immigration policy from the 1880s to the 1920s.[6]

Prior to the 1880s the United States had possessed a remarkably liberal immigration policy that constituted one of the finest expressions of its civic nationalist creed. During this period America welcomed virtually anyone, regardless of his or her national origins, who wished to make the United States his or her home. In the forty-year period from the 1880s to the 1920s, however, Congress and the executive branch replaced the nation's open borders policy with a "closed border," one grounded largely in a series of racial exclusions. Congress banned Chinese immigration in 1882, and President Theodore Roosevelt banned Japanese immigration in 1907. While both actions were responses to regional anxieties, notably white westerners' worries that "yellow hordes" were taking over the Pacific Coast, they became national policies, endorsed and sustained by the federal government. Frankly racist justifications underlay such discriminatory practices: Chinese and Japanese were so different from Americans of European origin and were so primitive, restrictionists argued, they could never be civilized or acculturated. Their biological constitution was such, their opponents alleged, that they needed no rest and little food. They thus would outperform American workers on a sliver of an American workingman's wages and thus drive the latter to ruin. These Asians were also alleged to know (or to care to know) nothing about democracy and citizenship and to be oblivious to the value of family life or moral probity. They were thought to be sexual predators (on white women) and the carriers of debilitating drug habits. They would contribute nothing to the American nation and had already harmed it by their presence. Fortunately, in the eyes of America's Asian immigrant enemies, no immigrant from East (and South) Asia could become a citizen, thanks to the 1790 law limiting naturalization to those who were free and white. The American nation had no place for these groups.[7]

In 1924 Congress extended its ban on immigration from East Asia to most of the world. And, for the first time, it struck at Europe and, in particular, at groups from southern and eastern Europe who were also thought to be racially inferior and thus damaging to America's "Anglo-Saxon" or "Nordic" stock. Here is how legislators in the House of Representatives described eastern and southern Europeans in 1924: "There is little or no similarity," declared Congressman Fred S. Purnell of Indiana, "between the clear-thinking, self-governing stocks that sired the American people and this stream of irresponsible and broken wreckage that is pouring into the lifeblood of America the social and political diseases of the Old World." Purnell quoted approvingly the words of a Dr. Ward, who claimed that Americans had deceived themselves into believing that "we could change inferior beings into superior ones." Americans could not escape the laws of heredity, Ward argued. "We cannot make a heavy horse into a trotter by keeping him in a racing stable. We cannot make a well-bred dog out of a mongrel by teaching him tricks." The acts that Ward dismissed as "tricks" included the learning by immigrants of the Gettysburg Address and the Declaration of Independence.[8]

Congressman J. Will Taylor of Tennessee, meanwhile, approvingly read to his colleagues a *Boston Herald* editorial warning that America was entering the same period of eugenical decline that had doomed Rome: "Rome had [mistaken] faith in the melting pot, as we have. It scorned the iron uncertainties of heredity, as we do. It lost its instinct for race preservation, as we have lost ours. It forgot that men must be selected and bred as sacredly as cows and pigs and sheep, as we have not learned." "Rome rapidly senilized and died," the editorial concluded, and so would America unless Congress took note of eugenical principles and passed the 1924 restriction legislation. The law passed both houses of Congress by overwhelming margins, drawing votes from congressmen and senators from every region of the country, East and West, North and South, urban and rural. It remained on the books until 1965, giving a decidedly racial cast to America's new nation.[9]

I do not want to suggest that no one opposed this law or generated alternative conceptions of nationhood at this time. In the first three decades of the twentieth century sizeable and varied groups of Americans drawn from the ranks of liberal reformers, ethnic and racial minorities, and socialist radicals labored to invigorate the civic basis of their nationhood and to insist that equality and inclusion ought to remain the governing principles of their polity. Many Americans were drawn to Israel Zangwill's vision of America as a melting pot in which the races of many lands would be drawn together and forged into a single people. A much smaller group, but including individuals whose writings and politics would gain influence in subsequent decades (the philosophers Horace Kallen and Alain Locke, the literary critic Randolph Bourne, the anthropologist Franz Boas, the educator Rachel Davis-DuBois, and the Indian reformer John Collier), pushed their thinking beyond inclusive programs of assimilation and began to argue that ethnic and racial pluralism would strengthen the egalitarian and democratic foundation of the American nation. But the eloquence with which these proponents of "pluralist nationalism" expressed their views should not blind us to their marginality in the 1910s and 1920s. The racial boundaries of the American nation grew stronger in the early twentieth century, not weaker. The country's urbanization and modernization at this time went hand in hand with the deepening of American's racial nationalism.[10]

This development was apparent not just in domestic politics but also in international relations, as an industrializing America extended its economic, political, and military influence abroad. It wasn't just that America's racial nationalism influenced the country's foreign policy but that its very nature and strength emerged from encounters between the United States and foreign countries. This process is especially apparent in U.S. relations with Latin America. The pivotal episode in that relationship was the war between the United States and Spain and the subsequent U.S. occupation of Spain's former colony, Cuba.

The U.S. rout of Spain in 1898 regenerated an American nation ground down by economic depression and class conflict and still suffering from the aftershocks of its civil war. The victory fueled a conviction that the United States was indeed a superior nation that could accomplish great feats, and this, in turn, energized both imperialists who wanted to flex America's muscles abroad and social reformers who wanted to improve U.S. society at home. But the war against Spain also shaped American nationalism, and especially its racial nationalist tradition, in more particular ways.

In Cuba in 1898 Northern U.S. white soldiers and Southern U.S. white soldiers fought alongside each other for the first time since before the Civil War. This development was itself a key act of sectional reconciliation and racial nationalist regeneration and underscored what was happening in politics and society in the United States: the repudiation of the Reconstruction promise of racial equality and the embrace of white unity and superiority as the basis of American nationhood. The significance of white Northerners and white Southerners fighting together increases in light of accusations emerging from the war itself that black soldiers then serving in the U.S. Army were inferior to white soldiers and should no longer be permitted to represent the United States in combat. These accusations were false, but they nevertheless damaged the reputation of black soldiers, who, after 1900, were systematically excluded from combat roles in the U.S. military. By World War I the U.S. Army permitted very few of the hundreds of thousands of blacks it had drafted to fight. This exclusion from combat devastated many blacks and their standing among whites, especially in an era when a nation's prowess was thought to rest on the quality of its military. The refusal to let black warriors join white ones on the field of battle underscored the strength of racial nationalism and the tenuousness of the black claim to be part of the American nation.[11]

Mexico, 1880–1940: The Racialist Residue of *Mestizaje*

Mexico had been a sovereign nation since the early nineteenth century (1821). But, as Eric Van Young notes in his essay for this collection, nationalist consciousness at the time of Mexican independence barely penetrated the ranks of the Mexican masses and especially of its large Indian majority. In the early years of independence, even efforts to fashion a polity in Mexico out of the minority of the population that was Creole and propertied proved difficult, as centrifugal regionalist forces frustrated efforts to unify the Creole elite around a common political authority and identity. Nevertheless, Mexican nationalism of the nineteenth century, like virtually all nationalisms of the period, did contain integrative and democratizing impulses that gained strength over the course of the nineteenth century and that made questions of incorporation—including that of Indian incorporation—inescapable.

Nations, to use a Benedict Anderson formulation, depend on a broad and deep horizontal comradeship. For a nationalism to work, the majority of people residing in a territory calling itself a nation have to be able to look at each other and say, we are all Mexicans, we are all Cubans, we are all Brazilians. In historical terms, such declarations of common nationality meant inviting the masses onto the political stage—to participate in movements for independence, reform, national defense, conquest, and economic development. These invitations often unleashed democratic enthusiasms, as groups within the nation, as a result of their mobilization, imbibed discourses about political rights and popular sovereignty. Nationalist mobilization did not always amplify democratic practice; indeed, by the late nineteenth century some nationalist regimes, such as the one developing in Germany under Otto von Bismarck, embraced authoritarianism as the best way to achieve social order, territorial expansion, and national glory. But even Bismarckian-style regimes had to contend with the instability that nationalist mobilization unleashed, for the shared and special nature of national identity allowed individuals who possessed it to press democratic claims on the state in the name of the nation.[12]

In Mexico the consequences of nationalist mobilization began to unfold in the middle decades of the nineteenth century. Mexico's defeat by the United States and the consequent loss of half its territory in 1848 shook the nation's established political and social order and led to the Ayutla Revolt of 1854, which brought Mexican Liberals to power. These Liberals quickly passed laws that legislated a free-market economy, a regime of private property rights (and individual landowners), a constitutional democracy, and a secularized system of education. When the country's Conservatives responded with force, the Liberals raised a popular army to defend their new state. A civil war ensued (1857–60), followed by the arrival in 1861 of invading armies from France, whom Conservatives had invited into Mexico in the hopes of restoring monarchy to their nation (in the anachronistic and ironic form of an Austrian archduke, Maximilian, who served Louis Napoléon of France). The Liberals waged years of guerrilla warfare against this Conservative-European alliance, finally emerging victorious in 1867 due in part to their success in mobilizing Indians and mestizos into National Guard units. Although many of the latter fought to defend their particular land or territory or to serve a military strongman, they also, through their struggle to defend Mexico, developed a popular nationalism hostile to foreign intervention and committed to the principles of individual rights and popular sovereignty.[13]

After 1867 some Indian and mestizo groups turned their arms on the Mexican state and the regional elites that supported it for privileging the propertied and powerful over the rural poor. The liberal Laws of Reform passed between 1855 and 1857 had outlawed the communal forms of property ownership then prevalent among Mexico's indigenous peoples and—in a manner that anticipated the Dawes Act in the United States—called for such land to be broken up into plots owned by single individuals or families. As would happen in the United States, this Liberal law became a pretext for large landowners and merchants to accumulate huge stretches of village lands. Such seizures, in turn, provoked the anger of poor Mexican peasants who now defended their lands using the new nationalist language of popular sovereignty and individual rights. Nationalism, in Mexico, had intensified democratic aspirations.[14]

In 1876, after several years of popular rebellions, regional resistance to central government consolidation, and infighting among liberal elites, Porfirio Díaz came to power and ruled the fragile nation until 1910. Díaz had originally built his reputation as a man of the people, specifically as a military leader of a popular alliance that had fought and then defeated the European invaders. But increasingly Díaz fancied himself a Bismarck or Napoléon of the New World, intent on restoring order and stability to Mexico and pursuing economic development and modernity through authoritarianism.

To modernize Mexico and make it more like those nations that were, in the late nineteenth century, regarded as the world's strongest (the United States, France, England, and Germany), Díaz and his technocratic advisors (*científicos*) first hoped to whiten the Mexican population. Spencerian ideologues of the late nineteenth and early twentieth centuries had turned the coincidence between national vigor and predominately white populations into evolutionary law: the fittest races naturally had built the strongest and most civilized nations. Porfirian nation builders wanted to make this law work for them, which meant finding a demographic strategy for turning Mexico's population white. Impressed with the U.S. and Argentine model, they hoped to encourage Europeans to immigrate to Mexico. The Porfirian intellectual and state builder Justo

Sierra wrote in the 1880s that Mexico's "impoverished blood" could only be improved by "large doses of strong blood, supplied in the form of [European] immigration."[15] But Sierra and the other *científicos* never managed to convert their desire for increased European immigration into a successful policy. Meanwhile, the economic modernization projects of the Porfirian state were drawing more and more Indians and mestizos from isolated rural areas into commercial, mining, and industrial regions, making the nonwhite character of Mexico all the more visible.[16]

The reaction of the Porfirian elite to Mexico's nonwhites was complex. On the one hand, its members found themselves appalled by the primitivism and poverty of the rural Indian and mestizo populations and used social Darwinist arguments to explain the "failure" of these people to succeed under conditions of capitalist competition. On the other hand, some members of this elite understood that a Mexican nation, unlike its U.S. neighbor, had somehow to incorporate these Indian masses. They initiated this process of incorporation by reviving an older nationalist narrative about how the Aztecs of the 1300s and 1400s had built a civilization rivaling those of ancient Greece and Egypt. The Aztecs, in other words, had already demonstrated how Indian peoples could fashion Mexico into a mighty nation and a glorious culture. How, then, to explain the gap between the superiority of the Mesoamerican Aztecs and the squalor of Indian life in the 1880s? Porfirian intellectuals laid this responsibility at the feet of the Spanish conquerors, who, even as they brought European civilization to Mexico, destroyed Aztec society in such an indiscriminate manner so as to trigger a process of Indian degeneration. This degeneration could not be easily reversed, but it could not be ignored. If Mexico were to succeed as a modern nation, Indians—or at least those who could claim an association with the Aztecs—had to be rehabilitated and incorporated. In the process, the greatness that the Aztecs had once bestowed on Mexico would be reclaimed.[17] This reclamation project took symbolic form in 1887, when the Porfirian regime erected in Mexico City a huge statue honoring Cuauhtémoc, the last Aztec emperor and, most important, the man who inspired the Aztecs to resist the Spanish conquistadors. Francisco Sosa, a government publicist at the time, declared that the "magnificent monument" would "honor permanently . . . the first and most illustrious of the defenders of the nationality founded by Tenoch in 1327."[18]

The Porfirian state builders often dealt harshly with Mexico's Indian populations and could be ruthless in their policies of incorporation—through, for example, the waging of war against and conquest of tribes that resisted central state authority.[19] Nevertheless, by the early twentieth century this governing elite had gone considerably further than had U.S. nation builders in acknowledging how central Indians were to the making of their nation. Their efforts to recognize the importance of an Indian heritage to the construction of Mexican nationhood allowed more and more Mexicans, including those outside elite circles, to glimpse that their nation's greatness lay in the racially mixed character of its population. If Mexico were one day to rival the great nations of Europe in its modernity, culture, and prosperity, it would do so by celebrating rather than by denying its mestizo character.

While the Porfirian elite launched the discourse on mestizo nationalism, it could never fully embrace it. That embrace would be the work of the Mexican revolutionaries who overthrew Díaz in 1910 and, with extensive Indian support, consolidated their power over the next twenty years. These revolutionaries celebrated the concept of *mestizaje*—the mixing of European and indigenous Indian stocks—and argued that such mixing had endowed their nation with uncommon vigor and valor. The United States feared the Mexican Revolution and invaded Mexico in 1913 and again in 1917 to subdue its most radical elements and, in the process, to protect U.S. economic interests.[20] The United States never secured the influence in Mexico that it had gained in Cuba after 1898, but its actions nevertheless impelled Mexican revolutionaries to frame their concept of national belonging as a repudiation of the one dominant in the United States. Mexico rejected the nationalism of its northern neighbor through its veneration of *mestizaje*.

Scholars often treat *mestizaje* as a uniquely Latin American product, which it was not.[21] The equivalent term in the United States, the "melting pot," gained popularity at precisely the time that *mestizaje* did, during the first twenty years of the twentieth century, though its conceptual roots can be traced back to the eighteenth century and, in particular, to the musings of the French immigrant J. Hector St. John de Crèvecoeur. In 1782 Crèvecoeur had asked, "What, then, is the American, this new man?" and he had answered, "He is neither an European nor the descendant of an European; hence that strange mixture of blood, which you will find in no other country. I could point out to you a family whose grandfather was an Englishman, whose wife was Dutch, whose son married a French woman, and whose present four sons have now four wives of different nations. . . . Here individuals of all nations are melted into a new race of men, whose labours and posterity will one day cause great changes in the world."[22] One hundred thirty years later Israel Zangwill updated this hybrid definition of the American for the twentieth century: "America is God's Crucible, where all the races of Europe are melting and reforming," the protagonist of Zangwill's 1908 play, *The Melting Pot*, proclaims. "Germans, Frenchman, Irishmen and Englishmen, Jews and Russians—into the Crucible with you all! God is making the American."[23]

Crèvecoeur and Zangwill were both forward-looking thinkers of their own times. The former conceived of an America open to Europeans who were not English and the latter of an America welcoming to Europeans who were neither

Anglo-Saxon nor Nordic. But neither could imagine an America emerging from a population mix that included not just Europeans but non-Europeans as well: Africans, Asians, and Native Americans. The idea that became so central to Mexican nationalism—that Indians were not only part of the melting pot but formed one of the fundamental metals out of which the Mexican national alloy had emerged—was inconceivable north of the Rio Grande. Thus, it was not the idea of *mestizaje* itself that distinguished Mexico but the idea that the best hybrid had emerged from the interaction of indigenous and European stock. The Mexican conception of nationality broke from notions of Europeanness and whiteness in ways that those in the early-twentieth-century United States never did.

It did not take long for Mexican revolutionary intellectuals to make *mestizaje* a defining characteristic of their nationhood. Manuel Gamio, a Columbia University–trained anthropologist and Mexican revolutionary, called on his fellow insurgents as early as 1916 "to take up the hammer and gird themselves with the blacksmith's apron, so that they may make rise from the miraculous anvil the new nation of blended bronze and iron."[24] José Vasconcelos, the Mexican secretary of public education from 1921 to 1924 and a key architect of the revolutionary regime's cultural policies, celebrated racial hybridity not just in Mexico but everywhere in the world. "All the great periods of history," he declared, "have been the work of a mixture of races, of peoples and colors, rather than the work of any privileged pure-blood nation." Hybridity "in man, as well as in plants," tends to produce better types, Vasconcelos argued, "as it tends to complement the weaknesses of a particular stock through interchange and assimilation with all the world." So thorough and rich was the process of mixing the blood of peoples as different as the Indians and Europeans, Vasconcelos averred, that the resulting hybrid race really did contain "all the world." Mexicans constituted nothing less than the "cosmic race," a race superior both to more narrowly based hybrids and to the "pure" races of North America and Europe. The future, in Vasconcelos's telling, lay with the mestizo nationalities of Latin America and not the "unmixed" ones of the United States and France.[25]

Mexican revolutionaries developed an ideology of *indigenismo* to honor the native peoples of Mexico and articulate the progress that would result when the latter's contributions to Mexican nationality were properly recognized. These revolutionaries undertook a variety of initiatives both to bring their transformed nation and its ambitions to the attention of Indian populations and to incorporate the Indian story and experience into the history and culture of Mexico. In the 1920s the Mexican state took control of elementary schools in remote areas and began teaching students literacy, hygiene, sobriety, patriotic virtue, nationalist history, and modern sports while countering the influence of the Church and local caudillos. To emphasize the Indian contribution to the making of the new nation, the revolutionary state rehabilitated Indian customs and folklore and encouraged urban and rural artists—musicians, balladeers, muralists, dancers, playwrights, and others—to mark the Indian presence and contributions in their work.[26] The revolutionaries did indeed spark a cultural revival in many areas, even as they often lost control of the programs they had set in motion. Popular artists who had been inspired by government initiatives used the cultural space that those initiatives opened up not to pursue revolutionary agendas but to create art grounded in the particularities of their experience and of their regions. Yet in the largest sense many Mexicans believed that their nation's cultural renaissance in the 1920s and 1930s, evident in everything from the symphonies and ballets of Carlos Chávez to the murals of Diego Rivera, expressed the richness and vigor of mestizo nationhood.[27] This mestizo renaissance, in other words, was understood to be the realization of revolutionary nationalist dreams.

In truth, this renaissance was far more an internationalist project than many nationalists could admit. Whether we point to the influence of the cosmopolitan Parisian painting milieu on the work of Rivera, or the importance of Afro-Caribbean rhythms and melodies to dance music in Mexico City, or the influence of U.S. big bands on mariachis, we can discern the importance of transnational flows of artists and cultures. Yet in this archnationalist age Mexicans usually insisted that the critical cultural mixtures were indigenous rather than international, an expression of Mexican rather than global *mestizaje.*

The emphasis on *mestizaje* marked Mexican nationalism as different from its North American counterpart. Even as the arrival of a reform government in the 1930s and the appointment of John Collier as head of the Bureau of Indian Affairs made U.S. policy toward its own Indians more liberal than it had been, the notion that American national greatness emerged from the mixing of its native and European stocks remained as heretical a thought during the New Deal as it had been in the 1880s. And even as diverse groups of Americans—eastern and southern European immigrants, Catholics, Jews, and Protestants, whites and blacks—were coming together in U.S. cities to create a vigorous mass culture of song, jazz, and dance and to form an eager audience for Hollywood movies, the Euro-American *mestizaje* that lay at the foundation of this cultural effervescence was denied far more than it was celebrated or even acknowledged.[28] The United States still aspired to be a white Anglo-Saxon nation, an aspiration that found expression in the maintenance of Jim Crow and a racialized system of immigration restriction. This aspiration manifested itself, too, in the expectation that those whites who were not Anglo-Saxon would hide markers of their ethnic difference (and inferiority) and seek to acquire the physical and cultural qualities that denoted Anglo-Saxons and Nordics as superior.[29] Thus, despite a convergence of political and cultural trends in Mexico and the United States after World War I, the articulation of nationhood in the two countries remained far apart.

Mexican nationalism, however, resembled its North American counterpart in at least three important ways. First, despite its progressive and inclusive character, racial essentialism lay at its core. Most Mexicans, even the revolutionary-minded ones, had not yet figured out how to separate nation from race. The Mexican people were thought to constitute a race, *la raza*, all of them marked by defining and enduring characteristics. Vasconcelos, for example, celebrated the mestizo for his "great vivacity of mind," his "boldness, universality of thought and sentiment," while at the same time worrying that his "unsteady" temperament made him hotheaded and irrational.[30] Most instructive about Vasconcelos's writing on this subject are not the particular adjectives that he chose to describe mestizos but his conviction that the characteristics he had identified as "Mexican" appeared in all those who were the product of *mestizaje*: northerners and southerners, urban dwellers and rural campesinos, workers and shopkeepers. Seen in this way, Vasconcelos's thinking differed little from that of the U.S. senators and congressmen who, in the 1920s, ascribed inborn characteristics to entire "races" of people from eastern and southern Europe and from East Asia. While Vasconcelos adhered to a more progressive vision than did the U.S. legislators who imposed a racist system of immigration restriction on America and favored a racial science that was Lamarckian rather than Mendelian in approach, he partook of a racial essentialism similar to the one that shaped North American thought.[31]

The second way in which Mexican nationalism resembled its American counterpart was in its emphasis on homogeneity: all Mexicans were expected to be fundamentally alike, just as all Americans were expected to fit into an Anglo-Saxon mold. Manuel Gamio wrote that successful nation building depended on "a solemn cry of shared blood, of shared flesh, that cry which is above all else, since it is the voice of life, the mysterious force which pulls material together and resists disintegration."[32] Gamio and fellow revolutionary nationalists differed from their U.S. counterparts, of course, in their belief that Mexico's "mysterious force" would emerge from the mixing of European and indigenous blood rather than from a Europeans-only melting pot or a campaign for racial purity. Nevertheless, they shared with North American nation builders a commitment to uniformity. Gamio was unambiguous on this point: "Racial homogeneity, that advanced unification of physical types, that advanced happy fusion of races, constitutes the first and most solid basis of nationalism."[33] It was the job of the revolutionaries to bring that happy fusion, that racial homogeneity, about.

This emphasis on uniformity and homogeneity led directly to the third resemblance between Mexican and U.S. nationalism: a hostility to those within the nation who were either racially or culturally different from the mestizo mainstream. Significant numbers of Indians regarded the emerging Mexican nation-state and its ideology of *mestizaje* as an unwelcome imposition on their way of life. A modernizing, "civilizing" ambition underlay the *mestizaje* project, many Indians believed. While the proponents of *mestizaje* sought to cultivate aspects of Indian life they liked (folk art traditions, the commitment to communal and cooperative labor), they were also intent on eliminating aspects they abhorred (diets lacking in nutrition, poor hygiene, folk medicinal practices that relied on potions and incantations to cure disease, and perhaps most of all a deep attachment to Catholicism and clerical authority).[34] Many Indians did not want to be modernized if it meant that they were going to be stripped of their ways of living, so they asserted their right to be left alone. This stance, in turn, infuriated many Mexican nationalists who feared that an insistence on cultural difference would weaken Mexico and imperil its future. These nationalists began using both propaganda and state power to impose modernity on these recalcitrant populations. By the 1930s a small group of anthropologists and educators, sometimes called Indianists, came to defend indigenous cultural preservation and autonomy within the nation, but they were as marginal in interwar Mexico as were their cultural pluralist counterparts, Horace Kallen and Randolph Bourne, in the United States.[35]

This intolerance of difference emerged in Mexico as well in connection to those groups who were thought to be so unlike Europeans and indigenous peoples that they simply could not be included in the *mestizaje* project under any circumstances. Blacks, for many Mexicans, constituted one such people. Mexico's African heritage and peoples of African descent were ignored by revolutionary nationalists, many of whom disdained the rage for "jazz" in the 1920s, by which they meant the popularity of the Charleston, fox-trot, and ragtime, and Mexican popular music deeply influenced by Afro-Caribbean, particularly Cuban, trends.[36] When these nationalists worried about the cohesion and strength of Mexico, they would often comfort themselves with the thought that at least they did not have a "Negro problem" on the scale of the one afflicting the United States. This fear of the Negro may also explain the reluctance of Mexican revolutionaries to explore in any depth the linkages between their own *mestizaje* and the *afrocubanismo* version of it taking shape in nearby Cuba.

The most dramatic manifestation of Mexico's intolerance of difference, however, occurred in connection not with blacks but with the Chinese. As many as forty thousand Chinese immigrants lived in Mexico by 1910, many of them concentrated in the northwestern state of Sonora. Chinese entrepreneurialism in Sonora had brought these immigrants disproportionate influence and visibility as a regional petite bourgeoisie: they were small manufacturers (shoes and garments), merchants, and small businessmen. In their middleman role they became well known both to the area's Mexican population and to U.S. corporations that were investing in Sonoran mining, railroads, and cattle raising.[37]

Chinese immigrants had come to Sonora for a variety of reasons: some had wanted to go to the United States but no longer could, owing to the 1882 Chinese Exclusion Act. The Porfirian regime had invited others to come to Mexico to remedy a regional labor shortage generated by the exodus of Sonoran men to California and the U.S. Southwest in the late nineteenth century. Still other Chinese came once they learned that their countrymen who had gone to Sonora at an earlier time were prospering. In nine Sonoran towns Chinese immigrants owned all the businesses.[38]

Mexican resentment of the Chinese escalated as the latter's regional prominence and affluence grew. Sonoran migrants who returned to Mexico from California brought with them the virulent anti-Chinese sentiments then gripping the U.S. West as well as a desire to create a society in Sonora in which white Creoles were dominant, much as their U.S. counterparts had done across the border in Arizona, New Mexico, and Texas. The revolution intensified immigrant Chinese vulnerability in part because the Chinese Mexicans were seen as favoring the interests of U.S. corporations over those of the Mexican poor and in part because a disproportionate part of the revolution's leadership had grown up in a Sonoran petite bourgeoisie that had been eclipsed by the Chinese newcomers. Anti-Chinese agitation coalesced into a regional movement in Sonora between 1916 and 1919 and then into a national movement as the "Sonora faction" of Mexico's revolutionary movement, led by Mexican presidents Álvaro Obregón and Plutarco Elías Calles, took power in the 1920s. By 1931 the revolutionary Mexican state had begun expelling the Chinese from Mexico even as it continued to glorify the wonders of *mestizaje*. By 1940 it had reduced a Chinese population of Mexico that had once numbered forty thousand to a mere five thousand people. José María Dávila, the Baja California Norte representative to the National Congress, justified the expulsion of the Chinese in these terms: they "do not represent a step forward in the ideal of *mestizaje* . . . but rather signify a step backward in the anthropological search for the prototypical [Mexican] man."[39] Just as the populist nationalism of the revolution "sought to 'forge the nation' by integrating the Indian," Alan Knight has written, "so it also sought to cleanse the nation by expelling the Chinese."[40] In the discrimination against, scapegoating of, and then expulsion of the Chinese, Mexico had become indistinguishable from the United States.

The Chinese experience in revolutionary Mexico underscores a general point: that even nations that had gone much further than had the United States in opening themselves to nonwhite peoples could not free themselves altogether from the nexus of nation and race. The Chinese appeared to Mexicans to be so foreign and so racially different that they could not possibly be assimilated into Mexican culture or incorporated into the Mexican nation. Their incorporation would undermine the racial superiority that *mestizaje* had bestowed on Mexicans.

It mattered, too, that Mexican nationalists, like those of virtually every country, believed that their people possessed a character that was singular and indivisible. Even as the scientific racism that underlay nationalism began to wane in the 1930s, the notion that each nation possessed a powerful and encompassing "national character" gained life. Anthropologists and public intellectuals such as Franz Boas, Manuel Gamio, Ruth Benedict, and Margaret Mead insisted that every people possessed a "personality," the result of deeply rooted and extensively practiced patterns of culture. This ascendant school of cultural anthropology had substituted, in effect, a cultural essentialism for a racial one and thus helped to preserve the fiction about the cultural unity and uniformity of nations for another generation. Only slowly did an alternative, pluralist conception of nationhood begin to enter political thought: that nations contained a variety of peoples, not all of them alike or possessing the same traits, and that such nations could accommodate their diversity without sacrificing political unity, sovereignty, or muscle. This conception belonged to the post–World War II era. Nowhere did it emerge without profound conflict and struggle, a mark of how much the early-twentieth-century history of nationalism, and especially the era's near-universal emphasis on what Gamio had called "racial homogeneity" (and later modified into cultural homogeneity), lived on into our own time.[41]

Cuba, 1880–1940: Resisting Jim Crow, Fearing a Black Republic

At first glance, the radical supporters of Cuban independence and nationalism in the late nineteenth century seem to have escaped the Mexican and U.S. preoccupation with racial homogeneity, whether produced through purity or hybridity. Revolutionary nationalists there repudiated both the ideology of white supremacy, then fastening its hold on the U.S. South, and the Mexican revolutionaries' celebration of *mestizaje*. José Martí and other leaders of the independence movement insisted instead on "racelessness" as the defining characteristic of Cuban nationhood. Cuba Libre, Martí declared, would not be composed of different races—blacks, mulattos, and whites—but only of raceless individuals bound to each other by their common status as Cuban citizens. This was a bold pronouncement for Cuban nationalists to make in an age in which racialist thought suffused nationalist discourses and in light of Cuba's proximity to the United States, where racial nationalism was growing in strength and looking to include the Caribbean in the scope of its discursive influence.

Few people in Cuba, it turned out, would be able to escape U.S. power and prejudice. Imperial circumstances would frustrate the anti-imperial and revolutionary dream of establishing a raceless republic in Cuba. But the failure cannot be attributed entirely to U.S. interference with Cuban affairs. Even the most progressive groups in Cuba, those that had done the most to free their nationalism from ideologies of racial supremacy, could not escape the race-nation discursive nexus altogether. Some of their insistence on "racelessness" masked a fear that too much emphasis on race would expose a fact that they preferred to disguise, namely, that a very large portion of Cuba's population was of African descent. If Cuba showed its African face to the world, they worried, Cuba would come to be categorized, designated, and denigrated as a black nation, much as Haiti had been. Thus even Cuba's revolutionary nationalists were quick to condemn efforts by Afro-Cubans to assert a distinctive racial identity and to call attention to their group's particular needs. Those needs, many Afro-Cubans argued, grew out of a singular *racial* history—especially the ordeal of their enslavement and the unfinished business of their emancipation—and demanded a singular response. Among the legatees of the Martí nationalist tradition, opposition to this position congealed not around explicit claims that Afro-Cubans were racially inferior but around warnings that any acknowledgment of difference, racial or otherwise, would weaken the solidarity on which the Cuban nation rested. A fear of blackness, however, did lie at the root of Cuban hostility to difference, which also helps to explain why a Cuban version of *mestizaje*, what would become known in the 1920s and 1930s as *afrocubanismo*, emerged much more slowly in Cuba than in Mexico or other Latin countries.[42]

Cuba gained its national independence in 1902, almost a century after its South American neighbors and Mexico had won their independence from Spain and Portugal. Two facts about Cuba help to explain its tardy arrival on the nationalist stage: first, the lucrativeness of its sugar economy, which made it one of Spain's prized colonial possessions; and second, the heavily African and enslaved character of its population, which inclined Creoles to put aside their hopes for independent nationhood. In 1846 Afro-Cuban slaves and free people of color comprised more than half of the Cuban population.[43] That demographic reality conjured up for white Cubans the nightmare of a second black republic in the Caribbean and one that would resemble the first, Haiti, in its poverty, hostility to whites, and alleged corruption and ungovernability. At bottom, this Creole fear of black rule expressed a racist conviction that Africans were a people too primitive to govern themselves or others.

From the perspective of Afro-Cubans themselves, national independence would mean little—and would not be worth the sacrifice of time and blood that it would inevitably entail—without the simultaneous abolition of the Cuban slave system and the incorporation of the Afro-Cuban population into a polity on equal terms with its Creole counterpart. National independence from Spain, in other words, required nothing less than a revolution in Cuban race relations and a transformation in property and social relations. This double project of freeing Cuba from Spain and Afro-Cuban slaves from their owners was a major undertaking and one that was going to take time—in Cuba's case, much of the nineteenth century.

Pressure for independence and emancipation built steadily, however, especially from the 1860s on. The abolition of slavery and the defeat of the Confederacy in the United States fatally damaged the credibility of the remaining Western Hemispheric slaveholding regimes and helped to spark the first anticolonial insurrection in Cuba. Creoles and Afro-Cubans took up arms against Spain in 1868 in what became known as the Ten Years War. This struggle lasted not ten years but thirty, progressively weakening the legitimacy both of Cuban slaveholders and Spanish imperial authority. Spain formally abolished slavery in Cuba in 1886 and had lost virtually all of its political control over Cuba by 1898.[44]

The struggle against Spain was not an easy one for Cuban nationalists to wage, and the scale of fighting left tens of thousands dead, imprisoned, or displaced while devastating a once-prosperous colonial economy. But the struggle was invigorating for Cuban rebels, nevertheless, and prompted the liberation movement's more radical elements not only to insist that there would be no compromise with Spanish authority on questions of independence but also that racial distinctions would carry no significance in Cuba Libre, the free Cuban nation. This insistence on eliminating race as a social and political category had incubated with particular force in the Cuban Liberation Army, in which, since the late 1860s, white and colored Cubans fought side by side and in which colored Cubans claimed a proportion of the officer corps—40 percent—that by the 1890s had outstripped their percentage of the population.[45] This integrated and egalitarian military experience did not lead to the organization of separate black political groups with primarily Afro-Cuban agendas, however. Nor did it culminate in *mestizaje*-like calls for the mixing of the white, mulatto, and black races. It led instead to the embrace of racelessness as a defining characteristic of the Cuban nation.

The most eloquent spokesperson for "raceless" nationalism in the 1890s was José Martí, a Cuban Creole and the acknowledged leader of the Cuban revolutionary struggle until his battlefield death in 1895.[46] Believing that race had deformed colonial Cuban society, Martí wanted to create a sovereign Cuba in which racial divisions had no place. Martí refused to concede to any group "special rights because they belong to one race or another." For Martí, "the word man defines all rights," and "man" meant "more than the white man, mulatto, or black man." Cuba meant "more than white man, mulatto, or black man." It meant the opportunity to be free, to develop one's character and humanity, to strive for economic improvement, and to cultivate "greatness in Cuba." Thus, to harp "on racial divisions and the differences between races in the case of an already divided people impedes the attainment of national and individual well being, which are to be secured by the greatest coming together of the racial elements that form the nation."[47] Martí did not advocate that whites, blacks, and mulattos in Cuba should mix with each other and produce a hybrid race; he imagined that the three races would remain separate but that the salience of their racial identities would atrophy as the affinity of Cubans to their nation increased.

Martí's vision of a raceless Cuba granted Afro-Cubans a more central place in their nation than African Americans were being offered during that period in the United States. Indeed, Martí deliberately embraced a form of national belonging very different from the U.S. race-conscious one. Not many white Americans living in the 1890s United States, North, South, East, or West, would have celebrated the fundamental unity and equality of white and black citizens as Martí did in 1893 when he spoke about the "souls of white men and Negroes" who rose "together from the battlefields where they fought and died for Cuba."[48] Cuba Libre was unimaginable apart from the sacrifices made by Negroes and whites to bring it about.[49]

Martí knew the United States well, as he had lived there as a Cuban exile for most of his adult life, in New York City and Tampa in particular. Both his commitment to egalitarianism and his opposition to racism took their mature form during these North American years. His desire to establish a raceless republic in Cuba revealed how much the civic nationalist ideals of the American Revolution—and in particular the Declaration of Independence—had influenced his thinking, as they had many other Cuban exiles. Yet Martí also believed that America by the early 1890s had reneged on the raceless and egalitarian promises of its republican heritage. Capitalism was undercutting America's commitment to economic equality, while the resurgence of a white supremacist South had destroyed Reconstruction's promise of racial equality. America had become a "monster," a model of nationhood to be repudiated, not emulated, by Cubans.[50] And so Cuban "racelessness" became his response to North American racial nationalism. It was a courageous stance.

Yet Martí could not free himself entirely from fears of black inferiority or from an anxiety that Cuba would never succeed as a nation if it marked itself—or was marked by others—as black. Martí made no allowance for blacks in Cuba calling special attention to their problems or for celebrating their African heritage. He rejected the proposition that slavery had saddled Afro-Cubans with particular problems—poverty, lack of skills and education, political inexperience—that had to be named and addressed.[51] He defined racism not simply as discrimination against blacks by whites but as the proclamation by blacks of their "special character."[52] While this stance can be interpreted as a radical—even admirable—attack on all forms of racial essentialism, it also seems a bit strained given the practical problems faced by an Afro-Cuban population emerging from slavery. Problems ignored were ones likely to persist and to undercut efforts to make the island's Afro-Cubans truly free and equal citizens. Martí's reluctance to address Afro-Cuban difficulties stemming from the slave experience arose in part from the homogeneity imperative that disfigured nationalism everywhere, even on the Left: cultural difference had to be eliminated in order to achieve civic equality and national solidarity. But Martí's refusal to contemplate the solution to the problem of cultural diversity emerging in Mexico and other Latin countries—homogenization through cultural mixing—also points to his enduring anxiety about the large African presence in Cuba. A brown nation could become great; a black nation could not.

Martí died in 1895, killed in a battle between Cuban and Spanish forces. But his legacy lived on, evident both in the stout resistance Cubans displayed toward U.S. conceptions of racial order and in their anxiety over revealing the African basis of their nation to the world.

The explosion of the USS *Maine* in Havana Harbor in 1898 brought the United States directly into the Cuban anticolonial struggle. Prior to 1898 many white Americans had not only supported the Cuban independence movement but likened Cubans to the American revolutionaries of 1776: oppressed by a haughty colonial power, struggling for their freedom and independence, and largely European (and white) in origin. The substantial Cuban Creole exile community in cities like New York successfully encouraged such comparisons, using the connections its more prominent members had established with the Hearst and Pulitzer newspaper media empires headquartered there to turn Cuban insurrectionists into reincarnations of the Lexington and Concord Minutemen. New York's powerful yellow press and its allies across the country trumpeted the cause of Cuban freedom and stressed the similarities between the U.S. and Cuban wars of independence. The Spanish imperialists, meanwhile, were depicted in the American press as brutish and corrupt, their capacity for goodness, liberty, and equality diminished by their Catholicism, popery, and dark skin and features.[53]

White American soldiers and journalists arriving in Cuba in 1898 brought these media preconceptions with them only to discover a world apparently turned upside down: many Cubans and a disproportionate number of those fighting for independence from Spain were black or mulatto. Most Cuban soldiers were poor—many of them had to fight without proper uniforms, arms, or provisions—and appeared to U.S. soldiers to lack education, discipline, and deference. They lived off their Spanish enemies, taking guns, clothing, and other useful items from those they had killed. Americans found their sympathies drawn to those they were told to fight—the Spanish soldiers, who appeared to be (at least in the officer ranks) educated, disciplined, and white. The audacity and the lack of "civilization" among the Afro-Cuban soldiers, meanwhile, aroused fears among Americans that the conditions that had allegedly prevailed in their own country during Reconstruction—irresponsible and incapable blacks on top—had taken root in Cuba.[54]

Neither individual U.S. soldiers nor the U.S. military authority took well to these discoveries, and the U.S. decision, soon after its victory over Spain, to occupy Cuba and to shape the new Cuban nation to its liking was informed by the conviction that the Cuban people, with its large population of African descent, could not be trusted to govern themselves. Lt. Gen. Leonard Wood, head of the American occupation authority and Theodore Roosevelt's close friend, did everything he could to impose American racial practices on the Cubans. He dissolved the integrated Liberation Army and attempted to replace it with an all-Creole guard. He reserved important jobs in the new Cuban government for Creoles and Spaniards and attempted to restrict the right to vote and other political rights to those who were white. Under this U.S. pressure more conservative elements of Cuban society came to the fore in 1899 and 1900. The middle-class and upper-class Creoles and Spanish settlers who dominated these conservative ranks wanted to sustain social arrangements in Cuba as the Spaniards had left them—Creoles on top, Afro-Cubans on the bottom. Some were enamored of the white supremacy arguments gripping the United States and hoped to make Cuba if not an Anglo-Saxon nation then at least one dominated by superior (and white) European stock. When the Cuban census of 1900 revealed that fully one-third of the Cuban nation was colored, conservative whites in the Cuban provisional government, with the support of the United States, passed a Europeans-only immigration policy meant to whiten the population.[55] Wood encouraged these efforts. And in order to secure the United States' ability to influence Cuban politics over the long term, Wood, before taking his occupation army home in 1902, compelled the Cuban Constitutional Convention to write the U.S. Platt Amendment into their constitution, giving the United States a perpetual and unchecked right of intervention into internal Cuban affairs.[56]

Yet even with their extraordinary power Wood and his U.S. occupation force often found themselves on the defensive against Cubans who refused to capitulate to U.S. racist imperatives and who reaffirmed the "raceless" conception of Cuban nationhood. Thus, Cuba rejected Wood's attempt to limit suffrage to whites by writing the principle of universal manhood suffrage into its constitution.[57] The U.S. effort to exclude blacks from the new nation's military also failed. When Cuba's first president, Tomas Estrada Palma, a social conservative elected in 1902 and much taken with America's Jim Crow policies, went too far in his determination to break with Martí's egalitarian tradition by excluding colored Cubans from the military, government, and economic opportunity, he provoked a political backlash. Organized by Cuba's Liberal Party and drawing heavily on Afro-Cubans, this opposition sparked the Revolution of 1906 that drove the conservatives from power.[58] In such ways did Martí's dream—and the determination among Cubans not to let U.S. Jim Crow policies shape the racial politics of their nation—live on.

But the United States was in no mood for capitulation either. The 1906 revolution brought the U.S. army back to Cuba to restore order and reimpress U.S. social views on the Cuban people. This time, the influence of the Americans deepened a racial fissure within the Cuban population itself. As Afro-Cubans found their path to equality blocked again, a significant minority among them jettisoned Martí's ideology of racelessness and joined a separatist colored party, the Partido Independiente de Color (PIC), insisting that the particular needs of Afro-Cubans had to be addressed. The PIC became a magnet for political fury within Cuba, emanating from nationalists on both the Right and the Left who charged that its Afro-Cuban supporters had abandoned Martí's dream of a "raceless" Cuba. In 1912 government troops, with the tacit support of the United States, massacred thousands of insurrectionist PIC supporters. Aline Helg and other scholars have argued that this was one of the darkest days in the history of the Cuban Republic and in its colored people's struggle for racial equality.[59]

The extreme nature of the government's reaction to this black protest reveals how much Cuban nationalists remained discomfited by the African presence in Cuba and by the possibility that Cubans might, at some point, wish to declare their blackness to the world. This discomfiture was itself part of Martí's revolutionary legacy and expressed his worry that any effort to mark or legitimate racial difference in Cuba risked highlighting the sizable African population in Cuba Libre. Such highlighting, Martí had feared, could easily imperil the entire nationalist and republican project.

Is it too much to expect that the Cuban revolutionaries, especially the Creole ones, would have overcome entirely their prejudice against Afro-Cubans? Perhaps. Simply keeping U.S. Jim Crow policies out of Cuba at a time when the United States was exporting its ideologies, commodities, and military to the island republic was a tall order. Racism, increasingly sanctioned by science, had, by the early twentieth century, suffused so many nationalist discourses in the Eastern and Western Hemispheres that it was difficult to escape its influence. And the subjugation and colonization of Africa by European colonial powers at this time intensified international perceptions of Africans as too weak and primitive to become independent and self-governing. This condescending posture in turn prompted people of African descent in the Caribbean and the United States in the early twentieth century to proclaim the blackness of their culture and identity—a move apparent in the actions of the PIC in 1912 Cuba and, only a few years later, in the black nationalist movement led by Jamaica's Marcus Garvey in the Anglophone Caribbean and the United States.[60]

Some historians have argued that the PIC insurrection and defeat, despite the tragedy of the massacre, left a positive long-term legacy by opening up a political space for Afro-Cuban activism that had not been there before. Thus, by the late 1920s, a populist general and president, Gerardo Machado, not only appealed to the Afro-Cuban population for its support but also granted Afro-Cuban organizations a legitimacy and a freedom of operation not previously available to them. As Alejandra Bronfman has noted, Machado made it possible for Cubans to question the "notion of a raceless Cuban nationalism" and to invoke instead "images of distinct ethnic and racial groups, united in harmony."[61] Soon after some Cuban artists and intellectuals began popularizing a particular form of Cuban *mestizaje*, often captured by the word *afrocubanismo*, which, for the first time, publicly celebrated the mixing of African and Spanish heritages in Cuban culture. Acknowledging the existence of separate cultures had, finally, it seemed, made it possible for Cubans to talk about how the interpenetration of the two had given Cuba its distinctive and proud character.[62]

Still, neither the separatist conceptions of black nationalism nor the *mestizaje* celebration of cultural hybridity developed as fully in Cuba by 1940 as the former had in the Anglophone nations of the Western Hemisphere or as the latter had in Mexico and other Latin American countries. Blackness in Cuba remained a volatile subject, and fears that revealing its face could undermine the nationalist project endured. In this continuing fear of Cuba's blackness we can detect the continuing influence of racialized nationalist discourses on Cuba's quest for identity and culture.[63]

This essay has stressed both difference and similarity in its analysis of U.S., Mexican, and Cuban nationalisms in the years between 1880 and 1940. Difference is apparent in the distinct ways in which each country addressed the question of its own racial diversity, with the United States embracing an ideology of white supremacy, Mexico celebrating the mixing of the European and Indian races, and Cuba trumpeting its racelessness. The Mexican advocates of *mestizaje* and the Cuban supporters of racelessness acted boldly in developing formulas of belonging and integration that repudiated the racial nationalism of the United States, their physical neighbor and their region's geopolitical policeman and ideological hegemon. The Mexican and Cuban rejection of the U.S. model should be understood in terms of both demographic imperatives and the dynamics of nationalist ideology. The demographic imperative is clear. The United States could pursue its path to racial nationalism by excluding a relatively small percentage of its people—about 10 percent—from the nation. But in Mexico and Cuba, pursuing the U.S. strategy would have meant excluding or subordinating a majority (in Mexico) or near majority (in Cuba). Some conservative nationalists in each country favored such an approach, but their plans for whitening their nation through European immigration or through drastic restrictions on who could become citizens of their nations met with little success.

A key reason for this conservative failure lay in the dynamics of nationalist mobilization. In the late nineteenth and early twentieth centuries nations were expected—and nations expected themselves—to be big, powerful, and unified. How could a new nation such as Cuba make a convincing case for its strength if it denied a large minority of its people participation in its polity? How could Mexico resist the imperial advances of France or the United States or build a modern industrial economy if its indigenous and mestizo populations had no stake in the country's defense or economic development?

Nationalism's injunction to be strong created a parallel one to be inclusive. The drive toward inclusion did not necessarily translate into democratic ideas and practice, but often it did, especially in situations when nationalism became bound up with social revolution—as was the case in both Mexico and Cuba. Thus, leading nationalists in Mexico and Cuba became determined to include nonwhite peoples in their nationalist projects and to do so in ways that invigorated republican institutions and practices. Thomas Holt has argued that this drive to include nonwhite peoples in the nation, apparent not just in Mexico and Cuba but in many other Latin American countries as well, did something fundamental to the European- and North American–centered discourses that dominated nationalist thought: it "challenged the exclusive association of modernity [and nationhood] with whiteness" and "decoupled racial mixture from the idea of racial degeneration." It may be that Latin America's chief contribution to nationalist thought is to be found here—breaking the connection between whiteness and national greatness—far more than in the nation-building activities that Benedict Anderson has attributed to the continent's eighteenth-century "creole pioneers."[64]

And yet, ultimately, the nationalists in Cuba and Mexico could not escape the racializing implications of the North American–European nationalist discourses they had embraced and, in some ways, transformed. The similarities between Cuban and Mexican nationalism, on the one hand, and U.S. nationalism (and, by extension, European nationalisms), on the other, were as impressive as the divergences. In all three countries national strength was thought to require racial or cultural homogeneity. In all three certain groups were identified as incapable of overcoming their difference from the homogeneous mainstream; they would therefore have to be subordinated, expelled, or hidden. Thus, even as Mexican nationalists were welcoming Indians and mestizos into the Mexican nation, they were distancing themselves from groups—blacks and Chinese— who were thought to weaken or contaminate the Indo-European basis of *mestizaje*. And even as Cuban nationalists were insisting that race would not be a defining characteristic of their nationhood, they were engaged in a sub rosa process of racialization, rendering invisible the African elements of their population and culture.

Why did Mexican and Cuban nationalists end up reproducing racializing tendencies that they were, in other respects, so determined to repudiate? One thinks of Marx's aphorism that people make their own history but not always in circumstances of their own choosing. To become a nationalist in the late nineteenth or early twentieth century was to enter a force field of potent and interpenetrating global discourses on nation, modernity, and race. Here one encountered powerful attractions and repulsions, not all of which could be controlled or overcome. In the late nineteenth century fashioning a strong and modern nation almost everywhere meant building an industrial economy and transforming the country's population into a vigorous, productive, and disciplined citizenry. Even under the best of circumstances this was not easy work. And nations in the 1880s and 1890s seemed beset by sharply deteriorating conditions: economic turmoil and depression, unemployment, class conflict, war, and regional and cultural resistance to national consolidation. In these circumstances of economic and political uncertainty and amidst the developing conviction that nation building was a zero-sum game, one nation's advance requiring another nation's decline, nationalists everywhere sought assurance that their nation was destined to succeed. Many found this assurance in racialized discourses that spoke with conviction about the special qualities that either inhered in or could be imparted to their people. As long as conditions were created (unity, homogeneity, and racial integrity) for those special qualities to flourish, then the nation's future would be secure.

If we understand that Mexican and Cuban nationalists had to operate within this force field of globalized discourses just as much as U.S. and European nationalists did, then their failure to free themselves entirely from racializing tendencies becomes more comprehensible. A full reckoning with the racist elements and the homogeneity principle of nationalist discourses would come, but only after nationalism's force field had been ruptured by two world wars, the Holocaust, and both the successes and failures of scores of new states emerging in Africa and Asia. That it took so much to disrupt these discourses speaks to the extraordinary power that the nexus of race and nation once exerted over the imagining of national communities.

NOTES

I wish to thank Mark Levengood, Linda Noel, and Daniel Gerstle for their research assistance on this essay and Ira Berlin, Don Doyle, Linda Noel, Marco Pamplona, and the anonymous reviewers for the University of Georgia Press for their comments on earlier drafts of this essay. A special thanks to Mary Kay Vaughan for encouraging me to move ahead with this exercise in comparative history, for reading multiple drafts of this essay, and for educating me in Latin American and especially Mexican history.

1. For one of the most interesting explorations of this paradox see Edmund Morgan, *American Slavery, American Freedom* (New York, 1975). On the 1790 law see James Kettner, *The Development of American Citizenship* (Chapel Hill, N.C., 1978), and Matthew Jacobson, *Whiteness of a Different Color: European Americans and the Alchemy of Race* (Cambridge, Mass., 1998).

2. On the promise and failure of Reconstruction see Eric Foner, *Reconstruction: America's Unfinished Revolution, 1863–1877* (New York, 1988); Steven Hahn, *A Nation under Our Feet* (Cambridge, Mass., 2003); Ira Berlin et al., *Slaves No More: Three Essays on Emancipation and the Civil War* (New York, 1992). On the restoration of elite white power in the South and the implementation of Jim Crow see C. Vann Woodward, *The Origins of the New South* (Baton Rouge, La., 1971); C. Vann Woodward, *The Strange Career of Jim Crow* (New York, 1955); Edward L. Ayers, *The Promise of the New South: Life after Reconstruction* (New York, 1992); David Blight, *Race and Reunion: The Civil War in American Memory* (Cambridge, Mass., 2001).

3. On the late-nineteenth-century history of American Indians see Philip Weeks, *Farewell, My Nation: The American Indian and the United States, 1820–1890* (Arlington Heights, Ill., 1990); Francis Paul Prucha, *The Great Father: The United States Government and the American Indians* (Lincoln, Neb., 1984); Robert Mardock, *Reformers and the American Indian* (Columbia, Mo., 1971). On the Indian image in the white mind see Philip Deloria, *Playing Indian* (New Haven, Conn., 1998); Richard Slotkin, *Regeneration through Violence: The Mythology of the American Frontier, 1600–1860* (Middletown, Conn., 1973); and Richard Slotkin, *Gunfighter Nation: The Myth of the Frontier in Twentieth-Century America* (New York, 1992).

4. Leonard A. Carlson, *Indians, Bureaucrats, and Land* (Westport, Conn., 1981); Christine Bolt, *American Indian Policy and American Reform* (London, 1987); Francis Paul Prucha, *The Indians in American Society from the Revolutionary War to the Present* (Berkeley, Calif., 1985).

5. On Croly's and Roosevelt's New Nationalism and its connection to the American tradition of civic nationalism see Gary Gerstle, *American Crucible: Race and Nation in the Twentieth Century* (Princeton, N.J., 2001), chap. 2.

6. For a sampling of historians who celebrated this new nation see George Mowry, *Theodore Roosevelt and the Progressive Movement* (Madison, Wisc., 1946); Arthur S. Link, *Woodrow Wilson and the Progressive Era, 1910–1917* (New York, 1954); and Arthur M. Schlesinger Jr., *The Age of Roosevelt* (Boston, 1957–60), 3 vols.

7. On Chinese and Japanese exclusion see Andrew Gyory, *Closing the Gate: Race, Politics, and the Chinese Exclusion Act* (Chapel Hill, N.C., 1998); Lucy Salyer, *Laws Harsh as Tigers: Chinese Immigrants and the Shaping of Modern Immigration Law* (Chapel Hill, N.C., 1995); Erika Lee, *At America's Gates: Chinese Immigration during the Exclusion Era, 1882–1943* (Chapel Hill, N.C., 2003); Yuji Ichioka, *The Issei: The World of the First Generation Japanese Immigrants, 1880–1924* (London, 1988); Roger Daniels, *Not Like Us: Immigrants and Minorities in America, 1890–1924* (Chicago, 1997).

8. *Congressional Record,* 17 March 1924, 4389.

9. Ibid., 8 April 1924, 4389.

10. Gerstle, *American Crucible,* chaps. 2–3; Israel Zangwill, *The Melting-Pot: Drama in Four Acts* (1909; New York, 1923); Gary Gerstle, "The Protean Character of American Liberalism," *American Historical Review* 99 (October 1994): 1043–73; Jeffrey C. Stewart, ed., *The Critical Temper of Alain Locke: A Selection of His Essays on Art and Culture* (New York, 1983); Randolph Bourne, "Transnational America," in Olaf Hansen, ed., *The Radical Will: Selected Writings, 1911–1918* (New York, 1977); George W. Stocking Jr., *Race, Culture, and Evolution: Essays in the History of Anthropology* (New York, 1968); Lawrence C. Kelly, *The Assault on Assimilation: John Collier and the Origins of Indian Reform Policy* (Albuquerque, N.M., 1983); Rachel Davis-DuBois, "Adventures in Intercultural Education," Ph.D. dissertation, New York University, 1940.

11. Gerstle, *American Crucible,* chap. 1; Cecilia Elizabeth O'Leary, *To Die For: The Paradox of American Nationalism* (Princeton, N.J., 1998); Blight, *Race and Reunion.*

12. On the importance of horizontal comradeship to nationalism see Benedict Anderson, *Imagined Communities: Reflections on the Origins and Spread of Nationalism* (London, 1983). On the importance of nationalism to the unleashing of democratic enthusiasms see Eric Hobsbawm, *Nations and Nationalism since 1870: Programme, Myth, Reality* (New York, 1990); and Gerstle, *American Crucible,* 148–49. Claudio Lomnitz has reminded us that the homogenizing and democratizing effects of nationalism should not prevent us from understanding how nationalism can simultaneously reproduce relationships of hierarchy and inequality in families, communities, and corporations ("Nationalism as a Practical System: Benedict Anderson's Theory of Nationalism from the Vantage Point of Latin America," in Miguel Angel Centeno and Fernando López-Alves, eds., *The Other Mirror: Grand Theory through the Lens of Latin America* [Princeton, N.J., 2001], 334–37). Another version of this essay appears under the same title in Claudio Lomnitz, *Deep Mexico, Silent Mexico: An Anthology of Nationalism* (Minneapolis, 2001), 3–34.

13. See Mark Wasserman, *Everyday Life and Politics in Nineteenth Century Mexico: Men, Women, and War* (Albuquerque, N.M., 2000), 91–157; Florencia E. Mallon, *Peasant and Nation: The Making of Postcolonial Mexico and Peru* (Berkeley, Calif., 1995), chaps. 2–5.

14. Ibid.

15. Quoted in Charles A. Hale, *The Transformation of Liberalism in Late Nineteenth-Century Mexico* (Princeton, N.J., 1989), 236.

16. For more on the attitude of Porfirian state builders toward the question of European immigration see William Raat, "Los intelectuales, el positivismo, y la cuestión indígena," *Historia Mexicana* 20 (1970): 415–21. For general background on the policies of the Porfirian regime see Wasserman, *Everyday Life and Politics,* 159–228.

17. Mauricio Tenorio-Trillo, *Mexico at the World's Fairs: Crafting a Modern Nation* (Berkeley, Calif., 1996), 91–99.

18. Quoted in Barbara A. Tenenbaum, "Streetwise History: The Paseo de la Reforma and the Porfirian State, 1876–1910," in William H. Beezley, Cheryl English Martin, and William E. French, eds., *Rituals of Rule, Rituals of Resistance: Public Celebrations and Pop-*

ular Culture in Mexico (Wilmington, Del., 1984), 139. On the colonial, protonationalist roots of Aztec celebration see D. A. Brading, *The Origins of Mexican Nationalism* (Cambridge, 1985).

19. Porfirian state builders could also be ruthless in their approach to questions of Indian acculturation and modernization, though many such efforts in the late nineteenth century were ineffective. For the limitations on educational reform, for example, see Mary Kay Vaughan, *The State, Education, and Social Class in Mexico, 1880–1928* (DeKalb, Ill., 1982), 9–78.

20. John S. D. Eisenhower, *Intervention: The United States and the Mexican Revolution, 1913–1917* (New York, 1993).

21. For an exception to this tendency see Thomas C. Holt, "Foreword," in Nancy P. Applebaum, Anne S. Macpherson, and Karin Alejandra Rosemblatt, eds., *Race and Nation in Modern Latin America* (Chapel Hill, N.C., 2003), xi–xii.

22. J. Hector St. John de Crèvecoeur, *Letters from an American Farmer and Sketches of Eighteenth-Century America* (1782; New York, 1981), 69–70.

23. Zangwill, *The Melting-Pot*, 33.

24. Quoted in Alan Knight, "Racism, Revolution, and Indigenismo: Mexico, 1910–1940," in Richard Graham, ed., *The Idea of Race in Latin America, 1870–1940* (Austin, Tex., 1990), 84–85.

25. Vasconcelos, "The Latin-American Basis of Mexican Civilization," in José Vasconcelos and Manuel Gamio, *Aspects of Mexican Civilization* (Chicago, 1926), 84. See also José Vasconcelos, *The Cosmic Race: A Bilingual Edition* (Baltimore, Md., 1997).

26. Mary Kay Vaughan, "Nationalizing the Countryside: Schools and Rural Communities in the 1930s," Desmond Rochfort, "National Identity in Mexican Mural Painting: Rivera, Orozco and Siqueiros," and Marco Velazquez and Mary Kay Vaughan, "Mestizaje and Musical Nationalism in Mexico," all in Mary Kay Vaughan and Stephen E. Lewis, eds., *The Eagle and the Virgin: National Identity, Memory, and Utopia in Mexico, 1920–1940* (Durham, N.C., 2006). See also David A. Brading, "Manuel Gamio and Official Indigenismo in Mexico," *Bulletin of Latin American Research* 7, no. 1 (1988): 79–80.

27. Velazquez and Vaughan, "Mestizaje and Musical Nationalism"; Rochfort, "National Identity."

28. To comprehend the *mestizaje* underlying U.S. mass culture in the 1930s see Michael Denning, *The Cultural Front: The Laboring of American Culture in the Twentieth Century* (New York, 1997); Lewis A. Erenberg, *Swingin' the Dream: Big Band Jazz and the Rebirth of American Culture* (Chicago, 1998); and Lary May, *The Big Tomorrow: Hollywood and the Politics of the American Way* (Chicago, 2000).

29. Gerstle, *American Crucible*, chap. 5; Matthew Jacobson, *Whiteness of a Different Color* (Cambridge, Mass., 1998); Michael Rogin, *Blackface, White Noise: Jewish Immigrants in the Hollywood Melting Pot* (Berkeley, Calif., 1996).

30. Vasconcelos, "The Latin-American Basis of Mexican Civilization," 92–94.

31. Though Lamarckian thought had a longer life in Latin America than in North America, support for eugenical approaches was widespread by the 1920s. See Nancy

Stepan, *The Hour of Eugenics: Race, Gender, and Nation in Latin America* (Ithaca, N.Y., 1991).

32. Quoted in Knight, "Racism, Revolution, and Indigenismo," 88.

33. Ibid.

34. Brading, "Manuel Gamio," 82–88.

35. On the Indianists see Knight, "Racism, Revolution, and Indigenismo." For a more sympathetic treatment of the *indigenismo* movement see Alexander Dawson, "From Models for the Nation to Model Citizens: Indigenismo and the 'Revindication' of the Mexican Indian, 1920–1940," *Journal of Latin American Studies* 30 (May 1998): 279–308.

36. Velazquez and Vaughan, "Mestizaje and Musical Nationalism"; Mauricio Tenorio Trillo, "Stereophonic Scientific Modernisms: Social Science between Mexico and the United States, 1880s–1930s," *Journal of American History* 86 (December 1999): 1156–87, 1174; Knight, "Racism, Revolution, and Indigenismo," 95.

37. Knight, "Racism, Revolution, and Indigenismo," 95.

38. Evelyn Hu-DeHart, "Huagong and Huahong: The Chinese as Laborers and Merchants in Latin America and the Caribbean," *Amerasia Journal* 28 (2002): 64–90; Evelyn Hu-DeHart, "Racism and Anti-Chinese Persecution in Sonora, Mexico, 1876–1932," *Amerasia* 9 (1982): 1–28; Eugenio Chang-Rodríguez, "Chinese Labor Migration into Latin America in the Nineteenth Century," *Revista de Historia de America* (December 1958): 375–97; Leo M. Jacques, "Chinese Merchants in Sonora, 1900–1931," in Luz M. Martínez Montiel, *Asiatic Migrations in Latin America* (Mexico City, 1981), 13–20; Lee, *At America's Gates;* Erika Lee, "Enforcing the Borders: Chinese Exclusion along the U.S. Borders with Canada and Mexico, 1882–1924," *Journal of American History* 89 (June 2002): 54–86.

39. Quoted in Gerardo Rénique, "Race, Region, and Nation: Sonora's Anti-Chinese Racism and Mexico's Postrevolutionary Nationalism, 1920s–1930s," in Applebaum, Macpherson, and Rosemblatt, *Race and Nation,* 223.

40. Knight, "Racism, Revolution, and Indigenismo," 97; see also Charles C. Cumberland, "The Sonora Chinese and the Mexican Revolution," *Hispanic American Historical Review* 40 (May 1960): 191–211.

41. For a thoughtful discussion of the racializing implications of *mestizaje* see Lourdes Martinez-Echazábal, "Mestizaje and the Discourse of National Cultural Identity in Latin America, 1845–1959," in *Latin American Perspectives* 25 (May 1998): 21–42; and for an incisive look at the way in which the ideal of "whiteness" survived in Mexico through both the Liberal and revolutionary periods see Claudio Lomnitz-Adler, *Exits from the Labyrinth: Culture and Ideology in Mexican National Space* (Berkeley, Calif., 1992), 261–81.

42. Cuban nationalists also sought to hide the presence of Chinese immigrants. Almost 125,000 Chinese immigrants had come to Cuba between 1847 and 1874, most as indentured servants, at a time when Spanish imperialists were searching for an alternative labor supply to African slaves. Thousands died in transit, during their period of indenture, or shortly thereafter, so that by 1900 the total Chinese population had shrunk to fifteen thousand. Still, the Chinese had formed a significant part of the nineteenth-century Cuban population (near 10 percent at its peak), made important contributions

to the economy, and participated in the anticolonial uprisings such as the Ten Years War. Nevertheless, their presence and contributions were all but erased from Cuba's historical memory by the founders of the Cuban Republic. See Hu-DeHart, "Huagong and the Huaohong," 68–69; and Chang-Rodriguez, "Chinese Labor Migration," 377. For a brief reference to their participation in the Ten Years War see Ada Ferrer, *Insurgent Cuba: Race, Nation, and Revolution, 1868–1898* (Chapel Hill, N.C., 1999), 48–63.

43. Ferrer, *Insurgent Cuba*, 2.

44. On this thirty-year struggle see ibid.; the standard work on the abolition of slavery is Rebecca Scott, *Slave Emancipation in Cuba: The Transition to Free Labor* (Princeton, N.J., 1985).

45. The colored proportion of Cuba's population had declined from more than half to about a third between the 1840s and the 1890s due to limitations on the slave trade that Spain reluctantly agreed to in the 1840s in response to international pressure. See Aline Helg, "Race in Argentina and Cuba, 1880–1930: Theory, Policies, and Popular Reaction," in Graham, *The Idea of Race*, 47.

46. John M. Kirk, *José Martí: Mentor of the Cuban Nation* (Tampa, Fla., 1983).

47. José Martí, *The America of José Martí*, translated from Spanish by Juan de Onis (New York, 1953), 310, 308.

48. Ibid., 310.

49. Ferrer, *Insurgent Cuba*.

50. On Martí's disillusionment with the United States see Philip S. Foner, "Introduction," in José Martí, *Inside the Monster: Writings on the United States and American Imperialism,* ed. Philip S. Foner (New York, 1975), 15–48. In a letter to Manuel Cercado in 1895 Martí wrote of the United States, "I have lived inside the monster and know its entrails—and my weapon is only the slingshot of David" (ibid., 3).

51. See, for example, Aline Helg, *Our Rightful Share: The Afro-Cuban Struggle for Equality, 1886–1912* (Chapel Hill, N.C., 1995).

52. Martí, *Inside the Monster*, 150.

53. On the importance to Cuban politics and culture of the Cuban exile community in New York see Louis A. Pérez Jr., *On Becoming Cuban: Identity, Nationality, and Culture* (Chapel Hill, N.C., 1999), chaps. 1 and 2. See also Allesandra Lorini, "Engendering 'Patria': Transnational Meanings of Late Nineteenth-Century Cuba Libre," unpublished essay, 2003. On American perceptions of the Spanish in Cuba see Gerald F. Linderman, *The Mirror of War: American Society and the Spanish-American War* (Ann Arbor, Mich., 1974).

54. Linderman, *The Mirror of War*.

55. Alejandro de la Fuente, "Race, National Discourse, and Politics in Cuba: An Overview," *Latin American Perspectives* 25 (May 1998): 47–48.

56. James E. Bradford, *Crucible of Empire: The Spanish-American War and Its Aftermath* (Annapolis, Md., 1993); Louis A. Pérez, *Cuba under the Platt Amendment, 1902–1934* (Pittsburgh, Pa., 1986); James H. Hitchman, *Leonard Wood and Cuban Independence, 1898–1902* (The Hague, 1971).

57. Alejandro de la Fuente, "Myths of Racial Democracy, 1900–1912," *Latin American Research Review* 34 (1999): 55–56; Helg, *Our Rightful Share*, 128.

58. Lillian Guerra, "From Revolution to Involution in the Early Cuban Republic: Conflicts over Race, Class, and Nation, 1902–1906," in Applebaum, Macpherson, and Rosemblatt, *Race and Nation,* 132–62.

59. Helg, *Our Rightful Share.*

60. On the influence of these international, scientific, and racist discourses on nationalism in Cuba see Alejandra Marina Bronfman, "Reforming Race in Cuba, 1902–1940," Ph.D. dissertation, Princeton University, 2000; and Stephan Palmie, *Wizards and Scientists: Explorations in Afro-Cuban Modernity and Tradition* (Durham, N.C., 2002), esp. chap. 3. On the rise of radical forms of black nationalism in the Caribbean see Winston James, *Holding Aloft the Banner of Ethiopia: Caribbean Radicalism in Early Twentieth-Century America* (New York, 1998).

61. Bronfman, "Reforming Race in Cuba," 142; de la Fuente, "Race, National Discourse, and Politics in Cuba."

62. Robin D. Moore, *Nationalizing Blackness: Afrocubanismo and Artistic Revolution in Havana, 1920–1949* (Pittsburgh, Pa., 1997); Bronfman, "Reforming Race in Cuba," chap. 5.

63. Vera M. Kutzninski, *Sugar's Secrets: Race and the Erotics of Cuban Nationalism* (Charlottesville, Va., 1993); Palmie, *Wizards and Scientists;* Martinez-Echazábal, "Mestizaje."

64. Thomas Holt, "Foreword," in Applebaum, Macpherson, and Rosemblatt, *Race and Nation,* xi. For critical approaches to Anderson's argument about the role of eighteenth-century Creole pioneers in the making of modern nationalism see Lomnitz, "Nationalism as a Practical System"; and Eric Van Young, "Revolution and Imagined Communities in Mexico, 1810–1821" in this volume.

Contributors

T. H. Breen is the William Smith Mason Professor of American History at Northwestern University. His most recent book is *Marketplace of Revolution: How Consumer Politics Shaped American Independence* (2004). He is now completing a study of American insurgency titled "Moments of Decision: Popular Mobilization and the Collapse of Empire, 1774–1776."

Phillip Buckner is Professor Emeritus, University of New Brunswick (Canada), and Senior Research Fellow, Institute of Commonwealth Studies, London. He is the author of *The Transition to Responsible Government: British Policy in British North America, 1815–50* (1985); editor of *Canada and the End of Empire* (2004); and coeditor of *Rediscovering the British World* (2005) and *Canada and the British World* (2006). He is also the editor of the volume *Canada and the British Empire* in the Oxford History of the British Empire series (2006).

Craig Calhoun is University Professor of the Social Sciences at New York University and President of the Social Science Research Council. His 1997 book *Nationalism* is a widely read introduction to the field. He has two forthcoming books: *Cosmopolitanism and Belonging* and *Sociology in America*, the American Sociological Association Centennial History.

Wilma Peres Costa is a professor of economic history at the University of Campinas, Brazil, and conducts research at the University of San Paolo as well. Her work on state building in nineteenth-century Brazil includes *A Espada de Dâmocles—o exército, a Guerra do Paraguai e a crise do Império* (1996), on the Paraguayan War. Her work on travel writing and national identity includes an essay on "Voyages et Pélerinages" in *Intellectuels, Société et Politique* (2006), edited by Denis Rolland.

Jeane DeLaney is an associate professor of history at St. Olaf College in Northfield, Minnesota. Her articles on Argentine nationalism and national identity have appeared in *Comparative Studies in Society and History*, the *Journal of Latin American Studies*, and several edited volumes. She is currently completing a manuscript on changing notions of nationhood in Argentina from 1810 to 1945.

Don H. Doyle is McCausland Professor of History at the University of South Carolina, where he also serves as Director of ARENA, the Association for Research on Ethnicity and Nationalism in the Americas, based at the University of South Carolina's Richard Walker Institute for International Studies. Among his several books are *Nations Divided: America, Italy, and the Southern Question* (2002) and, coedited with Larry Griffin, *The South as an American Problem* (1996). He has been a Fulbright Professor in Rome, Genoa, and Rio de Janeiro and is currently working on a broad interpretation of U.S. nationalism.

Hayley Froysland took her PhD at the University of Virginia in 2002 and is currently an assistant professor of history at Indiana University South Bend. Her work focuses on the social and cultural dimensions of nation building in Colombia, particularly elite concerns about the poor in the urban environment of Bogotá in the late nineteenth and early twentieth centuries. She is currently working on a book titled "Para el bien común: Charity, Health, and Moral Order in Bogotá, Colombia, 1850–1936."

Gary Gerstle is a professor of history at the University of Maryland. Among his works are *American Crucible: Race and Nation in the Twentieth Century* (2001), winner of the Saloutos Prize, and *Working-Class Americanism: The Politics of Labor in a Textile City, 1914–1960* (1989). His most recent publication is a coedited book, *Ruling America: A History of Wealth and Power in a Democracy* (2005).

Susan-Mary Grant is Reader in American History at the University of Newcastle-upon-Tyne, United Kingdom. She is the author of *North over South: Northern Nationalism and American Identity in the Antebellum Era* (2000), as well as the articles "Patriot Graves: American National Identity and the Civil War Dead," in *American Nineteenth Century History* (Fall 2004) and, most recently, "Raising the Dead: War, Memory and American National Identity," in *Nations and Nationalism* (October 2005).

Jack P. Greene is Andrew W. Mellon Professor in the Humanities, Emeritus, Johns Hopkins University. He has published widely on colonial British American history and on the American Revolution. Among his best-known books are *Pursuits of Happiness: The Social Development of Early Modern British Colonies and the Formation of American Culture* (1988) and *The Intellectual Construction of America: Exceptionalism and Identity from 1492 to 1800* (rev. ed., 1997).

Jorge Myers studied at Cambridge University (BA and MA) and Stanford University (MA and PhD). He is a professor in the Program in Intellectual History at the Universidad Nacional de Quilmes/CONICET in Buenos Aires, Argentina. Among his publications are *Orden y virtud: El discurso republicano del rosismo*

(1995); *Resonancias Románticas: Ensayos sobre historia de la cultura argentina 1820–1890* (2005), with Graciela Batticuore and Klaus Gallo; and numerous articles on romantic conceptions of the nation and of the River Plate in Argentina. He is currently preparing a study of the emergence of the cultural history of Latin America, "Tierra firme, los orígenes de la historia cultural latinoamericana 1900–1960," whose central theme is the interplay between "continentalist" and "nationalist" representations of Latin American culture.

Marco Antonio Pamplona is a professor of history at the Universidade Federal Fluminense and at the Pontifícia Universidade Católica, in Rio de Janeiro. He deals with topics related to state making and nation building, citizenship, and the idea of republic in the Americas from a comparative perspective. He has published *Riots, Republicanism, and Citizenship* (1996), later translated to Portuguese (2003), and *Revendo o sonho americano: 1890–1972* (1996), in addition to several articles comparing nineteenth-century intellectuals and nationalism in Iberian America. His is the director of the Fulbright Chair at PUC-Rio, in Brazil.

Heather Thiessen-Reily is a professor of history at Western State College of Colorado. She is the author of "Las bellas y la bestia: La educación de mujeres durante la era de Belzú, 1848–1855" in *Identidad, ciudadania y participación política desde la colonia al siglo XX* (2003), edited by Guillermo Delgado and Josefa Salmon. She is currently completing a manuscript on Manuel Isidoro Belzú and caudillo nationalism.

Eric Van Young, a professor of history at the University of California, San Diego, is the author of *The Other Rebellion: Popular Violence, Ideology, and the Mexican Struggle for Independence, 1810–1821* (2001), winner of the 2003 Bolton-Johnson Prize, among other books and articles. He is engaged in research for a biographical study of Lucas Alaman (1792–1853), a nineteenth-century Mexican historian, public intellectual, statesman, and conservative nationalist.

Barbara Weinstein is a professor of history at the University of Maryland and senior editor of the *Hispanic American Historical Review*. She is the author of *The Amazon Rubber Boom, 1850–1920* (1983) and *For Social Peace in Brazil: Industrialists and the Remaking of the Working Class in São Paulo, 1920–1964* (1996) and is currently completing a book on race, region, and national identities in twentieth-century Brazil, to be published by Duke University Press. She is president-elect of the American Historical Association.

Index

River Plate, 117–19; and Argentine
    nationalism, 123–25, 128, 129, 132, 134;
    and Brazil, 214, 225, 226, 227
Rojas, Ricardo, 150, 151, 152, 154, 155, 156
Roman Catholic Church. *See* Catholicism
Romans, 29, 32
romanticism, 12, 34; and Argentina, 121,
    122, 125, 126, 130, 132, 143, 144–48, 152,
    155, 156; and German nationalism, 12,
    31, 35, 144
Romero, José Luis, 121, 134
Roosevelt, Theodore, 273, 275, 276, 293
Rosas, Juan Manuel de, 123, 124, 126, 128,
    132, 144
Rush, Benjamin, 65, 71

Saint-Hilaire, Auguste de, 13, 214, 218,
    220–26
Saldías, José Antonio, 155, 156
Salón Literario. *See* Generation of 1837
Sarmiento, Domingo Faustino, 117, 126,
    136; *Facundo*, 123, 124, 132
Schultz, Kirsten, 255, 259, 260
Scots, 48, 58, 83, 86, 102, 109
secession, 8, 80, 81, 93, 133, 162, 225. *See
    also* Civil War (U.S.); Confederates
    (U.S.); Québécois; separatism
separatism, 7, 8, 9, 12, 105, 294, 295. *See
    also* Civil War (U.S.); Confederates
    (U.S.); Québécois; secession
Seton-Watson, Hugh, 31
Seven Years War, 49, 62
Shaw, Robert Gould, 85
Sickles, Daniel, 93
slavery, 4, 13; in Brazil, 215, 216, 219,
    220, 226, 227, 248–50; in Cuba,
    289–90, 291–92; defense of, 13, 95,
    249, 251–63; in United States, 62,
    64, 69, 83, 85, 91, 248–50, 273–
    74, 290. *See also* abolitionism;
    Africans
Smith, Anthony, 1, 5, 17, 30, 31, 33, 99, 100,
    235, 236, 240
Soto y Calvo, Francisco, 154

Spain, 4, 12, 13, 15, 18; and Argentina, 117,
    119, 121, 123, 125–29, 131–33, 144; and
    Cuba, 289, 290, 292; and European
    rivalries, 20, 21, 22, 62; and Mexico,
    185–86, 190, 191, 198; and War of 1898,
    148, 278, 282, 290, 292
Spanish. *See* language; Spain
Spanish-American War. *See* War of 1898
Spillman, Lynette, 89
St. John de Crèvecour, Hector, 81, 282
Strong, George Templeton, 80
Sumaj Urqu, 230, 233, 234, 235, 236, 240,
    242
Sumner, Charles, 80, 81

Taylor, Bayard, 88
Texas, 8, 287
Thomson, Charles, 75, 76
Tilly, Charles, 28, 33
Tocqueville, Alexis de, 13, 123, 212, 215
Toro y Gómez, Miguel, 154
Tourgee, Albion, 87, 90
Trenchard, John, 47
Trevor-Roper, Hugh, 236
Twain, Mark, 92

Unamuno, Miguel de, 136, 148
United States of America, 2, 11, 22, 43;
    and British, 46, 47, 48, 49, 54, 62–64;
    and Canada, 99, 100, 102, 103, 106, 109,
    110, 111, 114; and Civil War (*see* Civil
    War [U.S.]); and Cuba, 278, 282, 290,
    292–94; and immigration, 82, 86, 91, 94,
    275–77; and interstate conflict, 66–68,
    70–73, 75–77; and Mexico, 7, 282; and
    national government, 65, 73–77; and
    national identity, 62–63, 65; and race,
    50, 54–55, 62, 91, 256–57, 273–78, 283;
    and republicanism, 42–43, 45, 53, 55,
    56; and revolution, 11, 50–51, 54, 61,
    64–65 (*see also* American Revolution
    [U.S.]); and revolutionary nationalism,
    45, 53–54, 62, 65; and slavery, 54–56, 69,
    83, 85, 91, 248–50, 253, 258, 261, 273–74,